REGULATION IN THE WHITE HOUSE

An Administrative History of the Johnson Presidency Series

Regulation in the White House:
THE JOHNSON PRESIDENCY

By David M. Welborn

 University of Texas Press   Austin

First edition, 1993

Requests for permission to reproduce material from this work
should be sent to Permissions, University of Texas Press, Box 7819,
Austin, TX 78713-7819.

⊗The paper used in this publication meets the minimum requirements of American National Standard for Information Sciences—
Permanence of Paper for Printed Library Materials, ANSI Z39.48-
1984.

Library of Congress Cataloging-in-Publication Data

Welborn, David M., date
    Regulation in the White House : the Johnson presidency / by
David M. Welborn.—1st ed.
        p.   cm.—(An Administrative history of the Johnson
presidency)
    Includes index.
    ISBN 0-292-79078-3 (alk. paper)
    1. Independent regulatory commissions—United
States.   2. Trade regulation—United States.   3. Johnson, Lyndon B. (Lyndon Baines), 1908–1973.   4. United States—Politics
and government—1963–1969.   I. Title.   II. Series.
JK901.W46   1993
353.09'1—dc20   93-19982

For Aline

"La patience est amère, mais son fruit est doux."

Contents

Tables

Foreword

In this book David Welborn examines presidential management of economic regulatory programs. His purview extends to such matters as the independent regulatory commissions, banking, agriculture, the petroleum industry, and antitrust policy. Nowhere in the literature on the presidency and on economic regulation will one find such a comprehensive and insightful portrait of the president as manager of the regulatory state.

The book is the tenth in a series called "An Administrative History of the Johnson Presidency." Taking a broad view of administration, the series was designed first to present the infrastructure of presidential management—the structure, personnel, and operating relationships for decision-making and policy administration: Emmette S. Redford and Marlan Blissett, *Organizing the Executive Branch: The Johnson Presidency* (University of Chicago Press, 1981); Richard L. Schott and Dagmar Hamilton, *People, Positions, and Power: The Political Appointments of Lyndon Johnson* (University of Chicago Press, 1983); Emmette S. Redford and Richard T. McCulley, *White House Operations: The Johnson Presidency* (University of Texas Press, 1986); and David M. Welborn and Jesse Burkhead, *Intergovernmental Relations in the American Administrative State* (University of Texas Press, 1989). These books are paralleled by another on the exercise of the appointive power for judicial positions: Neil D. McFeeley, *Appointment of Judges: The Johnson Presidency* (University of Texas Press, 1987).

A second group of books have dealt with the presidential management of the policymaking and implementation process in particular substantive areas. This book fits generally into this category. Other studies include W. Henry Lambright, *Presidential Management of Science and Technology: The Johnson Presidency* (University of Texas Press, 1985); James E. Anderson and Jared E. Hazleton, *Managing Macroeconomic Policy: The Johnson Presidency* (University of

Texas Press, 1986); Harvey C. Mansfield, Sr., *Illustrations of Presidential Management: Johnson's Cost Reduction and Tax Increase Campaigns* (Lyndon B. Johnson School of Public Affairs, 1988); Paul Hammond, *LBJ and the Presidential Management of Foreign Relations* (University of Texas Press, 1992). This series will be completed with a book on presidential management of the Vietnam War.

A third group was planned with a more specific concentration on implementation. Although money and performance have fallen short, we still anticipate a volume on the implementation of civil rights legislation.

This series of studies has been financed by a grant from the National Endowment for the Humanities, with additional aid from the Lyndon Baines Johnson Foundation, the Hobitzelle Foundation, and the Lyndon B. Johnson School of Public Affairs of the University of Texas at Austin.

The findings and conclusions in the various works in this series do not necessarily represent the view of any donor.

EMMETTE S. REDFORD
Project Director

JAMES E. ANDERSON
Deputy Director

Acknowledgments

This exploration of the treatment of regulation in the Johnson presidency has spanned parts of the tenure of three of his successors. Over this period a number of debts have been incurred. Much is owed for their support and encouragement to Emmette S. Redford and James E. Anderson, director and deputy director of the Lyndon Baines Johnson Administrative History Project. Richard T. McCulley, a research associate in the project, was most helpful in several respects.

Archivists at the LBJ Library were unfailingly courteous and cooperative. Claudia Anderson, Linda Hansen, and Nancy Smith, while presiding over the reading room, handled requests gracefully, efficiently, and thoroughly. Mary Knill also provided useful assistance.

At the University of Tennessee–Knoxville, Tom Ungs as head of the Department of Political Science provided time off from teaching duties to facilitate research. Several graduate assistants made important contributions. These include Patra Bonham Rule, David M. Dickson, Steven Warren, and Michael Bobic.

Generations of secretaries have produced drafts over the years. For this, special thanks go to Irene Carney, Marie Horton, Naina Bowen, Debby McCauley, Phyllis Moyers, and Carolyn Gose.

There are still others to implicate. Paul J. Quirk critiqued the manuscript in an insightful and extremely useful way. In this and a prior project, Theresa J. May of the University of Texas Press was at the center of expeditiously moving from manuscript to print. Carolyn Cates Wylie and Kathy Lewis managed and performed the editing with great skill.

Finally, but not last, there is my wife, Aline, whose love, support, and patience are appreciated beyond words.

DAVID M. WELBORN

REGULATION IN THE WHITE HOUSE

1. The President's Business

The job of the President is to set priorities for the nation.

LBJ, 1971[1]

AS LYNDON B. JOHNSON OBSERVED after leaving office, the president's business does involve setting priorities, but that is not all. The president and his aides ordinarily are pushed and pulled in a variety of directions by forces they cannot control and, as a result, are regularly engaged in a complex of activities that involve more than setting priorities. Their variety and complexity are indicated by the president's agenda during the week of 8 March 1965.[2]

President Johnson was inundated that week with a number of important and delicate problems he could not ignore. The civil rights march from Selma, Alabama, to Montgomery precipitated more and more rancor and violence each day. Military and diplomatic actions on the Vietnam front were moving at a fast pace. There was a Marine landing north of Da Nang and active consideration of enlarging the Seventh Fleet in Southeast Asia. Secretary of State Dean Rusk was busy enlisting support from NATO allies. On the economic front, a poor balance-of-payments situation was of major concern. In domestic affairs, the Medicare and aid-to-education bills were at critical points in their movement through Congress, and other Great Society programs were in the final stages of preparation before submission for legislative consideration.

Meetings and consultations in regard to these matters with White House aides, top-level cabinet officials, members of Congress, black leaders, civil rights activists, Governor George C. Wallace of Alabama, and others dominated the president's schedule. Selma presented the most critical and immediate problems. It was important to calm the situation and to calculate how to take political advantage of it. Johnson was successful in both. By the end of the week the contending sides were beginning to back off and to moderate their stances. On 15 March, the start of the following week, the president made his historic speech to Congress and the nation calling for voting rights legislation.

Presidents are required to do more than grapple with pressing matters of state. Attention to these was interspersed with political and ceremonial tasks. There were meetings, for example, with a group of new U.S. ambassadors about to go forth to their posts, Great Britain's ambassador to the United States, the mayor of Chicago, and the master general of the Dominican order. Late Thursday afternoon came a press conference, a signing ceremony for legislation establishing the Appalachian Regional Commission, and an off-the-record visit to Capitol Hill. This was followed in the evening by the last of a series of White House receptions for members of Congress and their wives, the second such reception of the week. Throughout the day Johnson was also forced to act as crisis manager in his own residence. A group of civil rights demonstrators staged a sit-down protest in the White House after entering as tourists. The president directed the handling and removal of the protesters down to the smallest detail. But the week was not all work. On Saturday evening there was a White House dinner party in honor of the new ambassador to Spain, Angier Biddle Duke, and his wife. For the president, the dancing and other festivities did not end until 4:25 A.M. Sunday, dutifully followed by church attendance later in the morning.

Meanwhile the machinery of government ground on in Washington and in outposts across the country. A fair portion of its work involved regulation through which government requires or prohibits certain actions or behavior. At the time of Johnson's presidency, economic regulation of particular industries such as transportation, communications, and banking was ascendant. It focused on matters such as entry, routes, and rates. Regulation cutting across industries and aimed at realizing general welfare objectives such as environmental quality, often referred to as social regulation, was limited but beginning to grow in importance. During the week several departments and agencies announced important regulatory actions. The Treasury Department, the Federal Reserve Board (FRB), the Federal Aviation Agency (FAA), and the Securities and Exchange Commission (SEC) brought forth new rules. The Department of Health, Education, and Welfare (HEW) issued antipollution orders to cities on the south side of Lake Michigan. The Federal Power Commission (FPC) gave a license to Consolidated Edison for a new power production facility at Storm King on the Hudson River. Tougher standards for licensing UHF television stations were announced by the Federal Communications Commission (FCC).

Clearly, Vietnam, balance-of-payments problems, civil rights, and his legislative program were inescapably part of the president's business. What, if any, were the ties between the presidency and the scores of important regulatory decisions made at the working levels of government during the week? What considerations of presidential purpose went into the decisions? Were the president and his staff involved? The president was recorded during this week as spending little time on department and agency activities other than those related to civil rights, Vietnam, the economy, and the legislative program, probably no more than three hours all told. He broke away from a Camp David meeting on Vietnam to inspect a Job Corps camp and worked episodically on the selection of a new Treasury secretary, announced the following week to be Henry H. Fowler. Meetings were held with the FAA administrator, with the head of the Veterans Administration, and with a group of railway union executives on transportation policy and appointments to the Interstate Commerce Commission (ICC). These incidents are reminders that the president's business may include less-than-dramatic and even mundane questions of governance involving regulatory and other matters.

The analysis to follow aims at developing a fuller understanding of the president's business in regulation, especially as it is conducted in the White House. Its setting is the presidency of Lyndon B. Johnson, covering his entire time in office, from 22 November 1963 to 20 January 1969.

The Regulatory System

> The Executive Branch . . . has . . . grown up without plan or design like the barns, shacks, silos, tool sheds, and garages of an old farm.
>
> President's Committee on
> Administrative Management, 1937[3]

When Johnson became president, the national government had exercised increasingly important regulatory responsibilities at least since the passage of the Interstate Commerce Act in 1887. The elements of the regulatory system in 1963 for the most part still included the barns and other structures, some in the form of independent commissions, that the President's Committee on Administrative Management sought to modernize in 1937. It consisted of three basic and interrelated components: regulatory commissions, executive agencies with regulatory responsibilities, and the presidency. The commission and executive components are profiled in table 1.

A few points about this table should be underscored. As previously mentioned, at this time almost all of the regulatory programs of the national government were directed at private economic activity. This would change over the next six years. The table also shows that independent boards and commissions were the preferred means for administering regulatory programs, although programs located in executive departments and agencies were quite important. In some instances there were overlapping responsibilities. Most notably, the Department of Justice and the Federal Trade Commission shared antitrust enforcement duties, and the banking industry was supervised by two independent bodies and by the Treasury Department.

The presidential portion of the national system of government regulation, then and now, consists of the president and his aides when they are involved in regulatory matters. There are three basic foundations for their involvement. One consists of the powers and responsibilities associated with the president's role as chief executive. These provide a warrant for presidential engagement in the administration of regulatory programs, including commission activities, although legally the relationship is not the same as with programs of executive agencies. Major areas of engagement include appointments, budgets, and organization.

There is, of course, more to being chief executive than the performance of discrete executive functions such as these. Two transcendent aspects are of special relevance here. First, there is the implied responsibility to elicit, through a variety of means, lawful and effective government action in accord with presidential perspectives and preferences. Although by law and tradition regulatory commissions are to operate independently in making specific decisions, a strong argument can be made that an interest in the character and quality of commission regulation on the part of the chief executive is not inappropriate. The other aspect of the chief executive's role to note is the expectation that presidents promote coherence in governmental action through the provision of broad policy guidance and coordination efforts. Coordination is at times necessary among regulatory programs. Furthermore, they often have implications for other types of policies and programs. The relationship between regulatory actions and the president's economic policy goals is especially important.

Another foundation for involvement in regulation is the president's role as legislative leader. Regulatory policy problems are

Table 1. *National Regulatory Programs: 1963*

Organization	Fields of Activity
Commission	
Civil Aeronautics Board	Air carriers
Federal Communications Commission	Telephone and telegraph, radio and television
Federal Deposit Insurance Corporation[a]	Banking
Federal Home Loan Bank Board	Savings and loans
Federal Maritime Commission	Oceanic transportation
Federal Power Commission	Hydroelectric power, electric energy, natural gas
Federal Reserve Board	Banking
Federal Trade Commission	Antitrust, trade practices
Interstate Commerce Commission	Railroads, motor carriers, domestic water carriers, oil pipelines
National Labor Relations Board	Labor relations
Securities and Exchange Commission	Issuers of securities, securities markets and businesses, electric and gas holding companies
Executive	
Agriculture	Production and prices, commodity standards and exchanges, marketing practices and conditions
Federal Aviation Agency	Air transportation safety
Health, Education, and Welfare[b]	Food and drugs, water pollution
Interior	Oil imports, coal mine safety
Justice	Antitrust
Labor	Labor standards
Treasury	Banking

Note: this table is partially derived from Emmette S. Redford, *American Government and the Economy* (New York: Macmillan, 1965), p. 549. The Atomic Energy Commission is omitted because its major responsibilities were developmental and operational. The U.S. Tariff Commission is not included because its responsibilities were advisory in nature.

[a]Although not a regulatory commission in the strict sense, the corporation performed important regulatory functions.

[b]Air pollution control was added a short time after Johnson became president. He signed legislation with a regulatory element on 17 December 1963.

among the candidates for inclusion in the president's own legislative program. Beyond this, the president is expected to shape and control the legislative ambitions and stances of departments and agencies. The legitimacy of presidential control over commissions in legislative matters has been debated from time to time, but in practice they have stood in much the same relationship to the president in their dealings with Congress as agencies within the executive branch.

Presidents may have a regulatory agenda beyond their legislative program, and this agenda is the third foundation for their involvement in regulation. There are very few substantive regulatory matters that a president must decide. When Johnson was president, there were only four areas in which he was faced with regulatory decisions on a recurring basis: oil import control policy, strikes that might necessitate the invocation of emergency authority, international trade, and international air transportation. As will be seen, Johnson's regulatory agenda extended well beyond these areas. Its precise makeup varied from time to time, but two regulatory projects were of great interest to him throughout his presidency. In fact, both can be described as essentially presidential in character, because they were directly tied to Johnson's basic economic policy objectives and included government-wide efforts to influence economic behavior largely managed at the presidential level. Begun in the Kennedy presidency, they relied principally upon voluntary compliance with presidential policy, although established regulatory programs were used to support them. One employed wage-price guideposts to dampen inflationary pressures, and the other sought to improve the nation's balance-of-payments position through, among other means, limiting U.S. investments abroad.

Contextual Factors

It is not surprising . . . that shortly after assuming office, presidents so often conclude that their most difficult task is to inspire, persuade, cajole, urge, and, too rarely, order the federal bureaucracy to follow their policies.

Joseph A. Califano, Jr., 1975 [4]

Joe Califano, one of Johnson's top domestic aides, wrote these words shortly after leaving the White House. They suggest some of the subtleties and complexities in the conduct of the president's business in regulation or other areas when it includes the work of the various departments and agencies of the government. The character of the relationships linking him to other parts of the government is an important contextual factor shaping the operations of the presidency, as are the dispositions of the president and his aides toward them. Altogether, the received wisdom tends to emphasize the impediments to close, systematic, and effective linkages between the presidency and the ordinary flow of government activity, including that of a regulatory nature.

General Considerations

There are instances in which presidents may, in effect, command, as in making appointments. Presidents may also manage, as in the case of overseeing processes that link the presidency to departments and agencies. They may even administer or direct government operations in matters of special interest to them. Yet leadership suggests better than any other term what is involved in the president's relations with departments and agencies.[5] At a very general level, from the presidential point of view the basic *problem* of executive leadership is to elicit lawful and effective governmental action in accord with presidential perspectives and preferences. One part of the basic *task* of leadership, as Richard Rose says, is to influence officials below the president's level "so that their actions will contribute to the achievement of his objectives and to the fulfillment of his responsibilities."[6] But leadership is a problematic and reciprocal relationship involving exchanges. The second part of the leadership task (which affects success in the first) is, as head of the executive branch, to conduct the presidential office so that subordinate officials may fulfill their responsibilities. In successful performance of the executive leadership role, presidents both serve and are served by the permanent government. Neither task is easy to discharge.

When they go about their executive leadership business, presidents encounter several fundamental realities of executive government which condition their chances of success. If there are two points on which most of those who study or experience the modern presidency agree, they are that the executive leadership role is of enormous importance and that it presents presidents with enormous difficulties. Four basic realities must be faced: the scope and complexity of government severely tax leadership even under the most favorable conditions, while at the same time making its exercise all the more imperative; powerful forces compete vigorously with the president for influence over the executive branch and independent agencies; in the leader-follower relationship, there are disjunctions in what presidents and the permanent government want, need, and can easily provide; and, in any case, presidential resources for leadership are limited when weighed against the magnitude of the task.

At least since Franklin D. Roosevelt and the New Deal, the sheer bulk of the executive branch has challenged presidents as they attempt to place their mark upon it. As Hugh Heclo and others have pointed out, the domestic program explosion that began with the Great Society makes the problem more acute. Along with an increase in the scope and variety of government came an increase in the range of matters which attract presidential attention and overlapping responsibilities and intragovernmental rivalries which command it. Magnified "interrelatedness," to employ Roger B. Porter's term, accentuates the need for coordination from a government-wide perspective and for the executive branch as a whole in some sense to be managed.[7] But, as Stephen Hess notes, it is not always precisely clear what, in fact, is to be managed.[8]

Scale of operations itself would not be so great a problem if the president's preeminence in the executive branch was universally recognized and given deference. But that is not the case. He must contend with others to have his way. According to Godfrey Hodgson, "The executive branch is not really the President's branch. It is not effectively controlled by him. It marches to other drums."[9] In his view, some of the more compelling tattoos are sounded by the bureaucratic members of the permanent government themselves, stimulated by their sense of mission, expertise, policy preferences, and the deep-seated professional and organizational norms they have absorbed. Other tattoos are heard from Congress, resounding with its large responsibilities for the conduct of governmental affairs, and from various particularistic interests with stakes in department and agency activity. Not uncommonly, the bureaucratic, congressional, and interest group tattoos beat loudly and in proximate rhythm, overwhelming the often feeble and uncertain taps coming from the White House and its environs.[10] Whether or not the presidential office is as vulnerable as this characterization suggests, the reality of strong rivals to presidential influence is unquestionable.

Given the nature of the constitutional system, pluralistic politics, and complex modern organizations, it is not surprising that presidential views on substantive matters may clash with those of other actors. In the processes of executive leadership linking the presidency and the permanent government, substantive differences may be exacerbated by differences in institutional perspectives and in operating requirements. The two are closely related.

The perspective of the presidency is thought to be uniquely

government-wide in scope. This leads to a necessary preoccupation with problems in organizational interrelationships and policy integration, whereas the focus of officials within the permanent government is on discrete program segments. The presidential perspective is also distinctly political in character and concerned with broad lines of policy, whereas at operating levels rational-technical dimensions and the particulars of activity appropriately are of central interest. The four-year term and the political calendar force a short-run perspective on the presidency, whereas a long-term perspective dominates within the permanent government.[11] These differences make it difficult for the permanent government to serve the president as he would like and for the presidency to serve the permanent government as it would wish to be served.

Yet, as Louis W. Koenig points out, there are elements of "natural partnership" pulling the president and the permanent government together.[12] Each needs the other. A president ideally requires a variety of services from the permanent government—among other things, the opportunity to make the decisions he should make. He must receive timely information and analysis to allow him to determine, in the first place, what those decisions are, and then to make choices among options that are imaginative, substantively sound, and politically sensitive. He needs faithful implementation of those decisions so that, overall, the machinery of government in its day-to-day operations reflects his sense of the national agenda and his purposes.[13] The speed, imagination, adaptiveness, and sensitivity to presidential preferences and political interests which are expected to characterize responses are difficult for distant bureaucratic organizations to provide, even with the best of intentions. On the other side, the working levels of government need, according to Richard E. Neustadt, presidential decisions in matters critical to them, appropriate delegations of authority, support for their efforts, and a presidential "court of last resort" for the resolution of matters in dispute.[14] Presidents, from their elevated perspective, may elect not to perform such services in every case or may not be able to for reasons of politics, policy, time, or simple disinterest.[15]

Communication problems are an important intervening variable in the relationship, especially in rendering bureaucratic service to the president. For several reasons, departments and agencies may be uncertain as to what is expected of them.[16] Presidents may simply lack agenda and purpose relative to large chunks of government. Mixed or confusing signals may result when a number of not wholly compatible purposes are at work. The accommodation or mediation of conflicting policy objectives is a prime requisite in the presidency.

The clear articulation of integrated policy so that it may be executed by organizations naturally inclined to emphasize one or another of several particular objectives is understandably difficult. Also, presidential wishes may be imperfectly communicated because of the natural impediments found in complex organizations or because of intentional obfuscation. Richard Rose quotes a senior official of the 1970s as observing, "Presidential statements should be soft, fluid, vague, even tricky. There should be nothing in them to attract flak. We spend hours constructing paragraphs so that afterwards we can interpret them in different ways to different clients."[17] No doubt this overstates the case, but certainly political considerations may produce clouded presidential meanings.

Presidents, of course, have substantial resources to package and deploy in their relations with departments and agencies. But the resources are no easy match for the outward pull of the political centrifuge and the vast organizational and substantive complexity of the executive branch. Presidential ability to influence the executive mass, as Koenig says, is "highly imperfect."[18] Major instruments such as the budget and the power to hire and fire at political levels have many familiar limitations. The charismatic appeal of the office usually is moderated in some degree by the incumbent's personality, politics, and policies, although bureaucratic support for a president's efforts may develop despite initial reservations.[19] Presidential time and energy for investment in executive leadership are limited. Of first priority for presidents are the things they *must* do, and these alone make extraordinary demands on the person and the institution.[20]

A second contextual factor consists of the disposition of the president or the extent to which he wants to be involved and influential in department and agency activities. Discretion is not complete, of course. Presidents have two basic determinations to make in regard to executive leadership: the extent of presidential involvement in matters pertaining to department and agency activities and the approach to relations with the operating levels of government that will characterize their presidency. In neither do they have full discretion. Presidents have some executive functions which they must undertake, such as preparing a budget and making certain appointments. Other functions which they must perform in the domestic realm, such as presentation of a legislative program, involve relationships with departments and agencies. Conflicts and problems in coordination arise that simply cannot be ignored. There also is an enforced integration of concerns at the presidential level that enfolds executive leadership in the president's basic business of national leadership. The various aspects of the president's job are interconnected in such a way that ultimately they are not truly separable. Neustadt makes the point in this way: "In the American political system the President sits in a unique seat and works within a unique frame of reference. The things he personally has to do are no respecters of the lines between 'civil' and 'military,' or 'foreign' and 'domestic,' or 'legislative' and 'executive,' or 'administrative' and 'political.' At his desk—and there alone—distinctions of these sorts lose their last shred of meaning."[21]

Recasting the observation in terms of effects, presidential leadership in any sphere has repercussions in other spheres. No significant act, failure, or success is without some broadly diffused consequences for the conduct of government and the president's relations with departments and agencies.

The fact remains, however, that statutes and prevalent expectations allow presidents considerable room to maneuver in their leadership relationships with departments and agencies. They may be activists in the depth, intensity, and scope of their involvement; they may remain quite aloof; or they may place themselves at some intermediate point, depending upon their individual proclivities.

An LBJ Profile

Johnson is usually depicted as an activist president with sharply honed political skills and an overwhelming personality whose career reflected a fierce passion to gain power and substantive accomplishment through political leadership.[22] What kind of executive leader was he? Previous analyses and eyewitness accounts (though Johnson's own memoirs in *The Vantage Point* unfortunately are not among them) provide an impressionistic portrait. Depictions indicate considerable interest and investment of effort in executive leadership, frustration in regard to accomplishment, and flexibility in the conduct of relations with departments and agencies.

Analysts are inclined to highlight the legislative attainments of the Johnson presidency and to relate subsequent problems in implementation to a dominant interest in the legislative score card. Stephen Hess goes so far as to characterize Johnson as a "lifetime legislator, who viewed legislation as the end result of government."[23] Unquestionably, the legislative program was an area in which Johnson provided strong, driving leadership. Just as certainly, the particulars of governmental structures and processes usually were not of great interest to him for their own sake. But the evidence suggests that Johnson and those associated with his presidency knew that government meant more than the enactment of laws and that substantive accomplishment depended heavily on policy elaboration and implementation through the day-to-day operations of departments and agencies. They appreciated the importance of the executive leadership role. Perhaps Johnson's most emphatic public affirmation of this was in his "Quality of American Government" message to Congress in March 1967.[24]

Energetic executive leadership was apparent in three areas involving process innovations intended to strengthen the president's hand. One was the programming-planning-budgeting (PPB) system.[25] Another was the use of task forces for legislative program development.[26] Substantial organizational innovation, chronicled by Emmette S. Redford and Marlan Blissett, reflected a "comprehensive presidential management perspective."[27] Although Johnson himself was not the architect, he played an important part in shaping proposals for reorganization and in seeing to their approval. Finally, there was a concerted effort to build ties of loyalty within his administration.

One way of doing this was through the appointment process. Johnson himself was deeply involved. G. Calvin Mackenzie reports that he "was personally responsible for most of the important personnel choices made during his presidency."[28] His basic purpose was to find persons who not only were competent, but were personally loyal to him and receptive to his leadership.[29] Also, according to Hugh Heclo, "The White House could and did try to build loyalty based on presidential program commitments—the Johnson education program, the Johnson antipoverty program, the Johnson housing program, and a host of others."[30] White House meetings with members of the permanent government were one device. They were, in the words of a Heclo informant, a "massaging operation, a way of 'making them feel part of the family' and of recognizing that 'these were the people that made the machine go . . . people working for you and making the administration and its program a success.' "[31]

The Johnson presidency is typically seen as interventionist in its relations with departments and agencies. On the domestic side, portrayals, for the most part, are drawn from areas of obvious central interest to Johnson: economic policy and Great Society programs. In them, James E. Anderson finds that there was energetic use of all the means at the president's disposal in efforts to shape the conduct of affairs within the executive branch.[32] Neustadt characterizes Johnson as, at times, an "eager clerk," who turned "his enormous energies away from choices he could not escape to other people's choices that he wished they would make differently or better."[33] And he was a most knowledgeable clerk in the workings of government. Former House Appropriations Committee chairman George Mahon observed, "LBJ knew more about the federal government and the line items in the budget and had his finger in more agencies than any other president in this century."[34] One of his aides, James Gaither, commented on "the man's tremendous analytical ability and tremendous knowledge of the government and the government's programs—and . . . his tremendous grasp of figures and historical perspectives."[35] He described a meeting with White House aides, the secretary of Agriculture, and the director of the Bureau of the Budget on a particular program matter: "The President baffled every one of us. I thought I knew everything there was to know about those programs. He asked off of a memo that I had prepared for him—a briefing memo about the program—and he asked question [sic] that no one in that room could answer about impact on local government activities and the way the program would be operated, very direct, piercing questions going to the very heart of the proposal."[36]

Johnson's own activistic impulses were mirrored by his aides, who, according to Hess, "engaged in more operational and policy-formulating matters than ever before."[37] William D. Carey, who observed the Johnson presidency from the higher reaches of the Bureau of the Budget, points to the "needling and prodding" and attempts at "operational coordination" by presidential staff.[38] In Hess's view, the effects were not always positive; many "minutiae" invaded the White House.[39] The president relied on staff to "ride herd" over the executive branch, Thomas E. Cronin says.[40] In his view, this caused his agents to attempt "more than they were supposed to be doing"—"they came 'to give orders' rather than transmit requests."[41] Considerable tension resulted in their relations with departments and agencies, he reports.[42]

Great activism, no doubt, produced some satisfactory results, but it also is alleged to have produced great frustration. Johnson is said to have told president-elect Richard M. Nixon that one of his greatest mistakes was not moving early and firmly to gain control of the permanent government. Cronin records that the president "complained bitterly about the recalcitrance of the federal bureaucracy" and "expressed disappointment over seemingly slow and uncooperative departmental responses."[43] Califano's own book on the presidency suggests similar feelings at the staff level, as when he asserts, "Smaller federal agencies and numerous bureaus within large departments respond to presidential leadership only in the minds of the most naive students of government administration."[44] Frustration is also clear in the consideration given at the highest levels to plans and prospects for an ambitious restructuring of the executive branch. The major focus was provided by the work of the Task Force on Government Organization, chaired by Ben W. Heineman, which was organized in 1966 and completed its work in 1967. The basic thrust of its recommendations was to "presidentialize" the government.[45] It was left to the Nixon administration to move along the lines it set out.[46] Indeed, so far as is known, Johnson never expressed his views on the task force recommendations. The positive responses of aides close to him, however, are another indication of considerable dissatisfaction with the impediments to executive leadership embedded in existing arrangements. There are some indications that in another Johnson term steps would have been taken to strengthen the presidential hand.

Presidents and Regulation

The President's responsibilities require him to know and evaluate how effectively these agencies dispatch their business.

JFK, 13 April 1961[47]

Many students of regulation would agree with Johnson's predecessor, John F. Kennedy, that the president's responsibilities include some type of relationship with regulatory agencies. The precise nature of that relationship will depend upon a number of factors. They include the extent and nature of a particular president's interests.

LBJ in the Congress

Johnson's record prior to becoming president provides few clues as to his views on or his interests in regulation. Thus, beyond the energy that marked his overall approach to government and politics, there was little on which to base predictions about the extent to which regulation would be included in what was sure to be a generally "eager" clerkship and, to the degree that regulation was part of his business, the course that he would follow.

In 1937, at the age of twenty-eight, Johnson entered the House of Representatives after most of Franklin Roosevelt's major regulatory measures had been enacted. Two more would pass with the new representative's support soon thereafter. During his six terms in the House, Johnson's major legislative interest was the work of the Naval Affairs Committee. When legislation came to the floor to strengthen or refine regulation, he usually favored it. In no way did he indicate disagreement with the proposition that the national government had a major role to play in the regulation of the economy. In this, he was less a New Deal planner than a populist who felt that ordinary people and small businesses needed protection against vast concentrations of economic power. His closest connections with regulation while in the House were through constituent casework services and in relation to the Federal Communications Commission. The latter was animated by personal, not policy or political, interests. In 1943 Johnson and his wife, Lady Bird, purchased KTBC, a faltering Austin radio station. It was to serve as the foundation of the future president's considerable wealth and caused the commission to be of close, continuing interest to him.[48]

Johnson became somewhat more involved in regulatory matters when he moved to the Senate in 1949. As a freshman, his primary focus was on the work of the Armed Services Committee, but he was also assigned to the Interstate and Foreign Commerce Committee. This committee had jurisdiction over many important regulatory programs, but Johnson's Senate papers indicate that his involvement in its work was neither expansive nor intense with one exception: the regulation of natural gas.

The central issue of the time was the scope of the Federal Power Commission's jurisdiction over natural gas. It was quite complex. The Natural Gas Act of 1938 was subject to interpretation on the point. Early court decisions found the commission's jurisdiction to be limited, and this interpretation subsequently guided its implementation of the act. A later Supreme Court decision suggested the possibility of a more liberal interpretation, and in the late 1940s the commission began to move toward staking a broader jurisdictional claim. This prompted strong reactions from independent producers, who especially feared regulation of the price of natural gas at the point at which it was sold to pipelines or at the wellhead.

Congress engaged the issue in 1949 and 1950. Johnson was in the forefront in both instances. Up to this point, his relationship with the oil and gas industry had been mixed. Because of his identification with the New Deal and positions he took on naval oil reserves and the regulated price of gasoline during World War II, he earned the enmity of "big oil," the major integrated companies. They expended large amounts of money in efforts to defeat him in the 1944 and 1946 elections and backed his opponent in the 1948 Senate race. Johnson's relationship with independent producers, whose interests often conflicted with those of the majors and who also were important players in Texas politics, was more comfortable. In any case, during his congressional career, Johnson was generally supportive of oil and gas interests. Harry McPherson, a longtime Johnson aide, once observed that he was not a "friend" of either the majors or the independents.[49] He was constrained to support them because of the fact that petroleum was at the core of the Texas economy and many lives were dependent on it. This was the political reality that Johnson faced.

The 1949 struggle was over confirmation of Leland Olds for another term on the Federal Power Commission. Olds was a leader in the effort to expand the commission's jurisdiction over natural gas. Johnson chaired the subcommittee of the Commerce Committee that handled the nomination. After extensive hearings delving into his background and views, Johnson steered a report recommending against confirmation of Olds to the floor, managed floor consideration of the nomination, and won there by a substantial margin.[50]

In 1950 Johnson managed a bill amending the Natural Gas Act to settle, among other things, the dispute over jurisdiction in favor of the producers. It passed the Senate and the House but was vetoed by President Harry S Truman.

It is important to note that in neither case did Johnson assert that economic regulation in general was unwise or that reasonable regulation of natural gas was objectionable. His major arguments were that the commission and the courts were trying to usurp the power of Congress to say what the law is and that there were no economic or equity justifications for what the commission was attempting to do.[51]

This was the record as of 1953 when Johnson became the Democratic leader and shifted his interests in that direction. It showed basic acceptance of the regulatory system then in place. He had not, in any meaningful sense, sought to weaken it or to strengthen it. To the extent he actively attended to regulatory matters, it was essentially in response to constituency concerns. His legislative actions between 1953 and 1961 basically followed the same pattern.

Institutional Considerations

There are additional factors that transcend the dispositions of particular presidents. Most of those who write on the subject emphasize the relatively low level of importance presidents and their aides over time have attached to the regulatory activities of both executive agencies and commissions. This suggests the possibility that, under ordinary circumstances, there are inherent disincentives for presidential involvement in regulation. James Q. Wilson, for example, finds an absence of "close scrutiny or careful control" of regulation by the White House, or by Congress for that matter.[52]

Kenneth J. Meier concludes that the president is the "political actor least likely to intervene in a regulatory policy subsystem."[53] Randall B. Ripley and Grace A. Franklin see presidential involvement in making competitive (principally economic) regulatory policy as so limited that they do not treat this policy type in their general analysis of policy making. In the protective regulatory policy sphere, concerning environmental, health, safety, and consumer protection, they argue that the major policy decisions are made by the Congress, although presidents may exert some influence on them.[54] Furthermore, Ripley and Franklin judge the role of the presidency in the implementation of regulatory policies of both types to be quite limited.[55] Detailed case studies support the notion of limited presidential involvement and influence.[56]

There are competing explanations for limited presidential involvement in regulation, both essentially political in nature. One is that presidents are foreclosed from effectively participating in regulatory affairs. There are two versions. The first is the familiar capture theory: the view that regulatory agencies inevitably become the captives of those they regulate if they are not captives even in conception and establishment.[57] The second posits congressional dominance of regulatory agencies to the exclusion of other actors, including presidents. Members of Congress seek domination to secure resources for use in seeking reelection.[58]

The alternative explanation recognizes that presidents have a variety of resources at their disposal for becoming involved in and influencing regulation but have little interest in doing so. Resources include the prestige of office, constitutional authority, and certain statutory authorities conferred by Congress, as well as the control that may be exercised over budgets and legislation and the part played by the Department of Justice when regulatory decisions are taken to court. Of special importance is the capacity to appoint regulators and to designate the chairmen of regulatory commissions.[59] Appointment and designation are generally considered to be the most potent means at the president's disposal for exercising influence over regulation.

In the 1970s and 1980s presidents Gerald Ford, Jimmy Carter, and Ronald Reagan employed their resources in efforts to bring about deregulation in certain areas and otherwise to reform regulation.[60] Prior to this period such activism was rare. Marshall R. Goodman and Margaret T. Wrightson frame the conventional wisdom in regard to commission regulation in this way: "Empirical research suggests that presidents . . . made little systematic use of [their] powers to shape regulatory administration."[61] They arrive at the same conclusion in regard to executive regulation.[62] Even the appointment and designation powers are often thought to be used without system or substantive purpose.[63]

Several reasons are usually offered for this perceived presidential disinterest in regulatory matters. Clearly, the day-to-day activities of the Food and Drug Administration and the Federal Communications Commission are usually not presidential in nature. Even regulatory actions of considerable policy significance and modifications of regulatory statutes infrequently touch upon presidential priorities or core presidential concerns. Other explanations center on political considerations. William L. Cary, chairman of the Securities and Exchange Commission in the early 1960s, observes that superior management of regulatory programs brings no political benefits to a president.[64] There is no return for expending resources to that end. There also may be costs in indicating interest in particular regulatory matters, even for the best of reasons. Regulatory issues, by definition, involve clashing interests, often of individual parties, as in an enforcement action or a competitive licensing proceeding. A hint of presidential interest risks being taken as an effort to influence a regulatory decision in order to benefit a particular party. As history shows, presidents may suffer politically when there are such perceptions.

Even when presidential interest in a regulatory matter does not raise a propriety issue, political hazards are based on the pluralistic character of regulatory politics.[65] In recent challenges to the capture and congressional dominance models, Terry M. Moe has reaffirmed this characterization of regulatory politics. He finds that regulatory behavior is shaped by a number of endogenous and exogenous variables, including the agencies themselves with their distinctive structures, processes, and cultures as well as other actors such as the Congress, relevant interests, the courts, and the president.[66] Interactions among these in regulatory policy making and implementation tend to be conflictual in nature. The stakes are high for the competing parties. Presidents usually do not have a compelling interest of their own in the results. If Moe's analysis is correct, what do presidents have to gain by being drawn into the fray? Probably very little, if anything. What is to be lost? Losers in pluralistic contests may be alienated and withhold support for presidents in their efforts to attain their main objectives. There is also the chance of presidential failure, especially when the concerns of regulators, congressional committees, and interest groups—the "iron triangles" of legend—coincide.

In sum, from a pluralist perspective, presidents have resources for deployment, but they face risks in becoming involved in regulation. Thus, we are led to believe, they do so infrequently. But this does not necessarily mean that they are never involved or influential. Meier finds that "presidents can and do influence regulation."[67] A number of studies have related changes in regulatory policy and administration to changes in presidential administrations.[68] The Ford, Carter, and Reagan initiatives are still fresh in mind.[69] It may be that regulation simply came to occupy a fundamentally different place in political and governmental affairs during their times, or perhaps presidential distance and disinterest are overplayed as a descriptive theme for previous presidencies such as Johnson's.

Overview

Analysis of the Johnson years indicates that this may be the case. The following chapters examine the relationship between his presidency and regulation basically from a White House perspective. They are founded primarily on the memoranda and other working papers bearing on regulation that circulated among Johnson, his aides, and others in the administration. The cases and situations analyzed were identified through an examination of all the archival material dealing with regulatory agencies and regulatory topics, in an effort to examine the president's business in regulation comprehensively, rather than selectively.

The next two chapters consider linkages between the White House and the regulatory commissions. Subsequent chapters deal with the major regulatory matters that arose within the executive branch proper and came to involve the presidency, mainly involving the regulation of agriculture, oil imports, and banking and enforcement of the antitrust laws. These are followed by a chapter focusing on regulatory policy making, especially as it involved legislative initiatives, and a chapter providing a summation and analysis.

The picture that emerges confounds the conventional wisdom about presidents and regulation and also about Johnson the president in a variety of respects. Regulation was part of the president's business on a continuing and substantial basis. The energetic activism noted as characteristic of the Johnson presidency carried over, at least in part, to regulation. There was not a single day, it is safe to say, in which regulation was absent from the White House agenda. It was not unusual for several regulatory matters to be under presidential consideration concurrently. Almost all of his key aides were frequently engaged in regulatory business.

Despite his fairly extensive involvement, Johnson's basic views on regulation, in the end, remain clouded. In some instances he was an enthusiastic regulator, but in others he was wary and reluctant. Ironically, a good bit of White House interest in regulation was motivated by a desire to avoid or minimize presidential involvement, as opposed to seeking opportunities for intervention and broadened influence. In general, Johnson and his aides were inclined to respect the independence, the authority, and the expertise of both executive and independent agencies. As the analysis will show, a complex set of factors worked to shape the president's agenda in regulation, but in general terms the principal triggers were an obligation or duty of some sort to act or circumstances that, as a practical matter, forced Johnson and his aides to become engaged in regulatory matters. It was necessity, for the most part, not a desire to dominate or determine substantive outcomes, that was at work.

When conducting the president's business in regulation, Johnson and his aides ordinarily did not encounter recalcitrant regulators who resisted White House interest in their affairs. Relationships involved in transactions between elements of the presidency and agency officials were relatively close and normally cooperative. The agencies usually were responsive to presidential concerns and welcomed assistance in resolving problems affecting them. For Johnson, the permanent government and the tendency of officials to adopt departmental or agency as opposed to presidential perspectives did not seem to be a major problem, as reports indicate they often are.

Johnson himself was an active presence in regulatory matters. In handling them, he depended heavily on his staff. Despite his reputation to the contrary, on the whole Johnson and his aides seemed to work well together. He allowed them broad discretion in their undertakings with agency officials and in the way they represented his interests. One of their prime responsibilities, however, was to keep him fully informed on their activities. Johnson demanded and absorbed tremendous amounts of information provided by them and by others. He was interested in knowing what was going on in all quarters of the government, whether presidential stakes were involved or not.

As a decision maker, Johnson was decisive in some situations and indecisive in others. Before he acted, he insisted that his staff thoroughly consider the matter at hand and consult broadly. He appeared to want all relevant views to be aired and examined. Johnson's relations with his aides were open and marked by the candid expression of views. He welcomed their advice and seemed to be open to persuasion when his inclinations went against that advice. The decision-making environment was anything but closed and cramped or biased by skewed or incomplete information. Although he allowed his staff broad discretion, at the end of the day it was Johnson who had the final say. There was no doubt in anyone's mind who was president.

Although Johnson's basic views on regulation *qua* regulation may be unclear, there were certain objectives that drove the presidency in its attention to regulatory affairs. They were never formally stated as doctrine but are sharply implied by presidential comments, by the steps that were taken, and by the contexts of action. Three stand out in importance. The first was to ensure that regulation did not bring harm to the Johnson presidency. In this, Johnson relied heavily on the power to appoint and other means to gain the allegiance of regulators, and he did everything possible to ensure that the actions of regulators were perceived as reasonable, fair-minded, and based on the law, as opposed to being perceived as biased and intended to promote particular interests as part of a political agenda. Another basic objective was to enlist regulatory assistance in attaining basic economic policy objectives such as holding down inflation. A final objective was to extend regulation in order to enhance consumer, health, safety, and environmental protection.

Johnson and his aides were reasonably successful in attaining these objectives. There were no scandals. Politically harmful controversies or charges of biased regulation were kept to a minimum, given the basic nature of the politics of regulation. Most agencies did what they could to support economic policy. Congress, together with the president, took significant steps toward expanding regulation into new areas.

When considering regulatory matters, Johnson, as previously noted, tended to respect the substantive expertise of regulators and his advisers. He considered himself, with some justification, to be the superior source of political expertise in managing situations affecting his presidency. It was the political perspective that he brought to bear, focusing on what was possible politically and what needed to be done politically to obtain a desired result. His adeptness in the politics of regulation smoothed the attainment of his central policy objectives within the government and in the larger stream of politics that involved interest groups and the Congress.

The record of the Johnson presidency in regulation began to be established soon after he came to the office. In fact, his recognition of the importance of the regulatory aspects of government was clearly shown on the twelfth day of his presidency.

2. The Fourth Branch

You men are a very special group that have been assembled here this evening. You hold a great power but, more than that, you hold a great and noble trust. I believe and, yes, I know, that you will honor that trust by seeking greatness in your own efforts and by manifesting nobility in your own conduct; and if you do, that man that looks down upon us from Heaven this evening will be proud that you came his way.

LBJ, 3 December 1963 [1]

WITH THESE WORDS, the new president concluded his late-afternoon remarks in the Cabinet Room to the heads of independent regulatory agencies and his first major engagement with the enigmas of the president-commission relationship. The chairmen of the Civil Aeronautics Board (CAB), Federal Communications Commission, Securities and Exchange Commission, and several other agencies comprising the "fourth branch" of government—Kennedy appointees all—had been called to meet with the president in the White House as part of the process of transition. None were Johnson intimates. He knew some, such as Alan S. Boyd of the CAB, Newton N. Minow of the FCC, and Paul Rand Dixon of the Federal Trade Commission (FTC), from limited associations when he was senator and vice president. Others, such as William L. Cary of the SEC and Joseph S. Swidler of the FPC, were unknown factors to the president—as he was, in a sense, to them—accentuating ambiguities in institutional relationships which lay behind the meeting and Johnson's pledge of continuity and solicitation of support.

Paradoxes in the direction and control of regulatory activity account for the ambiguities that Johnson, like his predecessors, would face in relations with the commissions. As chief executive, he bore broad responsibility for the conduct of commission operations. His constitutional obligations were not vitiated by commissions designed to be, in some sense, independent. Yet the architecture of independence restricted presidential capacity to exercise responsibility through imposing legal restrictions on the appointment and removal of members. He had substantial means to affect the commissions by the designation of most chairmen and the appointment of members as seats became vacant and by controlling budgets and legislative programs. He had no clear warrant in law or tradition, however, for participating in regulatory decision making, except in a very few instances, most importantly in the certification of international air carriers. He might legitimately seek to provide overall leadership in regulatory policy and processes, but his actions would have to take into account the claims of Congress that the commissions, in a unique way, are its instrumentalities and the possibility that improprieties might be read into his actions.

For Lyndon B. Johnson, inherent constraints were joined by a set of special circumstances. He was quite aware of the political harm that regulatory missteps could do a president. Still fresh in mind was the effective Democratic exploitation of charges that in the Eisenhower presidency White House officials and some regulators had engaged in questionable conduct.[2] Johnson's role in the Senate's rejection of the reappointment of Leland Olds to the Federal Power Commission has been discussed. And he was acutely aware of potential hazards in the energy and communications areas. Many believed that his Texas political fortunes were tied historically to the economic interests of the oil and gas industry. "Just because I'm from Texas they think I own all the damned oil wells or that I have some special interest in the petroleum industry," the president told David S. Black, an FPC member and later an Interior Department official.[3] "I'm very vulnerable in the resource picture."[4] His broadcasting interests long had caused speculation about his relations with the Federal Communications Commission and the degree to which he might have received special considerations from it.

Another element was the Kennedy legacy of activism in the regulatory arena. The late president had responded vigorously to dissatisfaction with the Republican regulatory stewardship of the 1950s. Even before his inauguration, Kennedy set James M. Landis, the legendary New Deal regulator, to work on an assessment of agency performance. Landis's report was extremely critical of almost all the commissions and proposed a number of structural and procedural reforms.[5] A good many, such as strengthening the chairman's position in a number of agencies, were implemented through reorganization plans and agency initiatives, despite strong congressional concerns about expanded presidential influence in regulation. Per-

haps of greater importance was Kennedy's vigorous use of the appointment power to place his stamp on the agencies. Although Johnson would have his own opportunities to name regulators early in
his presidency, there were recently named Kennedy majorities on
most of the commissions and substantial numbers of his appointees
on the others.[6]

The presidential dilemma in regard to the commissions is as troublesome as it is clear. Regulatory activities neither can nor should
be ignored. Yet the paths to involvement are poorly marked and
treacherous. Johnson's commitment to continuity, in conjunction
with institutional and political impediments to presidential initiative, to some extent limited his options. But he did not turn away
from regulatory affairs. This and the following chapter chart the
paths to involvement in commission regulation followed in the
Johnson presidency and describe the nature of his business in this
sphere of government.

A Delicate Balance

> You and I, the Congress and the people, and all the special con-
> stituencies of your agencies, are challenged today to re-examine,
> reassess, re-evaluate the regulatory role. We are challenged to ele-
> vate our sights, to measure our performance by quality rather
> than quantity—to concern ourselves with new areas of coopera-
> tion before we concern ourselves with new areas of control—to
> take pride in how much we do rather than in how much there is
> to do.
>
> LBJ, 3 December 1963[7]

> See me. Last year this got in the paper and I had to see all kinds
> of other groups Pub Power, REA etc—This is com business not
> President I'll see Ed but I don't want this to be a utility president.
>
> LBJ, 11 May 1965[8]

One strain in the president-commission relationship was reflected in Johnson's meeting with commission chairmen just a few
days after assuming office: presidential attentiveness and measured
activism on the part of both Johnson and his aides. In the context of
a commitment to continuity, his remarks, especially those calling
for emphasis on the search for "new areas of cooperation before we
concern ourselves with new areas of control," demonstrated his interest and conveyed his views on the tone he wanted for regulation
in his administration.

There was another strain, a pull toward noninvolvement which continually played against and moderated activist impulses. It is exemplified by the president's scrawled reaction to a request that he see Edward Clark, Austin lawyer, longtime friend, and subsequently his ambassador to Australia. Johnson agreed to an appointment with Clark, but he was bothered by the purposes of the meeting. They were to introduce the new leadership of the Edison Electric Institute to the president, "a traditional custom," according to Clark, and to allow industry representatives "to talk about the relationship between the investor-owned electric companies and the Federal Power Commission."[9] Clearly the president did not wish to discuss such matters with representatives of the electric utility industry.[10]

The notion of a distinction between agency and presidential business, which Johnson referred to in his note, is of fundamental importance in understanding his relations with regulators of all types. It was partly rooted in the sense that the authority vested in regulators by Congress should be respected. It also reflected a concern for the proper allocation of presidential time and resources, including resources of a political nature. When it becomes known that the White House has been drawn into a situation, those with interests at stake tend to seek access and an equal opportunity to present their points of view, as Johnson had experienced following a session with utility executives the previous year. Not only is there a drain on time and attention, but the prospect arises of political losses as a result of being saddled with liability for regulatory outcomes, even when they are out of effective presidential control. Lee C. White, a White House aide who became FPC chairman in 1966, describes and explains such considerations and the presidential aloofness he experienced: "There were an awful lot of questions in the minds of many people as to whether he was pushing levers and making suggestions, but he never did. He never did. . . . He sort of treated me a little bit like I had leprosy, because I think he was fearful that it would appear, even if he weren't, that he would get the worst of all worlds—he would be accused of it without having the benefits of pushing me around."[11]

A president, in fact, cannot assign regulatory commissions to a leper colony far removed from the White House. But defining with some precision the nature of the president's business in regulation is not easy, either in theory or in practice. There are certain things he must do, such as make appointments, sanction budgets, and take stands on important legislative questions. There are certain things neither he nor his staff should do, such as try to influence the outcome of adjudicatory proceedings. But between these imperatives is a vast range of regulatory policy activity of national importance, of consequence for matters clearly within presidential purview, and capable of affecting a president's political base. It is in this vast middle ground that lines must be drawn and the problem of striking the balance arises.

There was continuing uncertainty in the Johnson presidency as to the appropriate and desirable kind and degree of presidential involvement in regulatory affairs. For example, doubt was generated even by proposed presidential communications with the commissions simply asking them to take into account balance-of-payments considerations in their conduct of regulatory affairs.[12] There was a similar concern in regard to pushing equal employment opportunity considerations. As Harry C. McPherson, Jr., special counsel to the president, said in this connection, those who were consulted "were concerned about getting the President, even in a hortatory way, into the regulatory business."[13]

The most explicit guideline was to stay away from particular "cases." It was never set out in formal terms, although Lee White recommended such a step shortly after moving from the White House to the FPC. His draft memorandum sent to Joseph A. Califano, Jr., special assistant to the president, prohibited "any contacts with members of regulatory commissions, bodies or agencies in connection with a particular case, proceeding or application which the regulatory body must act upon in a quasi-judicial fashion."[14] White's initiative was stimulated by congressional sensitivity expressed at his confirmation hearing, which he brought to the president's attention. Johnson's interest appeared to lead to the proposal.[15]

The failure to act on White's advice should not be taken as rejection of the principle. It seems clear that Johnson's preference, if not policy, was to keep the White House out of the kinds of proceedings to which White referred, despite frequent and numerous invitations to become engaged. His disposition was shown, for example, in his reaction to the effort by Robert Stevens to enlist White House help in getting the National Labor Relations Board (NLRB) to alter an order finding his textile enterprise guilty of "flagrantly unlawful" labor practices and requiring certain methods of communicating the decision to workers which Stevens saw as threatening to "ruin his reputation." Stevens, who had been "friendly" to the administration "on occasion," talked with McPherson in his White House office on the evening of 30 March 1966. Subsequently, McPherson sought background information from Frank W. McCulloch, the NLRB chairman, who explained and justified the novel remedies to which Stevens objected. McPherson reported all of this to Johnson on

1 April, concluding, "I don't believe the White House should get involved in turning an announced NLRB decision around."[16] The president concurred: "I agree with Harry on the Stevens memo"; furthermore, he recorded his objection to holding meetings in the White House on problems someone like Stevens was having in a regulatory matter.[17]

In addition to the personal dispositions of incumbents, other influences shape the conduct of the presidency. Among them are institutional norms infused in presidential operations by the Bureau of the Budget (BOB), now the Office of Management and Budget. One is that the president should have only "arm's-length dealings with the regulatories," as Elmer B. Staats, the deputy director of BOB, advised White House counsel Myer Feldman in 1964.[18] Feldman had asked for assistance in replying to a complaint about a matter before the CAB that the president received from a friend and supporter, the publisher of the *Denver Post*, Palmer Hoyt. The response, drafted by BOB and modified slightly by Feldman, concluded: "In any event, the President has no authority to interfere in the proceedings of independent regulatory agencies like the Civil Aeronautics Board, except on a formal basis as a litigant when foreign policy or other broad national interests are involved. Even then, it is usually the department concerned that interferes [*sic*], and it does so as a party in interest. I am sure you agree that it would be inappropriate for the president to make any informal representation to any member of a regulatory agency in connection with any matter before it."[19]

Staats felt it was especially important and timely "to speak emphatically," because of recent trade group gossip about the president-commission relationship. He enclosed a sample from *Aviation Daily* in his reply to Feldman's inquiry. "But possibly never before has there been so much definitive back stage political pressures and dictations as at the present time. More than one airline is feeling the brunt of these pressures through 'suggestions' and 'advice.' President Johnson is no one to step aside and let the agency act on its own and, if he is elected next month, it seems quite certain that the CAB will be a direct adjunct to the White House."[20]

As the next chapter shows, Johnson was not disinterested in air transportation matters, and there would be presidential policy initiatives at various points during his tenure, especially after Charles S. Murphy became chairman of the CAB in 1965. At this time, in late 1964, there were none. But the political point is the effect of the perception of a presidential agenda—hence the considerable sensitivity regarding involvement in regulatory affairs.

A policy of maintaining an arm's-length relationship was often referred to in memoranda and correspondence. For example, Lee White responded under the signature of W. Marvin Watson, also a White House aide, to a request for intervention in another CAB matter: "The President has a firm policy against White House staff involving themselves in any proceedings before regulatory agencies."[21] And from special assistant Robert E. Kintner: "Hy Gardner called me to ask if I could do anything about speeding up the clearing of channel 6 in Miami by the FCC. I told him I could not because the President had a rule against anyone in the White House making any representations of this character to independent agencies or departments."[22]

An informal and broadly stated policy of restraint incorporating such terms as "arm's length relationship," involvement in "proceedings," making representations in "cases," and the like obviously leaves much room for interpretation. This is especially true for persons poorly versed in the exotica of administrative law and without substantial prior exposure to regulatory cultures. Many of the White House staff could be placed in this category. Thus the policy was an imperfect means for guiding behavior, especially when there were pressing presidential interests associated with or affected by regulatory actions. In such circumstances, attentiveness, at the least, is almost impossible to avoid.

Two instructive illustrations of the dilemmas involved in getting in or staying out of the regulatory business, even peripherally, are set within a few months of one another in 1966 and 1967. One shows the implications that regulatory actions may have for a president's political position and concerns Henry Ford II. The other makes the same point and also suggests how regulatory actions may relate to a president's overriding policy interests. It concerns Frederick R. Kappel, chairman of the board of the American Telephone and Telegraph Company (AT&T) and former chairman of the Business Advisory Council.

Early in January 1967 the president had a group of businessmen to lunch. Among them was Henry Ford II, one of Johnson's strongest supporters in the business community. During the luncheon, Ford handed Joe Califano a letter addressed to the president in which Ford complained fiercely and at length about a recent and "unreasonable" Federal Trade Commission order that the Ford Motor Company produce information on warranty adjustments and customer complaints. His letter concluded, "Please consider this a purely personal letter which asks nothing of you except your thoughtful consideration of the present ventures and future courses of the regulatory agencies. If the recent action of the Federal Trade Commission is typical of the way it deals with business, it would be easy for me to understand why there may be growing strains on the Government-Business relationship."[23]

Califano held the letter because, as he later explained to the president, he took it to be a plea "for us to do something about the FTC request. . . . It seemed to me exactly the kind of thing that caused problems for Eisenhower and Sherman Adams."[24]

Because of Califano's protective action, Johnson did not become aware of the letter until almost two weeks after the luncheon. But in the meantime he learned of Ford's dissatisfaction from another assistant, Jack J. Valenti. Because "this man Ford was the first to come forward in 1964," Valenti recommended that Johnson talk to Ford to let him know his support was appreciated and "that though the government must do what it must do, Ford is not being singled out."[25] At this point the president did not want even peripheral involvement in Ford's regulatory problems, and he instructed Valenti that an appointment was not to be arranged.

That position changed later in the day when Johnson received a packet of material on Ford from yet another White House staff source, Robert Kintner, including samples of Ford's views gathered in a conversation with Kintner, a newspaper story reporting those views, and a recent speech by Ford in which he voiced his complaints. The matter had become public. This time the president said that he indeed would like to see Ford.[26] Shortly thereafter Watson elicited permission to set up a meeting.[27]

Johnson finally learned of the letter Ford had given to Califano the day after the go-ahead was given to Watson. He received a query from Ford sent through Kintner and William Schoen, on leave from Ford to work as a speech writer on Kintner's staff, as to "what action . . . [Johnson] had taken on the letter."[28] The caution flag went up again. The invitation to meet was not rescinded, but Kintner had Schoen call Ford "and say that the President was unfamiliar with any controversy Ford may have with the Federal Trade Commission and with the government, and that if Mr. Ford desires to talk to the President about government-business relations the President would be glad to see him."[29] A message also went back through the Valenti channel regarding Johnson's "personal concern . . . about Mr. Ford's feelings for the President," reiterating the invitation to visit.[30]

The Ford incident illustrates the rather intense pressure that may be applied to obtain at least presidential acknowledgment of a regulatory problem being experienced by an ally and the risks entailed if that occurs. If Ford talked to Johnson about the FTC matter, the president would be placed in a risky position. He would either have to say no to Ford or have a representation made to the FTC that might cause trouble. Even if he did say no, if a meeting at which a regulatory problem was discussed became public, there would still be trouble.

In this case, Ford's perceived political importance to the administration and capacity to influence the general climate of its relations with business persuaded the president to slide into the regulatory waters, although every effort was made to safeguard against going in too deeply and to finesse the FTC problem. Ironically, Johnson was saved from even a shallow wade by late-blooming caution on Ford's part. His response to the invitation to the White House was an expression of appreciation. He was still "for the President," but he begged off, because automobile safety standards were to be announced soon. Ford believed that "for the President's protection and his own it would be best to delay a meeting."[31]

Ford's persistence and use of varied channels to get his message through to Johnson were easily matched by Kappel's. Johnson became aware of Kappel's unhappiness with the Federal Communications Commission as early as the fall of 1965. On 27 October 1965, the day the FCC initiated the first investigation of AT&T rates in years, Kappel visited Secretary of the Treasury Henry H. Fowler to complain. Fowler reported the visit to Califano, who in turn told the president: "Ordinarily I would not bother you with this, but our control of regulatory agencies is incomplete and Joe Fowler believed that you should be informed in view of our good relations with the business community and Kappel."[32]

Several weeks later Valenti talked to Kappel at a dinner meeting of the Business Advisory Council. He passed on to the president the information that "Kappel was very disconsolate over the reaction to the FCC investigation of his company. This event is playing havoc with his $4 billion expansion program."[33] Attached was the Bell System petition to the FCC asking for reconsideration of its order, given to Valenti by Kappel.

As the FCC's investigation continued, Kappel sought an opportunity to air his complaints directly to Johnson. The first request for a meeting (16 May 1966 was suggested) came through Valenti. The president said no.[34] A few days later another channel was tried. This time it was James H. Rowe, Jr., Washington lawyer, old New Dealer, and longtime Johnson friend and adviser. He called Marvin Watson, who handled appointments. In forwarding Rowe's request to the president, Watson noted that the purpose of the proposed meeting was "to discuss in general the investigation started by the FCC. Mr. Rowe assured me that Mr. Kappel does not want to call names but will discuss the influence on business because of this announcement."[35] Again, the answer was no.

A short time later Rowe put the request in writing. His memorandum to Watson is worth reproducing in full, because it reveals something of the range of considerations at play in regulatory affairs at the presidential level, the nature of the diplomacy involved, and the role of intermediaries such as Rowe.

June 2, 1966

MEMORANDUM FOR: Marvin Watson

Fred Kappel

Dear Marvin:

This is just a reminder about our telephone conversation of last week about Fred Kappel, Chairman of the Board of AT&T.

Kappel wants to see the President. I said to you at the time that this seemed to me to be a case of "hand holding" by the President because Kappel, who will retire within a year, is personally upset by the FCC investigation of AT&T.

I am clear that Kappel does *not* want the President to do anything about it *except* take full advantage of his opportunity to recast the FCC. Kappel, without suggesting candidates, would, I think, point out Henry has gone. Loevinger is leaving, Wadsworth wants to be an Ambassador (or anything other than FCC) and this will be the first—and probably the *only*—opportunity for the President to put his mark on that Commission by the way of appointments.

Kappel would be well aware of the President's sensitivity about this particular Commission in view of the Johnson family interest in television—and he is smart enough not to push a President where he shouldn't be pushed.

But in his own way he is important to the President because he is still the symbol of big business which supports the President. Former Chairman of the Business Advisory Council, he is the king maker, the man who picks the new Chairmen like Murphy (a Kappel man). In a curious way he, as much or more than anyone else, sets the tone for the attitude of business toward the Administration.

Yes, I know the President has a few minor problems like Vietnam! As I told you on the phone, many years ago I told President Roosevelt a certain Senator was "off the reservation" and he had better talk to him. Roosevelt impatiently said "Do I have to hold Senators' hands while I am preparing for a war?" Before I could answer, he said "Don't answer; I know the answer is yes." Q.E.D.

James Rowe[36]

Watson brought the matter back to the president on 1 July. This time Johnson acceded, and Kappel came to the White House two weeks later.[37]

The reason for the president's change of mind can only be surmised. Perhaps it was simply the combination of Kappel's political importance and a persistence that wore away Johnson's reluctance. A brief background memorandum prepared by Califano the day prior to the meeting introduces another element, however. After describing the case before the FCC, he underscored the need for caution and the principle of noninvolvement. "You will recall that Newt Minow [former FCC chairman] was in to urge that we take some steps to make sure the case was speedily decided. In accord with your guidance, I told Minow that we would not become involved in any way."[38]

But there was a close tie between the outcome of the proceeding and the president's economic stabilization policy, which then had as its keystone the 3.2 percent wage-price guideposts. Califano and Gardner Ackley, chairman of the Council of Economic Advisers (CEA), reported that the CEA had been engaged in discussions with AT&T about negotiations with the FCC. The president of AT&T had "informed Ackley that AT&T was ready to settle for a total package of about 4%. However, they wanted to get Ackley's viewpoint because they recognize the difficult problems this presented in terms of the . . . guideposts."[39]

What a president might or ought to do under such circumstances is uncertain. There could be a considerable temptation to attempt to advance basic policy interests, such as restraining inflation, by bringing influence to bear on business or regulators to resolve a matter in a particular way. It would be better, however, not to have to act directly at all and instead to rely on sensitive regulators attuned to the president's policy interests. Thus the importance of the power to appoint.

The Power to Appoint

Tell Macy to get some more goddamned names. That son-of-a-bitch isn't going to take it.

Attributed to LBJ, January 1966[40]

The president barked these words to Marvin Watson as Lee White left the Oval Office without saying yes or no to the proposition that he move from the White House staff to the chairmanship of the Federal Power Commission. John W. Macy, Jr., who directed the staff work on regulatory and other presidential appointments, it seemed, would have to restart the selection process. The FPC position was important to the president for several reasons. Not only was it his personal responsibility to designate a chairman, but it was a politically sensitive office and presented the principal opportunity he would have to affect the commission's performance. Equanimity gave way to exasperation when his personal choice proved to be a reluctant bride, even after Johnson had been "at his very best," according to White, in application of the legendary treatment.[41]

The power to appoint members and to designate chairmen is probably the single most effective device presidents have for asserting their views in regard to the fourth branch. Others have large stakes in his appointment decisions, and there is wide-ranging interest in them. Consequently, there are political hazards as well as opportunities for presidents in their choices. The approach to staffing decisions of Johnson and his aides reflected sensitivity to the duality. Political caution was joined in the process with appreciation of the opportunities provided, not so much to control the agencies, but to bind them to the Johnson administration and to imprint them with Johnsonian perspectives.

Patterns

Johnson is quoted as once saying, "Nobody leaves Lyndon unless Lyndon wants him to go,"[42] and quite often the president preferred continuation to change in commission membership. Johnson had sixty-four membership selection opportunities on the eleven major regulatory boards and commissions covered in this analysis. Table 2 summarizes some aspects of the record.

The number of reappointments (twenty-nine) is only slightly less than the number of new members named (thirty-five). Counting appointments and reappointments together, Johnson majorities were implanted on two commissions in 1964, three in 1965, three more in 1966, and three in 1967. When reappointments are excluded, Johnson majorities were never established on the CAB (two of his three selections were for the same slot), the FCC, the Federal Maritime Commission (FMC), the FRB, and the NLRB. Johnson's reluctance to use the power of appointment with utmost aggressiveness is further indicated by the fact that almost all members who wished

Table 2. Appointments to Regulatory Boards and Commissions: 1964–1968

Agencies	No. Members	Appoint-ments	Reappoint-ments	Total	Year Majority Attained
Civil Aeronautics Board	5	3	4	7	1965
Federal Communications Commission	7	3	4	7	1966
Federal Deposit Insurance Corporation	3[a]	4[b]	0	4	1964
Federal Home Loan Bank Board	3	2	1	3	1967
Federal Maritime Commission	5	2	2	4	1965
Federal Power Commission	5	4	4	8	1966
Federal Reserve Board	7	3	1	4	1967
Federal Trade Commission	5	3[c]	3	6	1967
Interstate Commerce Commission	11	6	5	11	1965
National Labor Relations Board	5	1	4	5	1966
Securities and Exchange Commission	5	4	1	5	1964
Total		35	29	64	

[a]Includes the comptroller of the currency as an *ex officio* member.
[b]Includes Joseph W. Barr, named but not formally nominated by President Kennedy, and William B. Camp, named by President Johnson to be comptroller of the currency and *ex officio* member.
[c]Includes John R. Reilly, whose nomination by President Kennedy was pending in the Senate and who was renamed by President Johnson.

to continue were allowed to do so. Only three instances are recorded in which this was not the case. All three members denied reappointment held seats assigned to Republicans because of a requirement that no more than a simple majority of places be filled by members of one political party. The first to be rebuffed was Boyd Leedom of the National Labor Relations Board. Like most regulators, he had his congressional supporters, notably Senator Karl E. Mundt of South Dakota. As Leedom's term neared expiration in late 1964, Mundt talked to Johnson about him and followed up with written endorsements. When presidential action was not forthcoming, he wrote again, asking if reappointment was even a possibility.[43] Johnson instructed Valenti to "call him and tell him giving consideration but very doubtful because of protests."[44] The protests were principally those of George Meany and the AFL-CIO.

The congressional connection also was evident in the other two cases, mostly in the form of the Republican leader in the Senate, Everett M. Dirksen of Illinois, whose interest in Republican regulatory appointments was acute and constant. Despite a strong Dirksen endorsement, Abe McGreagor Goff was not reappointed to the ICC after his term expired in 1966.[45] More difficult was the matter of John S. Patterson of the Federal Maritime Commission. He was from Dirksen's home state of Illinois and was a close associate of the senator. Patterson was placed on the FMC in 1962, despite strong White House staff reservations.[46] His reappointment was opposed by the other Illinois senator, Paul H. Douglas.[47] More importantly, it was opposed by the commission chairman, Admiral John Harllee, who viewed Patterson as "a tremendous liability . . . because he had a habit of making difficulty and dissenting to absolutely everything that was done regardless of its merits." He "made as much trouble as possible" and "was a man of very little intelligence but a lot of stubbornness."[48]

The president was aware of the situation. According to Harllee, at a White House function, "President Johnson pulled me aside and told me personally and confidentially that he knew I had a problem about Dirksen and Patterson and that he was going to take care of it."[49] This was more easily said than done. Dirksen was not quickly convinced that a change should be made, and the memoranda flowed. "An enormous amount of time was spent on 'the Patterson question' in the . . . White House in early 1966," according to one study.[50] Finally a compromise was struck. Patterson would leave the FMC for a comparable position, membership on the Subversive Activities Control Board, which at the time was distinguished by almost complete inertness.

These instances in which persons were not reappointed suggest some of the reasons why so many were, including strong pressures for continuation, especially from congressional supporters, and the potential for disputes over replacement to escalate in ways that sapped time and energy, generated controversy, and forfeited or weakened political support. Changes might not be considered worth the candle, even if a disposition to make them was present. John Carver of the FPC is a case in point. As his term was expiring in 1968, Johnson took seriously White's complaints about Carver's lack of support for the FPC chairman and was inclined to replace him.[51] In the end, however, Carver was reappointed.

Similar considerations may fuel efforts to avoid changes, even when the regulator wishes to relinquish his position. John R. Reilly indicated in 1967 that he was going to resign from the Federal Trade Commission. White House efforts were made to persuade him to stay on, but without success.[52] Another result obtained in the case of Frederick W. Ford, a Republican member of the FCC. Several months before his term was to expire in June 1964 he decided that he did not wish reappointment and so indicated to the White House. But, for political reasons, the president did not want to have an FCC vacancy on his hands during the election campaign. People such as Representative Oren Harris of Arkansas, chairman of the House Committee on Interstate and Foreign Commerce, and Walter Jenkins of the White House staff spoke to Ford at the president's behest. Pressure grew. Johnson himself did not contact Ford, but the commissioner remembered the time as being "pretty tense." Finally he capitulated, indicated his willingness to continue (for which he received personal presidential thanks), and was quickly renominated and confirmed for a full term. Soon after the election Ford resubmitted his resignation, and it was accepted with alacrity and without complaint.[53]

The impact of a change on the conduct of commission business was also a factor which could make reappointment very attractive to the president. In 1967 the Federal Communications Commission had before it the controversial ITT-ABC merger proposal and was nearing completion of the AT&T rate investigation on which it appeared to be divided 4-3. Robert E. Lee, a Republican, was one of the majority, and his term was to expire on 30 June. That day came and went without word from the White House. Apparently no alternatives to Lee were considered; in fact, Macy cautioned the president well in advance that Lee's status needed to be clarified because of the cases.[54] Although wanting to be reappointed, the commissioner did not wish to dangle. He submitted his resignation on 3 July, much

to the consternation of the White House. It was felt that he was
placing the president in the embarrassing position of having to beg
him to stay. A meeting with Johnson was arranged for 11 July, but
canceled. Two days later Lee was summoned to see Watson, who
took him to the president. According to Lee, Johnson's first words
were, "What's this crap I hear about you wanting to resign?" Lee
said, "Mr. President, I am at your disposal," and Johnson concluded
the interview: "OK, that's taken care of." Lee's nomination was sent
to the Senate within just a few days.[55]

It is probably fair to conclude that there was a continuing tension
between the advantages of membership stability and change in personnel decision-making processes, even in the president's own deliberations. This is suggested by two situations occurring at about
the same time. In one, Johnson was reluctant to make a change, but
eventually did so. In the other, he apparently wished to make a
change, but circumstances caused him to relent.

In 1966 Secretary of the Interior Stewart L. Udall engineered personnel shifts that would bring Charles F. Luce, head of the Bonneville Power Administration, to Washington as his under secretary.
To allow this to happen, David S. Black was to go from the FPC to
Bonneville and John A. Carver to the FPC from the position Luce
was to assume at Interior. All was arranged, except for the president's approval. He was reluctant to act, and the matter dragged on.
He expressed his "considerable concern" in a White House session
with Black: "These are three very important resource positions that
are involved. Why should I take three men who are doing a good job
and—or, at least not creating problems—and shift them around like
this?"[56] Ultimately he acquiesced, but not before he was quite sure
that negative political reactions would be minimized and that no
problems would be created in concluding important cases then before the FPC.

Overlapping the Luce-Carver-Black fandango was consideration of
the reappointment of Gerald A. Brown to the National Labor Relations Board. In March 1966 NLRB chairman Frank McCulloch called
the White House to urge a new term for Brown. Marvin Watson duly
informed the president, who responded, "Tell him I'm considering
2 or 3 fellows to whom I feel obligated. I can't survive just reappointing people."[57] As he delayed action, pressure mounted in support of
Brown to counter pressure against him led by the U.S. Chamber of
Commerce.[58] In April Andrew J. Biemiller, legislative director of the
AFL-CIO, sent word through Califano that "the AFL-CIO and Meany
personally are very much for Gerald Brown." Still resistant, the
president wondered, "Why after Miami"—where the unions in con-

vention had strongly criticized the administration's economic policies—"does Biemiller think we should consult him?"[59] At about this time the NAACP and Roy Wilkins weighed in on Brown's side. But Johnson apparently still had other prospects in mind.[60] Meany himself called in support of Brown in June.[61] A month later the labor leader visited the president, with Brown being one of the items on his agenda.[62] Soon afterward Macy met with Johnson and thoroughly explored a rather detailed analysis of Brown's service on the board.[63] McCulloch remained a strong Brown advocate, forwarding endorsements to the White House and otherwise urging reappointment.[64] Finally, the president capitulated to the importuning, and Brown's reappointment was announced on 22 August 1966.[65]

A balance between continuity and change was also evident in the choice of commission chairmen, who are in many ways the keys to leadership in regulatory processes.[66] All the chairmen were presidential designees, except in the Interstate Commerce Commission and the Federal Deposit Insurance Corporation, where the members themselves made the selection. Informally, the president determined who would fill the FDIC post. And, except for the CAB, FPC, and FRB, chairmen designated by the president served in that position, but not as members, at his pleasure.[67]

Four Kennedy chairmen continued in their posts throughout Johnson's term of office: Admiral John Harllee at the Federal Maritime Commission; William McChesney Martin, Jr., at the Federal Reserve Board; Paul Rand Dixon at the Federal Trade Commission; and Frank McCulloch at the National Labor Relations Board. All except Martin were reappointed as members and redesignated as chairmen by Johnson at the expiration of their initial terms. Martin's term as a member of the FRB did not expire until 1969, and, when his four-year term as chairman expired in 1967, Johnson asked him to serve another.

Of the six new chairmen appointed by Johnson, three were promoted from commission membership: Rosel H. Hyde at the Federal Communications Commission; John E. Horne at the Federal Home Loan Bank Board; and Manuel F. Cohen at the Securities and Exchange Commission. Their appointment as members preceded Johnson's presidency. Kenneth A. Randall was selected by his colleagues to be chairman of the FDIC with Johnson's approval. Johnson initially appointed Randall to the board. Two of the "outsiders" brought in as chairmen were Charles S. Murphy and his successor at the Civil Aeronautics Board, John H. Crooker, Jr. The other was Lee C. White at the Federal Power Commission.

In no case would it be correct to say that a change in a chairmanship was forced by the White House. At one point in 1965 Johnson expressed some reservations about Harllee of the FMC, but he was soon reappointed without real problems or delay.[68] In the aftermath of a controversial FRB interest rate decision in late 1965, some in the White House explored the possibility of removing Martin from the chairmanship, a post he had held since 1951. His continuation on the expiration of his term as chairman in 1967 was not a foregone conclusion, but his standing was such that he was reappointed with little hesitancy. The one instance in which serious consideration was given to replacing a chairman who wished to continue concerned Paul Rand Dixon at the Federal Trade Commission. His term as a member was to expire in late September 1967. As early as the previous February his situation was on the president's mind, because of discord within the agency. There was a "possibility that he may not keep Dixon," a Macy assistant reported to Califano.[69] Donald Turner, who headed the antitrust division in the Department of Justice, was quite critical of Dixon's stewardship.[70] Macy ultimately endorsed Dixon's reappointment, "all things considered." Among those things considered was strong congressional support, including that of "Senator Morse, Speaker McCormack (who has repeatedly expressed a strong interest in Dixon), and by Congressmen Wilbur Mills, Joe Evins, and Jake Pickle," the last being the president's own representative.[71] Approximately two weeks before his term expired Dixon's reappointment was announced without fanfare at Johnson's ranch in Texas, and he continued to serve as chairman.

Voluntary departures precipitated all of Johnson's chairmanship changes. In three instances, chairmen went to other positions in government. Alan Boyd of the CAB became under secretary of Commerce for transportation; Charles S. Murphy of the CAB, desiring a less demanding assignment, moved to the White House to become counselor to the president; and Joseph W. Barr went from the FDIC to Treasury to be the under secretary. Both Boyd and Barr concluded their service in the Johnson administration as cabinet secretaries.

The others who left chairmanships returned to private life. William L. Cary of the SEC announced his departure for Columbia University, from which he was on leave, early in 1964. Joseph P. McMurray of the Federal Home Loan Bank Board (FHLBB) also left in 1964 for a college presidency. There are no indications that these departures were anything other than what they seemed—normal career transitions.

In the two remaining cases, there was considerable speculation about whether the chairmen left entirely on their own volition. When E. William Henry announced his resignation from the FCC in April 1966, a trade paper reported, "Word had been dropped repeatedly that it was hoped he 'would see the light' and quit," because of his Kennedy associations and the displeasure of broadcasters with his rather aggressive regulatory stances, among other reasons.[72] It is true that Henry felt a lack of rapport with the Johnson White House, and this was a factor in his decision.[73] It is also true that Johnson reappointed a number of commissioners who tended to check Henry's preferences for strong and innovative regulation,[74] but he was not overtly pushed to go. In the opinion of John Macy, "the President held him in high regard."[75] When Henry saw Bill Moyers in the White House to tell him he wished to leave in order to work in the campaign of his law school classmate, John J. Hooker, Jr., for governor of Tennessee, Moyers told him that the president was satisfied with his performance and asked him to reconsider.[76] But the resignation stood. Further evidence is Johnson's expressed "desire to give Bill Henry a good send-off," a gesture generally not afforded those in presidential disfavor.[77]

For Joseph Swidler of the FPC, the speculation was, to an extent, correct. His term expired on 22 June 1965. In the view of Lee White, his successor, "He would have been willing to remain as chairman if Johnson had asked him."[78] But he was a "tough, proud kind of hombre" and "fearful" that the president would not do so, because of his unpopularity in some sectors of the energy community. "So rather than run the risk . . . , he told me as the closest personal friend he had on the White House staff [White had worked for Swidler at the Tennessee Valley Authority] in May that he did not want to be reappointed, which I dutifully reported to the President and John Macy."[79] Johnson did ask him to stay on until a successor was named. As months rolled by, Swidler became anxious to leave. On 9 November 1965 the Northeast blackout occurred. He was asked to stay even longer to oversee an investigation, which was completed in early December; "then," according to White, "all of a sudden he was gone."[80]

Finding a replacement was especially difficult and frustrating. Many names were considered before the president settled on Lee White and finally got his acceptance. But this was not abnormal. In almost all cases, the process of recruitment and evaluation was a complex one undertaken with great care, with the president playing a central role.

The Process of Choice

In mid-October 1968 Johnson instructed one of his aides to "get me a name to send up as a recess appointment. Ask Bill Deason about his man—see if he knows anybody that is very dependable."[81] The appointment in question was a Republican vacancy on the Interstate Commerce Commission. It had existed since February, and, nearing the end of his presidency, Johnson wanted to push ahead and fill it.

At one point, former Maine governor John H. Reed, then a member of the National Transportation Safety Board, appeared to be the choice. Mike N. Manatos, in charge of Senate liaison, conducted soundings for the president. On the Democratic side, Senator Edmund S. Muskie of Maine did not object, but also did not see any "political mileage" for the president or the party in the appointment. On the Republican side, Manatos worked through Senator Dirksen. Senator Margaret Chase Smith of Maine would go along. However, Senator Norris Cotton of New Hampshire, the ranking minority member on the Senate Commerce Committee, was not immediately enthusiastic. According to Dirksen, Cotton "'wants to puzzle' over the . . . suggestion for a few days." Furthermore, Cotton "suggested the President may want to consider Bush Brooke," an aide to Senator Thurston B. Morton of Kentucky.[82] Reed's prospects faded because of senatorial indifference, Brooke was appointed a few weeks later to the Federal Power Commission and, in the meantime, Dirksen "was still searching for candidates for the Interstate Commerce Commission."[83]

While Dirksen was searching, so was John Macy. Although his efforts were supplemented in various ways, Macy's operation was extremely important in selecting regulators. Shortly after the 1964 election Johnson asked him to serve as his adviser on presidential appointments, in addition to chairing the Civil Service Commission. From a base in the old Executive Office Building, Macy and his small staff performed several key functions. Position profiles providing appropriate background and indicating needs were prepared as openings occurred. When profiles were completed, names of possible appointees were compiled from a variety of sources. After evaluation by Macy and his staff, information on a small number of top candidates and assessments of their qualifications, together with the position profile, were sent to the president. On the basis of material supplied by Macy and whatever else had reached him, Johnson would exercise one of a number of options, ranging from selecting one name to rejecting them all.[84]

In the case of the ICC position, Macy was ready to make a recommendation late on the afternoon of 30 September. He prepared a memorandum suggesting the selection of Noel A. Clark, a member of the Nevada Public Service Commission. It was typical of those he sent to the president when recommending an appointment. Clark had "performed well" as a state regulator and had "gained a reputation for competence, integrity and hard work."[85] A former president of the National Association of Regulatory Utility Commissioners, he was supported by that group. Favorable assessments had been received from Secretary of Transportation Alan Boyd, FPC member Carl E. Bagge, ICC member Wallace Burke, and former Nevada governor Grant Sawyer. Clark first had been put forward by Senator Alan Bible, a Nevada Democrat, but, according to Macy, Bible was no longer pushing the appointment, "apparently in the belief that such a request would jeopardize other appointments in which . . . [he] was interested."[86] However, Macy did not feel that either Bible or Howard W. Cannon, the other Nevada senator, would object to Clark's selection. If the president was not attracted to Clark, Macy provided four other possibilities, along with capsule evaluations, endorsements, and, as in the case of Clark, full biographies of each. Three of these, like Clark and the commissioner being replaced, were from western states.[87]

No one on Macy's list appealed to the president; as it turned out Johnson was not to find that "dependable" person he was seeking. The position was left to be filled by Richard M. Nixon. But several key features of the appointment process, as it typically functioned, are suggested by the effort. Decisions were not made casually. The search for possible candidates generally was wide-ranging, and credentials were evaluated with care. Macy's operation played an important role, but it did not dominate the selection process. Close attention was paid to political implications and to the acceptability of choices. The Senate's reaction, especially that of Republican members when a place was to go to one of that party, was carefully assayed.[88] Most importantly, although there was extensive White House staff work, the president himself was at the center of the process.

A thorough study covering several administrations concluded, "No President in recent times has been extensively involved in specific appointments to the major regulatory commissions . . . with the prominent exception of Lyndon Baines Johnson."[89] He recognized, according to John Macy, that "the character of my administration is going to be formed by the abilities of the people that work with me."[90]

The appointment of regulators was not a function with which Johnson was completely comfortable, however. Very soon after becoming president, he asked several aides to consider the wisdom of developing an advisory committee review procedure, like that used in selecting federal judges, to assess the qualifications of prospective board and commission members. White House aides used the bottom drawer technique for burying a presidential idea considered to be unwise: they simply failed to respond. Kermit Gordon, director of the Bureau of the Budget, was more forthright, making the point, among others, that appointment of regulators "who share your views and objectives is your most important formal lever for influencing the policies and activities of these agencies, many of which are vital to the success of your major programs."[91] This authority, Gordon felt, should not be diluted.

In practice, it was not. There were instances, to be sure, in which Johnson relied principally on first Ralph Dungan, then Macy. There were other instances in which he operated with great independence. Dungan remembered "a number of occasions . . . [when] lists of potential appointees were rejected in Johnson's mercurial and arbitrary style."[92] The president was particularly interested in the choice of chairmen. In selecting members, he seemed more interested in some agencies than others. Those of the highest priority included the Federal Communications Commission and the Federal Power Commission. At times, for positions he considered to be especially sensitive, Johnson served as his own prime recruiter and evaluator.

A rather dramatic example of the president assuming control is the appointment of James J. Wadsworth to the Federal Communications Commission in 1965: this was the position previously held by Frederick Ford, whose reappointment under presidential duress was discussed earlier. It was a Republican slot. Early in the year Johnson began to cast about for possibilities. Apparently he had in mind the appointment of a woman. Jack Valenti assisted through his Houston contacts. Oveta Culp Hobby of the *Houston Post*, secretary of Health, Education, and Welfare in the Eisenhower administration, was asked for her reactions to Dorothy (Buff) Chandler of the *Los Angeles Times* and Pauline Fredericks of NBC News, and for any other suggestions she might have.[93] There were other such contacts asking for nominations.

Several strong candidates were put forth by interested parties. Perhaps the strongest was Charles King of the Detroit University Law School, who had served a few months as a recess appointee to the commission in 1960. Indeed, he was mentioned favorably by Mrs. Hobby. But while on the FCC King voted for the renewal of one

of the Johnson television licenses. That alone was sufficient to dis-
qualify him.[94] The president was not about to appoint anyone from
the outside who could be connected in any way whatsoever to his
business interests.

Meanwhile, Macy had just undertaken his responsibilities in the
White House, and the FCC vacancy was one of the first presidential
appointments he tackled. He prepared several lists of possibilities
and submitted them to Johnson, but with no results. Macy came to
realize that the president was going to handle the matter himself.[95]

And so he did. Johnson's earlier consultations with Hobby and
others had come to naught, but he continued to have the problem in
mind. On 24 March he met with Ambassador Henry Cabot Lodge
on the situation in Vietnam. In the course of the conversation, he
asked Lodge for suggestions regarding the FCC post. Lodge recommended Wadsworth, who had been deputy U.S. representative to the
United Nations, then representative, in the Eisenhower administration. Johnson immediately saw him as *the* choice: a Republican blue-
blood with a prestigious record of public service, no connections
with broadcasting, and, to top it off, the brother-in-law of an influential Democratic senator, Stuart Symington of Missouri.[96] The
president immediately called Macy to initiate the necessary background check. The next morning he talked by telephone to Lodge,
to Macy, and twice to Wadsworth. At 12:50 P.M. Johnson called the
press into his office and announced Wadsworth's appointment.[97]

Although in the end Johnson acted independently in this case,
there was widespread consultation that was typical in the recruitment of regulators. Members of the White House staff often made
recommendations. The president, directly and through Macy, looked
for names from others in government and from close associates in
the private sector. Leonard H. Marks, the head of the United States
Information Agency, who once handled the legal affairs of Johnson's
broadcasting interests, usually was brought in on FCC positions.
Willard Deason, a member of the Interstate Commerce Commission
and friend since college days, was quite active, and not only in regard to ICC positions. Cabinet members were asked for suggestions.
Agency chairmen were important participants, especially when reappointments were at issue. In such cases, they usually opted for
the known and supported continuation. But not always. Lee White,
as noted previously, unsuccessfully opposed the reappointment of
John Carver in 1968.[98] Outside the government, attorneys and longtime confidants such as James Rowe, Gerald Siegel, and Edwin Weisel, Sr., peppered the White House with advice from their Washing-

ton and New York bases, as did Abe Fortas before and during his service on the Supreme Court.

Members of Congress played key roles. Senators were especially visible, in part because the necessity of confirmation added weight to their views. Quite often they were strong proponents of individual candidates and, even if not, were asked for assessments. Minority leader Dirksen and the ranking members of relevant committees were always interested in Republican appointments. At least seven of Johnson's thirteen Republican selections can be attributed to strong congressional sponsorship, and three of these appointees came directly from Senate staff positions.[99]

Patterns of involvement in the selection of chairmen were much like those for the selection of members and could vary considerably. At one extreme, the search process involved widespread consultation. In finding a replacement for Charles Murphy at the CAB, numerous persons were asked for suggestions. According to John Macy, some thirty names were proposed which merited serious consideration.[100] At the other extreme, the president was his own counsel. For example, it appears that he acted essentially alone in the choice of Rosel Hyde for the FCC chairmanship in 1966 after Henry's resignation and that no others were seriously in the running.

Wide-ranging consultation came into conflict with the president's interest in maintaining confidentiality in the appointments process in order to protect his options. Press speculation was not uncommon, as candidates and backers sought support, FBI checks were conducted, and journalists exercised their natural curiosity. Macy says, "I don't know of any single case where an individual who hadn't already been taken off the list was removed as a result of premature revelation in the press."[101] Nevertheless, Johnson could become highly irritated when his decisions were anticipated or when speculation seemed aimed at forcing his hand, and he would have the sources of stories checked.[102] In some cases appointments proclaimed as "sure things" came to pass, in other cases not. It is not clear to what extent prospects about whom stories were written remained on the list, but were passed over because of a breach of propriety which might indicate to the president a lack of reliability and questionable loyalty.

Criteria

What did the president want in a regulator? In 1965 a close friend of Johnson's suggested a young New York lawyer for a position on the FPC. The only connection drawn between the candidate and energy matters was brief service on special assignment with Senator John O. Pastore of Rhode Island in the 1956 fight over the deregulation of natural gas, which Pastore had opposed. Apparently this was enough to create presidential doubts. Johnson's response was: "Thank him [for the suggestion] but I want someone who can be fair and objective."[103]

The ultimate selection criteria were locked in the president's mind, as were the motives involved in particular choices. It is probable, however, that they were many and varied. In Ralph Dungan's view, the president "had 50 motivations for every political move he made, particularly in an election year."[104] The general character of operative criteria and motives can be implied, however, even if their specifics remain obscure.

There appeared to be three main criteria. One was basic competence. Macy and his associates provided Johnson with thorough analyses of candidates, their backgrounds, and their capabilities. James E. Marsh, who assisted Macy, says that Johnson told them, "Don't give me political advice. All I want from you guys is a qualitative assessment of whether a person can do the job, and I want only the very best people. If possible recommend two or three people for each vacancy, but make sure they're all the very best people available."[105] In Marsh's judgment, Johnson "was remarkably loyal to that concept."[106]

Another criterion was whether an appointment would advance the president's political interests. This was of particular importance when he came to make final choices. Johnson used appointments for building support, and, as one observer noted, there was an effort "to squeeze the last drop of patronage value" out of them.[107] The frequent delays in presidential decisions may have been related to this end, as Johnson presented the appearance of finally and reluctantly giving in on an appointment that he was prepared to make anyway, thus earning credit with those urging the action. There did appear to be some bargaining, especially with Senate Republicans, whose support he constantly sought on critical domestic and foreign policy matters. Sherwin Markman, who was responsible for liaison with the Illinois congressional delegation, comments on Senator Dirksen in this regard: "Dirksen had a shopping list. He'd come in the White House, periodically, with literally a list of things that he wanted; none of them normally of any great moment from a Presidential perspective, patronage kinds of things and so forth, which the President would more or less grant him."[108] In regulatory appointments, according to Lee White, Johnson "sometimes had to succumb to pressures, especially from Dirksen, who was a very hard bargainer, and I have a hunch he stole Johnson's pants a few times. And a few times it went the other way."[109] The kind of support that could be generated is indicated in Senator Wallace Bennett's expression of gratitude for the appointment of a candidate he sponsored: "While I will probably go on voting as a Republican, I hope there will be many of your proposals which I can support."[110]

The third set of criteria, and arguably the most important of the three, went beyond basic competence. For political and perhaps intellectual reasons, Johnson wanted regulators of a certain type, who would conduct themselves in ways that would not detract from his administration, create political problems or cost political support, or violate his preferences as to the tenor of regulatory activity. Several attributes were valued: relevant experience and expertise in governmental affairs, but no track record that would suggest the absence of an open mind on the regulatory matters to be decided; a background and temperament that would predict a judicious approach to regulatory responsibilities and behavior that would be seen as fair, objective, and reasonable, rather than vigorous and overt advocacy of *any* particular interest or point of view; and loyalty to the president and his administration.

Johnson went on record from time to time in describing what he wanted from regulators. When announcing his intention to name Manuel Cohen to head the SEC, he said, "I know that he shares completely my own philosophy of regulation, which is to be fair and equitable, applying the law with vigor and common sense."[111] At the swearing in of two FMC members, the president noted that they "have always placed cooperation ahead of control. . . . As President, I very much welcome this type of approach."[112] When Lee White was sworn in as chairman of the FPC, Johnson commented, "The chairman and the members of a commission must always remember that they are the judges for the public interest and not the advocates of a special interest. They should listen to both sides of a question, weigh all the facts and all the evidence available, then come to a decision—a decision that is objective and a decision that is fair."[113]

The president obviously saw a logical relationship between this type of regulation and his political fortunes. Advocacy regulation of whatever stripe on the part of a commission majority would exacerbate conflict within regulatory sectors. Even in the minority, advocates would be inclined to write dissents and otherwise make their views known, with similar consequences. The greater the prior participation in substantive matters under the jurisdiction of the agency involved, the more likely the presence of sharp views and special intellectual and other obligations and the less likely a regulator would be to maintain at least the appearance of judiciousness, to meld in with the administration as a whole, and to evidence loyalty.[114] It is clear from the record that for sitting members prior service was not a bar to reappointment, but for candidates to fill vacancies their prior record of advocacy was of great relevance.

For the most part, the backgrounds of new Johnson appointees indicate the absence of special obligations or tendencies toward advocacy. One group consisted of experienced and tested regulators. Two were promoted from staff positions, one became a commissioner after a brief stint as an aide to a member of another agency, and three came from state regulatory bodies. Another group of twelve was drawn from congressional staffs and executive agencies. Eight came from outside the government. Most of them had significant political and governmental experience, and none came from the ranks of those they were to regulate. Within these three groups, it would be difficult to find an appointee who, on the basis of the public record, could be comfortably classified as a partisan of anything other than thoughtful and reasonable regulation.

A fourth group, appointees to agencies regulating financial institutions, departed from this pattern. Most of them were drawn from the financial community. They included two securities attorneys named to the Securities and Exchange Commission; two bankers named to the Federal Deposit Insurance Corporation, one of whom was later moved to the Federal Reserve Board; and two mortgage financiers named to the Federal Home Loan Bank Board. Why was there a different approach in these instances? One clue is found in Johnson's remarks when Joe Barr was sworn in as chairman of the FDIC: "And now we are sending Joe Barr over to the FDIC with specific instructions to keep the experiences of the thirties in mind."[115] It may be that the president thought the best antidote to misbehavior in financial institutions was regulators who knew their intricacies. Furthermore, it seemed to be especially important for the regulators of financial institutions to have the confidence of the regulated.

There is another anomaly associated with the selection of regulators exercising jurisdiction over financial institutions, most notably when a position on the Federal Reserve Board was at issue. In this case, objectivity, especially in regard to economic policy, was not a desired trait. Johnson and his advisers were determined to name only persons clearly supportive of the administration's economic policies. Where there were doubts, intense inquiries were launched to resolve them.[116]

For prospective appointees to other regulatory agencies where policy commitment was not a criterion, special inquiries were made if doubts arose in the process of evaluation as to the overall reasonableness and objectivity of otherwise attractive candidates. When considering Columbia law professor William K. Jones for the Federal Power Commission, a book review written by him that was alleged to show bias came to the president's attention. Abe Fortas and Jack Valenti were asked for assessments. Fortas concluded that Jones appeared to be "an objective technician."[117] Valenti's view was that "Jones is a judicial mind, with leanings to the side of the consumer, or perhaps—to state it better—has a few misgivings about the gas producer's approval of depletion percentages while they fight other Federal guide-lines."[118] Whether the president was satisfied on the question of judiciousness is unknown, but Jones was not appointed.[119]

Fortas was also called on for advice in 1964 on the pending appointment of Mary Gardiner Jones, a Republican, to the Federal Trade Commission. He expressed some reservations, but did not believe that she was "an extreme trust buster," as the president had first thought him to say.[120] Rather, Fortas felt there already were too many antitrust lawyers, of which she was one, on the commission. Ralph Dungan gave further assurances to Johnson. "She has a very reasonable attitude toward the problems of the business community in their efforts to comply with the antitrust laws. She would be extremely reasonable and competent in applying the law."[121] Her appointment went forward.

Dungan's assessment was based upon conversations with Jones. Prior to a presidential decision, aides and other close associates often were employed to interview prospective appointees to ascertain rectitude and loyalty. The loyalty of Republican candidates was of special interest. Marvin Watson, after discussions with two Republicans being considered for the ICC, reported that one "does not need a job but he believes in what this Administration and President Johnson are doing in the field of transportation and would like to be a part of the program. . . . Although a Republican . . . he supported President Johnson in 1964 and will be a team player. 'That's the way I believe.'"[122] The other "reiterated his support of President Johnson's program on transportation. He is obviously eager to serve the President."[123]

Similar procedures and concerns were often evident in consideration of reappointments. For example, Watson and Macy met with Jones when her appointment expired in 1966. Watson reported, "She understands, and I believe, practices loyalty to the President."[124]

With former Tennessee governor Buford Ellington, he saw FTC chairman Paul Rand Dixon under similar circumstances the following year. Ellington reported that Dixon "is completely loyal to the President and the present Administration."[125] Watson's assessment was: "If he is truthful, he is a Johnson man."[126] Edwin Weisel, Sr., through Macy, supported the reappointment of Joseph Minetti to the Civil Aeronautics Board: "He believes in the principles of your Administration. He has been of considerable help in New York. He is *loyal*."[127]

In the case of Charles R. Ross, a Vermont Republican, it took almost a year for Johnson to decide on reappointment. Even before the expiration of his term in June 1964, there was open speculation that Ross would not be reappointed to the Federal Power Commission. He was known as a consumer's advocate, and segments of the oil and gas industry, especially gas pipelines, were pushing hard for his replacement. June came and went without presidential action. The death of one member added to the delicacy of the situation and to the president's problem. The commission was moving toward completion of the landmark Permian Basin area rate case, which would define the approach to be used in setting the wellhead price of gas. To reappoint Ross in the middle of a presidential campaign would elicit criticism from the industry. To name a more conservative regulator would be to invite controversy from the other side. To replace Ross with anyone and to fill the vacant position, also a Republican slot, might complicate completion of the case.[128] Johnson's response was to let the situation ride.

Ross continued to serve as an apparent lame duck on a four-person commission through the end of 1964 and on into 1965. While his reappointment was pending, a great deal of support developed for his continuation. He had strong backing in the Senate with George Aiken of Vermont at its core. The evidence suggests that Johnson spoke to a variety of people about Ross. By March the president had found a Republican he was ready to appoint to the FPC, Carl Bagge, a railroad attorney from Illinois and a Dirksen nominee.[129] It is not clear whether Bagge initially was to be named to the Ross position, to the vacancy with Ross continuing to serve on an interim basis, or to the vacancy to balance the Ross reappointment. It is clear, however, that Johnson continued to have doubts about Ross, but seemed to be moving toward renominating him. The situation came to a head on 16 March 1965. The president's breakfast was disturbed that morning by a Rowland Evans–Robert Novak column in the *Washington Post* entitled "The FPC's Doomed Men"—Ross and chairman Joseph Swidler. The heart of the column was the assertion that the two would probably go so that "a distinctive LBJ brand" could be placed on the agency.[130] This would mean "far more lenient regulation of natural gas prices than the present FPC wants."[131] According to the columnists, "Johnson tells intimates that the FPC need not be either pro-industry or pro-consumer, but should be neutralist— following his over-all concept of government by consensus. However, consumer interests regard regulation by consensus as utopian. They have no doubt that Mr. Johnson's commission would be neutral in favor of the oil and gas boys."[132]

The wheels began to turn, as the president moved to blunt the criticism by preparing to announce the appointment of both Ross and Bagge. Four days later Ross and Bagge spent the day at the ranch. They were present when their appointments were announced at a Saturday morning press conference, and they had lunch with the president.

It was unusual for regulators to visit the ranch. It was the practice, however, for persons about to be appointed or reappointed to meet briefly with the president before their selection was made public. The meetings served to forge ties between the officials and the administration through direct exposure to the president and whatever thoughts might be on his mind.[133]

Ross, Bagge, and several other officials whose appointments were announced at the Texas press conference learned the president's thoughts at the luncheon. According to Rowland Evans and Robert Novak, Johnson forthrightly shared his views on how regulators should go about their business and used the Ross situation to emphasize his points.

> As far as I'm concerned . . . every one of you people who are going to be on these regulatory agencies has got to act just like a judge. I get sick and tired of having people tell me that I have got to appoint someone . . . because they represent one of the interests that is concerned with the operations of the board. . . . You take Charley Ross here. . . . All of the liberal groups in the country kept telling me I had to reappoint Charley because he represented the consumer and I had all the conservative groups tell me *not* to reappoint him because he represented the consumer groups. . . . But then . . . the Governor up there [Phillip Hoff, a Democrat], one of the finest Governors in the United States, told me that he went to school with Charley and practiced with him and he told me that while Charley was a Republican, he was one of the fairest he ever knew and every decision he made, he made because he thought it was the right one, not because it was on

behalf of one group or another or because it was good for the Republicans or for the Democrats but because it was the right thing to do. . . . In every instance I've ever seen, what's good for the country turns out, in the long run, to be good for business and labor. That's why we've got this great economy and this great country of ours.[134]

Johnson, in short, was preaching the virtues of a government of consensus.

Ross's comments on that "memorable day" at the ranch suggest some of the effects that direct exposure to the president could have. In a letter to Valenti, he said, "To have been chosen by President Johnson to assist him in serving the people of American is naturally a honor I cherish. However, to have the opportunity to spend such a long period of time with President Johnson and to listen to him explain his philosophy of government was a particularly wonderful experience. It was not only gratifying to me personally and professionally, but it was stimulating beyond words to witness the real leadership qualities of our President. . . . I came back to Washington . . . convinced by his words and conduct that this Nation of ours is in good hands."[135]

Generally the meetings Johnson had with prospective regulators were devoted to presidential discourse on the proper conduct of governmental affairs. In an interview prior to the Texas trip, he admonished Bagge to be "judicious."[136] And he instructed the new regulator "to frustrate everyone who seeks an advocate rather than a judge."[137] In addition, he asked Bagge "to make one significant recommendation the first week after assuming . . . duties as a Commissioner."[138]

The experiences of two other appointees seem to be typical. Johnson spoke to Mary Gardiner Jones for about ten minutes "about the meaning of government service and the general way" regulators should conduct themselves.[139] James Nicholson reports that in his interview the president told him he would find work on the FTC "interesting and challenging" and that since the agency was an arm of Congress "he would receive no instructions as to his prospective performance." It was indicated, however, that the president was displeased with infighting at the commission and expected Nicholson to help bring it to a stop.[140]

Persons about to be named chairman also met with the president. After Rosel Hyde was told he was to head the FCC, he received a twenty-minute "lecture" from Johnson. Hyde recalled being "instructed . . . with comments such as: 'Maintain a steady, firm hand';

'no harassment'; 'don't be a public scold . . . no big publicity.' Yet . . . the President also indicated that he did not intend those remarks to mean that the Commission should fail to take action promptly and firmly to deal with issues generated by a rapidly developing and expanding communications technology."[141]

Orchestrating Acceptance

In mid-February 1968 Johnson was ready to announce the appointment of John H. Crooker, Jr., to replace Charles Murphy as chairman of the CAB, but there was trouble on the Senate Commerce Committee. Senator A. S. Mike Monroney of Oklahoma, chairman of the subcommittee that dealt with air transportation, had been plugging for the elevation of Robert T. Murphy, a member of the board who had formerly served on his staff. At the White House, W. DeVier Pierson, an Oklahoman and a former Monroney aide, was assigned pacification responsibilities. The president himself chipped in with a telephone call to Monroney that morning which "paid real dividends."[142] But that did not complete preparation for Senate confirmation. Pierson was directed to "get Murphy to take Johnny to meet each member Dem & Rep of Com as well as Mansfield Dirksen Long & Byrd of West Va & report to me."[143]

This orchestration of acceptance was common. Johnson wanted absolutely no problems in confirmation. Sponsors of unsuccessful candidates were assuaged.[144] Senatorial views on confirmation were surveyed and support was solicited by the White House staff and, when necessary, by the president himself. For example, shortly before the announcement of the appointment of H. Rex Lee to the FCC, the stances of at least ten key senators were reported in detail to Johnson.[145] The president himself paved the way with calls to the Democratic and Republican leadership.[146]

Generally there was a strong inclination in the Senate to ratify presidential nominations. In only two instances was confirmation anything more than a routine affair. Both involved Carl Bagge, the Republican FPC member. The first time it was charged after his appointment that he had taken a segregationist position on a housing project in his home town. The Senate Commerce Committee investigated the matter thoroughly; although he was exonerated and confirmed, there was unwelcome publicity and delay.[147] The second time Senate Republicans held up the process.

Johnson decided in late April 1967 to reappoint Bagge, two months before the expiration of the term to which he had been appointed following the death of one of the commissioners.[148] By the first week in August the Senate Commerce Committee still had not reported the nomination. Chairman Warren Magnuson had "adopted a 'go slow' policy," Mike Manatos told the president, in order to bring Norris Cotton, the ranking Republican on the committee, into agreement and to "prevent Cotton's taking a position of personal privilege."[149] It was no secret, Cotton acknowledged, that a part of his reluctance was Dirksen's disillusionment with Bagge. The Republican leader felt that Bagge had not reflected Republican views strongly enough. Dirksen's preference, he told Manatos, was to "let this just simmer a little while longer."[150] Johnson's response to this injunction was, instead, to "put heat on [the] fire!"[151] Bagge was later confirmed, but not before a period of delicate presidential dealings with Dirksen that involved, among other things, the artful use of correspondence with the commissioner's nearly blind mother, who did not understand the reasons for the embarrassment being experienced by her son, except that "our Senator Dirkson [*sic*] whom we all thought was working for the public interest has lost faith in Carl and thinks Carl is too liberal when Carl has cast his vote for the welfare of all."[152]

The president also monitored public reactions to appointments with some care. When he saw special political dangers in an action, such as in moving Lee White from the White House to the FPC, antennae were lengthened. In this instance, he asked to see all relevant correspondence coming to the White House and all press and congressional comments.[153]

Johnson himself, with the political effects very much in mind, usually determined the timing and circumstances of announcements. Appointments likely to gain general approval were highlighted. Those that might in some degree generate controversy were made public under conditions that would deflect criticism and enhance receptivity. One strategy was to pair them. White's was joined with that of Elmer B. Staats, a respected career civil servant and deputy director of the Bureau of the Budget, to be comptroller general. The designation of Rosel Hyde, generally viewed as a conservative regulator, to be the FCC chairman was announced along with that of Nicholas Johnson, a youthful and aggressive maritime administrator, to membership on the commission. Another strategy was to lessen attention by the timing of announcements. Robert Bartley's reappointment to the FCC was announced quite a while after his term had expired, despite the fact that no one else was considered for the position. The president had grounds to be especially wary. Bartley was a Texan and Sam Rayburn's nephew. He had voted on matters involving Johnson's communications interests and was strongly opposed by some in the industry. After a long period of silence the reappointment was quietly and routinely made public—on the day attention was focused on the launching of the *Gemini 5* space flight. It is not certain that this timing was planned, but it is difficult to explain it otherwise.[154]

The extent to which the president made a practice of wooing and disarming critics in connection with appointments is not clear, but in one instance the *New York Times* was the subject of special effort. The incident is interesting in and of itself, but it also illustrates Johnson's general sensitivities in regulatory matters and reveals something of his views on regulation.

The *Times* reaction to the Hyde-Johnson appointments was to suggest in a Sunday editorial that they raised "a real question . . . about how eager the White House is to have effective regulation" in either communications or maritime affairs.[155] That day Robert E. Kintner remonstrated with Jack Gould, who wrote on broadcasting matters for the paper, about the unfair treatment of Hyde.[156] Gould, in turn, asked for a backgrounder with the president on his communications policies. Kintner recommended an off-the-record conversation instead, with Johnson deciding after the meeting whether he wished Gould to use the material. The president agreed, and a meeting was arranged for the late afternoon of 27 June 1966.[157]

The interview was held, although on the previous day Gould had a long column also critical of Hyde.[158] The result was a lengthy and positive article appearing the next Sunday. Even a casual student of the president would have no difficulty in discerning the source of the views assigned, but not attributed, to him. In addition to reflections on communications policy, especially the vast potential of television for educational purposes, there was a spirited defense of the appointments. Johnson was to provide a "youthful perspective," Hyde the "steadying hand."[159] In communications matters, which were ranked as top governmental priorities along with defense and foreign affairs, Hyde would be a "calm and judicious leader," not "a provocative and articulate . . . [one] who may titillate the intellectuals while worrying the practical broadcasters."[160] According to the "source," there was a strong chance that Hyde "could achieve a record of practical accomplishment that might outdistance the scores registered by . . . [his] more controversial predecessors."[161]

Conclusions

No president can fail to attend to at least some aspects of the regulatory enterprises carried forward by the various boards and commissions. But there is great discretion as to the extent and the purposes of engagement and the means by which presidential interests are asserted. The nature of presidential views on regulation, if any, informs the uses of discretion. It seems evident that Lyndon B. Johnson had a number of basic views on the role of the presidency in commission regulation. He clearly saw regulatory programs as being an important part of government. There was also a notion that the presidential role in commission regulation was limited. Under ordinary circumstances, regulation should be left to the regulators. It would be inappropriate for the president and his agents to attempt to influence particular proceedings. Adverse political reactions could be expected if it was thought that there was tampering.

Further, Johnson appeared to have a regulatory model in mind that probably reflected his true preferences as well as his political interests. It was expressed in his first meeting with agency heads in early December 1964 and throughout his period in office in his detailed attention to appointment processes. It cannot be accurately grasped in conventional terms such as favoring or opposing either strong or weak regulation or in terms of advancing the fortunes of particular interests. Rather, the president was disposed toward regulation which transcended the advocacy of particular interests, which took the form of judicious and responsible application of the laws, and which would earn the approbation of all of those affected as being objective, fair, and reasonable. His core business in commission regulation was to shape its conduct along these lines. It was an effort to meld a consensus, as he was inclined to do in other areas as well. He sought the support of all in matters for which he was responsible. And perhaps it reflected an idealistic notion of the inherent nature of regulation. At the same time, it was a practical one from a political point of view, given the president's search for broad support for his major undertakings, such as the Great Society programs, his vulnerability in certain areas of regulation, and his reputation as wheeler-dealer and subtle manipulator of governmental machinery. For these reasons, it made some sense to apply the politics of consensus rather than conflict to regulation.

Johnson sought to advance his views on regulation through the performance of one of his primary duties in regulation, filling regulatory posts. This was a major part of his business in regulation. During his time in office he made more than seventy decisions of this type. He invested much energy in his appointment decisions and probably exerted his greatest influence on commission regulation through them. Whether a person was probusiness or antibusiness or likely to be a strong or weak regulator was not, at least not explicitly, a major consideration. Much more important were the character of the approach likely to be taken, the style of performance likely to obtain, and their fit with his view of the ideal.

In the selection of regulators, the president did not have a completely free hand. Commission chairmen were influential, as were members of Congress and interest groups. Their influence may account, in part, for the large number of continuations. But reappointments rarely were automatic. Johnson typically weighed his options with considerable care. Furthermore, even when the selection process concluded with a reappointment, he used it to make regulators aware of his interest in their work and to impress upon them his views on the proper conduct of regulation.

For most of Johnson's presidency, the selection process usually functioned in systematic fashion. He worked closely with John Macy and others, generally in open processes, consulting widely and seeking a variety of views and options.

Although the selection of regulators was perhaps the most important link between the regulatory commissions and the presidency and the most potent means for affecting the course of regulation, it was by no means the only one. White House–commission interactions in the conduct of regulatory affairs are the subject of the next chapter.

3. Attending to Commission Regulation

> I think this is a lot of gobbledygook—do you think this is all
> they should do . . . check it.
>
> LBJ, 4 September 1965 [1]

A TELEGRAM CAME to the president's attention shortly after it was
dispatched on the morning of 3 September 1965. It was from Representative Robert B. Duncan of Oregon to Representative Oren Harris
of Arkansas, chairman of the House Committee on Interstate and
Foreign Commerce, and to Charles A. Webb, chairman of the Interstate Commerce Commission, and concerned a shortage of boxcars
in Duncan's state. His complaints were that no House hearings had
been scheduled on Senate-passed remedial legislation and that the
ICC had not attacked the problem vigorously. Johnson reacted
quickly. At noon he called Duncan to report that he had directed the
ICC to investigate the situation and to report to the White House
immediately with a plan to correct the problem. By six that evening
a rather bland ICC response had traversed the few blocks from
Twelfth and Constitution to 1600 Pennsylvania Avenue. [2] It was, to
Johnson, "gobbledygook." He instructed Marvin Watson to pursue
the matter with the ICC, the oldest and perhaps most insular of the
regulatory commissions.

The presidential attention to the ICC in the boxcar matter did not
place the agency in a special category. It shared that attention with
other commissions. Although the president's wariness described in
the previous chapter was a constant factor, neither the president nor
his aides saw "independence" as always necessitating or allowing
indifference. A variety of forces pulled the commissions into the
presidential vortex with some regularity.

For the most part, the relationships between the presidency and
the commissions were loosely structured and relatively informal in
character, and there was a certain intimate quality to them. Contrib-

uting no little to the air of intimacy and to a sense of the president's proximity to regulatory affairs was the vast amount of information about the commissions that came to the White House. It arrived in myriad ways and forms: in conjunction with appointment and budget decisions; in regular and special reports from the commissions and advance notice of significant decisions; in the process of preparing and steering the legislative program; in congressional and private representations; and in the intelligence gathering and mediating activities of presidential aides and advisers. The range of information was extraordinarily broad. It extended from complex substantive matters of significant policy import, such as government policy toward the regulation of communications satellites, to whether Nicholas Johnson of the Federal Communications Commission was or was not mentioning the president in his speeches.[3] A sense of proximity was accentuated by the president's personal appetite for a rather astounding amount of information about the particulars of regulatory operations.

The president's awareness of commission affairs ordinarily was of much greater magnitude than his efforts to affect them. Nevertheless, the presence of the presidency was felt. As a prelude to considering the particulars, the following section depicts structures and channels linking the presidency and the commissions.

Linkages

TO: Larry O'Brien
Suppose you look at the attached from John Dingell. I agree with him that this letter is absolutely outrageous. Any thoughts?
Henry Wilson, 26 January 1965[4]

TO: Henry Wilson
I agree. I am not sure at this point who deals with Agencies along these lines unless it is Valenti.
Larry O'Brien, 28 January 1965[5]

TO: Jack Valenti
I have talked with Dingell again. This is so bad it just must be stupid instead of deliberate.
Henry Wilson, 10 February 1965[6]

TO: Lee White
May I have your recommendation on the attached?
Jack Valenti, 13 February 1965[7]

TO: Jack Valenti

There is . . . on the ICC a fellow by the name of Bill Tucker who is a moderate Democrat (a Kennedy appointee) who in the past has been willing to discuss on an informal basis some of the internal mechanisms and problems of the ICC. Either you or I could ask him to come over to have a little chat about the sometimes painful lack of political judgment by the commission and discuss with him what if anything might be done about it. So far as I know there is no direct or straightforward approach that holds any hope.

Lee White, 15 February 1965[8]

If you can talk with him off-the-record—good—Maybe I could join you.

Jack Valenti[9]

The dereliction of the Interstate Commerce Commission that precipitated these memoranda exchanged by presidential aides did not concern the nation's transportation policy or anything affecting it. It was simply a letter from the commission chairman to George Romney, the Republican governor of Michigan, lauding the state's efforts in emergency preparedness. But Michigan's Representative John D. Dingell, Jr., was "thoroughly displeased"—and felt that the White House should also be—"to see a government agency writing letters that are going to be used in Romney's campaign against a good Democratic candidate or against President Johnson."[10] His complaint obviously was shared by Henry Wilson, who was in charge of White House liaison with the House of Representatives, and his boss, Larry O'Brien.

As the memoranda suggest, the White House organization for dealing with the regulatory commissions was not always sharply defined, nor were the channels to employ in a particular situation always obvious. In part, the organizational imprecision reflected the president's general approach to the assignment of staff responsibilities and to staff operations. Flexibility and adaptability in the use of staff was preferred to neat and tight compartmentalization of functions and responsibilities. Johnson was once asked at a press conference to specify the exact assignments of one of several aides whose appointment had just been announced. His response was that White House staff "play any position here." In regard to the person in question, the president elaborated: "He will be at the service of the president, and if he needs to play first base or second base or third base, I hope that he can do it. He is equipped to do it."[11]

Johnson's preference for versatility in staff performance was reflected in practice. As Larry E. Temple, who served for a time as a special assistant, characterized it, "When he had something to do, something he wanted done, he would talk to whoever was the nearest and handiest. A lot of times I got involved in things that I guess on the organization chart were outside the realm of my responsibility, but I was there."[12]

Relations with the Federal Reserve Board were an exception. The prime channels of interaction were relatively clear. They ran from the president through the Council of Economic Advisers, the Treasury Department, and BOB. These constituted the Troika that dealt with basic economic policy, a group that became the Quadriad when joined by Federal Reserve officials.

For the rest, White House memoranda indicate that at presidential direction, in connection with ongoing responsibilities, or through happenstance, most principal White House staff members were involved in matters pertaining to regulatory commissions from time to time. Those concerned with policy development, such as Bill Moyers and then Joseph Califano and his associates, were among them. This was also true of staff focusing on congressional relations. The attention of aides whose interests were for the most part political, such as Marvin Watson and Jake Jacobsen, was also drawn to commission business on occasion. Others with general portfolios in subject matter areas often served as points for interaction with the commissions, as conduits for information on regulatory affairs, and as agents for presidential response and action when that was in order. For example, the portfolios of Lee White and then DeVier Pierson included such matters as communications, power, and transportation. Commissions with responsibilities in these areas came within their purview. Pierson described the dynamics in this way: "My work was not with the agency but was with what they were doing. I was involved in aviation problems and that involved the CAB, and in communications problems and that involved the FCC, and . . . natural resources problems might involve the FPC. I wasn't checking on the agency, but rather their part in the subject matter over which they and perhaps departments within the Executive Branch had jurisdiction."[13]

Despite much inconstancy in relationships, even for an aide such as Pierson, there was some regularity in linkages. For most of the period John Macy's office, of course, handled presidential appointments to the commissions. Throughout the Johnson presidency, the center for White House staff work on international air transportation matters and contacts with the CAB in this realm was the office of the counsel to the president, a position successively held by Myer Feldman, Lee White, and Harry McPherson. Starting in 1966 the president designated one White House staff person to serve as general liaison with the regulatory commissions. The activities of first Robert E. Kintner then E. Ernest Goldstein, who succeeded him in August 1967, on the whole supplemented rather than substituted for the work of other aides in handling regulatory matters.

Apparently the charters given Kintner and Goldstein were not finely drafted. Kintner, a former president of the National Broadcasting Company, also served as secretary to the cabinet. Presumably his background in a regulated industry was one reason for including regulation among his responsibilities. In practice, his major substantive involvement was in communications. For the rest, Kintner's main function was to receive the periodic activity reports and other materials submitted by the commissions, then to send them on, after flagging the more important parts, for the president's night reading.

Goldstein, who taught law at the University of Texas before entering private practice in France, was only asked by the president "to take care of the regulatory agencies."[14] In the process, Johnson told him "to walk softly and at the same time be useful" to them.[15] Presidential sensitivities in regulation were clearly conveyed to Goldstein. "I got a very distinct impression," because of Johnson's broadcasting interests, that "he did not want to be involved whenever a matter came up, for example, that dealt with the Federal Communications Commission; that he would rather I make a judgment if a judgment was necessary, and he would be completely insulated and divorced from it."[16] Although Goldstein did pick up other assignments—played other bases from time to time—he was quite active in commission affairs until Johnson left office.

The White House staff's interest in regulation complemented that of other presidential units. The Council of Economic Advisers kept a wary eye on several of the commissions and was alert to impending actions likely to affect the course of the economy. It also served as an in-house critic of regulation it judged to be excessive. The Office of Telecommunications Management (OTM) was very much concerned with actions of the Federal Communications Commission. The Office of Science and Technology (OST) also was involved in regulatory issues at times. Overshadowing CEA, OTM, and OST in importance was the Bureau of the Budget. Bureau officials occupied key listening and action posts. The agency's central role in budgeting, legislative clearance, and government organization and management thrust it deeply and consistently into the inner workings of regulatory bodies. Aides located in the White House, BOB, and other presidential agencies often functioned as independent links between the presidency and the commissions. It was not uncommon, however, for efforts to be integrated in *ad hoc* work groups involving one or more officials from the White House and other parts of the presidency.

Johnson gave his aides considerable discretion in the representation of presidential interests and views. "When you worked for him in looking after either an area or a department, or both, you did have a good deal of authority," according to Pierson.[17] There probably was little of consequence in White House relations with the commissions of which the president was unaware, however; staff members took special pains to keep him posted through informational memoranda and other means.

The president's direct working contacts with regulators in meetings or over the telephone, the Daily Diary suggests, were rare and for the most part restricted to commission chairmen, except for appointment interviews.[18] An exception, again, must be made for the Federal Reserve Board. Principally because of its important role in making and implementing macroeconomic policy, Johnson was in fairly frequent contact with its chairman. Among the other agencies, only four chairmen met with the president in business settings three or more times. Charles Murphy of the CAB and Lee White of the FPC had three recorded meetings with him. At the head of the pack were Manuel Cohen of the SEC with six and John Horne of the Federal Home Loan Bank Board with seven. The largest number of telephone calls from Johnson (seven) were to Murphy.

Whether it was Johnson, Kintner, Goldstein, or some other agent involved in substantive meetings or other types of contact, the linkage usually was with the chairman of an agency. Most of the time, interactions with them were on an as-needed basis, but Goldstein attempted to see all of the chairmen regularly.[19]

Members were not ignored, however. They too came to the White House, generally to attend ceremonies or to participate in other types of formal gatherings. In addition, Marvin Watson and Jake Jacobsen, with the president's approval, hosted a series of White House meetings with the full membership of each of the agencies to discuss administration policies and programs in general terms during 1965 and 1966.[20]

Extensive interaction with members usually had a strong foundation in personal relationships. Willard Deason of the ICC had been the president's close personal friend for years and also had special ties with many White House staff members. Not only was he the source of a continuing stream of letters and memoranda about ICC and other matters, but he was a regular White House visitor for lunch, dinner, and other social occasions. The Daily Diary shows that his visits and telephone conversations with Johnson were nearly equal in number to those of all other regulators combined. A fairly close relationship was established between William Tucker of the ICC and certain staff members. Nicholas Johnson, while at the FCC, was in frequent contact with friends who were presidential aides.

Although members were seldom involved in working contacts with the White House, there are indications of affective bonds formed between them and the Johnson presidency in the appointment process and through other means. Johnson and his associates consciously sought to create a sense of identification, a sense that regulators were integral parts of the administration. At a very personal level, George Hearn of the Federal Maritime Commission was made to "feel like one of the family" when he rode the presidential plane to New York.[21] For Philip Elman, the Federal Trade Commission's meeting with Watson and Jacobsen reflected "a vitalization of the proper relationship between the President and the federal administrative agencies." He went on to express the view that the "so-called 'independent' agencies would perform more effectively, efficiently, and more responsibly if they were less insulated from executive review and coordination." They should be free of dictation in their quasi-judicial role, he continued, but determinations in other realms should not be made "in isolation from, or in disregard of, basic national policy as expressed by the President."[22] NLRB member John H. Fanning, after attending a briefing session conducted by the president, responded, "Meeting you, Vice President Humphrey, and members of your Cabinet, and listening to your presentation of the key domestic and international problems confronting your Administration, was a most rewarding experience which will be of continuing inspiration to me in meeting the responsibilities of my job."[23]

Another regulator indicated that such reactions may be seen as more than polite expressions of appreciation. A liberal Republican, he had no special connections with Johnson or others in the administration prior to his appointment. His subsequent exposures to the president and the White House were no greater than that of the average regulator, but, limited as they were, they had a distinct impact on him and, the evidence indicates, on others. He interpreted the attention given to him and his colleagues through invitations to receptions and signing ceremonies as a special effort to acknowledge their contributions and to convey the president's view that the regulators and the work they did were important and appreciated. His reaction was to feel a strong and special sense of identification with Johnson and an obligation to be loyal to him.[24]

The precise nature and consequences of affective bonds between the presidency and regulators are, of course, very difficult to assess, but it is quite possible that they encouraged regulators to behave as they thought the president wished them to behave.

Working or action linkages are somewhat easier to specify. During the Johnson years, overt presidential action in regard to the commissions came in response to a variety of triggers and took several forms. The major precipitants of presidential involvement included commission requests for assistance; interagency conflict; administrative matters, such as budgets and organization, requiring presidential attention; a perception that presidential interests were at stake; and statutory mandates, especially in international aviation matters.

Playing Miss Fixit

> This is a day-by-day sort of Miss-Fixit—sort of an Eloise operation, with a few band-aids, that's what this is.
>
> E. Ernest Goldstein[25]

To describe much White House staff activity as playing Miss Fixit rings true. Much fixing took place, especially in helping commissions with their problems and in dealing with interagency disagreements in the absence of major presidential interests.

A Helping Hand

Goldstein's experiences in providing assistance are quite suggestive. "It's amazing how many things the agencies depend upon the White House for. For example, their fights with the Budget Bureau, or they just need more money, or they want a change in personnel, or they have an opening on the commission, and the chairman . . . has some idea of what he wants in the way of a replacement. . . . And that means coordinating with John Macy."[26] He interceded with BOB, for example, on behalf of the SEC and the FTC. In one case dealing with the latter, the agency's budget request had been slashed by $1,200,000 at a time when it was required to implement new consumer protection legislation. Goldstein strongly presented the FTC's "compelling" needs to the head of BOB and urged that "a new look" be taken.[27]

Assistance was often provided in the area of congressional relations. For example, Goldstein points out, "The SEC has no legislative liaison operation; so when they want to push on their legislative program, they'll call to Barefoot Sanders, Mike Manatos; and working with them and through them, try and push their legislative programs."[28] Congressional hostility to an agency could also spark action. Goldstein reports that during one period, "The NLRB was pretty much under attack from Senator [Sam J.] Ervin, and at that point I got involved in doing everything I could to relieve their burden and keep them all happy."[29] When there were forewarnings of a new onslaught from Congress, Goldstein, together with Manatos and other congressional liaison staff members, would try to provide protection by starting a "backfire" of supportive statements and by disseminating information that would counteract the expected charges.[30]

Another example of fixing a problem involved assisting the FTC when it began to implement new flammable fabrics legislation. According to Goldstein, "There were some very strange goings-on within the commission. And as a matter of fact, one of the commissioners was a particular friend of a Senator who had been one of those who had pushed hard for the legislation. And now he [the commissioner] was crippling the legislation by requiring the FTC to pay the costs of lab testing. And if the FTC had to do it, its budget would be totally inadequate and . . . enforcement . . . would be impossible. So Rand Dixon [the FTC chairman] called me and said, 'Pretty please, you've got to bail me out with my own commission.'"[31] And Goldstein did. The Senate sponsor of the rambunctious commissioner was asked "to get around and talk to his own guy, say, 'Look, I sponsored you . . . and you've gone ahead and messed up the things I've been for. Now, please don't make everybody's life a little harder.'"[32]

The Miss Fixit role was perhaps more difficult to play in interagency relationships than in dilemmas faced by commissions from time to time in regard to budgets and congressional relations. The problems often touched deep-seated and enduring policy questions that were of much greater importance to the agencies involved than to the presidency, but which seemed to require presidential assistance in their resolution.

On Conflict and Coordination

No regulatory commission was during Johnson's presidency or is now without sensitive relationships with other commissions and executive departments and agencies. Policy spheres are shared, and jurisdictions may overlap or conjoin. Not only may there be contention over prerogatives, but the actions of one entity may have profound effects for the work and responsibilities of another. Consider, for example, the Federal Communications Commission. A partial listing of the interagency dimensions of its activities during the 1960s includes the following: its decisions on spectrum allocation and rates affected government users, especially the Department of Defense; it regulated an important quasi-governmental entity, COMSAT; major portions of its work had international implications that were of interest to the State Department; and the Justice Department was at times concerned with the antitrust aspects of its decisions. A similar catalog could be provided for other commissions. Conflict and flawed coordination are typical of interagency relationships.

In Johnson's presidency, there appeared to be four levels at which interagency affairs involving independent regulatory bodies were handled. At the first level, department, agency, and regulatory officials grappled with problems, often in the context of formal proceedings. At the second level, the Bureau of the Budget intervened in an effort to forge acceptable accommodations of differences, as did the Office of Telecommunications Management and the Office of Science and Technology in their more limited spheres. At the third level, White House aides became involved. And at the fourth level, infrequently reached, the president himself was a participant. On matters of some policy significance, presidential intervention typically involved the joint efforts of White House and BOB staff. Conflictual relationships in the regulation of financial institutions and in antitrust enforcement are discussed in subsequent chapters. Here three cases involving the Department of the Interior and the Federal Power Commission suggest the dynamics of conflict and its resolution.

One case concerned the Department of Interior's WEST plan for power pooling in western states among a group of private and public utilities. Federal hydroelectric power was to be used for peak load purposes in the integrated system, a new steam-generating plant was to be constructed jointly, and public power enterprises were to get cheap and reliable power from private utilities. The substance of the plan and the propriety of the department's initiative caused no problems for the White House or for BOB. Questions were pushed up to the presidential level, however, regarding the participation of the Federal Power Commission and the Department of Agriculture in the negotiations. The second case involved the regulatory jurisdiction of the FPC over electricity sold by a component of the Department of Interior, the Southeastern Power Administration (SEPA), to the Tennessee Valley Authority (TVA). The department and the FPC were at loggerheads over the basis for the rates to be charged; as a result the sales went unregulated, contrary to clear statutory requirements. The third case arose from statutory provisions limiting FPC licenses for hydroelectric power projects to no more than fifty years. At expiration, the projects could be relicensed or the sites could be recaptured for public use. The licenses of many projects were due to expire in the 1970s and thereafter. How and on what basis would relicensing and recapture decisions be made? The FPC proposed a method to which Interior took partial exception. At issue were the prerogatives of the department and the commission.

Despite substantive differences, the cases are similar in some respects. Concerted presidential-level attention was sparked almost accidentally. The president himself was not involved. It was left to a White House aide, Lee White, and Bureau of the Budget staff to define and pursue presidential objectives in resolving differences. In the process, close bureau attention to the issues clearly appeared to be energized by White House interest. Somewhat surprisingly, in each case the presidential perspective was more in accord with that of the FPC than with that of the department.

White first learned of the WEST initiative in May 1965 when reading Secretary of the Interior Stewart L. Udall's weekly report to the president. He forwarded the report to Elmer Staats, deputy director of BOB, noting, "I am always apprehensive about quiet negotiations undertaken by the department with public and private utilities. I hope that you people are apprised of this and have some idea as to where it is heading."[33] The negotiations were announced in an Interior press release on 1 June. Two days later Staats responded to White with additional background gleaned by bureau staff and made the point that neither the FPC nor Agriculture was a participant. The commission, of course, had regulatory responsibilities bearing on the situation. The Department of Agriculture was relevant because it contained the Rural Electrification Administration (REA). Staats wondered whether he and White should have lunch with the Interior principals—or, if White thought it desirable, "we could get ourselves more deeply involved."[34] In a later memorandum, Staats again pointed to the lack of FPC and Agriculture involvement and, indeed, to the omission of the bureau as well. He was somewhat uncertain as to the course to follow. One reason was a new press release by Udall that referred to his talks with Johnson, "so we assume the President has been informed."[35] Staats asked White again whether "we should ask Udall to bring Agriculture and FPC into the discussions?"[36] After considerable delay White replied in the affirmative, saying, "It seems that we have had enough experience with the difficulties of pressuring agencies to support something when the basic decisions have already been made."[37] Thus a process of quiet persuasion began.

Bureau staff subsequently held informal discussions with Interior officials. Although, Staats told White, there were no plans in Interior to broaden participation in the negotiations, those "at staff level appeared to think it was a good idea."[38] The Interior officials promised to pursue the matter. If that approach did not work, "I will take it up with Secretary Udall myself," Staats promised.[39] It did not work. Udall's position, according to a BOB staff member, was that "Interior would not ask FPC and Agriculture to have representatives present at the discussions."[40] A departmental staff official, instead, was directed to keep the other agencies informed. Udall also said that Interior's approach had been discussed with and cleared by the director of the Bureau of the Budget.[41] In informing White of Udall's response, Staats said, "I know of no discussions between Udall and the Bureau on this. Do you think I should give him a call?"[42] Although White did not want "any big fuss," in his view a call from Staats would not hurt.[43]

Not long afterward Staats wrote a personal letter to Udall. A velvet touch was employed in the petition, but presidential preferences were clearly underscored. The key paragraph read:

> I realize how difficult and important these negotiations are, both from the standpoint of the Department as well as the Administration. Lee White and we have been concerned lest other interested agencies may have ideas which ought to be brought in at an early stage. Couldn't Agriculture and FPC have representatives in these negotiations? I am sure that you could work out arrangements with Joe Swidler and Orville Freeman to meet any confidentiality problems. I think you will agree that the joint work of all the agencies added materially to the successful conclusion of our Passamaquoddy study.[44]

Udall's prompt reply deftly turned aside this suggestion. He noted again that a member of Interior's negotiating team, Emil V. Lindseth, was designated to serve as liaison with Agriculture and the FPC, in effect shutting off further conversation unless others wished to escalate the level of conflict. Udall concluded, "I believe we can depend on Emil to keep interested Federal agencies completely informed as to the progress that is being made. We hope that these arrangements are satisfactory to all interested agencies."[45] Staats made an almost plaintive comment to White, attached to Udall's response: "Suppose this is about as good as we can do."[46] So much for a government-wide point of view in this instance; departmentalism prevailed, although the FPC and Agriculture were closer to the negotiations than would have been the case absent presidential efforts.

A more satisfactory conclusion was reached in the Southeastern Power Administration rate affair. Scores of General Accounting Office (GAO) reports are scattered through the White House files in the Johnson Library, most apparently unread. One did catch Lee White's eye in early 1964, however. It treated a ten-year impasse between the FPC and Interior over rates paid by TVA for SEPA power. He called the chief of BOB's Resources and Civil Works Division and asked for a draft reply to send to GAO.[47] The call ultimately produced an accommodation between the two agencies. In response to White's expression of interest, bureau staff had separate meetings with Interior and FPC officials. These, in turn, led to a new round of meetings involving both agencies, the first in April 1964 when Assistant Secretary of the Interior Kenneth Holm conferred with commissioners Charles Ross and David Black of the FPC. (Chairman Joseph Swidler disqualified himself, because of prior association with the TVA.)

The major differences to be resolved had to do with cost allocation methods and the interest rate on the power share of project investment assigned to the rate base. The department insisted on an incremental method of allocation and a 2 percent interest rate. The commission's positions were that the method was inappropriate and that the interest rate was too low. A rate proposal had been rejected by the commission in 1958 for these reasons, but the department stood its ground until 1964, arguing that the FPC had no warrant to substitute its judgment for the department's on the points at issue.

Discussion at the 15 April meeting indicated that a settlement might be reached by agreeing to Interior's position on cost allocation and to the FPC's position on interest rates. But new complications arose. One was an aspect of project financing not previously considered by the commission, but pending in a case it was to decide

within the next few months. Black and Ross preferred to delay further consideration of the SEPA-TVA matter until that case was concluded. There were other problems. It was uncertain whether another commissioner could be persuaded to join Ross and Black in
support of the compromise. Furthermore, Ross's appointment had
expired, and he might be replaced at any time. Such are the complexities in even small matters.

Staats and White kept in touch with the situation and stimulated
a continuation of the discussions.[48] The result was an Interior rate
proposal filed with the commission in October and November 1964
reflecting the compromise that emerged in April. In late December
the FPC gave its approval.[49] In White's words, the decision ended the
"long smoldering problem." Now, he told Staats, "we can forget
about it."[50]

The recapture matter was not so easy for White to forget. His involvement began just a month after Johnson became president and
did not end until the conclusion of his service as chairman of the
Federal Power Commission in 1969. On 23 December 1963 the
president gave White a letter he had received from Gus Norwood,
executive secretary of the Northwest Public Power Association.
Norwood criticized rules proposed by the FPC in November 1963
establishing procedures for handling the relicensing or recapture of
hydroelectric power licenses for facilities on rivers under federal jurisdiction. The rules provided for adversary proceedings before the
agency, in which executive agencies might participate, followed by
FPC recommendations to Congress, where the final determinations
would be made. Norwood's position was that the FPC's proposal was
a usurpation of the constitutional powers of the president; property
disposal or use falls within the responsibilities and prerogatives of
the executive branch, not an independent commission, he argued.[51]

White asked the departments of Justice and Interior for their
views. Justice's initial response underscored constitutional ambiguities and statutory silence on recapture procedures. While failing
to address squarely Norwood's constitutional argument, the reply
pointed out that "it is clear that the Congress must participate in
every recapture, at least through the appropriation process." But, it
was noted further, "the Executive Branch well could have a more
prominent role . . . than is anticipated in the FPC's proposed rule."[52]

Interior's response did not equivocate. Udall, in a letter to White
and in another shortly thereafter to FPC chairman Swidler, came
down fully in support of Norwood's position and against the FPC
proposal. The commission's approach compromised "the inherent

power of the President to make recommendations regarding the use and disposal of the Nation's water resources and public domain," Udall asserted.[53] Enlarging on the point, he continued:

> It is our feeling that policy decisions . . . in regard to . . . recapture simply are not suited to quasi-judicial proceedings before a regulatory agency. We do not believe that the recommendations of the Executive Branch of government regarding the future use of the public domain should be subordinated to and obscured by the presentations of adversary parties and the determinations of a regulatory agency. And we do not believe that one of the three great branches of government should submit its recommendations to its co-equal branch through the lesser offices of a regulatory agency. In short, we find the Commission's proposal inconsistent with Article II, Sec. 3 of the Constitution.[54]

In conclusion, he proposed that he and White personally discuss the matter and that executive branch procedures be developed for making direct recommendations to Congress.

To White, Udall's response raised "a pretty good-sized problem" involving "a fairly major issue."[55] Clearly, follow-up was required. He suggested to Elmer Staats the possibility of a meeting with Udall and Ramsey Clark, then an assistant attorney general, and asked that Bureau of the Budget staff "begin to grab a hold of the main issue."[56]

BOB completed preliminary assessment of the problem in May 1964. Staats reported to White that "our inclination is to feel that the procedural issue is not very difficult. . . . We do not see at this moment . . . any reason to be greatly disturbed by the Federal Power Commission proposal."[57] Federal agencies would be left with every opportunity to press their views and even to seek legislative authorizations for recapture independently of FPC procedures. Two months later the bureau completed a more thorough review. The conclusion, again, was that the proposal was "reasonable."[58] Buttressed by quiet presidential support, the commission promulgated its rules in October 1964. The bureau's imprimatur was placed upon them in that fall's director review session on the FPC's budget.[59] Subsequently, Interior and Agriculture, which also had an interest in the recapture question, were informed of the administration's support for "following the FPC procedures as a forum for settling the recapture question"[60] Although procedural issues were settled at this point, substantive policies on relicensing and recapture were not resolved until 1968, when legislation was enacted amending the Federal Power Act of 1920.

The Management of Commission Affairs

> Dear George:
> As you know, we have looked into the question of the budget for the National Labor Relations Board. I feel very strongly that it is essential to get prompt adjudication of cases before the Board since speedy action is essential to justice in this field. I am also familiar with some of the difficulties raised by an increase in the case load in some of the larger regional offices and I want you to know I have directed that action be taken to alleviate conditions in these areas.
>
> LBJ, 16 December 1963[61]

This letter to George Meany, head of the AFL-CIO, marked one of the few instances in which the White House evidenced interest in the management of a particular regulatory program in the absence of a substantive issue. Even then, given Meany's prominence as the leading trade unionist in the country and a Democratic stalwart, at root the interest, it is safe to say, was more political than managerial. By and large, the White House left commissions to manage their own affairs, although from time to time they were affected by presidential actions, most regularly in regard to their budgets.

A Miscellany

The commissions, of course, were subject to the general executive authority of the president. In his executive capacity, Johnson had his second and last meeting with the heads of ten regulatory bodies, joined by the heads of ten independent agencies, on 17 January 1964. The content of his actual remarks is not recorded, but the talking points prepared for his use indicate very modest objectives. They emphasized the importance of better relations with the White House in the release of information, cutting back on government publications as an economy, and placing more women in high-level positions.[62]

The commissions, along with all other departments and agencies, were subject to periodic presidential directives bearing on internal management. Many were of modest significance, concerning such topics as the exercise of employee voting rights and the review of employee safety programs. Others were of greater potential consequence and dealt with, for example, employing computer technology; implementing PPB systems; establishing and adjusting user fees and charges; tightening purchasing practices; and generally reducing the cost of government. Still others directed the commissions and other agencies to develop proposals for streamlining their operations. There are no indications that the commissions were any more or less receptive to these directives than other parts of the government.

Many presidential directives of the period were aimed at holding down the costs of government. The Johnson administration's position on expenditures for regulation also reflected a concern for economy. This is clearly suggested by BOB director Charles L. Schultze's letter to ICC chairman John Bush setting ceilings for the fiscal year 1967 budget. Although a modest increase in dollar amounts was allowed, a slight decrease in the number of personnel was required. Furthermore, Bush's attention was turned pointedly to the continuing importance of such economy measures as more effective position control, reduced travel costs, and the elimination of low priority programs.[63]

A rather tight-fisted approach to appropriations for regulation is clearly shown in a comparison of authorized positions—a more meaningful indicator than dollars—for ten regulatory agencies between the president's first budget, for fiscal year 1965, and his last, for fiscal year 1970. In six instances there was little change in personnel complements. There were large decreases in CAB and ICC staff (19.7 percent and 23 percent, respectively), largely because of the transfer of certain functions to the new Department of Transportation. Otherwise, they too experienced little change. Only the Federal Trade Commission and the Federal Deposit Insurance Corporation enjoyed substantial increases. A 25 percent increase in FTC staff is explained for the most part by its assumption of new responsibilities in the consumer protection area. The increase in the staff size of FDIC was a whopping 82 percent. A special executive affection for it was not the reason. Comparison of administration recommendations and legislative actions shows that the FDIC staff increases, funded as were the rest of its operations by the revenue it generated, were the work of Congress, not the president.

Fiscal conservatism reflected much more than BOB's institutional proclivities. For example, during the preparation of the budget for fiscal year 1967, the BOB's initial mark for the ICC was $27.2 million, less than the agency's request of $29.155 million but more than a 1966 appropriation of $26.915 million. The ICC then appealed for restoration of $405,000 and convinced the bureau staff to support

$300,000 of that amount, bringing the total back to $27.5 million. The president, however, decided to hold to the 1966 level, a parsimonious $600,000 less than even BOB was willing to allow.[64]

Budget determinations must be made, so some presidential effects on commissions through these actions are unavoidable. This is not the case for personnel management within the commissions. As in prior and subsequent administrations, some of the politically faithful were suggested in routine fashion for staff positions. Just as routinely, agency officials generally ignored the recommendations. Essentially, the commissions were left alone in personnel matters. Top level staff appointees—supergrades—were treated, however, to a White House interview with Marvin Watson or another aide to initiate them into the higher executive levels of the administration and, as in the case of the president's interviews with prospective commissioners, to cement their identification with the Johnson presidency.

On Organization

Notable presidential interest in organizational issues was restricted to agencies regulating financial institutions and transportation. Because attention to organization for regulating financial institutions was precipitated largely by the activities of the comptroller of the currency, it is addressed in the following chapter on executive regulation.

In transportation, some consideration was given to combining the functions of the Civil Aeronautics Board, the Federal Maritime Commission, and the Interstate Commerce Commission in a single transportation regulatory agency. A task force on government organization recommended this change in 1964.[65] The following year the idea received further attention. The context was the development of the president's transportation program for 1966, the centerpiece of which was a new Department of Transportation. The consolidation idea was opposed by the Bureau of the Budget at the time, because the statutes administered by the three commissions contained many substantive and procedural differences that would be difficult to reconcile. The bureau did agree that consolidation was a desirable long-term goal.[66]

Although the consolidation idea was dropped, the transfer of some functions performed by the CAB and ICC to the new department remained very much an issue. There was a modicum of opposition to parts of the administration's plan from both agencies. The CAB successfully resisted efforts to take away its authority for the payment of operating subsidies to qualifying airlines.[67] A minority of five members of the ICC took a public position against relocation of the authority to set *per diem* rates for the use of rail cars.[68] However, the commission unanimously supported the shift of related responsibilities for the issuance of rail car service orders and the establishment of demurrage charges. Industry opposition caused Congress to retain all rail car responsibilities in the ICC.

The most important changes made in 1966 were in transportation safety regulation. Both the CAB and ICC supported the president's plan for the transfer of their rather extensive safety responsibilities to the new department, even though this meant substantial losses in personnel and appropriations. After considerable debate and some adjustments in the president's plan, Congress approved the transfers.[69]

The ICC was the one commission whose internal organization was further affected by presidential pressure. Although the Bureau of the Budget was in the forefront, the White House and the president were more than just bystanders. The campaign to improve ICC operations through reorganization is an interesting illustration of the joinder of long-standing institutional concerns of BOB and the use of presidential influence in support of bureau objectives.

Starting in the late 1950s a series of studies revealed serious basic deficiencies in ICC operations and proposed a varied set of procedural and structural reforms.[70] Rather strong pressures were placed on the commission to make changes. In 1961 decision-making procedures were revamped. The implementation of field office reorganization began in January 1964. In addition to some backwash from this initiative, two structural problems remained on the agenda. One was headquarters reorganization, which the Johnson administration succeeded in achieving. The other concerned the chairmanship of the commission and was not corrected. ICC members still selected their own chairman each year. The law did not place administrative authority in the chairman, and the ten commissioners jealously guarded their collective authority to manage the work of the agency.

No sooner had field reorganization been announced than BOB began to urge the commission to take quick action to streamline headquarters organization.[71] But some commissioners were reluctant. A presidential word was seen as a way to generate movement. Johnson agreed to send a letter to the ICC chairman urging him "to give the most serious consideration to implementing a headquarters reorganization plan."[72] The presidential letter had the desired effect, and the commission named a committee to make recommendations. In the process, additional problems arose, and again the aid of the

White House was enlisted. The difficulty was that the commission was divided on the committee's plan. Several members, including the committee's chairman, were in opposition. The positions of two other commissioners were unknown. One of these was Everett Hutchinson, a Texan and old friend of the president's. Elmer Staats assessed the situation for Myer Feldman and suggested that "the White House . . . communicate" with the one opponent who was up for reappointment and the two who were uncommitted.[73] These three votes, added to the four who had announced in favor of the plan, would create a solid majority. Presumably, this suggestion was followed. Several months later, in June 1965, the ICC adopted a plan that BOB director Charles L. Schultze considered adequate, he told the president, although it did "not go quite as far as we should like." Still it was "another very substantial step forward."[74]

In the midst of the struggle over headquarters reorganization, implementation problems in field office reorganization compelled presidential attention. Staats alerted Lee White in February 1965 to the director of locomotive inspection's failure to cooperate with the changes that were underway. The director and his two assistants were appointed by the president and were vested by law with certain authority, although they were on the staff of the ICC. There had been conflict in the past, and it broke out anew when the director, with the support of the railroad unions, insisted that his functions not be placed under the authority of the new regional offices. He wanted to continue to direct field activity from Washington. On the other side, the ICC insisted on conformance with its organizational plan. Although Staats had several alternatives in mind, he made no concrete recommendations at that time.[75] By April 1965 the BOB had prepared a reorganization plan to abolish the three positions filled by presidential appointment, place the director's authority and responsibilities in the commission, and eliminate the statutory requirement that there be a locomotive inspector in each state.[76] The plan was presented to the president, who approved it.[77] Subsequently, careful checks were made in Congress and elsewhere as to its acceptability. They revealed the likelihood of strong union opposition and, consequently, some congressional squeamishness.[78] Nevertheless, the president allowed the plan to go forward, and it went into effect in July 1965.[79]

More serious problems were encountered in strengthening the chairman's position. On 2 March 1966 the president's transportation message went to Congress. Most of his proposals were approved, including the creation of the Department of Transportation. One that was not approved gave the president authority to appoint the chairman of the Interstate Commerce Commission and strengthened the chairman's executive authority. In fact, a reorganization plan along these lines was never submitted to Congress.

Those who worked on the message were quite aware that the ICC proposal would be controversial. Therefore, meticulous soundings were made in the transportation industry and in Congress, especially in the commerce committees of the two houses.[80] Concurrently, the Bureau of the Budget drafted a reorganization plan.[81] On 1 February 1966, when the president approved inclusion of the ICC proposal in the transportation message, he was assured by Joe Califano and Lee White of strong support for it. Six of the eleven ICC members were in favor, and indications were that the entire commission would give formal support. The chairmen of both the House and Senate commerce committees were positive, and the railroad and trucking industries would back the changes.[82] Subsequent congressional checks continued to be positive.[83]

As it turned out, the proposal's reception was not as predicted. Opposition arose among regulated carriers. Shippers were strong in their antagonism to changes in the chairmanship. Some members of Congress were concerned that too many reorganization plans were pending and advised delay. There were also hints that the plan in some way might endanger something much more important, the new department. The situation was still unsettled almost two months after the message. Joe Califano asked for a new assessment of congressional views. One of the most important votes recorded was that of Representative Chet Hollifield, who was to be the floor manager for the Department of Transportation bill. His advice was to hold off.[84] When Henry H. Wilson, Jr., who handled liaison with the House, transmitted this report to the president, he especially noted Hollifield's comment and advised Johnson, "This should be conclusive as to timing."[85] Apparently it was, and the ICC changes were placed on ice.

They surfaced again that fall. A task force on transportation was established under the chairmanship of Secretary of Commerce John T. Connor to prepare a program for the upcoming congressional session. The ICC chairmanship was on the list of matters that it was charged to consider.[86] The task force's recommendations included changes.[87] In a meeting of White House staff and key task force members, "all agreed that we should go with this year."[88] But again there was no action. The reasons are indicated in subsequent rounds of deliberations in both 1967 and 1968. In 1967 a Califano aide, Lawrence E. Levinson, asked Alan Boyd's judgment on sending up the plan. Boyd, by now secretary of Transportation, was negative. His reasons were the strong opposition of shippers, the railroads, and some truckers and the view of congressional friends of the administration that "no legislation of any type should be submitted this year . . . that is not felt to be essential."[89] Boyd's advice was persuasive. Early the following year Califano and Boyd again discussed the matter. The results of Boyd's initial contacts were somewhat optimistic in that opposition from carriers appeared to have faded. But doubts remained as to shippers and ICC practitioners.[90] Califano asked one of his assistants, Matthew Nimetz, to "stay with this one."[91] He did, but a later consultation with Under Secretary of Transportation John E. Robson indicated that the picture really had not changed all that much, except that prospective opposition had grown and prospective congressional supporters were more reluctant than before to become embroiled in the controversy.[92] So it was left to the Nixon administration to push through the ICC reorganization plan altering the chairmanship, which it did in 1969.

In Presidential Service

You . . . are directed to launch a thorough study of the cause of this failure. I am putting at your disposal full resources of the federal government and directing the Federal Bureau of Investigation, the Department of Defense and other agencies to support you in any way possible. You are to call upon the top experts in our nation in conducting the investigation.
A report is expected at the earliest possible moment.

LBJ, 9 November 1965[93]

The president's directive was to Joseph S. Swidler, chairman of the Federal Power Commission. Setting in motion a fast-moving and full investigation of an extensive electric power failure in the Northeast that affected 30 million people, it is one of the few instances of the public and forthright exercise of executive authority by Johnson that, in effect, directed the substantive work of a regulatory commission. The blackout was a critical event of such proportions and with such implications that a presidential response was unavoidable. Johnson's directive to Swidler put the FPC in presidential service. In other ways and in other contexts, the commissions served the presidency, or at least efforts were made to enlist their aid in matters of presidential interest.

Collaboration

On their own initiative or in response to requests, at times commissions willingly assisted in various endeavors of special presidential interest. The most important instances related to the administration's economic policy objectives and are discussed later. But there were others.

It is not unusual for constituent parts of government to relate their activities to major themes or interests of an administration and to emphasize their identification with presidential concerns. The Federal Maritime Commission reported, for example, that it had "persuaded . . . two steamship conferences . . . to effect substantial reductions" of charges in the Vietnamese trade.[94] As chairman of the FPC, Lee White vigorously pushed equal opportunity employment on regulated firms.[95] He also put forward ideas for crime prevention involving the use of electric power when the crime problem was high on the presidential agenda.[96] The Federal Trade Commission gave special attention to business practices in urban ghettos and attempted to ease the way for the local ownership of businesses there.[97] Discrimination in housing was a target of initiatives undertaken by the Federal Deposit Insurance Corporation.[98]

Another aspect of collaboration was the supply of information to the White House. Routine reports were supplemented by special notices about notable regulatory decisions.[99] From time to time, the White House attempted to tap the expertise of commissions for its own purposes. For example, ignoring the nonpolitical assumptions concerning commissions, the FPC was asked to supply suggestions for the 1964 Democratic platform and for presidential speeches.[100] It was also asked to address several questions pertaining to certain negotiations, in which it had no official role, involving the Bonneville Power Administration.[101] The views of the Civil Aeronautics Board were solicited on the site selected for a new airport in the Dallas–Fort Worth area.[102] The Securities and Exchange Commission supplied information on the publisher of *Look* magazine and on a former movie star turned financial adviser.[103]

Casework

Directly and through members of Congress, the White House received frequent invitations to intervene in regulatory proceedings. Inquiries and complaints usually were handled gingerly, reflecting both the propensity for avoidance discussed in the previous chapter and the political imperative of at least appearing to be responsive. Ernest Goldstein described his experience:

In a particular case we get lots of calls, here, either directly or
through the Congressional office . . . , or the lobbyists will come
in and say that they are worried about this, that, and the other
thing. . . . And the way you handle that is you tell them that the
decisions aren't made here; that the agency or department has its
mechanism for dealing with problems; that all we can interest
ourselves in is the fact that they're getting a fair shake and a fair
and expeditious hearing. This may even come from a letter
which is bucked in here—somebody will write a letter to the
President complaining that his application for an FM station . . .
has been held up unconsciously [*sic*] for X period of months. And
so what you do . . . is you find out what is actually happening
and if you feel that . . . the agency is dragging its heels, you suggest, well, . . . just be good to the public and get cracking with it.
And if you find that they're doing what seems reasonable, then
you write back . . . and say, "We assure you that everything is
being handled properly." . . . But this is the only involvement you
dare get into.[104]

Others in the White House also interested themselves in cases
from time to time. The more political of Johnson's aides were among
them; they may have been less discreet than Goldstein and certainly
less sensitive to admonitions against involvement in the particulars
of cases in ways that might suggest an effort to exercise influence.
For example, Jake Jacobsen elicited a status report on a bus proceeding involving a Texas carrier from a member of the ICC.[105] A member of the FCC reported, in response to an inquiry from Marvin Watson, that the application of a Texas radio station for an increase in
power "will be taken care of next week."[106] And, through an aide,
Watson was told by the general counsel of the Federal Trade Commission that it seemed possible to "work something out . . . that
will be mutually agreeable to the FTC and Coca-Cola" in a consent
decree negotiation then in process.[107]

Casework of a sort was also undertaken in support of presidential
as differentiated from constituent interests. Goldstein pressed the
ICC to regulate the household moving industry more aggressively
and invited the commission's chairman to the White House to discuss the problem.[108] Lee White, while still in the White House, sent
a memorandum, with Johnson's approval, to the FPC asking it to
examine Governor Nelson E. Rockefeller's disapproval of a contract
authorizing the sale of power produced in New York to a number of
rural electric cooperatives in western Pennsylvania.[109]

The president served as his own caseworker in some circumstances. For example, when an assistant secretary in the Department of Commerce was named, but not charged, in a Securities and Exchange Commission complaint concerning insider trading, Johnson called the SEC chairman for further information and "urged that the matter be pursued."[110] He also cleared, if he did not require, a letter from the SEC to the New York and American stock exchanges asking for an investigation into rumors circulated on the morning of 9 June 1965 that the president had suffered a stroke or heart attack.[111] The markets had reacted sharply. When later told that the rumors could not be traced, Johnson's response was a cryptic, "Looks like we could do better."[112]

Matters of Deportment

One of Johnson's major interests in regulation was the public demeanor of regulators. He carefully screened prospective appointees with this in mind, and, when presented with behavior he deemed inappropriate, he did not mask his displeasure. Perceived deportment problems could range from press leaks about forthcoming commission decisions to hints of disloyalty in advance of the 1968 presidential election.[113] FCC Chairman E. William Henry was made aware of presidential concern about a tiff with Frederick R. Kappel, chairman of the board of AT&T. Kappel believed, and told the president, that Henry had misled him about the timing of a rate case order. Henry, in a memorandum to the president, made sure that Johnson was aware of a successful meeting he had with Kappel that cleared away the misunderstanding.[114]

FCC commissioners Nicholas Johnson and Kenneth A. Cox also were recipients of a presidential reprimand. On their own, they sent a questionnaire to Oklahoma radio and television broadcasters on programming practices. The action was in anticipation of upcoming license renewal proceedings and reflected their dissatisfaction with the programming habits of broadcasters in general and the FCC's treatment of programming questions when considering renewals. Their survey raised the ire of broadcasters and Oklahoma Senator Mike Monroney and received considerable attention in the trade press. It also drew the attention of the Bureau of the Budget and the Advisory Council on Federal Reports, because the questionnaire had not been cleared. When the president learned of the situation from Ernest Goldstein, he instructed him "to talk to Johnson & say this highly irregular to have part of commission doing this."[115] Goldstein did talk to Johnson. As he told the president, "I emphasized the need for team work in a commission. I noted the obligation of Federal

Agencies to use regular procedures which do not harass the citizen. Nick got the message."[116]

Johnson reacted strongly to persistent public conflict among commission members. When Charles Murphy was appointed to head the CAB, the president told him "to reduce the number of split decisions by the Board."[117] At an interim point, although reporting success in reducing dissent, Murphy warned Johnson, "I don't know how long it will last."[118]

The most dramatic recorded presidential intervention to correct the deportment of regulators concerned the FTC. There was considerable publicly aired animosity—personal and substantive—among its members during much of Johnson's presidency. Conflict reached a peak in late 1967, when some members set out to block the appointment of the general counsel to a vacancy on the commission. He was the personal choice of the chairman. Within the span of a few days, the president personally indicated his displeasure to each member of the commission. On 8 December Commissioner Mary Gardiner Jones was called to the White House for a late afternoon meeting with Johnson. During a brief conversation, he talked about the appointment he had just made to the commission, James M. Nicholson. Jones "was astounded by the knowledge Johnson displayed concerning the internal affairs of the agency."[119] He asked her to assist Nicholson as he assumed his new responsibilities. Johnson also indicated that he was aware of her difficulties with one of her colleagues, Philip Elman, and assured her that if the problem got worse he would "take care of him."[120] Next came a session with Nicholson on 13 December. Again, Johnson showed his grasp of the commission's internal difficulties. Nicholson left with the impression that one of his responsibilities was to help reduce the personal conflicts.[121]

The next day there was a signing ceremony at the White House for flammable fabrics legislation. All the commissioners were invited. In the receiving line, the president told A. Everett MacIntyre that he was "displeased over all the adverse publicity the Commission was receiving . . . and the fact that certain persons were airing information to the press that should have been kept in confidence."[122] MacIntyre told Johnson that he was not one of those, whereupon he was congratulated on his "good judgment."[123] Elman, one of the principal antagonists, came along a bit later. Johnson grasped Elman's arm and looked him squarely in the eye. He said, according to Elman: "'This was good work signing this bill for the consumer, and the people ought to be told about it; speeches should be made; the adoption of consumer protection legislation was what the people should be reading about.' Then, there was a perceptible shift in emphasis. 'That's what they should hear, rather than the details of the bickering at the Commission.' Elman recalled the President stating the publicity was 'bad for me, bad for you, bad for the commission.'"[124] Perhaps, Johnson suggested, the FTC should follow the practice of the FPC. When differences arise, adjourn and come back the next day to work them out "in private."[125]

The signing ceremony ended with remarks by the president, but his FTC work was not yet done. Immediately afterward the chairman of the commission, Paul Rand Dixon, and Nicholson were with Johnson in the Oval Office.[126] One may presume that further presidential admonitions were on the agenda. As a result, according to Elman and others, a honeymoon spirit prevailed at Sixth and Pennsylvania Avenue NW for a few months. Unfortunately, it did not last until the end of the president's term, despite his extraordinary efforts.

Crisis

On an early November afternoon in 1965 the president, together with Mrs. Johnson and friends, was driving in the vicinity of the Moursund Ranch in the Texas hill country. Word of the blackout in the Northeast came over the car radio on the 5:00 P.M. news. Lee White describes the scene:

> When that big blackout hit, it was late in the afternoon—I think a Tuesday afternoon—on November 9, 1965. President Johnson was out somewhere on the Ranch, not in his house but running around in one of those Lincolns of his. And he heard on the radio that there was some great difficulty up in New York. . . . The President got on the radio and called up Califano and said, "What the hell is going on." Califano said, "I don't know. What the hell *is* going on?" He hadn't known about it. So the first word to the White House was by that world's great news follower Lyndon B. Johnson![127]

The president then told Califano, "For God's sake, get the FPC on it."[128] In White's view, without this directive the FPC would not have acted, because "it never occurred to them that reliability was one of their bags. . . . And it would never have occurred to them," except for the president's own reaction.[129] This was because he was "just a thirty-year professional bureaucrat, and in his mind the blackout . . . is automatically associated with the federal government responding and doing something. Within that framework, who should it be but the Federal Power Commission."[130]

Johnson was especially concerned with the national security implications of the power failure. In his first call, he asked Califano to check with Secretary of Defense Robert S. McNamara to see if sabotage was a possibility. His next step was to call the pilot of Air Force One to see if "the planes were standing by and ready to go" in case he was required to make an emergency departure.[131] Nine minutes after the president's initial call Califano called back—Johnson was still in the car—with information on the extent of the blackout and word that "the land-line to Moscow was not functioning."[132] During the next two and one-half hours Johnson placed and received fourteen telephone calls on the blackout, talking to various White House aides, McNamara, and the directors of the Office of Emergency Preparedness and the Office of Science and Technology. After dinner there were still more, including calls to the governor of New York and the mayor of New York City.[133]

While the president monitored the situation from Texas, Califano, among other things, searched for FPC chairman Joseph Swidler. According to White, Califano finally located the chairman at a reception and advised him, "The President said there's a goddamn blackout in New York. You'd better be doing something about it."[134] Swidler immediately started an investigation into the cause of the blackout. The FPC effort, supported by $50,000 from the president's emergency funds, was supplemented by coordinated inquiries undertaken by the Federal Bureau of Investigation and the Federal Aviation Agency. The various inquiries were followed closely by the White House. In less than a month the FPC completed its investigation. The reliability problem continued to occupy an important place on the commission's agenda thereafter, and a presidential task force in 1966 considered various alternatives for increasing the role of the FPC in insuring against large-scale interruptions in the supply of power. None became a part of Johnson's legislative program, however.

Advancing Basic Economic Policy Objectives

Although there were exceptions, Johnson, like other presidents, may have been largely indifferent to routine regulatory activities, but he was vitally interested in larger economic policy questions. In many respects, the economy performed impressively during his presidency. The 1964 tax cut was an important stimulus. Impressive gains were realized in the gross national product, in jobs creation, in disposable personal income, and in corporate profits. At the same time, there were signs of weakness due principally to the economic effects of the war in Vietnam. Inflation, as measured by the consumer price index, rose only an average of 1.3 percent a year between 1961 and 1965, but the annual average growth between 1965 and 1967 was 2.5 percent, and it shot up to 4.2 percent starting in 1967. The nation's trade surplus declined, and a balance-of-payments deficit grew into a major concern. Johnson was acutely sensitive to these developments.

The broad outlines of the administration's economic policy were forged, for the most part, in ongoing relationships linking the president, the Council of Economic Advisers, the Bureau of the Budget, the Treasury Department, and the Federal Reserve Board of Governors.[135] From time to time, however, regulatory commissions were enlisted in presidential service in pursuit of basic policy objectives, especially when economic stability was at issue. Threats to stability caused by troubled financial institutions drew presidential attention to the regulation of banks and savings and loan institutions. Other problems that pulled regulators into presidential orbit were inflation, labor disputes, and the balance-of-payments problem.

Johnson's concern with the soundness of financial institutions was reflected in White House relations with the comptroller of the currency's office, part of the Treasury Department, and are discussed in the next chapter. It was also expressed in relations with the bank regulators at the Federal Reserve Board of Governors and, in less restrained fashion, with those at the Federal Deposit Insurance Corporation and the savings and loan regulators at the Federal Home Loan Bank Board. The president emphasized his interest in sound banks to Kenneth A. Randall when talking to him about the chairmanship of the FDIC in April 1965.[136] Between 30 June 1963 and Johnson's meeting with Randall thirteen banks had failed, principally as a result of criminal behavior by management.

Not long after this meeting the problems faced by financial institutions intensified. There was a credit crunch of serious proportions caused by a tight monetary policy intended to restrain inflation, despite heightened demand for credit. The situation was aggravated in December 1965 when the FRB increased the interest rate banks under its authority could pay for time deposits. This created problems for banks outside its jurisdiction. Savings and loan institutions also were seriously affected, because of limits on the interest they could pay for deposits. As banks increased interest rates, funds began to flow out of savings and loans in substantial amounts.[137]

It was, Randall reflected later, a "crisis time."[138] At the FDIC, "At certain key points we were running checks on the flow of money two and three times a day."[139] While the crisis was building, he recalls meeting with the president in the White House. They were in a room in which a photograph of former president Herbert Hoover overlooked their conversation. Hoover, of course, was associated with many bank failures during the depression. At one point, Johnson "turned and he shook his finger at that photograph, and he said, 'I don't want them doing to me, like they did to old man Hoover.'"[140]

Beyond expressing his concerns to regulators, Johnson took positive steps to avoid the fate of "old man Hoover" by addressing weaknesses in the regulatory system. Legislation, treated in chapter 6, was proposed to strengthen the authority of regulators and to deal specifically with the shortage of credit. Steps were also taken to improve coordination among regulators. One source of problems was the operating style of James J. Saxon, the comptroller of the currency. Efforts to remedy this problem are described in the following chapter.

From the standpoint of the three independent agencies—the FRB, the FDIC, and the FHLBB—a fundamental problem until late 1965 was the absence of a framework for coordinating their actions with one another and with the Treasury Department. The FRB's December 1965 action on interest rates was taken without consultation with other regulators, who then had to cope with its effects.[141] Afterward, according to John E. Horne, then chairman of the FHLBB, "Johnson . . . very firmly requested, as a matter of fact it could be described . . . as a demand, that there be established a coordinating committee."[142] It included the FHLBB, the FRB, the FDIC, the comptroller, and the Treasury secretary, and it appeared to function rather effectively through 1968.[143]

Linked to interest rates and credit problems, but of more basic importance, was the larger question of inflation. Wage-price guideposts, established in 1962, were the cornerstone of the Johnson administration's struggle to minimize increases in the cost of living. Efforts to secure compliance with them were centered in the White House and in the Council of Economic Advisers. Several of the regulatory commissions were drawn into the effort. The Federal Trade Commission played a part in charting price movements.[144] It was also asked to study a rise in bread and milk prices in the summer of 1966 in order to ascertain whether they were associated with violations of the antitrust laws.[145] Reporting in October, the commission found a few possible violations, but it concluded that these did not cause the jump in prices.[146]

The course of cooperation was not always smooth, however.

Administration policy makers regularly expressed frustration about the failure of the Civil Aeronautics Board and the Interstate Commerce Commission to take the administration's economic policy objectives into account in their rate decisions. Transportation rates and wages were involved in a whipsaw relationship. A prospective increase in rates, whatever the justification, became an argument for wage increases in labor negotiations.

Of the two agencies, the CAB was the lesser problem, especially during the chairmanship of Charles S. Murphy from 1965 to 1968. Murphy, who served in the Truman White House and as under secretary of Agriculture until he moved to the CAB, was a longtime friend of the president. Shortly after he became chairman, Johnson asked him for "suggestions" in regard to air travel within the United States. In October 1965 Murphy responded in a lengthy memorandum to Joe Califano which emphasized lowering the cost of air transportation and expanding travel opportunities. He outlined a variety of steps that might be taken. One was to encourage promotional fares. He proffered an invitation to the president, not accepted, to meet with industry representatives and urge them to be innovative in designing fares.[147]

Johnson encouraged Murphy to proceed. The chairman dispatched progress reports to the president on a fairly regular basis. In late December he "could not resist sending" a newspaper clipping with the headline "Fares Are Falling for Airplane Travelers."[148] A month later he went with Johnson to visit Truman in Independence, Missouri. Four days later he sent Johnson a press release on air fares in response to the request "that I call your attention to new promotional fares instituted by the airlines."[149] Murphy wrote a few weeks later that "the CAB will approve a new excursion fare proposal which we expect to be filed 'voluntarily' by United Air Lines."[150]

Concern about the ICC's lack of cooperation crystallized in 1966. Early in October a small motor carrier rate increase pending before the ICC came to the attention of John Robson, who worked with Joe Califano on economic matters, and James S. Duesenberry, a member of the Council of Economic Advisers. In considering whether to make a representation to the ICC, Robson and Duesenberry felt that "we should save our guns for something more important."[151] At the same time, Robson expressed the need for a better relationship with the commission. "I think," he suggested to Califano, "that at your convenience we should sit down with Chairman Bush and set up a communication line and some device for assessing the significance of the increases."[152]

A need for effective lines of communication and, presumably, for opportunities to influence the ICC's thinking persisted as a theme throughout the remainder of the Johnson presidency. It was reiterated by Robson in November 1966 after Califano asked him to suggest discussion points for a meeting with Bush. One of Robson's ideas was the "institution of a reporting system so that the Council and I are advised of important rate increase requests as soon as they have been presented by carriers."[153] Califano raised the matter with Bush, but the communications problems were not resolved. Presidential aides continued to search for ways to convey their concerns about rates to the commission. In March 1967 Sanford Ross, now involved with Robson in wage-price matters, consulted with Califano on a prospective increase in rail rates. If they decided that the economic effects would be major, Ross said, "we will have to consider how the Administration should make its views . . . known to the ICC."[154] William Tucker, a member of the ICC who was more inclined than some of his colleagues to view ICC actions within a larger economic policy context and who talked to presidential advisers from time to time, was mentioned as a potential intermediary.[155]

Informal talks with Bush, Tucker, and Willard Deason were unsatisfactory means of achieving administration purposes. They were supplemented in June 1967 when Secretary of Transportation Alan Boyd wrote the three commissions regulating transportation. He asked them "to give heavy weight to the goal of over-all price stability . . . in rate decisions," according to Ackley's report to the president.[156] The replies, Ackley continued, were "generally disappointing," although "assurances were given that the goal of price stability would be considered, along with other goals."[157] Tucker, responding for the ICC, "said that all ICC decisions are based on a formal record, and urged DOT to intervene directly in the scheduled investigation of proposed increases by railroads."[158]

There were DOT interventions in ICC rate proceedings, but success was problematic. In a major motor carrier case not quite a year after Boyd's letter, the department's request for suspension of a rate increase was rejected. This, together with other developments, caused Arthur Okun of the Council of Economic Advisers to ask Califano, "Can anything be done to get the ICC to take price stability more seriously?"[159] His despair was almost complete. "DOT has tried to exercise its influence without success. We are thinking of inviting the chairmen of all the regulatory commissions . . . to a meeting to discuss the inflation problem. But I would not expect an enthusiastic response. It is ironic that, when any private businessman will at least listen to us plead our case, some government regulatory bodies seem to consider it an invasion of their territory. John Macy's office tells me that the President is about to make two ICC appointments. This might provide an opportunity to deliver the sermon on the urgency of price stability."[160]

Three weeks later Okun took his complaints and his suggestion to Macy and to the president. Macy took cognizance of Okun's views. So did the president, who noted, "Put on my desk to call Deason."[161] By this time, however, Johnson's presidency was near its end. The appointment power and the exploitation of informal ties, in the past, had not been enough to bring the commission into harmony with the administration, nor would they be in coming months. In wage-price stabilization, the ICC's independence was a reality.

There were a few situations with implications for economic stability, however, in which the ICC did ultimately cooperate. One of these concerned a shortage of rail freight cars, especially in the Far West and Midwest. As noted at the start of this chapter, Johnson himself placed the problem on the presidential agenda in September 1965. It remained there into 1967 when supply began to increase. Improvement in supply was the result of legislation backed by the president, ICC and industry actions, and reduced demand due to changed economic circumstances. But for more than a year the presidency and the ICC were in close communion in efforts to alleviate the problem.

The roots of the shortage were in a steady post–World War II decline in the number of available cars and in the ICC's limited authority to regulate their use. In the summer of 1965 the situation was aggravated by a bumper grain crop and the commitment of a large number of cars for shipment of military supplies to the West Coast and thence to Vietnam.[162] Vietnam's contribution to the problem was perhaps one reason for the president's energetic reaction, although the more immediate catalyst was a raft of congressional complaints and demands for action.

Obviously the White House neither could nor wished to supplant the role of the commission. Its response, however, indicates how the resources of the presidency may be employed in the resolution of a regulatory problem that falls within the jurisdiction of an independent agency. The basic overall purpose of presidential action was not to define and impose a solution, but to energize other actors and to accelerate movement toward some generally satisfactory conclusion. In regard to the ICC, the anticipated service to the presidency was not action along one particular line or another, but action that would remedy in some acceptable fashion a situation that had become a political problem for Johnson. There were several elements in the presidential response.

One element was simply to acknowledge the problem. This provided focus, underscored its seriousness, and accentuated the necessity for action. A second element was to take executive steps to reduce pressures on car supply. After being asked to take a leadership role in the administration's efforts, Vice President Hubert H. Humphrey reported to the president on actions of the departments of Agriculture and Defense. Secretary of Agriculture Orville Freeman agreed to minimize the movement of Commodity Credit Corporation stocks during the harvest season. Secretary of Defense Robert McNamara acted to minimize the adverse effects of military supply shipments.[163] A third element, in which the vice president also played a role, was directly expressing the administration's concerns to the railroads. Humphrey did so, advising the industry that it should "step up the movement of boxcars through its own program and its own policing of such program."[164]

The final two elements in the response involved the ICC directly. One was to aid the commission in the passage of a bill enlarging its authority. For years the ICC unsuccessfully sought legislation allowing it to impose realistic *per diem* charges on rail freight cars. In 1965, before the administration became involved, the Senate passed a bill that would "go part way toward helping our situation," the acting chairman of the ICC told Marvin Watson.[165] However, there were problems in the House of Representatives. In the days following Johnson's first indication of personal interest congressional liaison staff worked to stimulate House action.[166] Vice President Humphrey talked to the chairman of the House Interstate and Foreign Commerce Committee, Oren Harris, about the legislation. Harris, who did not like the Senate bill, was persuaded to schedule hearings; when the hearings were concluded, the White House urged him to report a bill promptly.[167] This was done on 20 October, but opposition from eastern railroads delayed enactment until 12 May 1966. Although the legislation was lacking in a number of respects, it was viewed as a step forward. The president's association with the issue and the passage of the legislation was reflected in a White House signing ceremony and presidential remarks on 26 May 1966.[168]

The last element was keeping pressure on the ICC to do the maximum administratively. From the day Johnson responded to Representative Duncan's telegram, the commission was continually reminded of the president's interest. That interest was expressed most acutely during September and October 1965. On 8 September Marvin Watson called John Bush to give him the president's view that the first ICC response was "gobbledygook." That seemed to have an effect, and thereafter the commission took the problem more seriously. The next day a communication was sent to the ICC's field offices pointing out the White House's interest and directing that "utmost efforts" be made to correct supply problems.[169] Bush promptly reported to Watson on this and other aspects of the situation.[170] In the meantime, the vice president pressed the commission to use its emergency powers to order the prompt return of western cars from the east. It did this on 1 October and followed up with additional car orders a few days later.[171] Information on these and subsequent actions was supplied to presidential aides and to the Council of Economic Advisers in periodic updates.

Presidential interest did not abate after the passage of the legislation. By that time price and wage stabilization was a major concern, and the car supply situation obviously affected prices. In August 1966 Robson inquired about the commission's progress in implementing the new law.[172] Several months later he was still concerned and asked Califano whether the ICC was "sure *everything* possible is being done to alleviate freight car tightness."[173] He urged Califano to raise the question with the ICC chairman at an upcoming meeting. Califano indicated that he would.[174] Shortly thereafter, the new chairman of the commission told Duesenberry that there were significant and positive changes in the car supply situation.[175]

Another example of cooperation between the White House and regulatory commissions on an economic policy matter, this time involving the ICC and the CAB, came in the summer of 1966. On 8 July a strike was called against five major air carriers after protracted negotiations broke down. On the day before, when it was clear there would be a strike, Johnson issued a statement outlining the administration's response. The CAB and ICC were "requested" to allow the air carriers still operating and rail and bus companies to expand their services in order to minimize the effects of the strike.[176] The ICC quickly authorized its staff to issue emergency on-the-spot grants for temporary operating authority.[177] The response of the CAB, undertaken in consultation with the White House, was a series of orders allowing the nonstruck carriers to fill service gaps.[178] It took other steps to lessen the adverse effects of the strike, and the White House was kept current on the board's progress.[179]

As the strike wore on, CAB chairman Charles Murphy was asked to work behind the scenes in the negotiations between the airlines and labor. These are discussed more fully in the next chapter. The point here is to highlight the role of the CAB chairman. Califano told the president that he and Secretary of Labor Willard Wirtz feared that at least one of the companies might be inclined to settle too generously and saw a need to "stiffen the spine of management a little."[180] They recommended that the president authorize Califano to have Murphy tell the presidents of American Airlines and Pan American World Airways (Pan Am) "that we are watching their cases and we want them to come in with economically sound settlements."[181] Johnson agreed to Califano's proposition, and Murphy talked to the two presidents, contributing to what was ultimately a successful negotiation.[182]

There was a mixed record of cooperation in regard to the nation's international balance-of-payments position, which had been deteriorating since the late 1950s. Johnson continued efforts begun by President Kennedy to improve the balance. Several regulatory commissions were asked to do their part, although it was not presumed that they could make major contributions. The president sent them letters on 14 May 1964 and 17 May 1967. The propriety of a letter was carefully considered on both occasions. When the second letter was being prepared Lee White, now at the Federal Power Commission but a presidential aide at the time of the first, was among those consulted. He thought the idea a good one, but advised caution. Califano summarized White's reaction for Johnson: "He does not recall your 1964 letter creating any problems. He points out, however, that the issue of the independence of the regulatory agencies is a delicate one, and we should avoid to the extent possible unduly publicizing the letter."[183] (Neither appears in Johnson's public papers.) Both letters basically requested that the commissions take balance-of-payments considerations into account in the exercise of their responsibilities. The second, in addition, asked their general cooperation with the Cabinet Committee on Balance of Payments.[184]

Several of the commissions contributed to the effort. A major role was played by the Federal Reserve Board, which participated with administration officials in framing policy and effectively used its relations with the banking community to restrain lending abroad. The Securities and Exchange Commission helped in a nearly invisible but interesting way. There were great pressures on the international monetary system in 1967 and 1968. Early in 1968 speculation in gold rose dramatically, threatening the monetary system and causing a large outflow of gold from the United States. One of the responses was to close the London gold market for the day of 15 March 1968. There was considerable uneasiness as to the effects of the closure. Among the possibilities were sharp reactions on stock exchanges in this country. The SEC has authority to suspend trading on exchanges, subject to presidential approval. The morning of 15 March found Manuel Cohen, chairman of the SEC, and several members of his staff ensconced in the White House situation room engaged in a "market watch" and ready to suspend trading if necessary. Fortunately, it was not necessary. As frequent reports to the president showed, it was a routine Friday in the markets. By 11:20 A.M. White House aides Lawrence E. Levinson and Ernest Goldstein could tell Johnson, "We have broken up our Command Post. . . . Manny Cohen has gone to the Hill to testify about mutual fund legislation."[185]

It was in the transportation area that the balance-of-payments stakes were largest, though modest in relation to the total problem. In effect, the ICC declined to help. Conversations between the secretary of the Treasury and the ICC chairman and other discussions involving the department and the commission drew a blank. The commission claimed that it was unable to supply information about the relationship between the flow of international trade and transportation rates. And it refused to undertake initiatives that would produce rate incentives for exports and disincentives for imports.[186]

The other transportation commissions, the Federal Maritime Commission and the Civil Aeronautics Board, were not so standoffish. The FMC worked cooperatively with the White House and others in the executive branch to eliminate freight rate disparities that discriminated against American exports. The president had pointed to this as a major problem in a message to Congress on balance of payments in 1965.[187] The CAB actively participated in efforts to increase foreign travel to the United States and to encourage Americans to substitute travel in this country for travel abroad, also called for by Johnson in his 1965 message.[188]

The general policy of the government, clearly set forth by Kennedy in 1963, was that international air fares should be reduced.[189] The policy was consistently asserted by the CAB, the Department of State, and the American carriers involved in International Air Transport Association negotiations. One of the policy's rationales was that lower fares would increase international travel, especially of foreigners to the United States, and thus have positive effects on the balance of payments. Other countries took a contrary view for precisely this reason. They wished to restrict foreign travel by their citizens.

In addition to participating in international negotiations on fares and pushing for reductions, the CAB undertook a number of special initiatives. One was the Visit U.S.A. program, which gave foreign travelers a fixed price for travel over a particular carrier's domestic routes for a specified period. The president pushed Visit U.S.A. in the 1965 balance-of-payments message and asked the vice president to help promote the idea.[190] Throughout, he kept in close touch with what the CAB was doing. Johnson's personal interest is shown by his reaction to an encouraging progress report from the CAB chairman on Visit U.S.A. fare proposals to be put forward by several carriers. "Tell Charlie Murphy I sure do love this, but I hope you can talk them into advertising the living hell out of it."[191] Several months later Califano wrote Murphy at the president's request to "express his deep appreciation for the tremendous job you are doing on your Visit U.S.A. program. He is just delighted."[192] Johnson also asked that Califano periodically get "reports from you as to the progress of this program and recommendations as to how we might be able to help you."[193] In addition to contacts between Califano and Murphy, the president's interest was reflected in the collaborative involvement of other White House staff and administration officials with the CAB and in the work of presidential task forces on travel established in 1965 and 1967.

Like the ICC, the CAB could only respond to rate proposals. Unlike the ICC, the CAB actively sought to persuade the carriers to file proposals to lower fares. And it was clear in the process that the White House stood behind the agency's efforts. Something of the board's approach is revealed in a memorandum to Califano a week after he asked for periodic reports. The board had just issued an order authorizing airlines to discuss joint Visit U.S.A. and joint Discover U.S.A. fares, aimed at encouraging Americans to forego foreign for domestic travel. "Our approach will be somewhat more aggressive than the order itself indicates inasmuch as we expect to invite the airlines to have their first meeting here," Murphy told Califano. He added, "And I plan to tell them something about the importance which the Administration attaches to this kind of activity."[194]

The President as Regulator

To: Joe Califano
  Pan Am is going to dive bomb my house (and me without an ABM system) if the President doesn't take action on its coterminal and Dublin applications. And of course he won't until he hears from you. Decide, decide.
                    Harry McPherson, 30 December 1966[195]

For a good part of the Johnson presidency, major changes in service between the United States and Europe were on the agendas of the

Civil Aeronautics Board and the president, who was responsible for approving board decisions in the international realm. Pan American World Airways was one of several persistent applicants for additional authority. As counsel to the president and aide closest to the proceeding, Harry McPherson was burdened by the rather intense pressures it generated. Hence his understandable interest in reaching a conclusion.

The case at hand was one of 185 CAB decisions on certificates and permits to U.S. and other carriers for service between this country and foreign points acted upon by Johnson during his presidency. Most of them were of limited importance, generated no controversy, and were handled in routine fashion. But some were extraordinarily complex and of great political and substantive significance. They concerned entire patterns of service between the United States and other regions of the world, including Europe and the Pacific. There were vast stakes for carriers as well as for the economic and foreign policies of the United States and other governments. Indeed, the reason for statutory delegation of final authority to the president is recognition of the important ways decisions on international air transportation may affect transcendent national interests. After describing in general terms the process by which this singular presidential responsibility in regulation was exercised during the Johnson years, some of the most important decisions of the period are examined for purposes of further illumination.[196]

The Process

In basic outline the process was a simple one. Cases ordinarily were initiated before the CAB by carriers or by the board itself, although in one instance the president was the initiator. At the conclusion of its formal proceedings, which typically included hearings, a recommended decision by a hearing examiner, and perhaps oral argument, the board formed its own decision. This was sent to the president, then forwarded to the Bureau of the Budget. The bureau coordinated review by interested departments and agencies, always including State, Defense, Treasury, and Transportation and at times others such as Post Office and Interior. Departmental views were summarized and transmitted to the White House along with the bureau's own position. The counsel to the president or his deputy, in turn, prepared a summary of relevant information and his own recommendations for consideration by the president and attached it to the material prepared by BOB. White House activity generally came two to three months after the bureau's review process began. At this stage, the aide might draw additional data and views from the board or other sources in government. And along the way, especially in the major cases, the aide would be confronted with sometimes intense lobbying and political pressures. U.S. carriers, both winners and losers before the board, were prone to anxiously urge the merits of their position on the White House through memoranda, other supporting material, and personal contacts. The White House files show that figures such as Booth Mooney, who had worked for Johnson in the Senate; Theodore Sorensen, from the Kennedy era; James Rowe, prominent Washington lawyer and Democrat; and members of Congress were enlisted as advocates. The president himself attempted, with apparent success, to avoid substantive contacts with outsiders on pending decisions. It was left to his aides, according to McPherson, to serve as buffers, "listening to the various claims and counterclaims of the industry."[197] Apparently, since there was formal presidential responsibility for decisions, it was considered appropriate for White House aides to hear out those with a stake in a matter, in contrast with situations in which final responsibility lay in a regulatory agency.

The decision memoranda prepared for the president often included a synopsis of the political dimensions of proceedings and the winners and losers created by the various options. But the extent, if any, to which political considerations and the extensive *ex parte* representations at the presidential level may have influenced dispositions or decisions is not altogether clear. There is one intriguing hint that personal presidential preferences may in some way have been made known to the board prior to its action, and with some effect. The day following release of the examiner's decision in the transpacific case, 17 April 1968, DeVier Pierson indicated for Johnson the "big winners" and those left "in the cold." In the list of six big winners, penned zeros were placed beside two, Eastern and United, in what is judged to be the president's hand. Three of the five in the cold are ranked 1 (American), 2 (Braniff), and 3 (Continental) in that same hand.[198] Perhaps coincidentally, except for United, whose domestic awards for Hawaii service were not subject to presidential approval, the board's decision departed from the examiner's along the lines indicated by the notations on the memo. Losers became winners. American got authority for Japan, Braniff was given Hawaiian authority, and Continental received the Pacific route the examiner awarded to Eastern, leaving it with nothing.[199]

The general pattern of presidential choice strongly suggests, however, the importance of basic policy considerations over personal or partisan political factors. Perhaps the most persuasive evidence in support of this conclusion is that throughout the process there was a very strong tendency on the part of those involved in the president's decisions to accept the CAB's judgment. In almost all the proceedings, the board's decision won the unanimous approval of the departments and agencies, the Bureau of the Budget, and White House aides. There appeared to be general conformance with the president's view, expressed to McPherson, that the CAB was "the principal determinant" in these matters.[200] Johnson's position, McPherson records, was that he would "intervene his judgment only for overriding reasons of national policy or foreign relations, where the CAB overlooked some major consideration, or where critical evidence was not available to the Board at the time the case was pending before it."[201]

The box score clearly reflects the exercise of restraint and a tendency to defer to the board. Johnson ratified the CAB's decision in 180 of the 185 cases that came to him. In a few instances approval came despite departmental and BOB reservations.[202] Each time the president overruled the CAB, there were policy reasons for doing so developed in the review process. The president insisted upon a more generous grant of authority to Air Afrique than the board first allowed.[203] In another case, he objected to a condition placed on Aerolíneas Argentinas.[204] Foreign policy reasons underlay both disapprovals. Three of the five disapprovals came in major proceedings dealing with the transatlantic and transpacific services of U.S. carriers.

Major Proceedings

These proceedings were among the most important in which Johnson and his aides were involved. They also were strands in a systematic and fundamental reexamination of the international authorities of U.S. carriers that originated in the late 1950s. Among the stimuli were growth in demand for international air transportation and the introduction of jet technology. A transpacific route case began in 1959, but was ended for all practical purposes by President Dwight D. Eisenhower's disapproval of the board's major recommendations in 1961, two days before his term expired. Shortly after Congress clarified the legal status of supplemental carriers in 1962, a proceeding was instituted regarding their charter authority to and from Europe. It grew into three proceedings worldwide in scope that would greatly increase the ability of supplementals to offer charter services. Then, in 1963, the CAB began a transatlantic route renewal case, which focused on the services of scheduled U.S. carriers. All of the proceedings dealing with Europe were concluded during the

Johnson presidency. Also, a new transpacific case was initiated at Johnson's direction in 1966, but it was not to be completed while he was in office. A CAB report reached him in December 1968, and Johnson approved almost all of the board's recommendations. However, Nixon withdrew approval shortly after he was inaugurated, and the result was changed not long thereafter.

The hallmark of these cases and additional proceedings dealing with other parts of the world was expansion of service by U.S. carriers. President Johnson clearly was in support of this basic objective and its intended benefits: an improved balance of payments; more travel options; and lower fares for the traveling public. This is indicated in tacit White House approval given to the CAB's expansion of the scope of the supplemental proceedings.[205] In his conversations with CAB chairman Charles Murphy and others, the president encouraged the CAB in its overall efforts.[206]

Presidential decision-making processes in the cases were similar in most important respects. One feature was that the central issues arose from exceptions to CAB recommendations taken within government and by segments of the industry. They were fairly limited and defined with relative clarity. In the supplemental proceedings, the key issue was whether the values of increased competition and travel opportunities for lower-income Americans through an expansion in charter flights offset possible adverse effects on the balance of payments; in the transatlantic proceedings, they were whether Pan Am should be allowed to provide West Coast to Europe service by way of New York and other East Coast points (the coterminal issue) and the number and identity of U.S. carriers to be authorized to serve Dublin; in the transpacific case, it was whether a third U.S. carrier should be authorized to serve Japan.

Only in the supplemental cases did the president ultimately come to full agreement with the board. At an early point, however, the authorization of one charter carrier was disapproved. It filed for bankruptcy after the CAB's recommendation was framed.[207] In the transatlantic case, the first time it came to the White House, he determined that only one carrier would be authorized to serve Dublin, rather than the three recommended by the board—Pan Am, Trans World Airlines (TWA), and Seaboard World Airlines. He also took exception to the board's failure to grant Pan Am coterminal authority. Johnson's disagreements with the CAB meant that further proceedings before the board would be necessary. In the transpacific case, the board was told to rescind its authorization of American Airlines, the third carrier, to serve Japan.

Those involved, of course, were fully aware of the large stakes of particular carriers in these cases. It could hardly be otherwise, given the tendency of many of the parties to lobby with intensity and vigor. But economic and foreign policy considerations were central. Parties succeeded in securing reversals when they were able to argue their cases on economic and foreign policy grounds instead of simple self-interest and when similar concerns were reflected within the government.

The decisions on Dublin and Japan clearly rested on foreign policy considerations. The Irish jealously guarded Dublin service for their own airline. The State Department felt that there would be impossible negotiating problems if three carriers were authorized as recommended by the CAB and only extraordinarily difficult ones if it were a single carrier. It was the view of both the departments of State and Transportation, in which BOB concurred, that the addition of a third U.S. carrier would cause serious problems in civil air relationships with Japan.[208]

Johnson's decision in the transpacific case stirred a great deal of public speculation and controversy about possible favoritism. In fact, his decision letter mirrors almost exactly the combined views of departments and agencies presented to him in the Bureau of the Budget summary.[209] Nevertheless, the relatively open lobbying by persons perceived to have "ins" with the administration raised questions. Johnson and DeVier Pierson, who handled staff work in the matter, felt that at least some of the suggestions of impropriety were intended to prevent a final decision until Nixon took office. In Pierson's view, Johnson took "a pretty bum rap" in media coverage of the case.[210]

According to Pierson, when the CAB's decision was announced in November 1968, consideration was given to whether it should be decided or left to the new administration. It was Johnson's "view that he ought to act on it, since he's ordered the case. In effect, it had been a baby of his administration. It was ready to go."[211] The case was then processed in the normal way. While this was occurring, the president "set down a number of guidelines. First, that he would not talk to any of the carriers or their representatives . . . ; second, . . . he would not talk to any Congressman about the case; third, . . . he would not attempt to second-guess the CAB on any matter involving the selection of carriers."[212] In this context, Pierson notes a special sensitivity about the award of routes to Continental in place of Eastern. "Continental had been a strong supporter of the President. The mills were grinding that there was some hanky-panky on this."[213]

At the conclusion of the review process, according to Pierson, "every department in the government recommended . . . that he approve the case with one exception, and that was the elimination of a third carrier to Japan. It happened that the third carrier . . . was American Airlines, the line that I guess had been more friendly to President Johnson over the years than any other. . . . So he took them out of the case. . . . I thought at the time, 'Well if there's any act that will ever make it clear that he had thrown politics aside in deciding this case it would be that action.'"[214]

But speculative comments in the press continued, dissecting the relationships between airline representatives and the president. Pierson says, "I must say in my naivete I thought, 'Well, this is just a little flak you have to go through.' But he told me the Sunday night before he left office when the bulldog edition of the *Washington Post* came out with a particularly gory story in it, he said, 'Now, I'll tell you what's going to happen. Those are planted for the purpose of getting President Nixon to intervene in the case, you wait and see—he'll intervene.' Sure enough, that Friday, the CAB got a letter from President Nixon."[215]

Other decisions did not create as much controversy, but they were not necessarily easier to make. There was division within the government on the balance-of-payments effects of expanded charter service by supplementals and the board's refusal of coterminal authority to Pan Am. In the supplemental proceedings, Treasury saw sufficient adverse effects to justify disapproval.[216] This position was echoed by the scheduled carriers.[217] On the other side, both the board and the Bureau of the Budget saw more limited negative consequences in the short run, and perhaps even positive consequences in the long run.[218] After these views were recorded McPherson, as he later told the president, "held three lengthy meetings . . . with representatives of Treasury, State, Budget and CAB trying in vain to get agreement on the facts."[219] His next step was to ask the Council of Economic Advisers for a study. It served little more than to underscore the uncertainties. The slant, however, was toward the position of BOB, the board, and approval, which McPherson recommended to the president.[220]

In regard to the coterminal issue, the merits of Pan Am's claim for authority had been debated for years. Its historic argument was couched principally in equity terms: foreign carriers were allowed to fly East Coast passengers to the Orient via West Coast points and, together with TWA, could fly West Coast passengers to Europe via intermediate points on the East Coast. Why discriminate against Pan Am and prevent it from picking up Europe-bound travelers at East Coast points on flights originating on the West Coast? One of its supporting arguments was that, in the transpacific case aborted by Eisenhower's disapproval, the CAB had sanctioned half the notion in its recommendation—eastern terminals for west-bound traffic—and that the board's staff in the current proceeding had supported coterminal authority, although the board did not approve it. Major opposition was from domestic lines. They would lose traffic immediately and, furthermore, they were fearful that coterminal authority would eventually result in domestic Pan Am service between the two coasts.[221]

In the 1960s Pan Am's equity argument was somewhat muted and a balance-of-payments argument was emphasized. James Rowe and Thomas G. Corcoran, Washington attorneys for Pan Am, pressed the balance-of-payments point incessantly on the White House, the Department of State, and the Bureau of the Budget. The airline claimed that the benefit would be in the range of $25 million per year.[222] The Treasury Department, through secretaries C. Douglas Dillon and Henry H. Fowler, substantiated the estimate and argued for granting Pan Am the authority.[223] In the Bureau of the Budget, Pan Am's claims were felt to be "grossly overstated."[224] While the matter was pending at the White House, McPherson asked Charles Murphy, still CAB chairman, for his views on the issue. Murphy reported that his staff members were of the opinion that coterminal authority for Pan Am would yield only "negligible" balance-of-payments advantages.[225] Other airlines also challenged the figures.

Despite support for approval of the board's position in the State Department and other places, the balance-of-payments argument proved sufficiently convincing for attention to turn to identifying the options available to the president, if he finally decided the airline should receive the authority.[226] After prolonged consideration— more than a year, in fact—that choice was made. The method was further board hearings in light of balance-of-payments considerations, together with a transpacific proceeding that would include the issue of coterminal authority in the other direction.[227] This, McPherson told the president retrospectively, was "as close as you could come to asking the Board to reverse itself."[228] And so the board did approximately eight months later, ironically in a decision in which the term "balance of payments" is not to be found.[229]

One other issue had to be resolved before the transatlantic proceeding was finally concluded: authorizing a single carrier to serve Dublin from among Pan Am, TWA, and Seaboard, CAB's original selections. This too was a source of difficulty in the White House. In short, the second time around the board chose Pan Am by a three to two margin. The minority, including chairman Murphy, preferred

TWA. According to the criteria employed by the CAB, the case was a "close" one, McPherson told Johnson.[230] The various departments and agencies that reviewed the board's choice all concurred or had no objection to it. But both McPherson and Murphy believed that TWA could perform the service as well as Pan Am and would lose more of its established business through Shannon, Ireland, than would Pan Am, also then serving Shannon, if it lost Dublin. Secretary of Transportation Alan Boyd shared their preference for TWA, but he did not recommend disapproval at this point, whereas both Murphy and McPherson did.[231] As a result of differences among his advisers, the president asked Califano, who did not ordinarily participate in such matters, for his view. It was finally recorded after McPherson's plea for action to avoid an aerial attack on his house. Califano recommended that the president "go along" with Boyd, Treasury, State, and the CAB majority.[232] The McPherson-Murphy reservations were not sufficient to counter the support for approval in other quarters and to overcome Johnson's expressed reluctance to impose his views on the board in carrier selection.[233] The CAB's choice of Pan Am was ratified.

Policy Matters

International aviation was in transition in the 1960s. Air traffic was growing rapidly, airlines were profitable, and distances were shrinking as a result of jet aircraft. Competition among the airlines of the world was intense, yet highly regulated. In the competition with foreign carriers, U.S. officials and carriers were of the view that often the playing field was not level. For example, before the transatlantic case was decided, two U.S. carriers competed with seventeen foreign carriers to and from Europe, whereas 70 percent of the traffic consisted of U.S. travelers. Other governments fought to prevent additional service by U.S. carriers to their countries, yet pressed the interests of their own carriers for additional service opportunities in the United States.

When he was a presidential aide, Lee White secured Johnson's assent for a general review of international air transportation policy.[234] This resulted in a White House meeting in the summer of 1965 involving Commerce, Treasury, the Federal Aviation Administration, the CAB, and presidential staff, but little momentum developed.[235] Several discrete changes in policy were considered subsequently, however.

One proposal was to give the CAB authority to regulate the international rates and rate practices of U.S. and foreign carriers. Its basic purposes were to place downward pressure on fares generally and to give the United States a tool to employ when other governments refused to allow U.S. carriers to lower fares. Kennedy had recommended legislation along these lines in 1963, and the Senate passed it. The matter was raised again in 1965 and lingered thereafter on the agenda for some time.

The major impediment to action was internal disagreement as to whether CAB actions employing the new authority would be subjected to presidential approval. A CAB proposal in 1967 did not provide for this. The State Department and the Bureau of the Budget objected strongly.[236] The Department of Transportation and Harry McPherson sided with the board. They felt that advance notification was sufficient and that the necessity to approve might place the president in difficult political situations that were best avoided. Failure to reach agreement at a White House meeting on 11 July 1968 ended consideration of the rate regulation option.[237]

Another proposed policy change that commanded considerable attention within the administration was initiated by Pan Am. In 1966 it backed legislation that would allow the CAB to grant U.S. carriers international operating rights on an exemption basis, after presidential approval, when foreign flag carriers obtained rights under bilateral agreements. The basic problem was that when the United States reached an agreement with another country foreign carriers could begin operations immediately, but the certification of a U.S. carrier to provide the agreed-upon service could take several years. The award of an exemption would mean that a U.S. carrier could provide service while a proceeding to award a certificate was underway.[238]

At first, the Bureau of the Budget was opposed.[239] A meeting of interested parties in the White House on 25 August 1966 showed that, although all agreed on the basic objective, there were significant differences within the government on the particulars. The bureau suggested that the various views be given a "no objection" clearance, leaving the differences to be worked out in the legislative process. McPherson secured the president's acceptance of this "hands off procedure."[240] Except for Pan Am, expected by all to be the prime beneficiary of such legislation, U.S. carriers were in opposition, and the proposal did not become law.

A third undertaking of considerable policy significance was initiated by the CAB. On 18 April 1966 it proposed to amend the permits of all foreign carriers through administrative action and with presidential approval. The change sought by the board would give it authority to require foreign carriers to file data about their operations and schedules and to get those schedules approved. The purpose was to neutralize a tactic employed by other countries in which the schedules of U.S. carriers were threatened or restricted as a lever for extracting new operating rights from the United States for their carriers.[241]

The State Department had a number of reservations but indicated that it would not object if there were two changes. One was to specify that the authority would be used only when there was clear justification for retaliation against another country. The other was to require that the president approve any action taken on the basis of the new authority. In a White House meeting on 24 April 1966, the CAB refused to budge. At this point all agreed to put the matter on hold to see what Congress would do with a bill then under consideration that would allow the CAB to take retaliatory action under certain circumstances.[242] That legislation did not progress, and in 1967 the board again suggested administrative action.[243] At the end of 1968 the CAB was still seeking presidential approval of its proposal.[244]

Conclusions

There was no fine-honed agenda and no sense of coherent, considered, and continuing objectives relating to the work of the regulatory commissions at any point in Johnson's presidency. The one constant, discussed in the previous chapter and evident here, was Johnson's insistence that regulators manifest the demeanor he considered to be appropriate. This was shown when he caused FCC members to be corrected and when he undertook to haul the FTC into line himself. To the extent there were objectives and an agenda, they seem to have fluctuated from day to day, based upon events and situations of the moment that defined the presidential business in regulation.

Direct presidential involvement in the work of the commissions, with few exceptions such as the annual budget cycle, the appointment of regulators, and international air matters, was limited and episodic in character. There was restraint, but not avoidance. For the most part involvement was subject to no plan. White House staff members could respond to requests for help on particular problems by regulators, as Goldstein did on numerous occasions. They could stumble across situations that seemed to merit attention, as did Lee White in the Interior-FPC conflicts. The completely unexpected could arise, as in the case of the blackout in the Northeast. From the president's point of view, probably the most important involvement was on matters with implications for central economic policy.

Even here, presidential involvement was largely episodic, reactive, and even opportunistic.

Only a minute fraction of regulatory commission activity was touched directly by Johnson and his aides. Although the norm of independence was generally observed, the relationships linking the White House and regulators are best described as relatively close, not relatively distant. One reason is the tremendous amount of information that flowed into presidential hands about what the commissions were facing and doing. The level of knowledge at the presidential level of what was happening day to day far exceeded the level of action, but it contributed to a certain familiarity. Another reason is the sense of an administration incorporating people at both the presidential and commission levels. A relatively small number of people were involved, with extensive personal ties. The most significant of these linked commission chairmen to presidential aides and to the president himself, who had selected them to serve, in effect, as his outposts.

Relationships were more cooperative than conflictual in nature. A good many of the interactions turned around presidential efforts to help the commissions with problems and to support their efforts. And when commissions were asked to help in matters of presidential interest, they were usually responsive. There were exceptions, of course. Both the CAB and the ICC defended some of their turf with success when the Department of Transportation was being planned. On the other hand, both freely relinquished their safety functions. Of all the commissions, only the ICC could be considered to be especially insular. Age and a tradition of independence were factors, no doubt. But the size of the commission (eleven members) was also important. In one sense, the problem was not commission unresponsiveness, but the unresponsiveness of some members. Probably the largest factor was that the chairman was the agent of the membership, not the president.

Congress and interest groups appeared to cause few problems in the presidency-commission relationship. There is, at best, very limited evidence of iron triangles at work frustrating the president in the conduct of his business. The only situation in which Congress and interest groups caused serious problems in attaining major presidential objectives concerned changing the character of the ICC chairmanship.

Taking care of the president's business in commission regulation seldom involved direct action by the president himself. In addition to appointments, the exceptions included international air decisions, the Northeast blackout, deportment problems, and times when basic economic policy was affected. Staff members were given wide latitude in determining what to do in regulatory matters, but they kept the president well informed along the way. Their organization was loose, and there was broad participation. There was lack of system, with few exceptions, in advisory and action processes. The *ad hoc* nature of staff operations, however, did not itself seem to be a limitation or a major source of problems. Indeed, staff arrangements appeared to serve the president as he wished to be served.

4. Executive Regulation

> Get Ackley to list all commodities & elements in price index
> that may be looking upward & get Wirtz, Freeman & Udall &
> Katzenbach busy quick.
>
> LBJ, 17 December 1965 [1]

JOHNSON'S HURRIED INSTRUCTIONS were to Joe Califano in response
to a memorandum from Gardner Ackley, chairman of the Council
of Economic Advisers. Ackley had reported an increase in consumer
prices and detailed an action plan to restrain them. Although consumer prices, in general, were not subject to direct regulation, a
number of regulatory programs administered by executive departments and agencies might be used to affect their dynamics. W. Willard Wirtz's Department of Labor, in addition to its capacity to influence the wage claims of organized labor informally, administered a
number of programs that affected labor costs, including the regulation of labor standards. The Department of Agriculture, headed by
Orville L. Freeman, was in charge of a massive regulatory complex
with control of the price and production of key commodities at its
core. [2] Stewart L. Udall and his aides in the Department of Interior
regulated oil imports. Enforcement of antitrust laws fell under the
purview of Attorney General Nicholas deB. Katzenbach and the
Department of Justice. The president's clear intent was to employ
these programs in securing price stability, a prime economic policy
objective.

Johnson's involvement in executive regulation fell into two categories. One, exemplified by his reaction to Ackley's report, can be
designated as essentially presidential in character. Regulation was
actively managed, if not driven, by the White House. Major efforts
of this type concerned wage-price guideposts, balance of payments,
and labor-management relations in some instances. Policies were
determined centrally, and executive departments and agencies, as in

the case of the commissions, were expected to reflect them in their program activities. There were also direct presidential efforts to affect the behavior of business and labor in relation to certain policy interests in these areas. In the second category, presidential involvement did not stem from central policy interests and was less intense and more sporadic. At best, the presidency was an occasional and perhaps reluctant participant, and there was a tendency to leave regulatory matters to the administrators with immediate responsibility. Distinctions between the two categories were not always clear-cut. For example, among the agricultural issues receiving attention, some were of concern because of their implications for prices, but others were not.

There were a number of well-established regulatory programs located squarely in the executive branch in addition to those just mentioned. They included banking, in which the Treasury Department played a major role; food and drugs, located in the Department of Health, Education, and Welfare (HEW); air transportation safety, the responsibility of the Federal Aviation Administration (an independent agency later placed in the Department of Transportation); and mine safety, another responsibility of the Department of the Interior.

To one degree or another, all of these programs attracted presidential attention. Much of it was routine, as in the case of annual budget reviews. In some instances the presidency played a major role in policy and program decisions. Its role in some areas, however, was quite limited. Food and drug matters were handled almost wholly at the departmental level. According to Wilbur Cohen, a top HEW official, the Food and Drug Administration "was not a part of LBJ's world."[3] The same could be said of other regulatory programs. Some FAA business involved the White House, but little of it concerned the agency's regulatory functions. There were regular policy debates at the presidential level on labor standards, especially on increasing the minimum wage and extending its coverage, but program administration matters rarely reached the White House.[4] From time to time, there were requests that the White House do casework in regard to executive regulation, but only a few, far less than in the case of commission regulation.

In executive regulation, the heaviest demands placed on the White House were in the areas in which the presidency was in the vanguard and in the regulation of agricultural prices and production, oil imports, and banking. Antitrust enforcement issues were also frequent and pressing items on the presidential agenda. These are the subjects of this and the following chapter.

The Presidency in the Vanguard

> We are, and we have been every week since I have been President, trying to find formulas and procedures that would be fair to the worker and the management. . . . Until we find something better, we will continue to follow it. We are constantly looking for something better.
>
> LBJ, 9 August, 1966[5]

Johnson was commenting on the wage-price guideposts in response to questions at a press conference. They had been much in the news in the preceding weeks as a result of complex labor negotiations, strikes, and prospective price increases in steel and other industrial sectors. Of all the areas of governmental activity that might be characterized as regulatory, Johnson was personally most active in effecting voluntary compliance with the guideposts. Other areas, linked in some ways to the guideposts, were regulating the flow of dollars out of the country and the flow of foreign currencies to the United States and dealing with major labor-management conflicts.

Defending the Guideposts

The concept of guideposts based upon productivity trends began to develop in the Council of Economic Advisers during the Kennedy administration. In 1964 a 3.2 percent standard was adopted for wage increases. Though periodically contested by labor and compromised by higher wage settlements, it remained in place as a target cap until the last year of Johnson's tenure when inflationary realities caused the administration to adopt a more flexible stance. The standard for price increases was never stated in exact terms. According to the CEA, "The general guide for noninflationary price behavior calls for price reduction if the industry's rate of productivity increase exceeds the over-all rate—for this would mean declining labor costs; it calls for an appropriate increase in price if the opposite relationship prevails; and it calls for stable prices if the two rates of productivity increase are equal."[6]

The guidepost initiative is difficult to assess. As Johnson's press conference remarks indicate, their weaknesses as devices for attaining economic stability were widely acknowledged in and out of the White House. And there was an ongoing quest for more effective policy and means of implementation. Some consideration was given to mandatory controls, but no agreement ever developed on a superior alternative. A start was made in the last year of Johnson's presidency with the establishment of the Cabinet Committee on Price Stability with its own staff. Its promising first steps in studying the problem were ended when Johnson left office.

From 1964 onward Johnson was at the center of internal policy deliberations and implementation efforts. Various organizational arrangements were employed for guidepost activities. No matter what the formal structure was at any particular time, however, *ad hoc* arrangements were usually preferred in dealing with particular situations such as an increase in copper prices or labor contract negotiations in the air transportation industry. In the White House proper, Joe Califano played the principal staff role. The Council of Economic Advisers was constantly engaged. The director of the Bureau of the Budget was an important participant, as were the secretaries of Agriculture, Commerce, Defense, Labor, and the Treasury. Their efforts were supported by numerous subcabinet officials, often working in interagency groups.

With no formal sanctions backing the guideposts, eliciting voluntary compliance was the focus of implementation efforts. It was, of course, a difficult and time-consuming task. James E. Anderson and Jared E. Hazleton describe a number of techniques used by the president and his aides to secure restraint, at times singly but more often in combination. Symbolism was employed, as when the government was presented as setting an example in its own wage determinations. Anderson and Hazleton distinguish further between intangible and tangible levers. Public pronouncements and private appeals fall in the first category. Although the president was moderate in his public advocacy, others such as the chairman of the CEA frequently spoke out on the wisdom of observing the guideposts. In particular situations, private appeals to business and labor decision makers via letters, telegrams, telephone calls, meetings, and conferences could be mounted in large volume. Johnson was often a participant in these efforts.[7] Techniques in the second category carried more force. As noted in the previous chapter, the commissions were asked to assist by taking stability considerations into account as they went about their regulatory business, albeit with mixed results. The involvement of antitrust enforcement and agriculture and oil import control programs are discussed later. Government procurement was employed as a lever, as was management of the government's stockpile of critical commodities. Export and import controls were used to expand supply and thus place downward pressures on prices.

Combating Imbalance

There was a close connection between wage-price concerns and the balance-of-payments problem. Both bore on economic stability. More specifically, to the extent that rising prices and wages reduced competitiveness abroad, payment imbalances would tend to grow.[8] During the early 1960s an imbalance of significant proportions emerged in the volume of dollars held abroad and the volume of foreign currencies held in the United States. At this time the dollar was backed by gold, and a growing imbalance had the potential of causing serious difficulties for the United States in the world economy. If the foreign holders of dollars became apprehensive about this country's ability to redeem dollars in gold, they would become reluctant to hold them. Consequently, the value of the dollar would decline. Neither the Kennedy nor the Johnson administration wanted this.

The imbalance took a jump in 1964, and the president dispatched a special message to Congress on 10 February 1965 laying out a set of corrective steps. Policy makers have a number of basic options to consider when they grapple with a deficit in payments. One is devaluation of the currency. Another is to deflate the domestic economy. Neither of these was attractive to Johnson and his advisers. The third option is to use a variety of direct means to limit the flow of dollars abroad and to increase the flow of foreign currencies in the other direction. This was the option chosen. Johnson's message focused on adhering to the guideposts, stimulating foreign investment and travel in the United States, limiting government expenditures abroad, and, most importantly, voluntarily restraining private lending and investment abroad.[9]

As in the case of the guideposts, Johnson followed balance-of-payments developments in considerable detail. On a day-to-day basis, the Treasury Department served as the lead agency. Several of the regulatory agencies were among a rather sizable group who worked with the Treasury and the White House on the problem. Their involvement was peripheral, except for the Federal Reserve Board, which was asked to exert its influence on banks to limit their foreign lending and did so in a cooperative spirit and with considerable success. The responsibility for persuading U.S. firms to limit their foreign investments was placed in the Department of Commerce.

This was the most contentious aspect of Johnson's response to the balance-of-payments problem. Many found fault with Commerce's efforts. In its actions and in policy debates over the guidelines for investment abroad, it became clear that the department was inclined to be more sympathetic to the interests of business than others thought appropriate.

A crisis point was reached in late 1967 when the British devalued the pound sterling and set off a rush for gold around the world. Ernest Goldstein of the White House staff became a key actor in developing new policy in the wake of devaluation. Emergency meetings were held at the ranch in late December, and Johnson announced a revised program on New Year's Day 1968.[10] The major innovation was the imposition of mandatory controls on investments, based on authority delegated to the president in the banking laws. The program was to be administered in the Department of Commerce by a new Office of Foreign Direct Investment. The first meeting of the interagency group assigned to oversee this office was at the White House, clearly indicating the president's vital interest in its work. In addition to Goldstein and Commerce officials, the group included representatives from the Council of Economic Advisers, State, Treasury, the Agency for International Development, and the Federal Reserve Board.[11] For a variety of reasons, including the mandatory program, the payments problem eased considerably over the course of 1968.

Resolving Labor Disputes

The development of a new balance-of-payments program in late 1967 came on the heels of a contract settlement ending a dispute in the railroad industry that had plagued Johnson for several months. He was required by law and circumstances to devote considerable attention to such problems in labor-management relations. Major contract negotiations were of interest because of the guideposts. In addition, the president was interested in avoiding or ending strikes that, in some sense, threatened the nation's well-being. This was conditioned by the necessity of preserving the delicate balance, crafted so carefully over the years, among labor, business, and governmental interests in the settlement of labor disputes.

During peacetime the president's primary tools for affecting the general tenor of labor-management relations and the resolution of particular disputes are the prominence and prestige of his office and other informal sources of influence at his disposal. These are backed, however, by potent but restricted legal authorities. One source is the Railway Labor Act of 1926, subsequently amended to apply also to the airlines.[12] It authorizes the president to postpone a strike for as much as sixty days, if the National Mediation Board certifies that transportation service to any section of the country is threatened. He does so by appointing an emergency board to investigate and, within thirty days, to report on the situation. During this period and for another thirty days the parties are expected to continue negotiations. Strikes and lockouts are prohibited. At the end of the sixty days the parties are freed of any restrictions on their actions imposed by presidential invocation of the law. The president can preclude a strike at this point only if Congress enacts legislation giving him additional authority.

The other source is a no-strike scheme based on the Railway Labor Act model contained in the Taft-Hartley Act of 1947.[13] If a strike or lockout affecting all or part of an industry threatens the health and safety of the nation, the president is authorized to appoint a board of inquiry. Upon receiving the board's initial report, he may then direct the attorney general to seek a sixty-day no-strike injunction. If it is ordered by a federal district court, labor and management must attempt to resolve their differences with the aid of the Federal Mediation and Conciliation Service. If no agreement is reached, the president may reconvene the board of inquiry. It is to file a report at the end of the sixty-day period containing management's final offer. The National Labor Relations Board then has fifteen days in which to conduct an election to determine whether the offer is acceptable to employees. Whatever the outcome, within five days of the election, the attorney general must seek dissolution of the injunction. As in the case of the Railway Labor Act, if the dispute continues, legislation is necessary to provide a basis for further governmental action.

Johnson employed a combination of informal influence and statutory authority in dealing with labor negotiations. In a number of instances he risked political embarrassment by becoming publicly involved without establishing a legal basis for action. At times he simply made public appeals for quick and reasonable settlements or asked officials in his administration to assist the parties in reaching an agreement. Twice Johnson went further and brought negotiations into the White House, in effect holding the principals hostage until there was an agreement. The first occasion, in 1965, involved the steel industry. Initial negotiations aided by the Federal Mediation and Conciliation Service were fruitless. A strike on 1 May was averted when the parties agreed to a four-month extension for further discussions. By mid-August, however, they were still far apart on wage and other issues. At this point, Johnson asked Senator Wayne Morse of Oregon and Under Secretary of Commerce Leroy Collins to meet with the parties and the mediators in Pittsburgh. Morse and Collins returned to Washington on 29 August and reported that, in their view, direct White House intervention was the only option to prevent a strike.[14] Johnson met with union and U.S. Steel representatives the next day as preparations for a shutdown were underway. That evening he went on national television to announce an eight-day postponement and the resumption of negotiations starting at 10 P.M. in the Executive Office Building.[15] They continued there in the public spotlight and under Johnson's watchful eye until 3 September, when he was able to go on national television again to report that a settlement was in hand.[16] From his perspective, its most important part was a 3.3 percent wage increase, tolerably close to the guidepost.

The other instance involved a copper industry that was racked with discord. After lengthy negotiations failed, a strike began on 15 July 1967 that shut down 90 percent of domestic copper mining production and, in the process, significantly reduced the production of lead, zinc, and silver. Fabricating plants were also struck. The effects of the stoppages, which ultimately involved 50,000 to 60,000 workers, were devastating in the areas immediately affected and soon began to be felt throughout the nation. Increased imports of copper, in addition, worsened the balance-of-payments problem.[17]

Administration efforts to restore peace began soon after the strike was instituted. In early September industry and labor representatives met in Washington with the secretaries of Labor and Commerce, but there was no progress toward a settlement. On 26 January 1968 Johnson appointed a fact-finding panel. Its recommendations were rejected by labor officials. Subsequently, the Federal Mediation and Conciliation Service was able to settle strikes against some small operators, but the great bulk of the industry remained comatose.[18] Johnson called the parties to the White House on 4 March to begin around-the-clock negotiations.[19] Under this pressure, agreements soon began to fall into place; in approximately a month the copper industry was once again mining, processing, and fabricating the ore.

Although the effects of the copper dispute might have justified the invocation of the Taft-Hartley Act, it was not employed. Johnson followed the example of his predecessors in his reluctance to apply it. From 1947 through Kennedy's presidency Taft-Hartley was used only twenty-three times.[20] Johnson invoked it in six instances. In three of them, there were threats to the production of vital military equipment, principally aircraft. The firms involved were General Electric and Union Carbide in 1966 and AVCO in 1967. The other three instances concerned the maritime industry. Strikes against Atlantic and Gulf Coast ports resulted in boards of inquiry in 1964 and

1968, and a board was established in 1967 to deal with a dispute affecting ship building and repair along the Pacific Coast.

Presidents have been less restrained in using the Railway Labor Act. Between 1945 and Johnson's assumption of the office it was invoked 140 times.[21] He applied its provisions in sixteen instances, twelve times in connection with railroad matters (six in 1964 alone) and four times in connection with airline matters. Three of these were in 1966.

Unrest in the railroad industry was a constant during most of Johnson's presidency and involved a variety of firms and unions. Prolonged nationwide strikes were narrowly averted in 1964 and 1967. For some time prior to 1963 the railroads sought adjustments, vigorously resisted by the unions, affecting train crews and work rules. Congress enacted legislation in 1963 in an effort to resolve the rules issue. It contained three main provisions. A panel was established to settle the central disagreements over the fireman's position and crew sizes. During the two years following enactment, strikes and lockouts over these issues were prohibited. In regard to numerous secondary issues, strikes and lockouts were banned for a 180-day period after the law went into effect.

Conflict over both primary and secondary issues intensified in early 1964.[22] The board established by the law announced an arbitration award on 26 November 1963. It was generally favorable to the railroads. By early 1964 the board's award had been upheld in the federal courts. At about the same time the moratorium on strikes and lockouts over secondary issues expired. The railroads began to press for the implementation of new work rules, and unions threatened to strike. Two emergency boards were appointed to facilitate the resolution of differences, but they were unsuccessful. In April Johnson intervened and persuaded both sides to accept a fifteen-day postponement of both new rules and strikes. Intensive negotiations followed, involving administration officials, and resulted in a basic agreement that Johnson announced on 22 April.[23] Despite this agreement, more limited disputes continued over work rules, wages, and benefit issues. These required the establishment of four additional emergency boards during 1964.

Although the industry remained unsettled in 1965 and 1966, widespread disputes were averted. Conditions changed in 1967.[24] Unions representing railroad shop workers made wage demands that management thought excessive. Johnson's problems intensified in January when the National Mediation Board ceased its efforts to secure an agreement and ended on 15 October when a special board established by Congress imposed a settlement. Prior to this point the recommendations of two emergency boards were rejected by the parties, and, at Johnson's urging, Congress twice passed legislation prohibiting strikes to give the negotiators more time. Early in May, as the situation continued to deteriorate, the president called for legislation providing for an imposed settlement. After this negotiations came to a dead end, and a strike was instituted. Two days after it began, on 17 July, Congress acted. Johnson named the five-member board established by the legislation the next day, and work toward the final resolution reached in October began immediately.

Troubles in the railroad industry were interspersed with troubles in the airline industry, as indicated in the previous chapter.[25] Early in 1966 the International Association of Machinists began contract negotiations with several carriers: Eastern, National, Northwest, Trans World, and United. It sought a substantial wage increase plus an improved benefit package. By April the National Mediation Board still had not been able to forge an accommodation. An emergency board was then established. Its recommendation for a 3.5 percent wage increase was rejected by the union. Contract talks continued, broke down in early June, and resumed when Johnson personally asked for their continuation. Still no progress resulted, and a strike began on 8 July.

Public and congressional unhappiness quickly grew as the five carriers ceased operations. Several bills were introduced in Congress to end the strike. (It was an election year, and the needs of members of Congress to fly were acute.) On 24 July Johnson announced that he too was considering a legislative solution. The threat of legislative action and the importuning of the administration caused the negotiations to resume. Secretary of Labor Willard Wirtz tracked them closely. Very early in the morning of 29 July he concluded that a settlement was within reach and that personal pressure from the president might make a critical difference in attaining it. Later that day Johnson met with the negotiators, and that evening he was able to announce that there was an agreement.[26]

The matter did not end there, however. Although the wage portion of the agreement was close to the union's figure, the membership rejected it on 3 August. The vote prompted a renewed barrage of congressional proposals for dealing authoritatively with the situation. In the context of these threats, negotiations quickly moved ahead; a final settlement went into effect on 29 August, bringing an end to the strike.

All in all, Johnson was a party to only a minute proportion of the labor disputes that arose across the nation during his presidency. Of those in which he played a part, he was reasonably successful in securing the results he sought. Arguably, the most difficult situations he faced were the 1966 airline strike and the 1967 railroad dispute. In both, the differences separating labor and management were substantial, and the economic consequences of work stoppages were great. In addition, a railroad strike of any real length would have seriously hampered the flow of war materiel to Vietnam.

Several other important matters were at stake. One was the integrity of the wage-price guideposts. There were implications in the settlements for the transportation industry as a whole as well as for other economic sectors. Settlements in both the railroad and airline cases exceeded the guidepost for wages, although the administration's efforts appeared to produce a lower rate of increase than would have resulted without them. Another consideration was to avoid, if at all possible, creating a basis for a larger, more authoritative role for the government in resolving labor disputes. Although imposed settlements were threatened in the airline strike and employed in the rail conflict, Johnson and others strongly underscored the exceptional nature of the circumstances and took pains to deny that new precedents were being set. Finally, there were the political interests of Johnson and the Democratic Party. The ambitions of both labor and management had to be considered with these in mind. Johnson was generally able to pursue an independent course without alienating important parts of his political coalition.

Enigmas in the Regulation of Agriculture

I am bleeding a bit on the price front. . . . As nearly as we can tell, the public has relaxed significantly where food prices are concerned, at least for the moment. The reaction of the farm community is not clear yet. I bracketed the price support increase announcements on dairy and soybeans with the news of lower food prices for the balance of the year. In this fashion I hoped to successfully walk the "tight wire" between producers and consumers.

Orville L. Freeman, 7 April 1966[27]

Freeman, a former governor of Minnesota, was constantly on a policy tightwire during his eight years as secretary of Agriculture, starting in 1961 under John F. Kennedy and extending through the whole of Johnson's presidency. The department was charged with implementing a host of programs, ranging from management of the national forests to the promotion of soil conservation and the administration of the food stamp and other domestic food distribution efforts. None matched the multi-billion-dollar commodity programs in importance. Regulatory decisions about production, price support levels, and related matters were major determinants of farm income and the costs of food and other products to consumers. They had important implications for the United States and other national economies and for the food supply in numerous countries around the world. Balancing the complex and potent interests and pressures playing on regulatory decisions was, to say the least, a politically harrowing task that fell mainly to Freeman and his colleagues as he walked the tightwire, under the president's watchful eye.

Contact between the White House and the Department of Agriculture was extensive and continuous. Freeman reported frequently and in depth to the president on a wide range of matters. Other departmental officials had regularized relationships with staff at the presidential level.[28] Presidential aides Myer Feldman, Harry McPherson, and then W. DeVier Pierson at various times were the principal conduits for the flow of communications between Agriculture and the White House. Still other presidential advisers, especially Bill Moyers, Joe Califano, and officials of the Bureau of the Budget and the Council of Economic Advisers, were participants in policy deliberations. Vice President Hubert H. Humphrey played an important role. Although Johnson was extensively informed about the work of the department, his active involvement usually focused on major policy matters of broad political significance. In the regulatory sphere, in addition to budget implications, he was most interested in the effects of agricultural prices on consumers, the shape of basic farm legislation, and commodity program decisions.

The Price-Income Conundrum

The regulation of agricultural prices and production was permeated by numerous technical and political difficulties. From the perspective of the presidency, the dominant problem was maintaining a politically viable balance between agricultural and consumer interests in the government's management of the agricultural economy. Thus the level of prices paid by consumers of processed food and other farm products was always a matter of concern. From 1965 onward, because of upward pressures on prices, the tension between the price of food and farm income was substantial. Johnson's resolve to fight inflation was unflagging and vital, he thought, in sustaining his political position. At the same time, however, agricultural producers were an important part of his political coalition. Freeman underscored the point in the aftermath of the 1964 elections, pointing out that rural America shifted "from a cornerstone of Republican strength into an area of enormous support for you and the Administration's programs."[29] The situation, from both political and policy perspectives, was an uncomfortable one.

In the absence of a ready solution to the price-income conundrum, the best that could be devised was a two-part coping strategy directed from the White House. The first part was to insist that the Department of Agriculture use its extensive discretionary authority over price supports and supply to moderate consumer price increases. The second part was to guide departmental officials, Freeman in particular, in political and public relations efforts to reduce the level of discontent voiced by consumers and by agricultural interests and their allies.

Warning flags were raised early in July 1965 when Gardner Ackley of CEA called Freeman's attention to a rather significant upward movement in farm and food product indicators. He asked "whether there are any actions the Department could take to halt or to temper these sharp increases in food prices? Are any dramatic measures possible that would express the Department's concern with the consumer's interest?"[30] Two days later Moyers relayed the president's concern about price increases to McPherson with the request that he "get together with Ackley and Freeman to see what, if anything, the Administration can do on this front."[31] Not long afterward Ackley forewarned Moyers that the soon-to-be released June wholesale price index figures would be up over May due in large part to increases in processed foods and farm products. Further increases were expected in the July figures. As for the request to Agriculture for corrective action, he said, "They have been able to propose none."[32] Although the situation eased somewhat in August, administration officials, including Johnson, continued to watch developments closely.[33]

Agriculture was not easily enlisted in anti-inflation efforts. Its basic position during this period was indicated in a memorandum from Freeman to Johnson in early October 1965. Two points stood out: that the American consumer did not pay enough for food and that farm income was too low.[34] Still the Council of Economic Advisers and the Bureau of the Budget pressed for action. In mid-October Kermit Gordon of BOB and Ackley jointly authored a memorandum to Califano. In their view the options available for reining in prices were "quite limited."[35] They included reducing feed grain support prices, lowering the price of sugar, and cutting Agriculture's purchases of commodities not governed by price supports. Freeman was not enthusiastic. A short time later he dispatched a lengthy memorandum to the president on the subject of "The Food Bargain."[36] He soon followed with a memorandum to Califano arguing that various actions under discussion would restrict farm income, but would not have significant effects on prices.[37]

Even as this memorandum was being processed, the situation was changing. Agriculture began to see shortage problems in wheat supply caused in part by the low quality of the 1965 crop and in part by protected P.L. 480 shipments of the commodity to India in the wake of extreme shortfalls there. It decided to counter with sales of wheat from Commodity Credit Corporation stocks.[38] The shift in the department's stance was completed in December. On the seventeenth Califano listed for the president a number of steps apparently devised by CEA that Agriculture agreed to take, which included lowering feed grains support prices, increasing the sale of grains from government stocks, and slowing purchases for the school lunch and other domestic distribution programs. These actions were to be supplemented by adjustments in the food purchasing practices of the Department of Defense.[39]

A month or so later Freeman was able to report that action was underway along a fairly broad front.[40] In passing the information along to Johnson, Califano observed that "Orville Freeman has moved out quite well on the food price situation."[41] During the next few months Agriculture reported to Johnson at least once a week on the price situation and its actions, and there were periodic meetings at the presidential level in which Agriculture participated. The department had shifted toward the presidential perspective on the price-income conundrum from its initial more parochial view.

The department's clientele was not pleased by this shift. At a White House staff meeting in late April 1966, according to a participant, "the Vice President spoke at length about a 'serious, first-class revolt among the farmers.' He said two of the primary problems the Administration has with the farmers are public announcements by Defense and Agriculture concerning Defense's non-purchasing of pork and butter and concerning Freeman's announcement that it was a good sign that agricultural prices were coming down."[42] The following day, a Friday, the deteriorating political situation in rural areas was underscored by a highly critical telegram to the president from a large number of Republican members of the House of Representatives who sought to capitalize on rural discontent.[43] At about the same time Johnson received the telegram Freeman described for him the farmers' unexpected, intense, and negative reaction to the anti-inflation efforts. His suggestions for a response were tentative and included more presidential meetings with farm interests and positive presidential statements on agriculture.[44]

Johnson and Freeman talked about strategy during the weekend. On the following Wednesday the secretary sent the president a progress report on nine major actions "taken or . . . underway pursuant to our conversations."[45] They fell into three prime categories: public statements by Freeman attacking critics; mobilization of support in Congress; and program initiatives that would be viewed favorably by the agricultural community. Less than a week later there was another progress report on the "counterattack."[46] Even as fairly aggressive anti-inflationary actions were underway, however, the political climate was complicated further by vocal and highly publicized protests against food price increases by "housewife" consumers in several parts of the country.[47]

At this point, June 1966, a basic pattern was set that would continue to the conclusion of Johnson's tenure in office. There was constant presidential concern about food prices in the context of general worries about inflation. The Council of Economic Advisers persistently advocated restraints. In its view farmers were relatively well off economically and were the prime beneficiaries of food price increases.[48] The Department of Agriculture was cooperative to a degree. Through jawboning and program decisions it sought price stability in agricultural markets. However, it remained a defender of the proposition that farm income was too low—and even if this was not the case, farmers could never be convinced of it.[49]

Tension between consumer and producer interests continued unabated. Food prices went up sharply in the summer of 1966, sparking strong public and congressional reactions.[50] Farmers began to feel an increase in their costs due to inflation.[51] For a number of reasons, farm income in 1967 was generally lower than in 1966. There was substantial anger in rural areas, including a dramatic milk strike in twenty-five states in early 1967.[52] Shortly afterward an aide to the vice president described an accelerating deterioration of the administration's position in the Midwest that raised the prospect of an electoral "catastrophe" in 1968.[53] This gloomy assessment was reinforced by Humphrey himself on many occasions. Pierson's diagnosis of "farm unhappiness" for Johnson said, "It always comes back to prices."[54]

The president continued to advise and direct Freeman on the tightwire in managing the politics of the situation. The emphasis was on explaining to farmers, members of Congress, and the public that American agriculture and the income of farmers had made striking progress in recent years, a task that Freeman undertook with great energy.[55]

One of Freeman's top associates observed that Johnson "escaped much of the rural troubles, because Orville absorbed them."[56] Unquestionably, Freeman drew heavy political flak from all quarters on the price-income issue. For his part, he felt that when he was "under attack" the president "rallied and he supported me very, very strongly."[57] That support became more public as the situation worsened in 1967 and the 1968 elections drew closer. Starting early in 1967 Johnson began to speak to agricultural groups and to meet privately with farm leaders with some frequency. He strongly advocated the interests of farmers in his last message to the Congress on agriculture in late February 1968. Despite the efforts of both Freeman and Johnson, however, contention and political difficulties would not go away.

A little more than a month after the message, on 31 March, Johnson announced that he would not be a candidate for reelection. No doubt many factors contributed to his decision, but perhaps the deteriorating agricultural situation played at least a small part. On Friday, 23 March, the Council of Economic Advisers had given him more disquieting news about food price increases.[58] He spent time with Freeman on Saturday and Sunday and directed the secretary to do a number of specific things to counter criticisms. On Monday he spoke at some length to delegates attending a conference on farm policy and rural life. His remarks promoted the legislative program recently sent to Congress and expressed optimism for the future, but they were colored by a tone suggesting personal weariness.[59] Freeman gave Johnson a progress report on 28 March following up on their weekend conversation, three days before the withdrawal.[60]

Subsequently, the president's concern for agricultural matters declined dramatically, as did his efforts to influence departmental decisions. Agricultural interests intensified their efforts to raise prices and, according to the CEA, won some legislative and administrative successes.[61] At the time Congress was working on an extension of basic farm programs. In that matter, as in other policy questions bearing on agriculture during Johnson's presidency, the price-income conundrum was a major unresolved and vexing contextual element.

Program Decisions

The White House periodically took up basic questions of agricultural policy involving legislation (discussed in chapter 6). Beyond basic policy issues, there was a constant flow of agricultural matters requiring presidential attention. Among the more important of these were commodity program decisions on price support levels, allotments, and diversion arrangements. There were also questions of import controls from time to time.[62]

The law vested broad discretion in the secretary of Agriculture for commodity program decisions. The secretary and his colleagues were very careful to keep the White House fully advised on these and other matters.[63] Their recommendations were assessed closely by presidential staff. Nevertheless, Freeman felt he was "pretty much left . . . alone." "We'd have our problems at budget time and program time, but almost without exception my recommendations were followed, and some times these were . . . very difficult decisions."[64]

Although Freeman was allowed a great deal of freedom, Johnson was a fairly active, if not always enthusiastic, participant in commodity program decisions. At times, however, he refused to participate. His stance in program matters, as well as other aspects of the agricultural enterprise, reflected Charles Schultze's view that every president is "upset" by it. Agriculture "drains the heck out of his resources . . . , and he normally finds that all the political chips are stacked against him."[65] Early in 1966, for example, a milk price issue arose in which the interested parties included Carl Albert, the Democratic leader of the House of Representatives, and Wilbur D. Mills, chairman of the House Committee on Ways and Means. The president's testy response to a request for his involvement was, "Get Mills & Albert with Freeman & get the President out of this."[66] Several months later a sugar price issue was turned away with the remark, "Earlier the President . . . said that he did not care to act on this."[67] But he could not avoid playing a role on most issues because of differences between the department and presidential staff. Typically the situation involved a recommendation from the department intended to have a positive effect on farm income to which BOB and CEA took exception on budgetary and price stability grounds. The record bears out Freeman's observation that the president usually supported the department.[68]

Johnson demonstrated uncharacteristic interest in one area: the price of beef. His personal association with cattle ranching no doubt was a factor. Although beef producers were not regulated, they were a vital part of the agricultural economy and played an important role in agricultural politics. In a variety of ways there were interrelationships between their situation and regulated commodities, feed grains in particular. Furthermore, the president had authority to regulate most imports, including meat, and there was pressure to do so from time to time. The administration resisted, however.

The first concrete agricultural issue Freeman presented to Johnson after he became president was a rather precipitous decline in beef prices.[69] The president immediately sparked a far-reaching campaign to correct the problem. Tactics included the negotiation of voluntary limits with exporters of beef to the United States, stepped-up purchases of beef by Agriculture and Defense, and the promotion of exports and domestic consumption. For a considerable period the president monitored these activities through detailed weekly reports prepared by Agriculture.[70] The effort was successful, and the imposition of import limits was avoided.

Judging by the volume and character of memoranda, dairy price issues regularly occupied a major place on Johnson's agricultural agenda, because of continuing downward pressure on milk production and producer income. Between October 1964 and May 1968 there were ten major price support decisions.[71] The saliency of dairy issues was accentuated by the electoral significance of dairy states, by the vigorous political activism of dairy interests, and by the prominence and influence of their supporters in Congress. In this and in other areas, the broad political implications of regulatory policy could not be ignored.

In dealing with dairy and other commodity matters, at times Johnson consciously used pending decisions as opportunities to strengthen his hand with Congress by creating credits that could be cashed in later. He was not always successful. During 1967 Wilbur Mills was among those pressing hard for an increase in milk price supports, a move that Agriculture favored. Johnson was then trying to enlist the powerful Ways and Means chairman's support for a tax increase. He was prepared to accept the departmental recommendation but wanted Mills to take the matter up with him personally. If Johnson appeared to give in to the chairman's request for help on milk prices, he would have an additional chit to use on taxes.[72] The president's aides tried to maneuver Mills into a meeting, but the chairman avoided the trap, knowing very well the nature of the game.[73]

The political artifice employed could be fairly elaborate. Pierson describes a situation in which acreage allotments for rice were under review. The president had Pierson leak a story that he was considering reducing them. That upset the congressional delegations from rice states, who sought a meeting. When it was held, Pierson followed Johnson's instructions and presented a strong case for cutting the allotments, and the president hinted that he was inclined toward that side of the argument. A few days later he had Pierson call the congressmen and relay his message: "I have decided in view of their personal interest in this that I won't do it, but I'll be needing their help on some other matters."[74]

Another example is found in the efforts of representatives of some cotton states to secure revision of cotton-planting regulations that had important production implications. The Department of Agriculture was willing to go along. Johnson appeared to have no particular preference one way or the other, but he had his budget director, Charles Schultze, call several of the congressmen and tell them that from his budget perspective he "didn't see how" he could support the change, because it would increase the cost of the cotton program substantially.[75] Pierson reported to Johnson: "His telephone calls did their work. The interested Congressmen are now very nervous about your decision."[76] Following this, as in the rice case, the members were invited to a White House meeting. Afterward Johnson endorsed their position, as he had intended to do all along.

These minor though revealing episodes highlight the extent of the president's rather large political stakes in agriculture. Decisions had immediate effects on consumer interests. They also had major implications for Johnson's overall political standing and the level of political resources available to him for, among other things, dealing with Congress. There were similar stakes in another hazardous and sensitive area, the regulation of oil imports.

Oil Import Controls

> I must not bring oil into W. H. & tell them not to insist. Ask them to see Ellington if they won't see Udall.
>
> LBJ, 29 April 1965[77]

A group of New England senators once more pressed to see the president to protest a decision not to increase residual fuel oil imports. Prior conversations with Secretary of the Interior Stewart Udall, in whose domain oil import control matters fell, gave no satisfaction. Their request to see Johnson was channeled through presidential aides Mike Manatos, then Jack Valenti, to whom his defensive response was directed. The president was more than a little bit sensitive about oil issues. As an astute and experienced Washington politician, he knew that, in the words of Douglas R. Bohi and Milton Russell, "Oil policy was a political disaster. Any action which satisfied a single group angered many more."[78] In addition, the widespread public suspicion of the oil industry and the fact that the interests of its domestic component coincided neatly with import controls presented a special hazard to Johnson because he was a Texan. His public involvement in the program certainly would be interpreted, at least by some, as reflecting parochial rather than national interests and would be subjected to political attack on those grounds. It is not surprising that early in his presidency he let it be known that he had "moved" oil import policy responsibility out of the White House to the Department of Interior, where the program was administered.

Although Johnson might attempt to disassociate himself publicly from the important and controversial problems that laced the program, he could not remove them from his presidency. Nor, as it turned out, could he insulate himself personally from them, if indeed he truly wished to do so. In fact, the decision the senators protested, seemingly made by Udall, actually was made by Johnson against all advice.

Processes and Issues

Oil import controls began on a voluntary basis in 1957 in the aftermath of the Suez crisis. Their essential purpose was to safeguard national security by limiting dependence on foreign petroleum supplies, which events in the Middle East showed were subject to disruption. Voluntarism did not work, and a mandatory program was instituted two years later by a presidential proclamation based upon authority delegated by Congress. When Johnson became president, its basic aim was to limit imports to approximately 12.2 percent of domestic production. Periodic administrative determinations of projected production by the Interior secretary were required as a basis for setting the overall level of imports and for allocating them. Decisions were based upon estimates of the Bureau of Mines and the application of allocation formulae by the Oil Import Administration.

Although substantial administrative discretion in setting annual import levels was delegated to the Interior secretary, the periodic and necessary revisions of policy through revisions of the proclamation itself required presidential action. Furthermore, the proclamation assigned certain correlative responsibilities to a part of the Executive Office of the President, the Office of Emergency Planning. It was to this agency's director, Buford Ellington, that Johnson referred the disgruntled senators. Finally, many of the decisions made in the administration of the oil import control program could be described as presidential in character. They were of major political and economic significance, both domestically and internationally, and bore heavily on other governmental responsibilities, such as national defense.

Several persistent and thorny policy issues were intertwined in policy and in program administration. One, of course, was the level of imports. Since foreign oil was considerably cheaper than domestic, domestic producers were intensely interested in minimizing imports by adhering strictly to the 12.2 percent target. They resisted any liberalization, no matter how slight, that might serve as a wedge for future increases. Consumers and foreign producers understandably were of a contrary view. A second persistent issue was the allocation of imported oil among refineries and other users. A third concerned treatment of oil from Canada, Mexico, and Venezuela. Good relations within the hemisphere were not well served by restricting imports from close neighbors who desired to sell in the U.S. market. Also, there were grounds for claiming special treatment based upon the rationale of the program itself, for these were rather secure sources, especially when imports came overland. A final issue was the extent to which the program should be modified to alleviate particular problems and to serve other goals, such as environmental quality and economic development in U.S. possessions, even though the level of imports might rise and the national security justification for the program might be compromised.

In its execution of the oil import program and in its decisions bearing on these issues, the Johnson administration had two basic and related effects. Controls were relaxed and important contributions were made to their eventual demise, with formal internment coming in 1973. The rise in the level of imports precipitated oil industry criticism that the principal purpose of the program, national security, no longer was served. This, added to growing consumer irritation and changed economic circumstances, prompted review, then termination, in the Nixon presidency.

It is impossible to specify the extent to which the movement toward the end of controls was purposive. Certainly there was opposition to controls in some government quarters. The manner in which decisions were made suggests, however, that the course of policy was as much (if not more) the product of the currents of the moment as of the systematic pursuit of a coherent policy objective.

There were seven major presidential decisions. The most important were Johnson's veto of a relaxation of controls over the importation of residual fuel oil in March 1965, the revision of the proclamation in December 1965, and the termination of residual controls in early 1966. Four subsequent proclamation revisions, three in 1967 and one in 1968, involved limited and relatively minor adjustments.

In these, Interior's recommendations were reviewed in the White House, and changes were required in only one instance. Controversial allocation and exemption decisions were made periodically by Interior, but presidential involvement in these was usually quite limited, if there was any at all. Other departments and agencies, however, might express intense interest in limited proclamation changes and other oil import decisions.

Decision making, especially on major matters in 1965 and 1966 soon to be examined, did not proceed smoothly. Problems arise when presidents have regulatory responsibilities and political interests at stake, but are reluctant participants or refuse to become involved at all. The point was made clearly, if belatedly, to Johnson by DeVier Pierson early in May 1968: "The oil import program is a mess."[79] Criticism was mounting in Congress. "We are . . . drawing heavy fire from all parts of the industry—and the administration of the program is not pleasing anyone. While 'scandal' is too strong a term, evidence of shoddy administration, poor coordination and questionable policy decisions is growing."[80] Pierson went on to discuss a number of recent and troublesome Interior decisions. "The heart of the problem," he asserted, "has been the policy that the White House does not participate in oil decisions—that Udall is the final authority. As a result, coordination and clearance with other affected departments has been almost non-existent."[81]

Initial Exposures

In late March 1965 Udall warned the president's appointments secretary, W. Marvin Watson, of controversial changes in residual fuel oil imports he planned to announce the following day. On a cover note he wrote, "Marv, Bar the door, Man!"[82] As it turned out, quite a different announcement was made as a result of White House intervention. This was the second major action of the Johnson administration on residual oil imports. The first came just a year before, on 6 March 1964, when Udall revealed that there would be a modest increase in the quota for residual oil. Negative reaction to that decision immediately drew the White House into the fray, where it remained solidly implanted until control over residuals was in effect abandoned, starting in 1966.

Residual oils are the heavy viscous residuum of the refining process, used principally as utility and industrial boiler fuel. Domestic refiners produced very little except on the West Coast, where the characteristics of heavy California crude dictated otherwise. For a variety of reasons, including the economics of shipping, refineries in

the central portion of the United States found it profitable to minimize the production of residuals. Consequently, the major source
was imports transported by water, and the major use of residuals was
along the East Coast.

Inclusion of residuals in the control program was a sticky problem
from the start. They were not a part of the voluntary program and
were placed on a separate footing in the mandatory program. The
national security argument for their limitation was not as strong as
for crude oil or for lighter products. Residual imports, for which Venezuela was a major supplier through Caribbean refineries, were sub-
stitutes for domestic coal and, to an extent, natural gas. In addition
to the relative security of the hemispheric supply, there was the
ready reservoir of domestic coal to be exploited if oil supplies were
interrupted.

The political division attending the residuals issue was stark,
with potent forces aligned on both sides. In favor of ample imports
were East Coast users and consumers wanting to hold down the cost
of energy, and Venezuelan and Caribbean interests. In opposition
were natural gas, coal, and affiliated interests. Each year when the
Interior secretary was required to specify the level of imports for the
next twelve months, strong political pressures were mobilized to
affect the outcome.

Udall's announcement on 6 March 1964 was that the basic program would remain unchanged, but that the level of residual imports would increase from 575,000 barrels per day to 638,000, because of an anticipated increase in domestic production. The
previous year, when Kennedy was still president, serious attention
was given to removing controls altogether. A thorough Office of
Emergency Planning analysis found no continuing national security
reasons for their extension.[83] However, in White House discussions,
according to Udall, it was decided to make "no move either to
tighten the program to meet the demand of the coal people or to
relax it to meet the demand of the consumer groups."[84] This was
essentially the basis for the 1964 decision, he reported to presidential aide Myer Feldman.

Leaders of the United Mine Workers of America, major coal companies, and coal-hauling railroads, directly and through coal-state
members of Congress, made strong representations to Interior and
the White house both before and after Udall's 1964 announcement.[85]
Their position was that, if residual imports were not restricted, the
industry's capacity to respond to national security emergencies
would be seriously impaired and, furthermore, that an increase was
inconsistent with the War on Poverty because of the negative eco-

nomic effects it would have in Appalachia. Although for a time these arguments had the effects intended by their proponents, the review they precipitated turned out to be a major step toward the removal of controls altogether.

Protests after the particulars of the program announced in 1964 became known prompted Myer Feldman, the presidential aide who dealt with energy matters at the time, to reach for some sort of accommodation through negotiation with the National Coal Policy Conference. His efforts to find a basis for agreement continued through April and May, but without success.[86] On 5 June 1964, when Johnson was scheduled to meet with National Coal Policy Conference representatives, Feldman was still searching. Discussions with conference officials prior to the meeting, Feldman informed the president, indicated that there was the possibility of a plan that would involve creation of a permanent National Energy Commission, increased coal exports, and accelerated development of new coal-based products and services, in exchange for coal's acceptance of increased residual imports. Since the details had not been fleshed out, Feldman recommended as an interim step the creation of a cabinet committee to study the residual oil question.[87] In a late afternoon meeting Johnson reportedly told the assembled coal advocates of his intention to give the matter his personal attention. Shortly thereafter he established a committee, chaired by Secretary of Defense Robert S. McNamara, with the secretaries of State, Commerce, Interior, and Labor as members. The coal group was satisfied for the time being.[88]

Completion of the cabinet committee study came before it was time to announce the following year's program. Four members, with Secretary of Labor Willard Wirtz in dissent, not only rejected a reduction in residual imports, but recommended that controls be lifted completely. With the report buttressing his own doubts about whether restrictions could still be justified on national security grounds and the necessity of revising the program, Udall prepared for a bold move.[89] The East Coast was divided into three parts: New England, the Middle Atlantic area, and Florida. In the Middle Atlantic area, where there was substantial competition between coal and fuel oil, controls would be retained, although the quota would rise. In New England and Florida, where coal was used in lesser quantities, essentially free imports would be allowed.[90]

The president was informed of the plan in late March 1965, and he did not like it. He made what an aide characterized as a "firm and unequivocal decision" against relaxation on the grounds that it would be "politically disastrous" to him in Appalachia and to a certain extent in the Middle Atlantic region.[91] Although Udall "never knew what happened," he surmises that "Senator Jennings Randolph and Senator Byrd of West Virginia crashed through to the White House."[92] White House staff members Lee White and Harry McPherson were dispatched by Johnson to see Udall on the evening of 30 March, the day before the secretary was to make the new program public at a news conference. White and McPherson represented the president's political concerns as being their own. "At no time," White reported to Johnson later that evening, "did we indicate you had been involved in this matter." They "confronted" Udall with their "view that he should reverse his decision." His response was, "I will do whatever you tell me to do—I am the President's boy."[93] But Udall so persuasively argued his position that White and McPherson returned to the White House convinced that it was substantively and politically correct. They advised Johnson that Udall should be allowed to proceed as planned.

The president, however, was not swayed, and White went back to Udall the next morning with the suggestion of a thirty-day delay. Udall's view was that such a move "would put the problem in the White House immediately."[94] The approach Udall would take, White told Johnson, was to announce the continuance of the program for another year with some increase in the level of imports. The secretary planned to say, if asked, that the president had not been involved, but there had been discussions with the Bureau of the Budget and White in regard to a need for a presidential proclamation to effect the major changes that were known to be under consideration.

Udall's announcement precipitated the expected querulousness from all sides and widespread speculation about the last minute change of mind and the role of the White House in it. New England senators were especially disturbed, because they had been led to believe that there would be an exemption for their region.

A line of defense was quickly established. What Udall first proposed to do, it held, was legally questionable under the proclamation and the national security foundation upon which it rested. A formal determination was necessary to ascertain whether national security would be impaired by relaxing residual import restrictions.[95] There may have been such legal considerations, but the evidence is clear that they did not figure in White House deliberations or the president's decision. Nevertheless, subsequent activity proceeded as if the legal problem was central. It featured a national security assessment by the Office of Emergency Planning. As this study progressed, so did consideration of other changes in the oil import control program, culminating in December 1965 with the promulgation of a new presidential proclamation and the announcement that residual controls would be liberalized.

The First Proclamation

On 10 December 1965 the president signed his first proclamation amending the formal provisions of the oil import control program. The 1965 revision was quite significant in that major policy questions were considered and severe political problems had to be finessed. When the matter was concluded, Johnson received the approbation of Texas independent oil man Jake L. Hamon, who wrote, "This is just a note to thank you for the new oil import program for 1966. It is fair and equitable, and it will enable the domestic industry to grow." Johnson grudgingly had seen Hamon on oil matters, along with another producer, W. A. Moncrief, a few months before.[96] Hamon's letter prompted Johnson to instruct Jake Jacobsen, one of his aides: "Call him and tell him I appreciate it very much and put him and Moncrief on the park list."[97] Their cost for gratitude was an opportunity to contribute funds toward the purchase of land for a new state park adjacent to the LBJ ranch.

The proclamation had other positive consequences for Johnson. In its aftermath Udall emerged in industry eyes as the dominant figure in oil matters, taking attention away from the White House and from the residuals decision.[98] At the same time, observers saw the decisions and the processes through which they were developed as an impressive display of political adeptness, "an amazing feat of Johnsonian legerdemain," as one commentator put it.[99]

The accolades came because the proclamation avoided the restrictions sought by oil interests, yet it received substantial industry support. Starting early in 1965 the oil industry pushed hard for its restrictive approach to imports. It urged Congress to pass legislation to establish a stronger statutory base for controls and to tighten them. At Interior hearings on the program in March, Governor John B. Connally of Texas, speaking as chairman of the Interstate Oil Compact Commission (IOCC), proposed a 10 percent cut in imports, a position reiterated at the group's June meeting. Then, in late October, the Independent Petroleum Association of America (IPAA) added its weight to the campaign for further curbs.[100] But even as these efforts were underway, restrictive measures under consideration for the proclamation were being stripped away within the government. Others went by the wayside still later, at the point of presidential approval.

When that approval was given, the president was at the ranch and the IOCC was in session not far away in Corpus Christi. In an abrupt turnaround from their March position, which demanded substantial cuts, the representatives of oil-producing states accepted a substitute resolution offered by Texas Railroad Commission member Jim C. Langdon. It proposed simply to hold imports to present levels. The provisions of the proclamation were compatible with this stance, so Udall was able to claim broad industry support for the new program when it was made public shortly thereafter. In turn, Langdon was able to commend the program as a major improvement, leaving the IPAA, as one columnist said, looking "in vain for any improvement at all."[101]

The process leading to issuance of a proclamation in December 1965 was not as elegant as the political results were taken to be. The manner in which program revisions evolved was shaped at the presidential level only to a limited extent, and the effort stumbled and stalled at various times due to the president's inattention or dissatisfaction with the choices given him. Johnson's continuing discomfort with oil questions was indicated during this period by the serious consideration given to delegating formal authority for proclamation changes to the Interior secretary. This was suggested by Attorney General Nicholas deB. Katzenbach in an early April 1965 meeting with Lee White and Interior solicitor Frank Barry. White was still handling oil matters in the White House. Udall endorsed the move in mid-May because, he told White, the recent flap over the residuals program indicated that no matter how "skillfully we handle it . . . some of the journalists will readily infer that the President was deeply involved in the decisions embodied in any proclamation which bears his signature."[102] The secretary enclosed a draft executive order establishing the delegation. Subsequently, despite Katzenbach's early sponsorship, the idea was killed after a technical review in Justice concluded that, although delegation was legal under the statute, it was unwise on policy grounds.[103]

Lead responsibility for framing program changes to be incorporated in a proclamation was exercised by Interior. When the process began in early 1965 Udall hoped for a conclusion by the middle of June, but that target date was not met. After public hearings were held, Interior prepared a list of recommended program changes. There was close consultation with the State Department in evaluating them. By mid-May this had produced joint positions on some points and disagreements on others. The process was snarled in early June when Buford Ellington stoutly protested the exclusion of the Office of Emergency Planning from meaningful involvement in it.[104] This failure in coordination was one of a number of reasons that forced Udall to continue the oil import program without change from June to December. The seriousness of the coordination problem was underscored in late June when the Bureau of the Budget intervened to set out concrete procedures to assure proper and timely interagency review of changes under consideration.[105] As a result an interagency task force chaired by Udall was established, which functioned with relative effectiveness for the remainder of the year, although Interior and State continued to be the dominant forces.[106]

When finally approved, the proclamation made four major changes in the import control program. They themselves did not alter the overall level of imports, although the volume was increased for 1966 due to the projection of expanded domestic production. One of the changes was restrictive in character and prohibited unlicensed imports into U.S. foreign trade zones. The others altered or promised to alter the allocation of imported oil by authorizing the assignment of quotas to mainland petrochemical plants and to Puerto Rican petrochemical operations and by enlarging the discretion of the secretary to adjust the amount of imports arriving in the form of unfinished oils. The first three changes were among Interior's initial recommendations and the fourth was an outgrowth of another. Other changes proposed by the department were lost, some before and some after a draft proclamation was submitted for presidential approval. One notable loss was an adjustment in the proclamation to address problems in hemispheric imports. The main reason was that Johnson would not provide policy direction.

Under existing arrangements, oil from Canada moving overland was not restrained, although the amount expected to be imported was figured in the total allowed. Between 1959 and the first part of 1965 the volume of Canadian imports rose from about 90,000 barrels per day to more than 300,000. Two major problems resulted. The lesser one was that refineries with access to Canadian crude gained a competitive edge over others. Of much greater significance was Venezuela's perception that it was being discriminated against, because its oil was not allowed into the country on the same basis as Canada's. From the standpoint of U.S. policy, the dilemma was that the steps necessary to satisfy Venezuela would sharply attack vital Canadian interests, while maintaining the status quo, although beneficial to Canada, offended the Venezuelans. Washington officials judged the situation to be extraordinarily sensitive. Assistant Secretary of State Anthony M. Solomon told the president's national security adviser, McGeorge Bundy, that in his view oil import control was "the hottest political issue in both Canada and Venezuela *vis à vis* the U.S."[107] Indeed, the future of the governments of Lester Pearson in Canada and Raul Leoni in Venezuela were seen to depend, to a substantial extent, on how import questions were handled.

In early 1965, when it became known that program changes would be under serious consideration, Venezuelan officials began to bargain for treatment equal to Canada's. Interior and State officials held preliminary discussions with Canadian and Venezuelan representatives in Washington in March and April and began to develop options. By late May the two departments were able to report to the White House their agreement on a plan that was expected to satisfy neither country. The basic notion was to give Venezuela comparable but not identical treatment to that accorded Canada. The Canadians would be asked to hold imports to an annual growth rate of no more than 5 percent and would be told that, if voluntary measures did not work, the United States would take whatever steps were necessary to attain this result. In addition, the proclamation would be revised to give the Interior secretary a modest sanction to apply in the form of requiring permits for overland importers of petroleum products. There would also be a cosmetic change to assuage Venezuelan feelings: the term "overland exemption" would be replaced by "controlled and coordinated pipeline movements." Venezuela was to be given a preference in the form of bonus import licenses to refineries using oil from offshore Western Hemisphere sources. Also, it would be pointed out to the Venezuelans that they would benefit from the special consideration to be given to the development of a Puerto Rican petrochemical industry and from anticipated relaxation of residual oil controls.[108]

Two impediments stood before the plan. The Canadian and Venezuelan governments had to accept it; prior to that the president had to approve it. In early June Lee White outlined the suggested approach for Johnson and, along with Francis Bator of the National Security Council staff, recommended that State and Interior officials be allowed to begin serious talks with the other countries involved. Udall was still attempting to meet a mid-June deadline for proclamation revisions; if he was to do so, discussions had to start immediately. Perhaps anticipating the president's reaction, White acknowledged, "It is always distasteful to be offered an agreed-upon package involving such a delicate matter with short notice and with no alternatives."[109] Johnson withheld his assent; despite repeated requests, it was not until the end of August that he allowed Udall and Under Secretary of State for Economic Affairs Thomas Mann to go to Canada for discussions.[110] As it turned out, only Udall went—and he went without knowledge of the president's substantive views on the questions at issue. The meeting, White reported to Johnson, "was perfectly harmonious," but there were no agreements because "Udall was not authorized to make any commitments, even tentative ones, pending an opportunity to discuss this with you."[111]

By mid-November the Canadians had agreed to the 5 percent limit on their exports. Even after extensive talks, however, the Venezuelans remained quite cool.[112] They stoutly pressed for a country quota. To provide this would mean a fundamental change in the nature of the control program that would be opposed by domestic refiners, because their costs would increase, and by U.S. oil investors in Venezuela, because of fears that they would be exposed to significantly greater governmental control and taxation.[113] During this period Secretary of State Dean Rusk made a final stab at an agreement when he stopped in Caracas on his way to a conference in Rio de Janeiro. After his talks there, the secretary was forced to conclude, as he put it in a cable to Under Secretary of State George Ball, "No formula is in sight which offers a solution regarding Venezuelan oil."[114] At this point, in late November 1965, proclamation provisions dealing with hemispheric problems were dropped from further consideration.

There appeared to be no major disagreements between Interior and State on an approach to hemispheric imports, but there were differences on other points. Interior's proposals were fairly ambitious and contemplated a number of restrictions calculated to appeal to the domestic oil industry. Most of them were opposed by the State Department based upon such considerations as the absence of national security justifications and incompatibility with international trade agreements and other foreign policy requirements.

Some rather basic and controversial reallocations of imported oil among users were also at issue. One involved special consideration for a new Puerto Rican refinery to be operated by the Phillips Petroleum Company under the sponsorship of the island's government and justified on economic development grounds. Its ultimate approval was fairly certain—in March Udall had announced his intent to provide it an allocation. Another was to give quotas to petrochemical firms, a move strongly supported by that industry and the Department of Commerce and just as strongly opposed by refiners who would lose access to imports in the amounts gained by the manufacturers of petrochemical products.

In the absence of presidential policy guidance, by the middle of the summer several proposed changes had fallen by the wayside as a result of disagreements within the government. They included bonus allocations for petrochemical exports, allocations for domestic wildcatters, and further restrictions on the importation of petroleum products and unfinished oils. Several restrictions remained, however, in regard to foreign trade zones, toluene, and aircraft fuel used in U.S.–Puerto Rican flights. These were emphasized in material going to the White House as parts of Interior's package with beneficial effects on domestic industry. Furthermore, between June and August Interior and State agreed upon two additional features designed to appeal to domestic producers. One would encourage the movement of crude produced in the central United States to the West Coast. This was expected to increase production in the Permian Basin by 40,000 barrels per day. The other would shift computation of the volume of imports to 12.2 percent of past production from a projection of production for the next year.[115] The revised formula was strongly favored by domestic producers because, in their view, future production was often overestimated, resulting in a higher level of imports than was justified.

The reasons for what appears to be increased solicitousness for the position of domestic oil interests are not clear. One possibility is that it developed in the processes of interdepartmental negotiations and reflected a realistic sensitivity to the politics of oil. Another is that cues came from the White House as the political dimension of proclamation changes was assessed. Still another was that Udall and others were making assumptions about presidential policy preferences in the absence of stated presidential views. Udall later commented in regard to oil that he and Johnson "never discussed it as a policy issue."[116] The secretary also maintained that the 1965 residuals decision was the only one shaped at the presidential level. Clearly, the president and his aides were aware of the course of deliberations through memoranda from Udall and others and through periodic representations by the oil industry. But in support of Udall's claim there is no evidence of presidential efforts to shape the recommendations being put together at the departmental level in this case.

As summer turned to fall and the December deadline for the proclamation grew nearer, the situation remained unsettled, but the direction began to turn toward relaxation of controls. One factor was Office of Emergency Planning reservations about the national security justifications for several of the proposed changes.[117] Political and economic uncertainty also appeared to be a factor as the president remained reluctant to commit himself in response to specific recommendations sent to him for approval.

Officials at the departmental level, especially Udall, now seemed to appreciate the need to create or at least define political circumstances not so much to force Johnson to act, but to make it comfortable for him to do so. One tactic was to absorb negative political reactions at the departmental level and concurrently to demonstrate external support for controversial provisions. Falling in this category were quota allocations for petrochemical firms that previously were not eligible for them. They were disadvantaged in competition with refiners that both had allocations and manufactured petrochemicals. Interior held a hearing on this change in October. Udall opened the proceeding with an announcement that the change would be made. As he expected, the approval of those who would benefit was expressed in no uncertain fashion. Another tactic was to search for a basic rationale for the proposed package that would appeal to Johnson. For much of the fall the rationale supplied emphasized benefits to domestic producers through a slight decrease in imports. Apparently acting on the premise that the president wanted significant restrictions, in mid-November Udall and Mann felt impelled to argue that an even greater reduction in imports than they had proposed would not help independent producers all that much and would require a national security determination that would be open to question. Still Johnson refused to act. When Lee White sent the Udall-Mann memorandum to the president with another in a series of requests that he meet with them, the president turned it aside with a request to White that he provide his own recommendations.[118]

The factor destined to break down the barriers to decision began to emerge at about the time the Udall-Mann memorandum was prepared: upward movement in the price of oil in the United States caused to an extent by Vietnam War demands. Four days after the memorandum was sent Udall followed with another to take advantage of price increases. He advised the president that "the issuance of the *new oil import proclamation* will give us strong leverage to control unnecessary price escalations." He argued further that *"there will be a minimum of Congressional or industry criticism if we act now,"* making references to the supportive attitudes of Judge Jim Langdon of the Texas Railroad Commission and to Texas oilman Jake Hamon, "our mutual friend."[119] The price situation also was featured the following day in a memorandum from Mann to Lee White. He reiterated State's previous positions, but with one important change. Rather than basing import levels on past instead of projected production, the Interior secretary would be given discretionary authority to decide which basis to employ. Basing imports on the secretary's projections could continue if a higher level of imports was necessary to hold prices in line.[120] This proposal contained the seeds for increasing imports rather than restricting them.

Now the arena of consultation enlarged to include those basically concerned with the broader economic implications of the pending proclamation changes, and the center of White House activity moved from Lee White toward Joe Califano, although White continued to be very much involved. On 23 November Califano received a memorandum from Udall summarizing the various means at his disposal for easing pressures on supply. Udall further suggested that permissive authority could be delegated to him to raise imports in any period if required by national security considerations. This would provide an additional economic stabilization lever. It would also have a liberalizing effect.[121] The next day, in response to a request from White for his views, Gardner Ackley, chairman of the Council of Economic Advisers, criticized several of the Interior-State recommendations that were restrictive in nature on the grounds that the proposed package "goes squarely in the opposite direction from the President's present strong concerns with price stability in the petroleum industry."[122] Ackley followed the next day with an assessment for Califano, also read by the president, of the oil price situation.[123] Thus, within less than a week, presidential attention shifted from the oil import control program per se to its implications for macroeconomic policy, and one group of advisers was set against another.

Around the first of December Udall sent Johnson a formal draft proclamation for approval. The specific proposals were those that Udall had urged since midsummer, plus the emergency national security authority to adjust levels of imports. They were supported, Udall told the president, by State, Justice, and the Bureau of the Budget, in addition to Interior. In presenting the proposals, Udall now downplayed the price problem, suggesting that any difficulties could be handled through informal cooperation with the industry. He indicated that the Texas Railroad Commission would be helpful, noting that he had spoken the previous day with Langdon and planned further conversations with him on production policies.[124] Lee White and Joe Califano were critical of several of the proposals. They felt that the delegation of authority to increase imports if required by national security would make no real difference in the situation and opposed changing the basis for computing the level of imports from future to past production and the jet fuel provisions as unduly restrictive.[125]

In the face of contrasting views, Johnson sought further advice, asking Jake Jacobsen to review the Califano-White position. Jacobsen's only reservation concerned the Phillips plant in Puerto Rico and was based upon negative comments he had gotten from people in the industry.[126] Through Jacobsen, who was with him at the ranch, Johnson went back to Califano with questions about arrangements for announcing the new oil import program and had the proclamation redrafted to meet the Califano-White criticisms.[127] Udall announced the changes in Washington on 10 December, and the president appended his signature to the document later that day.

Oil import policy had been under close examination for almost a year. The process began as a major policy review, and in a sense it was. Many possible changes were considered. In the end, however, the changes announced were relatively modest. Clearly Johnson's nearly complete failure to provide policy guidance was a major factor. Perhaps more significant than the contents of the proclamation was what was not included. Many restrictive provisions were dropped. The most important of them shifted the base for calculating quotas from future to past domestic production. In the process, a basis for future liberalization emerged.

The Demise of Residual Limits

One matter was still to be resolved in the aftermath of the proclamation: the residual fuel oil question. The situation had not changed significantly since March 1965 when Johnson refused to sanction the end of controls. Many officials still thought there was little, if any, justification for their continuation. Califano indicated the strength of their views to the president shortly after the new proclamation was approved. "It was extremely difficult to get Ellington, Udall and Vance to back off their position that residual fuel quotas should be terminated."[128]

Restrictions on residual imports along the Eastern Seaboard were ended shortly thereafter, on 1 April 1966, and in the rest of the country the following year. The April action was within the scope of the authority delegated to Udall and ostensibly was his initiative. But as was the case the previous March, the White House was very much involved. The most important presidential intervention was in December 1965, soon after the proclamation was issued. At that time Johnson rejected the advice of Buford Ellington, Deputy Secretary of Defense Cyrus R. Vance, and Udall that controls be terminated immediately. The president, though apparently not reluctant to see the end of controls at some point, wished for a more subtle approach and gave Califano the job of arranging one. The agreement that Califano negotiated with Ellington, Vance, and Udall was not easy to achieve, as Califano told the president. Ellington's view that there were no national security justifications for continued controls reflected a recently completed OEP staff study. He would go along with continuation only if Defense revised its recommendation to him on national security requirements to justify the phase-out formula that Califano wanted. Vance agreed to do this. Califano was able to report to the president on 20 December that "we now have everyone on board" and that Udall felt that the decision "will slide through pretty well because his action should be sufficient to hold the prices on residual oil and coal (both of which are slipping up) and at the same time is not the complete termination . . . that the coal interests . . . now expect."[129] Califano went on to describe the contacts that would be made to secure the most favorable reception for the announcement. With these assurances, the president approved the program revisions.

Reactions to the decision were just about as expected. Udall summarized them for Califano two days after it was made public. Those of the major coal associations and the United Mine Workers, he thought, were quite mild, given their traditional stances on residual imports. The only real problem was with members of Congress from New England who wanted a complete end to controls immediately. But, Udall continued, "after discussions with some of their principal representatives their disappointment has been toned down considerably."[130]

The "substantial relaxation" proclaimed in December 1965 was anticipated to lead to the end of controls in about two years. As it turned out, the period for the East Coast was approximately three months. In contrast to the December decision for gradual termination, which the president had insisted upon, the March decision evolved consensually out of interaction between presidential and departmental levels. The change was precipitated by two key and closely related developments: an effort by Venezuela to increase the price of residual oil and intensified political pressure from New Englanders in the House and Senate for faster movement toward the end of controls.

The principal actors at the presidential level were Califano and Lee White, with an assist from Gardner Ackley. It was Ackley who alerted Califano on 3 January to rumors of Venezuelan action and who confirmed this to the president the next day.[131] Subsequently, the State Department sent detailed assessments of the Venezuelan move to the White House, and Ackley was asked by Califano to "please pick this up with State . . . and Interior."[132] By 14 January the chairman of the Council of Economic Advisers was able to report the results of his consultations with Udall, Mann, and Solomon of the State Department, John W. Douglas of Justice, and representatives of Defense. "All agreed," he told Califano, "that scrapping the quota system for residual fuel tickets would be the strongest move we could make." Reflecting his long-standing antipathy to import controls, he cautiously pushed for action. "If it can ever be done, this is probably the best time to scrap the quota system entirely. The coal industry is producing at virtual capacity, and could not seriously claim to be adversely affected. But it would take a new Presidential Declaration [*sic*], which might be politically hot."[133]

On the political front, New England members of Congress intensified their push for decontrol in two moves early in February. First, Senator Claiborne Pell of Rhode Island gave the president a copy of a critical floor statement he intended to make that tied controls to inflation. Johnson immediately asked for and received reactions to Pell's position from various quarters. Udall's was: "The Senator has a point."[134] The State Department responded that "Senator Pell is essentially correct in saying that import quotas for residual fuel oil have resulted in higher prices to the U.S. consumer."[135] Second, Lee White was proffered an invitation to attend a meeting on residual oil with House Speaker John McCormack and New England senators and House members. He asked the president what he should do and was told not to go.[136] The invitation precipitated other conversations between White and Johnson that afternoon, culminating in a talk that evening on residual oil in relation to New England.[137] In its aftermath, White asked Udall to prepare a response to Pell in consultation with Justice and OEP.[138] This started the process that led to a concrete recommendation to the president for action the following month.

The substance of that recommendation actually originated with the New England senators. The plan they suggested had several positive features. It satisfied their policy objectives, gave a signal to the Venezuelans on prices, minimized negative reactions by maintaining the structure of control without the substance, and did *not* require the president to sign a proclamation to put it into effect. Basically it called for an administrative adjustment in the residual control program to require licenses for imports after rather than before the fact, in effect allowing unfettered importation.[139] As described by Bohi and Russell, "It was a backhanded sort of system, allowing importation of what had already been sold, and licenses for what had already been delivered."[140]

In less than two weeks after the plan surfaced, Udall and Attorney General Katzenbach both recommended to the president that he approve it.[141] Apparently an amber signal was given at that point. In the middle of March Udall told Califano, "I await your green light," as he asked the president's permission to announce the new program.[142] Califano sent Udall's request to Johnson, indicating that he, Larry O'Brien, and Katzenbach concurred. But the president not uncharacteristically wanted somewhat broader consultation. Particularly, he wanted Ferris Bryant, the former Florida governor and new OEP head, brought in. When Califano reported that there would be a meeting of Bryant, Katzenbach, O'Brien, and Udall, he was told to "have Jake [Jacobsen] sit in on this."[143]

Califano tried again for Johnson's approval after the meeting in which all, including Jacobsen, voiced support for the proposal and designated the contacts that would be made prior to an announcement. Still the president was not quite satisfied. He wanted to talk to Jacobsen himself and wanted checks with those likely to be put off by the decision before he made up his mind.[144] The next day Califano was able to report on Udall's talk that afternoon with Joe Moody of the National Coal Policy Conference, who told the secretary that "he was 'not too surprised. . . . I respect you fellows and guess we'll just have to trust you.'"[145] "As I recall," Califano told Johnson, this mild reaction was "consistent with some soundings Jacobsen took today with some of his contacts."[146] With these assurances, the president gave his assent.

There would be other difficult decisions on oil import controls prior to the conclusion of Johnson's presidency. From 1966 onward there was rather constant interest in the administration of the program based upon a determination to minimize inflation. None, perhaps, were as risky in their political implications as those that set the basic policy course between 1964 and 1966. During this period the president and his aides were also attending to contentious regulatory problems in another important economic sector, banking.

In Search of Coordination: Bank Regulation

Good job—stay on it.

LBJ, 19 July 1965[147]

Henry H. Fowler, the new Treasury secretary, had just reported on the successful first meeting of the Coordinating Committee on Bank Regulation. The committee was composed of the comptroller of the currency and the chairmen of the Federal Reserve Board, the Federal Deposit Insurance Corporation, and the Federal Home Loan Bank Board. Treasury participated "in a very modest observer role," according to Fowler.[148] Johnson's positive reaction to Fowler's news was not surprising. The committee was a promising step away from turmoil in bank regulation that had continued without major respite practically since the first days of the Kennedy administration.

The principal sources of conflict were pressures for fundamental change in the structure of financial institutions and in banking practices. Dilemmas presented by these pressures were exacerbated by a fragmented system for the regulation of banks and by the distinctive policies and personality of Comptroller of the Currency James J. Saxon. The resulting controversies roiled through the banking fraternity, regulatory agencies, and Congress, and at times crashed over the protective levees encircling the presidency. They often took the form of conflict among various parts of government with responsibilities for bank regulation. Although independent agencies were involved, the problem of coordination focused on the office of the comptroller, located within the executive branch, because, paradoxically, it was Saxon's strong thrust for independent action that often catalyzed discord.

Regulatory Arrangements

In early 1964 the president's budget director and the chairman of the Council of Economic Advisers summarized for him the organizational disarray in bank regulation and the major problems they perceived in coordination: "The organizational structure is a mess."[149] Then as now, core responsibilities for the regulation of banks were divided among three federal agencies and the fifty states. Banking is frequently described as a "dual" system,[150] with national banks and banks chartered and supervised by state regulatory agencies. However, state banks are also subject to substantial federal regulation. The resulting pattern of control, as Gordon and Heller implied, often was less a regulatory duet than an unharmonious chorus.

At the national level, the Office of the Comptroller of the Currency, located in the Treasury Department, chartered and supervised national banks and approved their branches, as well as mergers and conversions in which the resulting institution was a national bank. The Board of Governors of the Federal Reserve System controlled the admission of state-chartered banks to the system, examined them, and, with state regulators, supervised them and approved their branches, plus mergers in which the resulting institution was a state-chartered member. It also regulated bank holding companies. In addition to providing deposit insurance for all types of commercial banks and mutual savings institutions, the FDIC admitted state-chartered banks that were not members of the Federal Reserve System to insured status, examined them, and, with state officials, supervised them and approved their branches. It also approved mergers and conversions that produced nonmember state banks. There were still other agencies with stakes in bank regulation, including the Federal Home Loan Bank Board (basically concerned with savings and loan associations), the Securities and Exchange Commission, and the antitrust division of the Department of Justice.

In their memorandum to Johnson, Gordon and Heller laid out some of the major problems that resulted from existing organizational arrangements. No agency had "authority commensurate with its responsibility."[151] The FDIC, for example, was not responsible for admitting all banks to insured status and did not examine all insured banks. Because of overlapping responsibilities, two or three agencies might be required to act when a bank was in difficulty or involved in a proposed merger. In some areas agency policies and practices differed, producing inconsistent federal regulation. Bankers attempted to play off "one agency against the others," and each agency tended to serve as a "spokesman for its banks."[152]

Similar assessments had produced a stream of proposals for reorganization over the years. In 1949 the Hoover Commission recommended shifting FDIC to Treasury. The Commission on Money and Credit, reporting in 1961, wanted to consolidate the examination and supervision of commercial banks in the Federal Reserve. The following year Governor J. L. Robertson of the FRB suggested the creation of a new commission to supervise banks, and the comptroller's advisory committee, echoing the Hoover Commission's view, concluded that all authority over state-chartered banks should be placed in an FDIC relocated in the Treasury department.

Although some members of Congress from time to time translated such proposals into legislative form, they went nowhere. The problems were obvious, but the diverse interests with stakes in bank regulation preferred the status quo to the uncertainties of reorganization. This disposition was manifested clearly in President Kennedy's Committee on Financial Institutions, which completed its work in 1963. The committee was highly critical of existing organizational arrangements and took note of numerous operational deficiencies in regulation. But no real solutions emerged, in major part because the heads of the three principal regulatory agencies sat on the committee and could not agree on an alternative. The best that could be done was to call for improved voluntary coordination, the tenuous mastic traditionally relied upon for cohesion in bank regulation.[153]

The Limits of Voluntarism

Although located within the executive branch and subject at least to the nominal direction of the Treasury secretary, the Office of the Comptroller of the Currency possesses many attributes of an independent agency. The comptroller is appointed by the president for a term of five years and can be removed only for cause. Because of statutory provisions and the generation of revenue through fees for services, he has a measure of freedom in the personnel and budgetary realms.

James J. Saxon, who maximized the elements of independence inhering in his office and who pushed voluntary coordination to the limits, was appointed by President Kennedy in 1961. Born and educated in Ohio, he migrated to Washington during the New Deal. After pursuing a civil service career in the Treasury from 1937 to 1952 and completing a law degree in 1950, he began to move in a political direction. During the presidential campaign year of 1952 he was special assistant to the chairman of the Democratic National Committee. Subsequently, he served as Washington representative of the American Bankers Association, as a Senate committee staff member, and then, returning to the Midwest, was in charge of governmental affairs for a major Chicago bank from 1956 until selected to be comptroller. There are suggestions that his sponsor for the position was Mayor Richard J. Daley of Chicago.[154]

As comptroller, Saxon combined distinctive views on banking with an aggressive style of operation. The past performance of federal regulators, he felt, was deficient in many major respects. The FRB, in particular, he considered "very myopic and very outdated" in its approach, according to his deputy and successor, William B. Camp.[155] Among the premises guiding his actions were that banking was a closed industry unable to meet a growing demand for necessary services; that more numerous and larger banking institutions and more extensive branching would remedy this condition and contribute to greater economic prosperity; that banking was too closely regulated to the detriment of desirable levels of economic growth and development; and that banks should not be prohibited from performing any financial function. During Saxon's tenure as comptroller, these views were translated into approximately 700 charters for new national banks, approval of a large number of new branches, a liberal stance toward proposed mergers, and extensive revision of regulations to give banks considerably more operating freedom.[156]

Saxon's actions put him at odds with state banks, with other state and federal regulators, and, in regard to mergers, with the Department of Justice. State bankers justifiably saw the expanded scope of national banking as a threat to their business. State regulators reflected the concerns of their constituents. They further reacted against being pressured to follow the comptroller's lead, which at times contradicted state banking laws, or risk seeing large numbers of conversions from state to national charters. Numerous rules promulgated by Saxon were judged to be contrary to law by other regulators, especially the Federal Reserve Board. There was deep division in the government on bank mergers, as shown by the figures on merger applications submitted to the comptroller in 1962. Of 118, 100 were approved, including more than 50 which Justice advised against and about 30 to which the FRB took exception.[157]

Saxon's independence or, in the words of Gordon and Heller, his propensity for "riding rough shod over the other . . . agencies" cropped up in several areas.[158] He broke with established procedures and resisted consultation with the FRB and FDIC on charter and branch applications. He chafed against the methods preferred by his regulatory colleagues for eliciting annual reports of condition from banks. Although by law an *ex officio* member of the FDIC board, most of the time Saxon refused to participate in its meetings on the specious grounds of official conflict of interest. Instead he sent an aide to represent him. And he fought openly with other agencies in the legislative arena. A not untypical case concerned legislation before Congress on savings bank charters. Saxon took a position contrary to that shared by Treasury, the FDIC, and the FHLBB. Moreover, to strengthen his own stance, he let out a confidential FHLBB draft of a revised bill while it was still under consideration within the executive branch, a serious breach of administrative etiquette.[159]

Because of what Gordon and Heller described as the comptroller's "highhanded behavior," Johnson had not been in the White House long before some of Saxon's opponents began efforts to secure his removal.[160] Meanwhile, others concerned with the breakdown in coordination began to push for corrective steps.

Catching the Presidential Eye

The first initiatives were taken by the bankers themselves. In late January 1964 S. E. Babington, president of the Independent Bankers Association, wrote to the president: "Please give serious and favorable consideration to this request, on behalf of a delegation of representative bankers, leaders in the Independent Bankers Association, and all of them Democrats, who desire to talk to you about the political liability . . . involved in the administration and continuation in office of James J. Saxon. . . . He is intemperate, possessive, and has stirred controversy and confusion through the Nation's banking system. . . . Mr. Saxon seems determined to revolutionize the traditional dual banking system, and remold it into what he thinks it should be by edict, regulation and, irrespective of, and even contempt for, banking laws in the respective states."[161]

The complaints of the state banks represented by Babington were joined soon afterward by those of William F. Kelly. Kelly was president of the American Bankers Association (ABA), the principal organization of the national banks, once Saxon's employers, and now his major constituents. In a public statement, Kelly complained about ruptures in coordination among regulators and asked the president to take a hand. He followed a few days later with a letter to Johnson covering the same ground and suggesting that the Treasury secretary, C. Douglas Dillon, be assigned responsibility for seeing to it that there was adequate cooperation, consultation, and discussion among the regulators.[162]

Unlike Babington's, neither Kelly's public comments nor his letter to the president were personally critical of Saxon. Nevertheless, he drew a sharp response from the comptroller. It was, Dillon told White House aide Kenneth O'Donnell, characteristic of "the frankness with which he tells off any one who happens to disagree with him."[163] Saxon equated Kelly's support for coordination with approval of "thirty years of inaction in banking policy." In truth, Saxon asserted, the development of sound public policy required the free exposure and discussion of issues that were stifled by an emphasis on coordination. He concluded by suggesting to Kelly that the ABA "would make a much more constructive contribution if it would speak out clearly on the substantive issues instead of calling for imposed solutions chosen by others."[164]

The bankers' complaints and a good bit of press discussion struck a White House still in transition. Responses to Babington and Kelly took several months to develop and did not go out until April and May, respectively. In the process, their letters ricocheted around the Bureau of the Budget, Treasury, and a raft of presidential assistants. At one time or another, there was participation by Kennedy holdovers Myer Feldman, Kenneth O'Donnell, and Lee White and Johnsonians Clifton C. Carter, Walter Jenkins, Bill Moyers, and Jack Valenti.

Despite a certain disorganization, several points became fairly evident. First, there was considerable support at the presidential level for Saxon's policy objectives, if not for his methods. According to Joseph W. Barr, who became FDIC chairman in January 1964, many shared the comptroller's view that bank regulation was choked with anachronisms.[165] Even Gordon and Heller, despite their criticisms, thought that Saxon was right on the issues more often than not. Second, there was no strong thirst to replace Saxon, at least not without giving him an opportunity to mend his ways. Third, the situation was seen as something of a political minefield which the president personally should avoid. Persistent efforts to arrange meetings between the independent bankers and the president or, failing that, with White House staff were deflected just as persistently. The advice Walter Jenkins gave to Jack Valenti on one such request is indicative: refuse, "because it will give us nothing but trouble."[166]

Minefield or not, the president was aware of the situation, contrary to the independent bankers' suspicion that he was being kept ignorant of it by Kennedy aides trying to protect Saxon.[167] And action was not far away. On 24 February Treasury Secretary Dillon talked about coordination problems with Johnson. He proposed that the president request him to "ask the various agencies to establish procedures which would insure a maximum degree of cooperation consistent with the legal setup," Dillon later told Moyers. Johnson was amenable. "The President agreed that something should be done and suggested that it might be more helpful if he himself wrote a letter either to the various agencies or to me. He asked me to think about this matter and advise him as to what I thought most appropriate."[168]

On reflection, Dillon concluded that a presidential letter to him would be the better course. He had a draft prepared, together with draft letters from him to the heads of the various affected agencies. The letters reported the president's directive and outlined the new procedures to be followed. The packet of material was sent to the White House for approval two days after the president and Dillon conferred.

Gordon and Heller gave Johnson a different perspective while Dillon's plan was under review. They argued for a more decisive intervention, recommending "that you arrange to meet—preferably alone—with the Comptroller. . . . We urge that he be told in no uncertain terms that he has a choice of (a) working in harness with the FDIC and the Fed—thereby ending a situation which makes the Administration look ridiculous—or (b) leaving—that you then meet with the heads of the three agencies, Secretary Dillon, and the undersigned—to stress the importance of consistency in banking regulation and to urge regular consultations and negotiations to resolve policy differences."[169] They further suggested that in the second meeting Johnson refer to a bill pending in Congress to create a single banking agency "and indicate that legislative action may be the only solution if the present chaotic situation is not ended."[170]

Johnson chose Dillon's softer course. FDIC chairman Joe Barr observed that the president had "no stomach" for the kind of encounter urged by Gordon and Heller.[171] And if there ever was a conversation between the comptroller and the president in which coordination problems were discussed, there is no record of it.

Dillon's letter was signed by Johnson on 2 March 1964. In it the president recognized that each of the agencies "has been granted authority directly by Congress" and "enjoys considerable independence of action." Nevertheless, the letter continued, "from a standpoint of overall public policy, it is important that they follow orderly procedures and that all agencies work together to try to accommodate the views of the others."[172]

The procedures the president sanctioned were rather simple. Basically, Dillon told him, the agencies were "asked to give notice and an opportunity to comment to each other and to me ten days prior to public announcement of any rule, regulation, or policy which might involve conflict with one of the other agencies."[173] The agencies quickly agreed to comply, and the procedures went into effect in mid-March 1964.

Next Steps

In essence, the new procedures required only that differences in views "be carefully considered and accommodated as practicable," as Dillon's letter informed the bank regulators.[174] The poor likelihood that the comptroller would be harnessed by such modest restraints was indicated by a serious dispute within the government that re-erupted about the same time the coordination procedures were established. The problem concerned legislative positions. In 1963 the SEC proposed extensive changes in the securities laws. One of them was to extend disclosure requirements to all widely held stocks sold over the counter, including those of banks. All of the agencies concerned, including the FDIC and the FRB, favored placing administrative responsibility in the SEC—except for the Office of the Comptroller of the Currency. A compromise was molded with the help of the White House, or so it was thought. Each of the banking agencies would apply the disclosure requirement to the banks under its supervision. A bill so providing passed the Senate. Support for this approach was affirmed specifically in the president's 1965 budget document and in his consumer message of 5 February 1964.

Notwithstanding the clarity of the administration's position and the assumption of others that the comptroller was in agreement, Saxon continued his opposition. His view of the requirement was that it was unnecessary and burdensome. In a letter and statement of 19 February 1964, he communicated this position to the House Committee on Interstate and Foreign Commerce and in the process enraged the chairman of the SEC and the director of the BOB. Their ire was heightened even more when Saxon sent letters to all national bank presidents, "in effect inviting their opposition to portions of the bill affecting banks," Gordon of the BOB complained to Dillon.[175]

Gordon reported to the president on the situation the next day:

> To keep you abreast of developments relating to the behavior problems of the Comptroller . . . , I am attaching copies of letters I sent yesterday to Chairman Oren Harris and Secretary Dillon.
>
> The letter to Oren Harris helped to induce Chairman Cary of the SEC to tone down a letter which *he* is sending to Mr. Harris. In its original version, Cary's criticism of the Comptroller's behavior was so strongly worded that it might have been read by the press as the public eruption of a first-class brawl within the Administration. In its final version, Cary's letter is much more diplomatic.[176]

The letters to Harris, especially Gordon's, appeared to have a purpose other than simply to reiterate support for the compromise. It was to warn Saxon that he "should either get in line or get out." This sentiment was attributed to unnamed officials in a *New York Times* story about the letters appearing on 17 March, four days after they were sent. It noted that the letters "could not possibly have been written without personal knowledge and consent of President Johnson." Government officials confirmed that there was an intent "to serve warning on Saxon that further challenges to Administration policies would not be tolerated."[177]

In the midst of this controversy, others in the White House were considering a direct approach to Saxon. Kenneth O'Donnell asked both Gordon and Dillon for their advice about a conversation he planned to have with the comptroller. Both responded on 19 March 1964. Gordon provided a list of specifics with which the comptroller should comply "if he is to fall in line as a member of the Johnson Administration." They included observance of legislative clearance requirements and other procedures whereby Saxon could "seek to avoid open conflicts with other agencies."[178] From Dillon, O'Donnell received a detailed description of the "aggressiveness" with which Saxon "pursues his ends without any thought to the consequences to others in government," and the comptroller's view that efforts to compose differences were a "waste."[179] Noting that Saxon even disregarded internal Treasury coordination processes, Dillon suggested that the best thing O'Donnell could do would be to ask Saxon simply to adhere to established government procedures, which, he ruefully noted, "I have done without any conspicuous success."[180]

Whether O'Donnell met with Saxon is not known, but other White House aides did see the comptroller. Larry O'Brien, head of congressional liaison, was vexed by confusion about the administration's position on legislation. He set out to persuade Saxon to change his ways and brought in Myer Feldman and Walter Jenkins for support in the effort. On 25 March Feldman gave the president a detailed summary of a meeting the three aides had with the comptroller. Saxon was forthright, according to Feldman, about his suspicions of BOB. He complained about the critical newspaper stories he thought originated there and the ultimatum that he cooperate or resign. Feldman felt the situation could be salvaged, despite the strong feelings of both the comptroller and officials with whom he was in conflict. A major reason was that he, O'Brien, and Jenkins "have always found the Comptroller cooperative. When he is told by the White house what to do he follows instructions."[181] On the basis of the meeting, Feldman felt that three steps should be taken: make it known that Saxon was not in the "doghouse"; make certain that legislative clearance procedures were followed in the future; and "caution" administration officials not to snipe at one another.[182] He recommended that the White House group should now meet with Saxon, Dillon, and Gordon to affirm the president's confidence in the comptroller and to put regular clearance procedures back into place.

The president's letter, Dillon's efforts, White House staff interventions, and the attempts of Joe Barr on his own initiative to play a "peacemaker's" role in the relationships among bank regulators may have contributed to improved relations for a time.[183] But tension remained and conflict was never far away. Saxon grudgingly began to comply with clearance procedures, but was quick to react when dissatisfied with the treatment he received. Approximately a month after the talk with O'Brien, Feldman, and Jenkins he complained to Gordon about a particular legislative proposal he charged was "languishing" in the Bureau of the Budget. Indicating that he was quite unhappy with being subjected to such controls, he concluded, "We do not believe that the apparent necessity for clearance by your office . . . should be a basis for unwarranted delay in the disposition of these matters."[184]

The effectiveness of Dillon's coordination procedures began to erode rather quickly. In fact, nine months after they were established they were "dormant," Treasury's general counsel reported to the secretary.[185] Among other factors, conflicts over the interpretation of relevant laws were too deep-seated to be resolved through the exchange of views. In August 1964 Gordon brought two recent incidents to the president's attention. In one, the Federal Reserve Board refused to allow a state member bank to absorb a smaller one on antitrust grounds. The comptroller promptly invited the larger bank to shift to a national charter and promised to approve the merger if it did so. In the other, Saxon ruled that national banks could own stock in foreign banks directly. The Federal Reserve Board, however, took the position that this was unlawful.[186]

It was clear to Gordon that additional steps were called for to secure more uniform application of banking laws, but concerted White House attention to the matter would have to await conclusion of the presidential election season then underway.

Options

Just a few days after the election Herschel Schooley, Washington representative of the independent bankers, wrote Bill Moyers: "Dear Billy D., Under the mandate it would now be most timely, and deserved, should the President . . . decide to give the big, overdue heave-ho to the contentious and arrogant Currency Comptroller, Gentleman Jim Saxon, soonest."[187] In the months after Johnson won his own presidential term replacing Saxon was an option often discussed. Reorganization was another.

The replacement of Saxon was still a much more popular idea in certain quarters outside the White House than within it. There is no indication that this option received serious official consideration in late 1964 or in 1965, when purposive steps to improve coordination were under close review. As for Saxon himself, rumors circulated prior to the election that he was about to leave voluntarily. They were incorrect. After one such report in the *New York Times*, the comptroller's special assistant for public affairs sent Walter Jenkins other newspaper stories outlining the reforms Saxon was preparing to push, with the note that, "The Times notwithstanding, the Comptroller . . . does have some plans for the months ahead."[188]

Saxon was to remain as comptroller until his term expired in late

1966. Not everyone was pleased. In April 1965 the Independent Bankers Association publicly asked for his removal.[189] More serious, and more interesting in its lack of desired effect, was the threat posed by Wright Patman, chairman of the House Banking and Currency Committee and a firm Johnson ally. Patman was a vociferous foe of big banks and a vigorous supporter of small, local financial institutions. In January 1965 Dillon passed word to the president that Patman intended to make an all-out attack on Saxon and "believed his investigation could very likely lead to the impeachment of the comptroller" for persistent actions contrary to law.[190] Although Patman did not follow through fully with his threat of investigation, his position on Saxon did not change. In the latter part of 1965 Marvin Watson reported to Johnson on Patman's frame of mind. It was very simply that "the Comptroller . . . has got to go. He continues to violate the law."[191]

In contrast to the possibility of replacing Saxon, the reorganization option was given careful scrutiny in the White House. Preliminary work started well before the election. In August 1964 Gordon told the president that bank regulation was one of the items on the agenda of the Task Force on Government Reorganization, chaired by Don K. Price of Harvard University.[192] Others also were thinking about structural changes in bank regulation. In late October both Saxon and Barr attended a meeting of the ABA in Miami. Saxon was first out of the blocks. He proposed to the bankers that authority to approve state bank charters be removed from FDIC and the Federal Reserve Board and left exclusively with the states. Barr reacted vigorously. He indicated his own preference for a single board to exercise federal regulatory responsibilities in banking. And at a press conference in what was seen as an "open slap" at Saxon, he made it clear that the comptroller's idea had not been sanctioned by the administration.[193]

On 3 November Douglass Cater summarized for the president a raft of reorganization proposals prepared by the Price task force. In regard to banking, it recommended consolidation of all supervisory and examining functions of the three principal federal agencies in Treasury under a new position at the assistant secretary level.[194] In subsequent discussions between the Bureau of the Budget and the White House, however, another approach was elected: to consolidate bank regulation functions in an independent agency headed by a single administrator. By mid-February 1965 the necessary general staff work was completed on this option, and a reorganization plan and message were in draft form.[195]

Apparently Johnson was sympathetic to reorganization. But before he finally made up his mind, he wanted word on the bureau's "spade work" with the agencies, Congress, and bankers. This was the message to Kermit Gordon on 21 March from Bill Moyers, who was coordinating consideration of a variety of reorganization proposals from his post in the White House.[196] There was a measure of support in Congress for a change, evidenced by reorganization legislation introduced independently by some members. But overall the omens were not encouraging. Johnson still held forth the possibility of action in a press conference on 1 April, but it seems that he had just about decided that the political equations would not solve satisfactorily. In responding to a question about a Senate inquiry into recent bank failures, he said that the administration was "giving most serious consideration" to organization for bank regulation.[197] But the next day the *New York Times* reported government officials' view that there was a problem in "the near unanimous opposition of bankers to . . . centralization." This, according to the story, was "the only thing that kept President Johnson from proposing a consolidation of the banking agencies long ago. . . . The President did not think Congress would permit it."[198]

The firm opposition of major segments of the banking community was further indicated the next week in a letter to Johnson from the president of the ABA, Reno Oldin, arguing against centralization and for renewed efforts at voluntary coordination.[199] Not long after the news conference a subcommittee of the House Banking and Currency Committee held hearings on reorganization legislation. An administration position was not presented. In their testimony, both Saxon and Kenneth A. Randall, who had recently become the FDIC chairman when Barr was named Treasury under secretary, were cool to organizational changes. Again, bankers expressed strong reservations.[200]

Although the events of April 1965 affirmed the considerable strength of antireorganization forces, the reorganization idea did not die completely. The president's response to Oldin's letter, which went out in May, was guarded, but it did not foreclose any options. Avoiding comment on substantive issues, it basically promised further presidential "comment" and "action as appropriate" based upon consultation with senior economic advisers.[201] Such consultations as occurred, however, never carried reorganization any closer to presidential approval than in late 1964 and early 1965. The next time there was serious consideration was in late 1966. Joe Califano reported to Johnson that he, Joe Barr, and Charles Schultze, who was now head of BOB, were "looking at ways to end the present confusion and overlapping in the three bank supervisory agencies." The president approved Califano's recommendation that the alternatives be refined and another round of soundings be taken.[202] Inquiries showed that the politics of the situation had not changed, and once again the presidential imprimatur was withheld.

Toward Normalcy

The impulse for direct action also was lessened by an easing of tension. In mid-1965 Fowler reported an improved situation to the president. In his view, "The atmosphere among bank regulatory agencies seems to have settled down somewhat."[203] After the serious flirtation with reorganization, and perhaps in part because of it, interagency relationships had begun to resemble less a brawl than normal competition among organizations with overlapping responsibilities. To be sure, the comptroller still sparred with the FDIC and the Federal Reserve Board over interpretations of the law. A breakdown occurred in late 1965 when the Federal Reserve Board raised the interest rates banks could pay on time deposits without consultation with other regulators. There were differences on legislative matters, especially in 1965 and 1966 when Congress enacted new laws on bank mergers (discussed in the following chapter); on interest rates paid on savings deposits (examined in chapter 6); and on the powers of regulatory institutions in the wake of a number of bank failures. But there was no return to the tempestuousness and chaos of 1964 for the remainder of Johnson's presidency.

Several factors account for diminishing tension, in addition to previous presidential interventions. Saxon's distinctive views and his style of operation were familiar now, even though not always applauded. Others were able to take into account his likely reactions and "to seal him off" to a certain extent, according to Barr.[204] The comptroller himself made some positive adjustments. He announced in February 1965, for example, that all or parts of thirteen states and the District of Columbia were now "closed" to additional national bank charters.[205] He also began to take a somewhat more active role in FDIC matters.[206] Joe Barr was by this time a practiced middleman in disputes among bank regulators and on occasion was called upon for purposes of conflict control. In January 1966 he wrote to Califano on his involvement in two disputes between Saxon and the FDIC, based upon his "mandate to mediate" conferred by the White House.[207] New formal procedures for voluntary coordination were put into place in 1965. Then, in November 1966, Saxon's term expired and he was replaced. Finally, concern for overall economic conditions at the presidential level, in Treasury, and in the other agencies may have diverted attention from fundamental problems in coordination and contributed to a mood of accommodation in parochial rivalries.

The new coordination procedures came at Fowler's initiative in the summer of 1965. With the approval of the president and after consultation with the parties involved, he established the Coordinating Committee on Bank Regulation. In concept the committee was much like that proposed some years before by the Kennedy Task Force on Financial Institutions and more recently by the American Bankers Association. It was made up of the heads of the three agencies regulating banks plus the chairman of the Federal Home Loan Bank Board, with Treasury as an observer. The members nominated matters to be discussed quarterly or at special committee meetings. The secretary of the Treasury was to be informed if the committee could not come to agreement on matters before it. Members were assured that the secretary, in dealing with disagreements, would respect their independent statutory authority and responsibilities.[208]

The procedures were of some interest to the president. Fowler gave him a full synopsis of the committee's inaugural meeting in June 1965 and received in return Johnson's encouragement: "Good job—stay on it."[209] The president's continued interest in the coordination problem is indicated by the periodic reports he received on the committee's activities and by public statements emphasizing the importance of coordination efforts, as in his 1967 economic message.[210]

The committee continued to function until the conclusion of Johnson's presidency. By all accounts it was a relative success, meeting more often than originally planned, generally every two weeks, according to William Camp, who replaced Saxon. In the meetings, he said, there was "a free and frank exchange of views." Furthermore, a cooperative spirit was at work. "We don't always agree," Camp noted, "but it's all done in the spirit of good fellowship and understanding."[211] The committee's discussions of major policy questions with cross-cutting implications, such as the levels of interest rates to be paid on savings and their impact on the soundness of financial institutions of all types, made important contributions to the development of administration policy. Specific aspects of regulatory operations were also examined. A query from Senator William Proxmire in February 1967 provided an opportunity to sum up a series of positive steps, such as issuance of joint regulations under the Financial Institutions Supervisory Act of 1966; improved coordination of examinations, investigations of suspected illegal practices, and bank borrowing from the Federal Reserve; common guidelines governing bank advertising; and joint studies of several matters, including capital adequacy and liquidity.[212] A good many of these accomplishments were realized before Saxon's departure on 15 November 1966, again testifying to the changed climate of relationships.

It is not clear whether Saxon genuinely wished to end his service after a single term, although he announced his intention to do so before there was any public indication of a presidential predisposition in the matter. His successor felt that Saxon wanted to continue.[213] Joe Barr, however, thought that he wanted to leave. In regard to those on the presidential side of the decision, Barr's view was that Saxon was not pushed out, but neither was he begged to stay.[214] The separation probably was mutually satisfactory to a substantial degree. This is indicated by a memorandum from Henry Fowler to Jake Jacobsen of the White House staff suggesting a public exchange of letters between Saxon and the president. The secretary noted that the "circumstances of the termination" were "truly cordial and happy." In further justification he added that in his opinion the comptroller had "made a major contribution to the public interest in national bank regulation."[215]

Johnson announced William Camp's selection on 8 November 1966, election day, with the new comptroller by his side on the steps of the Pedernales Electric Cooperative after the president had voted. Camp was a Texan, but also a career civil servant who rose through the ranks to become Saxon's deputy. Reportedly he was Saxon's choice for the position.[216] Although he did not share his predecessor's abrasiveness, he did, for the most part, share his views on banking.[217] Nevertheless, there were some important differences between their regimes in regard to coordination, regulatory priorities, and attention to the political environment in which bank regulation took place.

Camp's approach was shaped in discernible ways by Johnson's sensitivities and directives. Presidential concern for coordination, of course, was well established, and Camp made a conscious and successful effort to further improve cooperative relationships among bank regulators. For example, in contrast to Saxon, he tried to attend all meetings of the FDIC board.[218] Bank examination was a high priority for Camp, whereas it was not for Saxon. Camp's own background was in examination. His natural inclinations were heightened by President Johnson's interest. Between 1961 and 1965 nineteen banks failed across the country. While only three were national banks, the total failure rate was much greater than had been experienced in recent years. This worried Johnson. Even before

Camp's appointment he personally made periodic requests to the regulators for reports on the health of financial institutions. In Johnson City, the president's wishes were expressed to Camp in no uncertain terms: "Bill, I want you to examine the banks very, very thoroughly. That's what I want. I want them examined."[219] This was followed in January by a strong and explicit admonition to the agencies in the president's economic report to make improvements in the scrutiny of banks.[220] In the political sphere, liaison with state regulators and with bankers was strengthened.[221] Again, Johnson was a factor. "The President has been very anxious that we keep close liaison with bankers," Camp noted. He and other regulators, at Johnson's "suggestion," regularly began to go out together from Washington on speaking tours.[222]

Conclusions

Perhaps the most striking feature of the cases discussed is the level and intensity of Johnson's interests. He was quite active and engaged in guidepost and balance-of-payments matters and, when circumstances demanded, in labor disputes. All related to macroeconomic policy, a distinctively presidential responsibility, and Johnson's response was to play an active leadership role that distinguished little between executive agencies and commissions when it came to seeking help. A large and diverse group of officials assisted the president. Differences arose among them from time to time. Representatives of the Department of Labor might have been more sympathetic to labor's position in contract negotiations than the Council of Economic Advisers, and officials in the Department of Commerce might have been more responsive to business interests in foreign investment than others wished, but on the whole presidential policy guided the actions of Johnson's subordinates. An important factor is that policy in those areas was stated with considerable clarity.

In contrast, Johnson displayed a notably lesser degree of interest in the regulation of agriculture, oil imports, and banking. He clearly wished to minimize, if not avoid altogether, public involvement in these controversial and politically hazardous undertakings. Even behind the scenes he often played a restrained role when policy or program issues of necessity rose to the presidential level even when he was pressed to act. He was inclined to procrastinate, as in the case of the oil import control proclamation in 1965. Johnson's reticence, or deference, was such that his personal views, if any, on regulatory policy in the three areas were often a puzzle even to his close associates. His interest in improving the administration of bank regulation was clear, however.

An absence of distinctly presidential policy objectives in the three cases did not mean an absence of presidential concerns. Johnson was clearly attentive to the larger economic and political ramifications of regulatory decisions or problems. He was most actively engaged in agricultural and oil import matters when they were related to price increases in the economy. When serious political problems threatened or erupted, especially when his relations with Congress were involved, his interest also was ignited. His decision not to end residual oil controls in 1965 is a prime example. Even then, Johnson preferred to remain outside the spotlight and to guide and direct the political maneuverings of his subordinates—presidential aides and secretaries Freeman, Udall, Dillon, and Fowler—in minimizing political damages.

When juxtaposed with prior chapters, these cases clearly show that Johnson's concepts of commission and executive regulation were different. Whereas he opposed advocacy on the part of commission members, he accepted it from executive regulators. Freeman, Udall, and Saxon were constantly in the position of advocating regulatory policies and defending their decisions in the political arena. They drew no criticism from the president for this.

Although there was no driving substantive presidential agenda at work, the relationship between the presidency and agriculture, oil imports, and banking could be described as relatively close. As in the case of commission regulation, there was constant interaction and exchange of views and information. With the possible exception of those involving Saxon, relationships could be described as more cooperative and responsive than conflictual. Saxon's independence was offset by the cooperative stances of other Treasury officials and of the FDIC and FHLBB. The strong and conflicting pressures on Freeman were a source of tension from time to time. Notable problems included his perceived reluctance at one point to combat increases in food prices with the desired vigor. Udall constantly sought to reflect presidential views. Even when embarrassed by Johnson's veto of his residual oil decision in 1965, he played the role of the willing presidential agent. For both Freeman and Udall, the problem was not so much that there were attempts to force strong presidential views upon them as it was the absence of presidential policy direction, which was a major source of discomfort.

In the vacuum, congressional and interest group pressures assumed considerable significance and had their effects. From presidential and departmental perspectives, they were not dominant, but they were factors with which to contend. Although influential, congressional and group interests did not appear to be impregnable barriers that prevented the White House from securing the kinds of responses it wanted from regulators. Rather, presidential and departmental officials attempted to maneuver together through sometimes troublesome political conditions.

Despite Johnson's wariness, or rather perhaps in part because of it, presidential aides played important roles. The Bureau of the Budget, of course, was a major presence. In addition, White House staff members monitored regulatory operations with considerable care. Patterns of interaction were fluid, changing as portfolios shifted among aides and with evolving economic and political circumstances. The involvement of aides, like that described in previous chapters, was basically *ad hoc* and reactive in nature. They usually did not appear to have strong, programmatic views on regulatory matters. Like the president, they were most sensitive to the broad economic and political implications of regulatory decisions. On the whole, their role, in addition to monitoring, can be described as involving mediation, playing the honest broker, and keeping Johnson informed. The role of presidential aides tended to diminish somewhat in the banking area when the coordinating committee began to work with some effectiveness.

The Bureau of the Budget and the Council of Economic Advisers also played prominent roles. They had certain general policy biases that caused them to be generally supportive of the comptroller's innovations and critical of agricultural subsidies and oil import restrictions. They had some effect as departmental recommendations moved through presidential decision-making processes. The Office of Emergency Planning exercised some influence in oil import control matters. When the advice from his aides differed from departmental views, Johnson usually sided with his aides.

All three cases show the importance of conflict within the government as a trigger of presidential involvement. In none of them, with the possible exception of bank regulation, were the conflicts as intense as in antitrust enforcement. One area where there was major conflict was bank mergers. Here, in place of his fellow bank regulators, Saxon took on the Department of Justice.

5. Tenuous Ties: The Case of Antitrust Enforcement

I think he (Ramsey) is out of step to [*sic*]! Call Ramsey at *once* & tell him I strongly agree with Boyd but I will not force him to act against his conscience as I told him.

LBJ, 5 May 1968[1]

AT ISSUE WAS WHETHER the government would attempt to halt the Interstate Commerce Commission–approved consolidation of the Great Northern; Northern Pacific; Chicago, Burlington and Quincy; and Spokane, Portland & Seattle railroads—the Northern Lines merger. Secretary of Transportation Alan Boyd, among others in the administration, favored the merger and argued against the challenge that Ramsey Clark, the attorney general, intended to mount. Despite the clear expression of the president's views, the next day the Department of Justice went to court.[2] Ironically, in one of the few instances in which Johnson personally took an unmistakably clear position on an antitrust question, he was overridden by departmental regulators.

This outcome was less an act of insubordination than the reflection of a rather consistent presidential disposition, in the end, to defer to regulators and, in this case, to leave decisions on antitrust enforcement to the attorney general and officials in the antitrust division. Even here, where the president held a strong opinion, he was willing to allow his attorney general's "conscience" to dictate what the government's position would be.

The president's attention turned to antitrust in a number of instances, especially to antitrust activity related to the immediate economic policy objectives of the administration and to mergers in banking and rail transportation on which there was division within the government. Nevertheless, during Johnson's tenure the ties between the presidency and the antitrust endeavors of the Department of Justice were tenuous, even at the most general policy level.

From a policy perspective, there was a basic question that was not, and perhaps could not be, answered during the Johnson presidency: Whose views should shape the application of antitrust laws in important public policy matters? In the case of banking, the primary competitors for dominance were the comptroller of the currency and the Department of Justice. In railroad mergers, they were Justice and administration officials with transportation policy responsibilities.

The Course of Antitrust: An Overview

> I see these as the main tasks of Federal economic policy
> today: . . . To maintain and enhance healthy competition.
>   LBJ, 27 January 1966[3]

No policy on antitrust was openly articulated at the presidential level during the Johnson presidency. The president's own public pronouncements almost never touched upon this important area of economic control. One of the few exceptions was in his 1966 economic report to Congress—and even then there was no more than a simple recognition of the importance of "healthy competition."

Not much more is discernible in the reports of the Council of Economic Advisers. The 1965 document did look in some detail at a fundamental challenge to antitrust policy, the post–World War II merger and acquisition trend, specifically conglomerate mergers, which came in increasing numbers during the 1960s. Two points about the treatment of conglomerates by the presidential advisers are especially interesting. First, the council accurately noted the considerable uncertainties existing at the time about precisely how the antitrust laws applied to mergers of companies that were not substantial competitors or in a supplier-customer relationship. Second, it took an ambivalent position on such mergers. In contrast to those for whom big, by definition, was bad, and others who judged conglomerates to be a means for increasing economic efficiency, the council saw both negative and positive features in the new aggregations of economic power and neither criticized nor applauded them.[4]

This 1965 discussion was the fullest exposition on antitrust problems by officials at the presidential level, although the 1967 report did treat in general terms the importance of vigorous antitrust enforcement for a healthy economy.[5] In 1968 a presidential task force completed an examination of the antitrust laws and recommended several fundamental changes. The movement toward a distinctive administration policy on antitrust, to be examined in the next chapter, was cut short, however, by Johnson's decision to forego another term. Submitted to the president just a few weeks before his return to Texas, the task force report joined the mound of potential initiatives left pending.

In the absence of clear presidential policy on conglomerates and other antitrust questions, the clash of values inherent in antitrust enforcement played directly upon the regulators in the Department of Justice. This is not unusual. It is probably the case, as Robert M. Goolrick has observed, that "generally speaking, . . . the tenor of antitrust policy at any particular moment has depended primarily upon the philosophy and fervor of the Antitrust Division chief (and sometimes the attorney general)."[6] One might add that it is the "philosophy and fervor" of these officials in conjunction with those of the antitrust bureaucracy, composed for the most part of attorneys with a prosecutorial bent, that account for the resulting pattern of enforcement.

During the five plus years of the Johnson presidency there was a measure of discontinuity in antitrust leadership. Three men served as attorney general and three as assistant attorney general for antitrust. Under the procedures in place at the time, the attorney general's approval was required for the antitrust division to act. This was not just a formality; at times division recommendations were rejected. Through this means, and through other opportunities to push the division in particular directions, attorneys general may have a significant effect on antitrust policy and its implementation.

Robert Kennedy served for just a few months as attorney general under Johnson before departing to become a candidate for a seat in the U.S. Senate from New York. His successors, Nicholas deB. Katzenbach and Ramsey Clark, were more influential than he was in setting the tone for antitrust enforcement under Johnson.

Katzenbach had been Kennedy's deputy. According to some, he was not much interested in or sympathetic to antitrust enforcement. Several instances have been reported in which he turned aside recommendations for action, including one to separate Western Electric from AT&T.[7] In her analysis of antitrust enforcement in the 1960s, Suzanne Weaver questions whether such instances are properly understood as reflecting antipathy to antitrust or differences over substantive economic goals, such as protecting jobs versus maximizing competition, and doubts about the strength of the legal premises undergirding proposed actions.[8] Donald F. Turner, who headed the antitrust division under Katzenbach, says that the attorney general did reject a number of complaints prepared under the supervision of his predecessor, because they were poorly developed.[9] For whatever reasons, however, it seems clear that Katzenbach's enthusiasm for antitrust was substantially less than his successor's.

Clark moved into the top spot in 1966 from his position as deputy attorney general when Katzenbach became under secretary of State. Described as a "populist" by the two assistant attorneys general for antitrust who served under him, Clark was an antitrust activist.[10] Interest in antitrust ran in the family. His father, Tom Clark of Texas, headed the antitrust division before moving on to become attorney general, then an associate justice of the U.S. Supreme Court. Ramsey Clark's activism was reflected in a variety of ways. He encouraged U.S. attorneys scattered about the country to bring price-fixing suits.[11] He was receptive to antitrust division initiatives and prodded the division to act with more vigor on conglomerates in general and in several specific situations, including the International Telephone and Telegraph and American Broadcasting Company merger and the massive power of the International Business Machine Corporation (IBM).[12] The most striking indication of activism, as will be seen, was his insistence on moving ahead with several cases over opposition from other parts of government and even from the White House. But Clark was not always insensitive to competing concerns. For example, he refused to approve a division recommendation to challenge the merger of the McDonnell and Douglas aircraft companies.[13]

William H. Orrick, Jr., was in charge of the antitrust division when Johnson became president. He had replaced Lee Loevenger not long before. A San Francisco attorney, Orrick served in the Kennedy administration as assistant attorney general heading the civil division and as assistant secretary of State for administration before returning to Justice in the antitrust post. He had no particular background in antitrust, in contrast to his successor, Donald F. Turner, who took office in 1965.

Turner was a professor at the Harvard Law School, an economist as well as a lawyer, and one of the country's leading antitrust scholars. He had known Katzenbach since student days at the Yale Law School and Ramsey Clark since clerking for Tom Clark at the Supreme Court. Turner served from June 1965 through May 1968 and in his three-year tenure probably had more impact on antitrust activity than any other single individual during Johnson's presidency. When he returned to his Harvard position, he was replaced by his top aide and former Stanford law professor Edwin M. Zimmerman, whose views were much the same as Turner's.

These officials presided over a good bit of antitrust activity. A respectable number of enforcement actions were instituted: an average of forty-one a year from 1964 through 1968, just below the average of forty-three from 1961 through 1963 and above the thirty-four averaged by the Eisenhower administration.[14] Traditional concerns in areas where the law was relatively well established were reflected in boycott, market allocation, and price-fixing cases. Other emphases, especially in regard to mergers, reflected major transitions underway in industry structure, antitrust law itself, and views on the place of economic reasoning in antitrust policy and implementation.

One of the most distinctive aspects of antitrust enforcement during the Johnson presidency was an effort to rationalize the efforts of the antitrust division. It was a time in which there was considerable tension and uncertainty in the antitrust and business communities, caused by developing merger patterns in conjunction with the powerful discretionary weapons against vertical and horizontal combinations created by judicial interpretations of the 1950 amendments to the Clayton Act.[15] Efforts to reduce tension and remove uncertainty began with Katzenbach and Orrick. Both were of the view that in the early 1960s there was no coherent policy to guide the division's efforts or to inform the decisions of business. Rather, there was a "scattergun" approach to enforcement that did not sufficiently take into account economic considerations.[16] Orrick began a search for coherence with the creation of a policy planning and evaluation staff.

Turner built on Orrick's initiatives in several ways. The policy planning and evaluation functions were expanded, strengthened, and staffed by persons brought in from outside the division. Added weight was given to the analysis of economic effects in case assessment and selection. In the construction of cases, considerable emphasis was placed on further developing and sharpening antitrust law where there were ambiguities, rather than simply compiling a good won-lost record. Merger guidelines were prepared as an aid to voluntary compliance and to channel division activities.[17]

Turner's regime and the policies and processes associated with it did not enjoy universal popularity. Like the comptroller of the currency, James J. Saxon, he attempted to bring fresh thinking into an area of government regulation where traditional approaches were increasingly called into question by a changing economy. Although there was not the intense acrimony produced by Saxon's distinctive personality, there was "widespread hostility" to Turner's approach in several quarters, according to Richard Posner. Writing some years later, Posner considered Turner to be on the right track and "the most distinguished head of the Antitrust Division since Thurman Arnold."[18]

One quarter from which there was opposition, Posner reports, was the antitrust bar, and another was a segment of the division's staff. The bar was not pleased because Turner's views implied a diminished volume of antitrust litigation. Trial attorneys in the division were discomfited for the same reason, but they also had other complaints. They chafed at circumscription of the wide latitude they traditionally enjoyed in shaping the enforcement process and at economic critiques of the cases they proposed. Some of them, together with congressional and other advocates of a tough antitrust program, believed that, taken together, the various parts of Turner's effort at rationalization amounted to permissiveness.[19]

A major sore spot was Turner's view that the purpose of antitrust was to increase and strengthen competition. He was not interested in attacking even large-scale mergers which did not appear to alter the competitive balance, although there might be a legal foundation for challenging them. Accordingly, he overrode the staff and refused to allow complaints to be filed against several highly publicized mergers, including Continental Oil and Consolidated Coal, Atlantic Refining and Richfield Oil, and Pure and Union Oil.

Another sore spot was the slippery problem of conglomerates. There was sentiment among the staff, shared by Clark, for vigorous action against them. Turner, on the other hand, took the position that, for the most part, conglomerate mergers were not illegal under the law as then written. Consequently, any campaign against them would have to be preceded by congressional action. Some staff members disagreed with Turner on the legal point and with his theory as to how selected conglomerates might be challenged under the law as it stood—if the parties involved could be shown to be potential competitors. Foundations for the theory could be discerned in certain judicial decisions, but elements of the staff felt potential competition to be a weak reed, difficult to prove, and resented its imposition from above. Nevertheless, some complaints were filed on this basis.

Still another of Turner's theories which some staff members did not accept was that of shared monopoly. Although Turner was not antagonistic to bigness per se, he was convinced that in certain highly concentrated industries with oligopolistic characteristics competition was in fact muted. He had studies made of the automobile, sulphur, metal container, and other industries that showed features of shared monopoly, but no complaints were filed. Staff members involved in litigation felt that proving the existence of the phenomenon in court was chancy at best.

Even the centerpiece of the rationalization effort, the merger guidelines, finally issued on 30 May 1968 just as Turner returned to Cambridge, did not sit well with the staff. Their basic purpose was to define the market circumstances in which a merger might be subject to attack. Staff criticisms were that the specifications gave away too much and unduly tied the hands of the division in enforcing the law. Nevertheless, for more than a decade the guidelines were to remain, without substantial change, an important element of the division's work.

Although the work of the antitrust division in selecting and preparing cases, grappling with ways to approach the conglomerate problem, preparing merger guidelines, and in other areas clearly was not subject to presidential direction, there remains the possibility of presidential influence. A basis for assessing the degree of that influence may be laid by examining interaction between the White House and the Department of Justice on antitrust matters.

On the Periphery

Talk to Ramsey and ask him to *try* to help.

LBJ, 8 April 1965 [20]

The White House was under pressure from Democratic senators Abraham Ribicoff and John McClellan to turn around the Justice Department's refusal to clear General Electric's acquisition of a small electrical appliance manufacturing firm with plants in their states, Connecticut and Arkansas. The plants were closed, and 1,000 people were out of work. The choice, as presidential aide Jack Valenti put it to Johnson, apparently was "between purchase by General Electric and permanent closing of the plants." [21] White House staff previously had made their own inquiries. In mid-March Mike Manatos, who worked in congressional liaison, talked to Orrick about the matter. Valenti relayed to Johnson Orrick's "hope . . . that the President will stay clear of this problem." [22] In the meantime, Lee White passed on to Ribicoff and McClellan a detailed summary of Justice's views. [23] White House staff subsequently had conversations with Katzenbach, after which Justice agreed to reconsider its stance if no alternative purchaser were found. [24] The president's instruction to talk to Ramsey Clark, then deputy attorney general, followed not long thereafter. Within a matter of days Justice cleared the acquisition.[25]

According to the authors of *The Closed Enterprise System*, Joe Califano said that Johnson made a conscious effort to stay away from antitrust matters because of his "wheeler-dealer" image.[26] Katzenbach says that Johnson was "insistent in all matters in the Department of Justice that political considerations be given no weight whatsoever. The best politics were no politics at all."[27] Although a certain gulf may have separated the presidency and antitrust, bridges were in fact established from time to time, as in the General Electric case. They were traversed in the selection of Justice Department officials, to a limited degree in enforcement, and in certain areas of legislation and policy.

The key Johnson appointment in the antitrust sphere was Turner; it is doubtful that the antitrust views of Katzenbach and Clark were factors one way or another in their choice to be attorney general. Turner was suggested by Katzenbach.[28] The attorney general initially found the president to be unenthusiastic, because Turner was not only an academic but on the Harvard faculty.[29] Given Turner's background and prior work in antitrust, it is likely that Katzenbach saw him as someone who could produce the rationalization he favored. Johnson, as was typical, consulted further. At a minimum, he talked to Clark Clifford about Turner. Clifford was a Washington lawyer, former aide to Harry S Truman, leading Democrat, and a close friend of the president. On 22 April 1965, five days before Turner and Katzenbach visited the president in the Oval Office, Clifford reported, in Valenti's words, "a valuable find." It was Turner's book, written with Carl Kaysen, *Antitrust Policy: An Economic and Legal Analysis*. "In this book, no doubt, this man has put down exactly what he feels about anti-trust policy," Valenti told Johnson. "Clark is reading the book tonight and will give us his analysis tomorrow."[30] Presumably both Clifford's reading and the Oval Office interview were satisfactory. Johnson announced Turner's appointment at a press conference just four hours after their meeting. In that announcement Turner's Harvard affiliation was pointedly overlooked; the president only identified him with Stanford, where he was then serving as a visiting professor.[31]

There was no antitrust portfolio as such in the White House, and antitrust materials crossed the desks of a fair number of White House aides at one time or another. But some focus of responsibility did occur in 1967 and 1968. Ernest Goldstein included antitrust in his range of interests, and Larry Temple served as general liaison with Justice.[32] Special relationships of some significance were also at play. Califano had been a student of Turner's, and that connection was important in some instances. One of the most important ties was between the president and Clark. Harry McPherson has described it as being quite intimate. "The President loved—and as far as I know—loves Ramsey. He has know him all his life, and has tremendous respect for him, for his moral character, for his capacity to speak succinctly and powerfully, to wrap up a tremendous amount of information."[33] There were reservations, however. "He thought Ramsey was too young; that he was wet behind the ears. That he had little understanding of how to get along with Congress."[34] On matters pertaining to the Department of Justice, "they talked a lot on the telephone." And "as to the President's relationship to Justice on . . . anti-trust if any, it was personal between him and Ramsey."[35]

Their relationship became quite strained in the last weeks of Johnson's tenure in the White House. A number of antitrust actions were filed, the most dramatic seeking to dismantle IBM. These were counter to Johnson's wish not to mount major initiatives in the last hours of his presidency. An overt indication of the president's irritation was Clark's exclusion from his farewell luncheon with the cabinet.[36]

Neither Turner nor Zimmerman received any policy direction from Johnson or others in the White House or experienced anything that they could call true interference.[37] In fact, Zimmerman was unique among subcabinet officials in that he never met the president, although he attended several White House functions. Turner's most intimate contact with Johnson was in the preappointment interview, and that session was entirely without substantive discussion of antitrust. He did receive one directive, however. Katzenbach warned him that Johnson was likely to be testy because of newspaper stories he felt came from the antitrust division which brought internal differences over the General Electric acquisition into the open. Indeed, these stories caused Turner's appointment to be moved up to April from June, even though he would not complete his assignment at Stanford until then. After bantering with Katzenbach, Johnson suddenly turned to his new antitrust chief and said, "Mr. Turner, I want you to remember just one thing. You work for Katzenbach. If at any time you don't think you can do this, then it is time to leave."[38] In other words, as Turner interpreted the president's admonition, if differences arise, go quietly and do not take them to the newspapers.

Neither Johnson nor his aides in the White House received regular and systematic reports on antitrust matters, except for the snippets that appeared in the attorney general's own periodic chronicles of departmental affairs. The information that might pique White House interest in antitrust questions arrived in various forms and in random ways, including newspaper stories of the sort that upset Johnson prior to his appointment of Turner.

Certain associates were alert to the political implications of the antitrust division's efforts and were quick to flag problems for the president's attention. For example, Warren G. Woodward, who had worked for Johnson when he was in Congress and was now a vice president of American Airlines, sent the president an article critical of antitrust activity through Valenti. It was accompanied by a message: "The President has made simply magnificent strides in getting businessmen on his side. It would be a shame if the various agencies were to inadvertently undo all the good that has been done by being less than sensitive to the President's stated objectives."[39] In another instance, Vice President Hubert H. Humphrey forwarded an article to Califano for the president's information. It attacked some of Turner's statements on advertising. Humphrey thought that precipitation of such fearful reactions did "the President a disservice."[40] Despite such representations, Turner says that from time to time he received compliments on his speeches from Johnson indirectly, and after leaving the White House Johnson let Turner know how much he valued his service.[41]

It was not unusual for the White House to receive advance notification of important antitrust actions. Advance notification appeared to be just that, and not a request for approval or clearance. Mark Green and his associates say that Johnson "did 'clear'" the filing of two cases, implying that he was asked for and gave his approval to filing politically sensitive undertakings.[42] There is no evidence of these actions in the presidential papers.[43] Notifications documented there, in fact, did not invite an expression of presidential views. An example is the information Johnson received from Katzenbach in early March 1965 on Justice's plan to file suit in three days against the Times Mirror Company, publisher of the *Los Angeles Times*. The intent of the suit was to force divestiture of the Sun Company of San Bernardino, publisher of three papers in that city and acquired less than a year previously. Katzenbach's memorandum set forth the basis and rationale of the suit in such a way as to make a negative response extremely awkward.[44]

At times the objects of antitrust actions attempted to use the

White House to influence the Justice Department. In April 1964, for example, two White House colleagues asked Walter Jenkins for his views on a request from a firm that its case be discussed with the antitrust division. Jenkins responded, "My advice would be to tell them it is a judicial matter and one we cannot appropriately get into."[45] Despite such advice, there were benign contacts in some instances with no notable indications of enthusiasm accompanying them. In most instances for which there is a record, the ultimate disposition of the matter went against the parties making the presidential contact.

One unsuccessful supplicant was Pierre Salinger, press secretary to president John F. Kennedy and to Johnson, appointed a U.S. senator from California, then defeated when he sought election in 1964. In July 1965 he wrote Johnson for help in securing revisions in a previously negotiated consent decree involving his new employer, the National General Corporation. The president directed Lee White "to reply at once and forward to Nick K for his personal attention."[46] After telephone discussions with Salinger and White, Katzenbach responded promptly to the White House inquiry. Unfortunately for Salinger, Justice was firm in its view that there was no basis for altering the restrictions contained in the decree.[47]

Robert A. Uihlein, president of Jos. Schlitz Brewing Co., working through Eliot Janeway, an economic consultant and syndicated columnist with White House connections, was similarly frustrated in an effort in 1964 to soften Justice's resistance to his firm's purchase of a controlling interest in LaBatt's, a large Canadian brewery. The White House staff learned that "the Department of Justice feels it has an airtight case," Myer Feldman told Walter Jenkins. Furthermore, Feldman said, "If the Department . . . granted this kind of consideration to Schlitz, our very good friend, Gus Busch, would hit the ceiling. He is always claiming that we favor Schlitz anyway. He has been required to divest himself of much less objectionable interests."[48] Justice held to its position and forced Schlitz to give up on LaBatt's.

Two years later a combination of circumstances caused comment suggesting presidential influence in Justice's decision to drop one of its suits against Anheuser-Busch. Busch and a number of his executives were heavy contributors to the Democratic Party and to Johnson's own President's Club. About the time the Justice Department's decision was announced, Turner flew with the vice president and others to St. Louis to the baseball all-star game in Busch's plane.[49] A number of Republicans, noting the timing of the action and the trip, charged political favoritism. In fact, there were no White House-Justice exchanges on the suit. To justify the decision, Katzenbach and Turner opened the entire case file to Republican members of Congress. It showed disagreement on the merits of the case within the antitrust division and a sound basis for dismissal based upon changed circumstances.[50]

Other unsuccessful efforts to work through the White House involved the communications media. Paul Miller, president of Gannett Newspapers, tried unsuccessfully to see Johnson in 1967 to discuss an imminent Justice Department suit against his company over ownership of a television station in Rockford, Illinois. Marvin Watson, through whom the request was passed, told Miller, "The President does not become involved in matters of this type." Watson, nevertheless, gave Johnson the opportunity to decide for himself on a visit by Miller.[51] Although the newspaper executive was not a stranger to the White House, no meeting was held there on the antitrust problem.[52] Less than three months later Gannett agreed to sell the station.[53] Ironically, at about the same time Gannett bought the San Bernardino papers the *Los Angeles Times* had been forced to relinquish.

In the previous year a proposed merger of the *New York Herald Tribune, New York Journal American,* and *New York World Telegram* was brought to the attention of the White House. Katzenbach reported the result of Justice's investigation in April 1966. As summarized for Johnson by Jake Jacobsen, the attorney general "made it perfectly clear that he thinks this action is entirely legal."[54] A strike held up the start of the merged operations. Toward the end of the summer, however, the issue arose again. Morris B. Abram, attorney for the Democratic *New York Post,* contacted the White House to stress the negative implications of the merger for his client.[55] Although Dorothy Schiff, who owned the *Post,* was in the Oval Office for forty minutes during the late afternoon of 23 August, there is no indication that her visit resulted in any White House contact with Justice on the matter.[56] The department persisted in its view that there was no basis for action. The arrangement among the three papers ultimately collapsed, but not because of government opposition.

In another newspaper situation, labor unions striking the *San Francisco Examiner* and the *Chronicle* asked the White House for assistance. They wanted the White House to pressure the Justice Department to challenge an operating agreement between the two papers on antitrust grounds. An inquiry was made. The department's position was that any action should await the appeal of a recent lower court decision in a similar situation to the Supreme Court and resolution of the legal issues there.[57] That procedure was followed.

There was a major exception to the general lack of presidential interest in attempting to use antitrust laws for policy or political purposes in connection with wage and price stabilization, especially during 1965 and 1966.[58] In September and October 1965 polls showed public dissatisfaction with Johnson's efforts to hold down increases in the cost of living. The White House asked Justice to explore the extent to which the rise in food prices, a major source of public concern, might have resulted from illegal practices and arrangements. Katzenbach's first response, passed to the president by Califano, was that the probable culprit was lowered production. He "has not found any collusions yet, but he is moving out to examine the situation in detail," Johnson was told.[59] The president approved Califano's suggestion that Califano have "a meeting with Katzenbach and Ackley indicating your great concern over increases in the cost of living generally and in food in particular and see if we can do something about this."[60] As a follow-up, a week later Califano received, through Bureau of Budget director Charles Schultze, a list of twenty-seven price-fixing cases brought by Justice against food companies since 1961.[61] There was no subsequent action in the food area at that time.

Attention turned to other industries in 1966. In March the president received a memorandum on price patterns in the automobile industry from Gardner Ackley. Johnson approved a proposal that Ackley, Califano, and Katzenbach talk further about the structure of the industry in relation to prices and antitrust.[62] Again, no action resulted. Not long before, Turner had reported to Califano on antitrust actions underway in the steel and construction industries, other areas in which prices were rising.[63] Staff in the antitrust division later looked at clothing and concluded that there was little to suggest that price hikes were attributable to factors within the reach of antitrust laws.[64]

In mid-1966 food prices and the use of the antitrust weapon were still of interest in the White House. In August Califano passed on to Johnson a list of actions pending against bread and milk companies.[65] Soon thereafter the president pressed for further consideration of the uses of antitrust laws. While still in his bedroom on the morning of October 12, Johnson saw a *Wall Street Journal* story on an outbreak of competition among grocery chains in the Midwest that caused substantial reductions in store prices. The article implied that in many areas of the country there was an absence of real price competition in the grocery business. Jake Jacobsen had bedroom duty that morning. He phoned from there to Larry Levinson of Califano's staff with the president's directive "to call Ramsey Clark first thing and ask him to get some Grand Juries to investigate food prices in about a half-dozen big cities. Ramsey is going to be reluctant to do this and should be talked to 'sweetly!'" Also, Jacobsen specified, "the Council [CEA] should also be brought into this," and "the question of bakeries should also be looked at."[66]

By the next day a plan had formed to send a formal presidential message to Clark, then acting attorney general. John E. Robson, who worked on economic stabilization matters in the White House, was given drafting responsibilities. His statement focused on food, clothing, and other basic consumer items. Recognizing that a variety of factors affect prices, Robson had the president pledge in the draft that he "would make certain that the failure of true business competition is not among these causes, so that neither collusion nor excessive concentration of economic power results in artificially high prices."[67] The statement ended with directives to Clark "to insure that the full resources of the Justice Department will be utilized to continue the vigorous enforcement of the antitrust laws; and . . . to analyze existing legislation and advise me whether it provides adequate tools to preserve free competition in all aspects of the economy."[68]

Robson was "not sure" that his statement "is what the President had in mind," he confessed to Califano. Furthermore, along with Clark, Turner, and Ackley, he did not "think that the issuance of the statement is a good idea."[69] Several reasons were given, including the probable absence of a significant tie between price increases and economic concentration. Turner, Robson said, believed "that present anti-merger policy is about as tough as it can get without embarking on some very novel theories."[70] The suggestion of legislation in order to attack the oligopoly problem was "fine *if* the President is willing to follow it through." It would be a long and difficult struggle. Finally, such a statement probably would draw a "drastic" reaction from the business community and the stock market.[71] Apparently the negative reactions of key presidential advisers killed the message, and the generally held view that the underlying problems could not be alleviated through antitrust activity, at least in the short run, ended any serious interest in employing that device in stabilization efforts.

The peripheral stance the White House generally sought to take in regard to antitrust questions could not be easily maintained in all instances. When various parts of the government were at odds over antitrust policy and enforcement, the president and his aides were forced to be more active participants in decision-making processes.

Tug-of-Wars

> We firmly believe . . . that banking, an intensively regulated industry, should not also be burdened by traditional antitrust concepts.
>
> James J. Saxon, 10 January 1966[72]

> There is every reason to be as concerned about undue concentration in banking as there is to be concerned about undue concentration in any other industry.
>
> Nicholas deB. Katzenbach, 14 September 1965[73]

Tension between the advocates of control of economic power through market mechanisms and, on the other side, through government regulation is constant in public policy processes. It was quite pronounced in the deregulation debates of the 1970s and 1980s. Even during the Johnson presidency, the two perspectives confronted one another when attention was given to relaxing regulation in several areas. These efforts are discussed in the following chapter.

A related problem is the application of procompetition precepts and the antitrust laws to regulated activity. It may become an especially vexing one from a presidential perspective when the zeal of antitrust enforcers for competitive arrangements is set forcefully against the protective disposition of industry regulators. In the Johnson administration such struggles occurred in a number of policy arenas, including communications, energy, agriculture, transportation, and banking.

One of the distinctive features of antitrust activity during the Johnson years was the antitrust division's increased attention to competition in regulated sectors and to regulatory proceedings. In energy and agriculture the antitrust division's interest was compelled by the efforts of other agencies to diminish the effect of antitrust laws through statutory changes. The Federal Power Commission sought authority to approve and to grant antitrust immunity to pipeline company mergers and to interconnects and pooling arrangements among electric utilities. Agriculture pushed for legislation to expand production controls in tandem with price setting by agricultural producers through collective bargaining with purchasers.

Presidential aides in the White House and the Bureau of the Budget found themselves caught between deep-seated differences in points of view as they tried to work out administration positions. The conflicts between Justice and the FPC, with BOB's acquiescence, were carried over into Congress, and neither the pipeline nor the pooling bill passed.[74] Justice's reservations on giving farmers collective bargaining power were joined with those of BOB and the Council of Economic Advisers.[75] Although the principle was endorsed by the president in his 1968 farm message, no specific proposal was forwarded by the administration.[76]

Antitrust division involvement in regulatory proceedings touched several areas. The division participated in two Federal Communications Commission cases. In one, the single daily newspaper in Beaumont, Texas, sought to acquire a local television station. Justice took the position that the transfer would eliminate competition unnecessarily, and the application was withdrawn before completion of FCC processes. Much more dramatic and well publicized was the proposed merger of ITT and ABC. The commission approved the merger over the antitrust division's opposition. With some moral support at the presidential level (namely, from the Council of Economic Advisers) Justice appealed the FCC's decision.[77] But before a court had an opportunity to rule, the merger agreement was terminated by the two parties.

Clashes within the government produced by different perspectives on competition in regulated industries were most persistent and consequential in regard to bank and railroad mergers. During the 1960s fundamental and far-reaching structural changes were underway in both industries. Hundreds of bank mergers were proposed to the three regulatory agencies sharing approval authority. The Interstate Commerce Commission considered a constant stream of rail merger plans. The antitrust division looked at these mergers through the lenses of the Clayton and Sherman acts. The regulatory agencies looked at them through the lenses of their own statutes, which required that when deciding on mergers consideration be given to a variety of factors, anticompetitive effects being only one.

A key administrative problem was the extent to which the actions of Justice should reflect a coordinated governmental position in its participation in agency proceedings and subsequent appellate processes. The problem was often dealt with by ignoring it, allowing the various agencies simply to execute their responsibilities as they saw them. At times, however, there were efforts at the presidential level to develop a coherent stance. Both tendencies are evident in the treatment of bank and railroad mergers. In banking, problems were exacerbated when the discord between Justice and the regulators spilled over into Congress.

Bank Mergers

FOR: THE PRESIDENT
Attached is the bank merger bill. Justice does not believe that the bill is a wise one, but in view of the background and struggle does *not* recommend veto. I presume that you do not want . . . a signing ceremony. However, Paul Porter has requested a pen for the Lexington, Kentucky bank, which is one of the three mergers approved by the compromise.

Lee White, 19 February 1966[78]

Two days after receiving White's memorandum Johnson, without fanfare, signed the bill amending the Bank Merger Act of 1960, and a pen was quietly dispatched to Lexington with his approval.[79] Ironically, if the White House had any large interest in the particulars of this measure, it was to prevent legislative approval of mergers that the antitrust division had attacked in the courts. But the legislation did have this effect. The Lexington bank was one of three beneficiaries of the congressional reprieve. The others were combinations of the Continental-Illinois National Bank & Trust Co. and City National Bank & Trust Co. of Chicago, and the Manufacturers Trust Co. and the Hanover Bank of New York. Courts had found the Lexington and New York mergers to be contrary to law. The Chicago merger was still in litigation.

The new law had several major features.[80] One made legal these three mergers, all consummated before 17 June 1963, when the Supreme Court, in a case concerning Philadelphia banks, ruled that mergers approved by regulatory authorities under the Bank Merger Act of 1960 remained subject to attack under the Clayton and Sherman acts.[81] A related provision concerned mergers consummated between 17 June 1963 and enactment of the legislation which had not been challenged by the Justice Department. These were protected from prosecution, except under the antimonopoly provisions of the Sherman Act. The Sherman Act also remained applicable to the Lexington, Chicago, and New York combinations. Other portions of the new law attempted to clarify the ground rules for future mergers. Those which otherwise would violate section 7 of the Clayton Act and section 1 of the Sherman Act might be approved if their anticompetitive effects were clearly outweighed by the probable benefits weighed in terms of community convenience and needs. Finally, bank mergers could not be consummated for thirty days after regulatory approval. During this period the government might seek to enjoin them. If so, a merger would be stayed automatically, unless a court determined otherwise.

The events leading up to enactment of the legislation illustrate normal regulatory politics and presidential involvement therein. The policy questions were important, and there were large implications in them for the structure of the economy and for banking and related endeavors. Major divisions existed within the government. Among the principal combatants were, on one side, the antitrust division and, on the other, the bank regulators, most notably the comptroller of the currency. He was joined in his position by powerful segments of the banking industry and their congressional supporters. It might be expected, given differences within the administration, that the presidency would be drawn into a leadership role to stop parts of the government from warring against one another. That did not happen, at least not in the conventional sense of leadership. Antagonistic approaches on the part of the administrative agencies involved were tolerated both before and after the 1966 legislation.

There is no evidence of White House involvement in particular bank merger cases. During 1965 and 1966, when changes in the law were under consideration, departmental, industry, and congressional actors were dominant, although there was presidential activity on the periphery. The discussion of the 1966 legislation is illustrative in regard to two basic points about the presidency and regulation. One concerns the nature of disincentives for presidential involvement. The other is how the presidency may be pulled into the fray and the nature and effects of participation in the face of disincentives.

Intragovernmental and legislative conflicts over bank mergers were precipitated by ambiguity in existing law.[82] The Bank Merger Act of 1960 purportedly set forth the rules by which mergers would be judged, reflecting the view that special standards applied to combinations in regulated industries. This legislation arose out of uncertainties created by 1950 amendments to section 7 of the Clayton Act that barred the acquisition by a corporation of the assets of another subject to Federal Trade Commission jurisdiction if competition would be lessened substantially or if a tendency toward monopoly would result. Because banks were not under FTC control, it was assumed by many that the new provision did not apply to them. Starting in 1956 the Eisenhower administration urged Congress to extend the 1950 law to banks. Congress was reluctant to do so. But in 1960 it did pass general legislation on bank mergers. The three bank agencies were authorized to approve mergers found to be in the public interest. The legislative history was fairly clear that competitive effect was a factor to be weighed in the public interest calculus along with others, such as the financial circumstances of the banks involved and community needs. As subsequent developments showed, however, much remained unclear. Two key questions were the relative weight to be given to competitive effect and to the several other factors set forth in the law and whether mergers could be attacked in the courts as Clayton and Sherman Act violations or only on the basis of the 1960 legislation, which was somewhat more permissive.

The issues were joined in the early 1960s when regulators sanctioned a large number of mergers, many over the objections of the Justice Department. The antitrust enforcers did not accept the results passively; they went to court on the basis of the Clayton and Sherman acts. Between 1961 and mid-1965 seven approved mergers were attacked. They were a minuscule portion of the approximately seven hundred sanctioned, but the sensitive point was not the number opposed. Rather, it was the legal theories and statutory interpretations asserted by the antitrust division, which, if accepted by the courts, would make mergers more difficult than many regulators and bankers thought wise or anticipated by the law as they understood it.

In 1963, as previously noted, the Philadelphia case reached the Supreme Court and was resolved in favor of the antitrust division. Regulatory approval of a merger under the 1960 act, the court held, did not bar subsequent challenge founded on the Sherman and Clayton acts alleging undue anticompetitive effects. The following year the Lexington case was decided by the court, and again the division won.[83]

Consternation among bankers escalated to action in March 1965, when a district court ruled against the Manufacturer's Trust–Hanover merger. The two banks had gone ahead with the amalgamation, despite the suit. Within a month Senator A. Willis Robertson, chairman of the Banking and Currency Committee, introduced S. 1698, which, much changed, became the 1966 act. His proposal simply did three things: first, it saved two accomplished mergers already judged to be illegal; second, it exempted from the Sherman and Clayton acts all past bank mergers, including those still in the process of litigation; and third, it exempted from these laws all future bank mergers.

The early clashes between the Justice Department and the comptroller in the merger suits appeared to be of no concern to the White House, according to antitrust officials.[84] Robertson's bill, however, eventually forced the president and his advisers to consider the merger issue. It was brought to Johnson's attention soon after Robertson introduced it. Robert Anderson, secretary of the Treasury in the Eisenhower administration, contacted Bill Moyers to ask that the president take no position on the measure. Anderson provided a lengthy memorandum giving his reasons in full. It ended, interestingly, with reference to remarks by the Senate majority leader when the 1960 law was passed. Johnson's words at the time were that bank mergers "are now and will continue to be exempt from the antimerger provisions of Section 7 of the Clayton Act."[85] This interpretation was contrary to that now embraced by the antitrust division and seemed to be in accord with Robertson's bill.

Anderson's request prompted Moyers to ask the Bureau of the Budget, specifically Phillip S. (Sam) Hughes, who was in charge of legislative clearance, where matters stood. Hughes responded that "there has been no activity on the bill as yet, but my guess is that a consensus may be rather difficult to achieve. Justice is almost certain to oppose legislation, and I imagine the bank regulators will have mixed feelings about it."[86] He indicated that the bureau would proceed to gather agency views. Seeming to accept Anderson's contention that the Robertson bill "reinstates the original purpose of the Bank Merger Act of 1960," Moyers advised the president that he did "not believe there is anything that should or could be done at this time."[87]

When Senate hearings began a short while later, on 19 May 1965, nothing, in fact, had been done toward framing an administration position. The Federal Reserve Board chairman testified for the bill, but Justice, the comptroller, and the Federal Deposit Insurance Corporation did not appear or otherwise present their views. Robertson suggested to Senate majority leader Mike Mansfield that this was because BOB was slow in authorizing their appearances.[88]

Only after the conclusion of the hearings did a serious effort begin to construct a uniform stance. In late May Attorney General Katzenbach, Treasury secretary Fowler, and Bureau of the Budget director Gordon met "to hammer out an administration position," Jack Valenti informed Johnson, who was preparing to return a call to Senator Everett M. Dirksen, the Republican leader, on the subject.[89] Justice was against any bill, but that position was compromised in the negotiations. Hughes summarized the position agreed to at the meeting for Lee White a few weeks later. It included "provision for immunity against all further antitrust action for all mergers consummated prior to enactment of S. 1968, or as to which no antitrust suit had been filed during the proposed sixty day moratorium, *ex-*

cept for cases where antitrust suits are pending or have been adjudicated prior to the time of enactment."[90]

Justice, on balance, was the winner in the agreement. Its successful challenges to bank mergers would not be vitiated. In the future antitrust laws could still be the basis for complaints. From the antitrust perspective, the major concessions were that in the future challenges would have to come within sixty days of regulatory approval and there could be no attacks on unchallenged mergers approved by regulators before legislation was passed.

On 8 June BOB advised Justice that a measure amended along these lines "would be consistent with the Administration's objectives."[91] This was the day, however, on which the Senate committee unanimously reported Robertson's bill. One change was made in his version. An amendment offered by Senator William Proxmire removed the absolute bar to antitrust suits and allowed Justice to attack mergers within thirty days of regulatory approval. An effort failed to expunge the language that negated prior antitrust actions. Three days later the bill passed the Senate by voice vote. Up to this point in the legislative process, it should be emphasized again, the administration, the Justice Department, and two of the three regulatory agencies concerned had not been heard officially in Congress on the issues.

There was substantial ferment in bank regulation that summer. Congress was investigating several recent bank failures and also was considering amendments to the Bank Holding Company Act. Treasury secretary Fowler was trying to produce some degree of harmony among regulators through his new coordination procedures, discussed in the previous chapter. The merger issue was only one element of controversy. It flared, however, with increasing intensity as the summer progressed into fall. One factor was a new suit concerning two St. Louis banks whose merger was approved by the comptroller, then promptly attacked by Justice shortly after the Senate acted. This increased to seven the number of cases initiated by Justice that would be abrogated if the measure became law as it was now written.

During the first part of the summer the White House waffled somewhat in its approach. Not long after the Senate vote Harry McPherson expressed his concern about the approval of questionable mergers through legislation to Lee White, then the counsel to the president: "When and if the bill gets here you will have a problem advising the President on whether or not he should sign it, if this protection clause for past mergers remains. This is only to alert you to it. If you think it is bad policy, as I do, maybe we should have Henry [Wilson] check Patman to see if he will try to strike it."[92] White asked Sam Hughes of BOB for background. The response summarized the May negotiations within the administration, Senate deliberations, and prospects in the House. Hughes did not see any objections to exempting past unchallenged mergers, as Justice, Treasury, and BOB had previously agreed. He foresaw the possibility of a tradeoff between this and Proxmire's thirty-day moratorium on consummation and reasoned that it probably was more important to retain the moratorium than the opportunity to question approved mergers that as yet had not been attacked in court. He too wondered whether Wilson "should . . . work with Patman to achieve [the] Fowler-Katzenbach-Gordon compromise."[93]

Representative Wright Patman was chairman of the Banking and Currency Committee and obviously in a position to have a major say in House consideration of the Senate bill. No friend of big banks and generally considered to a supporter of the smaller "independent" banks, he had expressed opposition to protecting bank mergers from antitrust laws shortly after Robertson's bill was introduced. Not surprisingly, he was in no hurry to schedule hearings when the Senate measure reached his committee.

Around 1 July former president Dwight D. Eisenhower contacted Johnson and asked that he request Patman to hold hearings. Eisenhower was acting, McPherson told Marvin Watson, "on behalf of Gabriel Hauge, who is now with the Hanover-Manufacturers Bank in New York."[94] Hauge had served Eisenhower as a presidential aide. McPherson weighed the situation. Although he still found the portions of the bill providing antitrust exemptions to have "no basis in conscience or reason," he recommended to Watson "that in order to satisfy General Eisenhower, you call Patman and say that it would be helpful if he would try to schedule a hearing . . . sometime in the next two months. . . . We certainly don't want to be in a position, in my opinion, of pushing hard for this Hauge-Eisenhower proposal, but we can ask for a hearing."[95] After several conversations with Watson, Patman agreed to "have this hearing if it will in any way assist the President," although the chairman made clear that he still opposed the bill.[96]

Hearings before a subcommittee chaired by Patman began on 11 August and continued intermittently until late September. They were almost over before the administration's position was clarified, and even then some doubts remained. Katzenbach testified on 18 August and took a strong position against the bill, saying that because his testimony had been cleared he believed that he spoke

for the administration. The press reported his views as if that were
the case. An immediate response came from Charls Walker, executive vice president of the American Bankers Association. The next
day he wrote to Marvin Watson expressing "great shock" at reports
"that the Administration opposed the bill lock, stock, and barrel . . .
in view of my discussions with you, with Joe Fowler, Kermit Gordon, and even with the Attorney General."[97] Confusion increased
the following week when Saxon, with Fowler's authorization, dispatched his views in support of the bill in a letter to Patman.[98]

The process of clarification began on 30 August when the president asked for a report on the situation in the House.[99] He was under
some pressure from bankers who otherwise supported him to
straighten out his administration's position and not to oppose the
bill coming to a vote, and it is plausible to assume that he was concerned about the effect of his handling of the legislation on that support.[100] Walker, in his letter to Watson, indicated some of the ways
in which the bankers had been useful to Johnson. "When the President called me . . . to ask me to help get a good reception for Joe
Fowler's appointment . . . he told me that he knew of this cooperation, that the ABA had been 'perfect,' that he was grateful, and that
he hopes we would keep it up. We've tried to—on everything from
balance of payments to silver coin, from Presidential appointments
to loans on higher education."[101]

The House hearings were now in recess. Shortly before they resumed there were two important developments. Fearing that Patman intended to kill the Senate bill in his subcommittee, Representative Thomas L. Ashley, a Republican, introduced a House bill that
required courts to base decisions only on the 1960 act, permitted the
antitrust division to contest mergers within thirty days of approval
only under the 1960 law, and saved just the Manufacturers Trust–
Hanover and Lexington mergers. Eighteen other committee members introduced identical legislation. A majority was now clearly on
record in opposition to the chairman.[102]

From the other side, the White House was pressured further to
take a stance by Patman and others within the government. Both
Kenneth A. Randall of FDIC and Turner of the antitrust division
talked about the situation with Joe Califano. Katzenbach followed
Turner's visit with a letter to the president's special assistant reiterating Justice's position.[103] Califano reported these contacts to the
president and sent forward another BOB background memorandum
from Sam Hughes. Hughes noted that up to this time the various
agencies had presented their own views, but that "in the advice

given . . . we have leaned in Justice's direction." "I think this is still the proper course," he concluded, "unless the President wants to be heavily involved."[104]

Califano was persuaded that the president should become involved to "get this situation straightened out," he told Johnson.[105] There were two reasons. First, "The Administration does not look good when three different executive agencies . . . are not working towards the same objectives." Second, "I do not believe you should get tagged as allowing a bill to pass which would in effect reinstate bank mergers found to be violations of the anti-trust laws by the Supreme Court and strongly opposed by the . . . Attorney General."[106] Califano asked permission to meet with Katzenbach, Turner, Fowler, and Randall—Saxon was notably excluded—to work out a definitive position. The next day Saxon testified for the Senate bill, and the day after that Katzenbach and Fowler began negotiating their differences. Both were more moderate in their views than their subordinates. Katzenbach, for example, earlier had told McPherson in regard to the Manufacturers-Hanover merger that he did not "think we should have brought it in the first place and doesn't see how we won it."[107] In fact, as the negotiations on an administration position proceeded, the Department of Justice was working out a settlement of the antitrust case with the bank. Soon an administration position in the form of a letter from Katzenbach to Patman was before the president for his review.

Drafted by Katzenbach, revised by Fowler, then put in final form by the attorney general and cleared with Califano, the letter was presented as representing the views of Justice, Treasury, and FDIC. On the whole, it reflected Justice's position. The one dissenting note was Saxon's continued support for wiping away litigation in the seven cases, despite the willingness of his superior, Fowler, to defer to Justice on the point.

The secretary had tried without notable success, however, to shape the letter in other ways. He sought to include endorsement for review on the administrative record in certain situations as an option to *de novo* judicial proceedings. Most importantly, he sought to include language admitting that the regulatory agencies and courts had in fact employed different standards in evaluating mergers. To make such an admission would implicitly endorse statutory language requiring that appeals and judgments be based on the 1960 law.

Katzenbach's strategy in the letter was to deny that such inconsistency existed, but to recognize that some disagreed. He also asserted that the courts did consider criteria such as those spelled out in the bank merger law in deciding cases brought on the basis of the Clayton and Sherman acts. Although the attorney general saw no real problem that required correction, he did not object to new statutory language stating that agencies and courts should apply the same criteria. Given his reasoning, a general provision of this type would not bar future actions based upon the Sherman and Clayton acts. Katzenbach's major concession in the letter, one he had made all along, was to forego the opportunity to attack mergers that had not been challenged prior to the enactment of legislation. Not addressed was the question of a deadline for filing suit after a merger received regulatory approval.[108]

Califano included the letter in the president's 20 September night reading along with a memorandum strongly endorsing its content and the political wisdom of sending it. Califano feared that silence would be a signal that Johnson would go along with anything Congress chose to do. If there was something on the record, he wrote, "in the unlikely event that you would be presented with an intolerable bill, you could not be accused of failing to give notice of the Administration position. At the same time, it is the Attorney General and Secretary of the Treasury who are presenting that position, not the President himself."[109]

Johnson seemed reluctant to go even this far. His first response was to ask Califano to see him in regard to the comptroller's position.[110] Califano had not mentioned Saxon in his memorandum. The next evening Califano prepared another memorandum, once more arguing strongly for approval of the letter. He concentrated on the forgiveness issue, on which Saxon maintained an independent stance. Califano's major point was that giving in to legislative approval of mergers found to be illegal *"will subject you to severe criticism in the liberal press and in a large segment of the conservative press* [Califano's emphasis]. You would almost certainly be accused of having made some kind of private deal with Manufacturers since it is generally known that this is the bank pressing for this legislation."[111]

A little over three hours later, at 10:55 P.M., Califano wrote still another memorandum for the president's night reading, accompanied by still more information: a history of the legislation, the Senate committee report, and the Senate debate from the *Congressional Record*.

The main topic of Califano's memo, however, was a leak of Katzenbach's letter. Johnson had just learned that, although he had yet to approve it, Patman had been informed of its contents, and the president was not happy. Califano promptly canvassed the principals, who all denied that they or the few associates working with them had talked to Patman. Katzenbach thought that the antitrust division, which opposed the letter, might be the source, but the most likely possibility there denied culpability. Fowler remained convinced that the division was responsible and that the leak was intended "to get Nick not to send the letter . . . , because the Anti-Trust Division believes the letter is too weak," Califano told Johnson.[112] In conclusion, Califano reiterated his own opposition to the Senate bill and support for the Fowler-Katzenbach position. But he also provided alternatives to sending the letter as a statement of the president's position: have Katzenbach send the letter as his position; have Fowler give the substance of the letter in testimony as his position; and have the two of them lobby to get special treatment for certain mergers out of the legislation.[113]

The strategy decided upon had two parts and strongly suggests Johnson's desire to stay out of the fray, perhaps because, as Joe Barr noted some time later, he had "too many good friends on both sides of the issue."[114] The letter was sent on 24 September, but the content was not linked to the White House. Each use of the term "the Administration" was stricken from the draft.[115] What Patman received were the views of Katzenbach, in which Fowler and Randall concurred. The second part of the strategy was to play for time. When Califano sent Johnson a copy of the letter dispatched to Patman, he summarized the plan:

> If Congress adjourns without action on the legislation, Manufacturers/Hanover will complete its settlement with the Justice Department and the provision in the bill which puts you on the spot . . . will not be in the bill again next year because there will be no pressure for it. At the same time, you will become in no way involved. Katzenbach, Fowler, Barr and I believe that this can be done. If a bill is passed this year, it will almost certainly contain that provision (unless you intervene). Katzenbach, Fowler and Barr believe they can take care of occupying the Committee through the end of this session without involving the White House.[116]

First indications were that the plan might work. The negotiated settlement of the New York merger case was in sight, and chaos abounded in the House committee. A majority of members had rebelled against its strong-willed chairman and tried to force full committee consideration of the permissive merger legislation before it. On 7 October Treasury under secretary Joe Barr summarized the situation for Johnson as "a state of almost complete confusion."[117]

This augured well for delay, although there was still movement in the committee. Patman "was not particularly happy" with the content of Katzenbach's letter; nevertheless he would try to report a bill along those lines.[118] Some chance remained, however, that Ashley's bill would be reported. There was also a new complication. Patman and others were considering adding an amendment to bring all the bank regulatory agencies, including the Federal Reserve, under the audit authority of the General Accounting Office and the appropriations authority of Congress. The chairman's desire to make the FRB more accountable to Congress was fierce and long-standing. Barr was not greatly concerned about the effects on the agencies other than the Federal Reserve. An appropriations limit would restrict its abilities to conduct necessary international and domestic transactions. Equally important, "an audit of the international operations of the Federal Reserve," Barr warned the president, "would be roughly equivalent to auditing the covert activities of the CIA. The Fed operates as our agent in many of these activities and without absolute secrecy most of these operations would be doomed to failure."[119] This was another reason for caution.

Soon thereafter, serious difficulties were encountered which threatened the plan to delay and to negotiate an accommodation in the New York bank merger. On 19 October the House committee, in a meeting Patman and others claimed to be illegal, reported a bill that, though less extreme than the Senate measure, was still unacceptable to those who were against concessions to the banks. Then on 5 November a district court rejected the plan negotiated by Justice and Manufacturers Hanover Trust for the sale of forty-six branches, because of disagreement between the two sides on the meaning of language and timing. The parties were given another opportunity to resolve their differences, but it was evident that the bank still hoped for legislative relief.[120]

There was no further congressional action until early January 1966, when Katzenbach modified his position somewhat in another letter, this time to Henry S. Reuss, a senior Democrat on the House Banking and Currency Committee. Saxon countered with a strong critique, the main point being that the attorney general's proposal, instead of reversing the case law as Robertson's bill intended, would write that law into the statute.[121] He once more spelled out in detail his own legislative preferences. Coordination clearly had faltered again.

Reuss, a Patman ally, put Justice's revised proposals into an amendment to the Senate bill, and the chairman called a committee meeting for 18 January to consider it. Ashley objected on the grounds that a bill already had been reported. He was backed on his point of order by a majority of the committee.

That evening House Speaker John W. McCormack called together Patman, Ashley, and several key committee members in an effort to end the impasse. It was agreed that Ashley and Reuss would draft a compromise. They did, and the next day it was accepted overwhelmingly by the full committee with Patman joining the majority. Within a short time the bill traveled unchanged through the House and Senate to the president's desk. Although, as Lee White advised Johnson just prior to attachment of the presidential signature, Justice had reservations about the bill because the three bank mergers were saved, it had been remarkably successful in shaping the legislation to reflect its point of view.[122]

The new law, as it turned out, actually strengthened the application of antitrust laws to bank mergers. The compromise clearly established the ability of Justice to file suits based upon the Clayton and Sherman acts. It established the principle that for mergers to be approved adverse effects on competition must be clearly outweighed by community needs and convenience, clarifying the language of the 1960 law that listed anticompetitive effects as just one among a number of factors to be considered. Finally, the provision that Justice must act within thirty days of regulatory approval, accompanied by an automatic stay against consummation of a merger until litigation was concluded, proved to be an important addition to the antitrust arsenal. In practice, it allowed automatic injunctions against mergers that Justice itself could invoke simply by instituting a case. The difficulties encountered before 1966 had been most severe when banks went ahead with mergers while litigation proceeded, producing the thorny problem of separation if the judgment went against them. Now institutions wishing to merge were denied this strategic advantage, except in unusual circumstances.

It took a number of judicial decisions to make clear that the antitrust perspective had won over that of bank regulators, or at least that of the comptroller, in the legislative process.[123] In the meantime, the level of antagonism remained high and undisguised. Banks, the comptroller, and their congressional allies stoutly asserted, in the aftermath of enactment, interpretations of the law that minimized threats to mergers. Justice proclaimed contrary interpretations and asserted them not only in pending litigation but in new cases filed against mergers approved under the revised statute. As might be expected, this did not sit well with the comptroller, who branded such action initiated not long after the bill passed "a new low in antitrust enforcement."[124] Conflict, furthermore, was carried directly into the courts, with attorneys from regulatory agencies fighting antitrust division attorneys, a condition made possible by a provision in the new law allowing the bank regulators to intervene in antitrust suits. Regulatory politics persisted on the issue through other means after Congress acted, but ultimately the courts endorsed the views of the Department of Justice.

The key presidential problem in bank mergers was to promote the development of a legislative policy position to guide antitrust enforcement. In the case of the railroad industry, the issues were the government's stances in particular merger cases.

Railroad Mergers

> They haven't liked the Committee's advice, and . . . have been operating independently without even keeping the members of the Committee informed.
>> Gardner Ackley, 28 November 1966[125]

"They" were the antitrust division, the committee was the Interagency Committee on Transportation Mergers, and the complainant was chairman of the Council of Economic Advisers. Unlike bank mergers, where any coordination was on an ad hoc basis, there was a formal mechanism to employ in rail mergers. The committee, established by President Kennedy in 1962, had members from Justice, Commerce, Labor, and the Council of Economic Advisers. It functioned spasmodically as a means for settling upon a government position in important merger cases until the Department of Transportation began operations in 1967. Thereafter, positions were worked out, for the most part, in consultations between DOT and Justice.

Ackley's complaint about Justice's tendency to go it alone, lodged with Califano, came in the period between passage and implementation of the law creating DOT. It was not the first time, however, that discord had arisen within the government on railroad mergers. Nor would it be the last. These disputes tended to be of greater presidential interest than those in the bank merger field, perhaps because rail mergers were much more sensitive politically and singly they had broader economic effects. Yet again, there was considerable presidential reticence in dealing with them, even when Justice insisted upon a course of action questioned by other parts of government and the White House itself.

The source of conflict was the same as in bank mergers. The antitrust division tended to focus basically on competitive effects.

Table 3. *Major Rail Merger Cases: 1963–1969*

Justice Position Uncontested	Coordinated Position Achieved	Coordination Failure
Atlantic Coast–Seaboard	Norfolk & Western–Nickel Plate–Wabash	Penn-Central
	Western Pacific acquisition	Northern Lines
	Norfolk & Western–Chesapeake & Ohio–Baltimore & Ohio	
	Chicago & Northwestern–Chicago, Milwaukee, St. Paul & Pacific	

Other officials were inclined to take additional factors into account. The criteria spelled out by Kennedy, later elaborated by the committee, included, for example, "the realization of genuine economies" that would produce "economic, efficient, and adequate service to the public—and reduction in any public subsidies."[126] In particular, officials concerned with transportation policy were inclined to take a more positive view of mergers than the antitrust staff.

While Johnson was president, Justice participated in seven major rail merger proceedings.[127] In four instances, there were successful efforts to accommodate differences and to hold to a coordinated position that the antitrust attorneys asserted before the Interstate Commerce Commission and in the courts. In one case, Justice determined the government's position on its own without a contest. Coordination broke down in two merger cases, creating serious problems between Justice and the White House. The cases are identified in table 3.

Efforts to merge the Atlantic Coast and Seaboard lines began in 1961, before creation of the interagency committee. On its own initiative, the antitrust division opposed the merger before the ICC and held to that position until the merger was sanctioned by the Supreme Court in 1966.[128]

In two instances in which a coordinated position was developed, Justice was required to change its stance. The first shift occurred just before Johnson acceded to the presidency. When the Norfolk & Western–Nickel Plate–Wabash merger came to the ICC in 1962, the antitrust division opposed it. The following year the interagency committee concluded that the merger might have desirable consequences if conditions were specified to protect smaller lines. The division adopted this position and in mid-November 1963 asserted it before the ICC. Ultimately, the commission authorized the merger along the lines suggested by the committee and argued by the division.

A second shift was necessitated in the competition between the Santa Fe and the Southern Pacific railroads to acquire the Western Pacific. Originally, Justice opposed any acquisition. In September 1962 an ICC hearing examiner found for the Santa Fe. Subsequently, the interagency committee took a position unanimously opposed to control by the Southern Pacific, and all members but Commerce were against control by the Santa Fe. In early January 1964, because of disagreement in the committee, the White House became involved. E. Barrett Prettyman, Jr., White House liaison with the committee, set out a number of options for Myer Feldman.[129] The White House sided with Commerce, where transportation policy responsibilities were placed at the time. The Justice Department was directed to oppose control by the Southern Pacific, but to indicate to the ICC that control by the Santa Fe would not be resisted. It did so, but a year later the commission denied both applications.

During the period in 1966 when Ackley complained that Justice was ignoring the interagency committee, the Norfolk & Western–Chesapeake & Ohio–Baltimore & Ohio merger proceeding began. The Justice Department, acting independently, did not at first take a position on the merits, although it did assert that no decision should be made until the fate of several smaller lines was determined. Later on, in 1968, a common position was worked out with the Department of Transportation that basically reflected Justice's original stance. A similar accord was reached that same year on the combination of the Chicago & Northwestern and another midwestern railroad.

Coordination faltered in the Penn-Central and Northern Lines mergers. The joinder of the Pennsylvania and New York Central railroads was the most dramatic of the decade. Near the end of the Kennedy administration and not long after the merger was formally proposed the interagency committee took a position against it. This stance was then ratified in the White House. Not long after Johnson became president the heads of the two lines and labor representatives pressed strongly for a change in the government's position. One of their stops was the White House. They met with the president on 10 July 1964 and presented their case.[130] Apparently, Johnson's response was to refer them to the Justice Department. When Pennsylvania board chairman Stuart Saunders wrote a thank-you note to the president on 14 July 1964, he reported that he had seen Attorney General Robert Kennedy the previous day. "I believe Mr. Kennedy is sympathetic to our position," Saunders said. "I am, of course, hopeful that some way can be found to change the opposition of the Department of Justice."[131]

Saunders had met with Kennedy, Katzenbach (then deputy attorney general), and Orrick. Kennedy, just about to embark on his New York senatorial campaign, refused to sanction a change in position at the time. "I did tell Mr. Saunders," Kennedy recorded in a memorandum for the files, "that I would inform my successor by memorandum . . . that if the hearing examiner's recommended decision should be contrary to the Government's position and favorable to the merger and the merger applicants have by that time formulated terms for inclusion of the New Haven in the proposed Penn-Central system which are satisfactory to the New Haven's trustees and to the District Court, then unless circumstances have materially changed it would be my recommendation that the Department of Justice not continue opposition to the merger beyond that point."[132]

After Katzenbach was named acting attorney general, he indicated his agreement with Kennedy's position in a letter to Saunders.[133]

In July 1965, approximately a year after the conversations which produced Kennedy's memorandum, an ICC hearing examiner's report and recommended order approved the merger. Along with others, despite the informal commitments of Kennedy and Katzenbach, Justice filed exceptions and participated in oral argument before the commission in opposition to the merger and in support of certain conditions if the commission should approve it. After the ICC decided for the merger in April 1966, several parties, including Justice, petitioned for reconsideration to determine if the conditions specified were adequate. In September the commission agreed to further proceedings, but authorized immediate consummation of the merger if the two railroads would accept whatever modifications and conditions the regulators might subsequently require. A district court refused to stay the commission's order. On 18 October 1966, however, the Supreme Court did so and set oral argument for early January.

What position would the government take before the Supreme Court? Between the first formulation in 1963 and this point in the proceeding, Justice essentially had been on its own, although the White House was generally aware of developments, and there was some consultation with presidential aides at various stages. But, as the case neared a climax, internal dissatisfaction with Justice's orientation became more acute, precipitating serious presidential involvement.

The issues in the Penn-Central merger were many and complex, but two were fundamental from the government's point of view. The first was the wisdom of this particular option for realigning rail service in the Northeast. The second was the protection of several affected lines, especially the bankrupt New Haven, the Erie-Lackawanna, the Delaware & Hudson, and the Boston and Maine.

Basically, the antitrust division did not like the merger and preferred another approach to restructuring the northeastern railroads. Others, including the Council of Economic Advisers, had come to the conclusion that the merger made sense.[134] The division also felt that the merger should not be approved until the fate of the smaller roads was determined. The ICC had ordered the freight operations of the New Haven and, pending final approval in another proceeding, its passenger operations to be included in the merger, so that issue was on the way to resolution. Questions remained in regard to the other three roads. Should they remain separate entities to be protected by constraints placed on the Penn-Central by the commission, should they be included in the Penn-Central system, or should they be included in the new Norfolk & Western system? The last option was before the commission at the time it approved consummation of the Penn-Central merger. In contrast to the antitrust division's predilections, others in government thought that the costs of delaying consummation outweighed the likely benefits. A major reason was the New Haven. The longer the merger was delayed, the greater the possibility that this important link in the northeastern railroad system would be forced to cease operations. From a political point of view, the future of the New Haven was probably a more important factor than the merger itself, because of the intense interest of the region and its political leadership in the continuation of threatened vital services.

The issue came to the White House during Thanksgiving week of 1966 while Johnson was at the ranch recovering from throat surgery and engaged in a round of meetings on Vietnam and the budget. Justice was disposed to continue its opposition, although Turner, Califano learned, was "not rabid about it."[135] On the other side, the Council of Economic Advisers and Commerce under secretary Alan Boyd thought the government should support the ICC's order and immediate consummation.[136] Certain railroads pressed for continued opposition, while Saunders diligently pressed for withdrawal of the government's objections.[137] As Califano reported to the president, the Pennsylvania board chairman claimed "that you told him if he ran into any problems delaying the merger, to get in touch with you and you would move things along."[138] Saunders also brought to bear Kennedy's memorandum and Katzenbach's concurrence with it.

Ramsey Clark (now acting attorney general) did not consider the memorandum to be binding and, as Califano reported to Johnson, "in the absence of any indication from the White House would file recommending a remand to the ICC for further hearings."[139]

Johnson's reaction was relayed to Califano through Jake Jacobsen the day before Thanksgiving. In the president's view, he had made no promises to Saunders, but he did feel that Kennedy's memorandum constituted a commitment.[140] Califano, his assistant Larry Levinson, Gardner Ackley, and Arthur Okun of the Council of Economic Advisers began a campaign to reshape Justice's position. They were guided in this by the president's views formed in several conversations with Abe Fortas, who was then sitting on the Supreme Court. The president's first preference was no brief. If that was not possible, the brief should say that there was no need for a remand and there should be immediate consummation of the merger.[141]

The main target of Califano and his associates was Thurgood Marshall, the solicitor general, who represented the government before the Supreme Court and who would define the position to be taken there.[142] Ramsey Clark was kept informed, but there was no direct contact with the antitrust division.[143] Ackley and Okun were the emissaries to Marshall. They spent more than an hour with him on Saturday morning, 26 November, arguing that the government should simply take no position before the Supreme Court. "Marshall is obviously unhappy with the situation in which he finds himself, and would like to find a way out," Ackley told Califano. "But he is being pressed very hard in the other direction by his staff." Furthermore, Marshall considered it inconceivable that the solicitor general should not take a position in such an important case. Ackley and Okun then urged that—if a position had to be taken—it be that the merger was in the public interest, that there were adequate devices for protecting the affected railroads, and that consummation should not be delayed.[144]

Apparently it was felt that a direct approach to the antitrust division would not be productive. On the morning of the meeting with Marshall, Turner called Levinson to give his personal view: on balance there was "a strong case . . . for opposing the merger in the Supreme Court." As he informed Califano, Levinson "did not tell Don about any of the meetings or anything else that was going on here."[145]

The White House efforts at persuasion were only partially successful. Marshall's memorandum filed with the Supreme Court did not "quarrel with the merits of the . . . merger" and noted that various government agencies "believe that the merger is in the public interest and that its consummation should be promptly effected."[146] But there was no backing away from Justice's opposition to immediate consummation. As Clark informed the president, the position remained that "the merger should be delayed until the fate of three smaller railroads is decided."[147] This, as it turned out, was what the court ruled in March 1967, and the case was returned to the ICC.[148]

The antitrust division continued its interest in the Penn-Central and related mergers, especially in the conditions for protecting the smaller roads. Not long after Marshall's memorandum was filed in late 1966 the division submitted a brief to the ICC suggesting an approach somewhat different from that previously outlined by the commission.[149] Edwin Zimmerman, the number two person in the division at the time, recalls that some progress was being made in the winter and spring of 1967 in developing receptivity for its point of view, even with Boyd and the new Department of Transportation.[150]

A change occurred in mid-May 1967, when Johnson met with the New England governors at Bradley Field, not far from New Haven, Connecticut. Among those accompanying him were Ramsey Clark and William Tucker, chairman of the ICC. One of the topics of conversation was the fate of the New Haven and the Penn-Central merger. The governors feared that the New Haven would be forced to cease operations if the merger continued to be blocked. Clark is reported as saying that the governors "yelled at me" for opposing the merger.[151] In a press briefing at the end of the discussion, Connecticut governor John N. Dempsey, speaking for his colleagues, reported that they were "delighted" with the president's "grasp" of the situation.[152] Johnson, in the meeting, issued a "directive that immediate action be planned" to continue services on the New Haven.[153] He suggested that the governors come to Washington the following Thursday "to plan action programs" with administration officials to keep the railroad going until the merger could occur.[154] The president rounded off his instructions on Air Force One while returning to Washington, telling Clark in no uncertain terms that he did not want any further action by Justice that would delay the merger.[155] The department was now effectively removed as a factor in the proceeding.

Not long after the Connecticut meeting Tucker passed word to the White House that in a few days the ICC would announce further orders in the Penn-Central and inclusion cases that should speed the merger along. Watson relayed the message to the president and noted, "This is a result of your recent meeting with the New England Governors."[156] He asked for and was given permission to call the governors with the good news.

Several months later the Supreme Court had before it the ICC's decision to include the Erie-Lackawanna, the Delaware & Hudson, and the Boston and Maine in the Norfolk and Western system and, once again, to allow consummation of the Penn-Central merger and to incorporate the New Haven in it. In contrast to the year before, Justice's brief, submitted by a new solicitor, Erwin N. Griswold, took the position that, although the fate of the three railroads assigned to the Norfolk and Western remained somewhat in doubt, that was no reason to bar the Penn-Central consummation.[157] Justice could not be accused now of trying to block the merger, and by so doing placing the New Haven in further jeopardy. The court upheld the ICC's orders.[158] The way was cleared for the merger. All that remained was a final decision by the Supreme Court providing for the inclusion of the New Haven, which came in June 1970.[159]

During the hectic days of November 1966, when the Penn-Central appeal problem was thrust on the White House, Gardner Ackley advised Joe Califano, "If you don't want to spend Thanksgiving Day 1968 on emerging problems involving a merger of the Union Pacific and the Santa Fe (or some such), I suggest you see to it that the Interagency Merger Committee gets back in business. Art Okun has been reminding Alan Boyd and Harry McPherson for the past 6 months that we were heading for a Penn-Central crisis, and urging that the Committee needed to dig into it. Nothing happened."[160] Ackley's advice went for naught, and not long thereafter the crisis he predicted arose, although not on a holiday.

The railroads involved were the Great Northern, the Northern Pacific, and three of their subsidiaries: the Pacific Coast Railroad Company; the Chicago, Burlington and Quincy; and the Spokane, Portland & Seattle Railway Company. Once these comprised James J. Hill's Northern Securities empire. Not surprisingly, when their recombination was proposed in 1961 Justice opposed it. This position was taken before creation of the interagency committee and was maintained through initial disapproval by the ICC in 1966, then approval on reconsideration in November 1967. As in the Penn-Central case, conflict arose over whether Justice should carry its opposition into the courts.

The Department of Transportation thought not and so advised Justice at the conclusion of commission processes.[161] Justice was not receptive, and Transportation appealed to the White House. Its under secretary, John Robson, summarized the department's views for

Joe Califano in May 1968. Community, union, congressional, and other opposition had evaporated, and there was "no compelling *transportation* argument for or against the merger." Robson felt that the government should "maintain a position of neutrality and save its ammunition for a case where the merit of opposition is less ambiguous."[162]

Justice's views were also relayed to the White House, mainly through discussions between Clark and Larry Temple. The position advanced by Justice was that "failure to appeal here would tend to mean the Department . . . no longer intends to apply the anti-trust laws to the railroad industry."[163]

Califano put the matter on the president's desk shortly before Justice planned to act in early May 1968. This was not the first time that Johnson had concerned himself with the Northern Lines merger. Several months before, in December 1967, not long after the ICC had approved it, he studied two single-page memoranda, one outlining reasons for supporting the merger and the other reasons for opposing it.[164] The memos were prepared on different typewriters and authorship was not indicated, but they appear to be the kind of statements he might request from persons outside the government who sought his involvement and support for their positions. It is not certain what resulted from his attention. Justice's course at the time was to petition the ICC to reconsider its approval. That was denied by the commission on 11 April 1968, setting the stage for debate over appeal.

Johnson's position on whether the government should appeal was clear. He was in complete agreement with Transportation. Nevertheless, as previously indicated, he left it to Ramsey Clark to act as "his conscience" dictated. Clark's conscience told him to appeal; at eleven in the evening the day after the president stated his position a Justice Department attorney appeared at the apartment door of Chief Justice Earl Warren with a request to stay the merger.[165] Warren granted a temporary stay, later extended so that a district court could consider the case on the merits.

Several months later, as the Johnson presidency was drawing to a close, the decision of the district court upholding the merger was announced. Another furious battle erupted between Transportation and Justice over whether to appeal to the Supreme Court. Transportation secretary Boyd went directly to the president with his arguments against further opposition, and Johnson concurred. Clark insisted on an appeal. According to Temple, "The President talked to Ramsey two or three times, and he had me talk to Ramsey two or three times about it." In all the conversations, "The President said to Ramsey his position was not the same as Ramsey's. He agreed with Alan Boyd and the ICC. Ramsey with the same fervor expressed his opinion in the same characteristic independence that Ramsey had."[166] In the end, the appeal was filed, but in 1969 the Supreme Court approved the merger.[167]

Conclusions

Johnson had little impact on antitrust matters while president. Probably his most important action was the appointment of Turner to head the antitrust division on the recommendation of Katzenbach. If the probing he initiated had found ways to use antitrust enforcement in fighting inflation, the record might read somewhat differently.

Most antitrust cases, although important, have limited economic or political significance. Their ramifications are such that it would be surprising if presidents indicated an interest in them. Indeed, expressions of interest might be alarming if they raised questions about presidential motivations. Some questions about antitrust policy, however, transcend the particular cases in which they arise. Presidents clearly are justified in addressing them. During the Johnson presidency, a rough distinction along these lines was maintained. The president and his aides were concerned with only a handful of cases and always within a policy context that unquestionably justified their interest. Almost all of them were associated with bank and railroad mergers and concerned the policies that were to guide antitrust enforcement in these areas. Furthermore, there were disagreements within the government as to what those policies should be.

The debates were not about whether mergers of banks and railroads were, in general, good or bad. They were not about whether, in general, antitrust enforcement was too vigorous or too slack. Those involved in the discussions about bank mergers appeared to share the sense that from a policy perspective fewer and larger banks were probably a good thing. The basic point of contention was whether the Sherman and Clayton acts still applied and, if so, how? Whether the presidency would have been drawn into the fray if legislation had not been introduced is uncertain. The fact that it was forced the administration to develop a position. In the end, it was the comptroller of the currency versus the White House and the Justice Department, with Treasury officials somewhere in the middle. The victory went to the presidential side.

In the dispute over bank mergers, the presidential complex confronted something resembling a subgovernment or subsystem, but a sharply divided one. The comptroller, the ABA, and a substantial number of banking committee members in both houses stoutly endorsed one policy preference. Against this array were the Department of Justice, some members of Congress, the small banks, plus the presidency. The forces that might be expected to win, based upon the conventional wisdom, lost.

In regard to railroad mergers, it was Justice versus officials involved in transportation matters who, backed by presidential staff, thought that the consolidation of railroads was often desirable from a transportation policy perspective. Between 1963 and 1969 there were six mergers in which differences arose. In two instances, Justice agreed not to mount challenges. In two others, the department did not intend to challenge the mergers, but wanted to act to protect smaller lines that were affected by them. The Department of Transportation was persuaded to accept Justice's approach. The most difficult situations were the Penn-Central and the Northern Lines mergers. In the latter, the Justice Department insisted on its position over presidential opposition. In the former, presidential views prevailed. Thurgood Marshall's cooperation in altering the Supreme Court brief was the key to the situation. Johnson orchestrated this result, and it was his only decisive involvement in an antitrust case.

There were practically no vestiges of regulatory politics as they are usually conceived in the rail merger conflicts. One reason is the nature of the process that moved individual cases from administrative to judicial arenas with no real opportunity or incentives for direct congressional and interest group involvement. The exception was in the Penn-Central case, in which an interest group—the New England governors—did have a major influence in stimulating Johnson to press for a quick, final resolution.

Beyond this case, the role played by the president was minimal, although he received a great deal of information about antitrust matters. Even so, it seems that monitoring by his aides was of lesser intensity than in many of the areas of regulatory activity examined previously. Problems required their purposive attention when coordination broke down below. This was seemingly inherent in the informal relationships that linked Justice and the comptroller in antitrust policy matters. Intractable conflict was not inevitable when there was a formal system for coordination in place, as when the Interagency Committee on Transportation Mergers was functioning. When the presidency became actively involved in an antitrust problem, Johnson's White House aides basically sought to facilitate an accommodation among competing positions. Although they may have had policy preferences, their interests were less substantive than political, and their advice to the president tended to focus on the politically efficacious rather than the substantively correct.

6. Further Explorations of Policy

> Keep this away from W.H. Let Udall do this if he and Clark agree
> it is desirable.
>
> LBJ, 31 May 1967[1]

THE PRESIDENT HAD before him a policy proposal from a group of prominent business executives filtered through Joe Califano. It was for a nonprofit corporation composed of major industries to attack air pollution problems. Although there were antitrust and political difficulties to be anticipated, Califano advised approval on the merits. Johnson turned the suggestion aside and away from the White House, as he often did in regulatory matters. There were often suggestions for policy change that he eagerly accepted, however.

In Johnson's presidency, a great deal of attention was given to innovation in regulatory policy, some of which has been treated in prior chapters. This chapter focuses on formal policy reviews that anticipated the possibility of legislative action, Johnson's legislative program in regulation, and presidential-congressional interaction in setting regulatory policy.

The legislative policy agenda of the Johnson presidency was dominated by initiatives linked to the concept of the Great Society—civil rights, education, health, and economic opportunity. Yet, despite the president's reserve on the air pollution proposal, there was a regulatory component. Employing the typology of Erwin C. Hargrove and Michael Nelson, in this sphere the Johnson presidency can be characterized largely as one of both consolidation and preparation and only to a limited extent as one of achievement.[2] Much policy activity involved refining or consolidating a regulatory framework that was essentially set in the 1930s. There were, in addition, signs of preparation for major policy changes. These were of two types, proceeding in different directions. One involved a contraction of national power through deregulation. The other, more pronounced, involved the expansion of national power. Some consideration was given to enlarging the realm of economic regulation, especially to protect consumer interests. Of far more importance, the foundations were laid for the massive emergence of what later was labeled the "new" or "social" regulation aimed at enhancing public health and safety and environmental quality. In the remainder of this chapter, after examining presidential-level policy machinery, these aspects of regulatory policy in the Johnson presidency are explored.

Policy Machinery

Expand air pollution control program.

Joe Califano, 22 September 1966[3]

Califano's instructions were to Gardner Ackley, chairman of the Council of Economic Advisers. Ackley was also chairing a task force on the quality of the environment that was to work on the legislative program for 1967. When the regulatory policy initiatives associated with the Johnson presidency took the form of legislative proposals, they went through one of two basic channels of development, the congressional or the presidential. As will be seen subsequently, a fair number of proposals arose in Congress before being taken up or adopted by the president, although prior to adoption executive branch officials may have played important roles in initiating and shaping them.

There are a number of explanations for congressional activism in regulatory matters during the 1960s. Traditionally, regulation—or the resolution of regulatory issues—tends to be of special concern for members of Congress.[4] During the 1950s Democrats in Congress formulated a policy agenda, much of which was still pending when Johnson became president, that included a number of regulatory items.[5] And in the innovative and expansive climate of the 1960s there were incentives for members of Congress to play major leadership roles in advancing proposals for new or strengthened regulatory policies and programs.

Presidential policy development took place in varied contexts. Essentially it involved aides and advisers assessing ideas and attempting to work out differences. Although aware of their progress, or lack thereof, Johnson usually gave them considerable latitude as they sought to forge agreements.

A primary presidential channel for policy development was the annual process for preparation of the president's legislative program. It featured the use of task forces, some involving persons outside the

Table 4. *Major Task Forces on Regulatory Issues: 1964–1968*

| | Type of Issue | | |
Year	Economic	Consumer, Health, Safety, and Environment	Totals
1964	2	4	6
1965	3	1	4
1966	7	6	13
1967	5	4	9
1968	1	4	5
Total	18	19	37

Note: This table is informed by the list of task forces provided in Nancy Kegan Smith, "Presidential Task Force Operations during the Johnson Administration," *Presidential Studies Quarterly* 15 (Spring 1983): 320.

government and others not.[6] Task forces gathered and sifted policy ideas, many of which called for regulation, and prepared reports to the president. These were evaluated by Johnson's aides in the White House, in the Bureau of the Budget, in the Council of Economic Advisers, and in other places within the government. After a process of winnowing and sharpening in White House meetings and review by the president, proposals typically were packaged in a series of messages to Congress. Table 4 indicates the magnitude of task force activity that dealt with regulation of one type or another.

The full flavor of task force activity and its fruits will be revealed over the course of the chapter, but some initial observations are useful here. The task forces varied considerably in the scope of their work. Some, such as the health group in 1964, dealt with numerous problems in a very broad substantive area, only a few of which were defined in regulatory terms. Others had a much narrower focus, as in the case of the task force on truth-in-lending in 1966. The relatively small number of task forces concerned with the environment does not do justice to the amount of work undertaken in this area. The four task forces established in the 1965–1968 period had very comprehensive charters to develop ideas for improving environmental quality, and each covered a large number of topics. There were rather ambitious, comprehensive policy reviews by task forces on antitrust, communications, and energy regulation. Systematic attention to regulatory issues peaked in 1966 and 1967. This was in part due to the budgetary effects of the Vietnam War. As the availability of funds was restricted due to the war and to the budgetary requirements of new programs established in 1964 and 1965, interest increased in regulatory initiatives that were relatively inexpensive to implement.

In addition to the task forces, there were other important elements in the central assessment of policy and the development of initiatives. A few public commissions were employed, including one on agricultural policy that examined regulatory issues. There was also the work of the presidential staff office assigned responsibility for representing consumer interests. It must be given major credit for stimulating many of Johnson's proposals in economic, health, and safety regulation and for the four consumer messages he sent to Congress. It also played an important role in developing public support for his initiatives.

A presidential focus on the interests of consumers began to develop early in 1962 when John F. Kennedy sent the first message to Congress that dealt exclusively with consumer protection.[7] In it, he directed the Council of Economic Advisers to establish a Consumer Advisory Council, formed in July 1962. With a membership that included well-known consumer activists, its first year of life was devoted principally to gathering information and studying issues. In July 1963 Walter Heller, who then chaired the CEA, assessed the work of the council for the president: it had "scattered its shots across a wide range of topics."[8] For the most part, he continued, the members "have dealt with subjects that are of interest to the Administration and have come up with compatible statements. In a few cases, however, they have gone pretty far off the reservation and have done some mischief."[9] Heller concluded on a positive note, asserting that the council "*can*, with good leadership, grow rapidly into a political asset and a valuable addition to the workings of democratic government."[10]

Some months earlier Heller had flagged an organizational problem he thought to be of some consequence: the council was advisory to the CEA, not to the president.[11] Even as Heller's November 1963 memorandum was being written, a corrective reorganization was under consideration. It was decided to attach the council to a cabinet committee on consumer affairs and to appoint a special assistant to the president for consumer affairs to supervise the council, to chair the committee, and to provide the requisite leadership. Heller described the plan for Johnson on 12 December 1963, just a few days after he became president.[12]

The prime candidate for the special assistant position was Esther Peterson. In 1961 she moved from the Washington office of the AFL-

CIO to be assistant secretary of Labor for labor standards and director of the Women's Bureau. A longtime labor activist, while with the AFL-CIO she worked on legislative matters in the Senate. In the process, she developed a close relationship with Kennedy that led to her joining his administration. The White House initiated discussions with Peterson about the new special assistant position well before Kennedy's death. These continued after Johnson took office.[13] A major problem, he was told by Heller, was that Secretary of Labor W. Willard Wirtz did not want to lose Peterson.[14] A compromise was arranged: she would be named special assistant and would also continue as assistant secretary but drop the bureau portfolio.

On 3 January 1964 Johnson announced Peterson's White House appointment and issued Executive Order 11136.[15] It created a sub-cabinet committee, the President's Committee on Consumer Interests, to be chaired by Peterson. The Consumer Advisory Council would continue as an adjunct to the new committee. Aided by a small staff, Peterson quickly became a lively, energetic, and often controversial adjunct to the presidency.

She began to make her mark in appearances around the country and before congressional committees as she set out to raise the level of consumer awareness. Some in the administration thought she went too far and created political problems for the president. Looking back, a few years later she observed, "I became very controversial. Businessmen complained loudly to the White House."[16] In addition to Peterson's personal stances, the Consumer Advisory Council was a strong and vocal advocate of protective action and contributed to apprehension in the business community. In the latter part of 1964 Peterson's discomfort peaked. Subject to political criticism, she felt herself to be on the periphery of the presidency. There was no direct contact with Johnson, and other White House aides with access to the president, she felt, were insulating him from her and her activities because of the concerns she raised. The weight of two sets of full-time responsibilities also began to wear on her.[17]

After the first of the year Peterson took two related steps to clarify her situation. On 22 February 1965 she sent a note to Johnson asking for new directions and also asking whether he wished her to continue in both posts, in one or the other, or in neither.[18] She also proposed several ideas for organizational change to other presidential aides. Lee White asked Arthur M. Okun of the CEA to assess them. One of Peterson's ideas concerned the general role of the consumer interest apparatus. Okun told White, "Most of the . . . members of the Consumer Advisory Council are 'professional consum-

ers,' with records of leadership in consumer organizations. They
want publicity for the consumer interest and they want to lobby for
the consumer movement. . . . They want Esther Peterson to be their
ambassador in the Administration."[19] She was uncomfortable in
this role, preferring to emphasize constructive collaboration with
her colleagues in the government in addressing and developing solutions to policy problems.[20]

Months passed with no substantive response to her personal note
to Johnson or to her ideas for clarifying her role. In October Peterson
heard that consideration was being given to moving the consumer
enterprise away from the presidency. She promptly outlined her own
views on organization. Essentially they were to abolish the special
assistant position, abolish the Consumer Advisory Council, and
shift responsibility to various departments and to a new cabinet
committee.[21] By this time, however, the popularity of consumer initiatives was perceived by some in the White House as having beneficial political effects. In reporting to Califano on Peterson's scheme,
Larry E. Levinson expressed doubts about major changes "in view of
the polls and the President's role in protecting and being interested
[in consumers] in the White House—why change now?"[22] Califano's
response was, "Tell Esther to do *nothing* till she hears from us."[23]

Nothing was heard for several months. In April 1966 Peterson
again expressed the desire to return to Labor on a full-time basis.
Bill Moyers relayed her request to Johnson and argued that a new
special assistant should be named if she left. The president seemed
to favor moving responsibility to the departmental level instead. He
responded, "Talk to Wirtz & Gardner & I'd think assign responsibility to one of them."[24] For a time serious consideration was given
to moving it to the Department of Health, Education, and Welfare.[25]
Thinking changed by late January 1967, when it was anticipated
that consumer responsibilities would be placed in the new department to result from combining Labor and Commerce.[26] It was not
long before it was clear that the consolidation was dead, however.

At this point the administration elected to follow a course of modest adjustment instead of making major changes. Peterson finally
gave up her White House responsibilities. Her replacement, announced on 4 March 1967, was Betty Furness, a well-known radio
and television personality with an extensive record of public service. She and her staff waged vigorous war in behalf of consumers
for the remainder of the Johnson presidency. Soon after the appointment of Furness, on 1 May, Johnson signed an executive order that
recast the consumer effort along the lines suggested by Peterson in
1965. The President's Committee on Consumer Interests, still to be

chaired by the special assistant, was raised to cabinet level. The Consumer Advisory Council was reestablished with a more representative membership to provide advice to the president and to the committee.[27]

Policy Reviews

> We need a national communication satellite policy.
> S. Douglass Cater et al., 13 May 1967[28]

Whether in task forces concentrating on legislative program development or in the day-to-day work of the Executive Office of the President, considerations of regulatory policy issues tended to be hurried and segmented in character. The broader context of policy was often neglected, and important policy problems could be overlooked. Adjusting to the emerging communications satellite technology was one such case, as Douglass Cater and two White House colleagues pointed out to the president in 1967. Only in a few instances were there measured, systematic, and rather comprehensive assessments addressing basic questions of economic regulatory policy. Four can be identified, which concerned, in rough chronological order, energy, agriculture, communications, and antitrust.

Energy

The energy review, in truth, does not precisely fit the criteria set forth above. Instead, it consisted of a series of loosely connected exercises, but collectively they constituted a fairly comprehensive examination of several aspects of regulation. The exercises included the work of the 1964 Task Force on Natural Resources; the National Power Survey, begun in 1962 and completed in late 1964; and the 1966 Task Force on Electric Power. In general, the result was extensive assessment, but little action. As James L. Cochrane observes, energy policy in the Johnson administration was marked, overall, by confidence in the surety of future supply and by "technological optimism."[29]

The work of the Task Force on Natural Resources was informed by a Bureau of the Budget paper on policy issues. A number of the issues identified in the paper related to energy, and two of them were regulatory in nature. One was whether rural electrification cooperatives should be subject to FPC regulation, and the other had to do with the regulation of electric power entities by the commission.[30]

Chaired by a distinguished economist, Joseph C. Fisher of Resources for the Future, the task force drew membership from several universities, the Department of the Interior, and the Forest Service. It was quite restrained in its recommendations on energy regulation, basically calling for further study. A presidential commission on energy policy was suggested. Among the items indicated for attention were oil import policy, state regulation of oil production and the national role in guiding it, natural gas regulation, and FPC authority over the generation and transmission of electricity.[31]

In consideration of several of the issues it raised, the task force noted the potential value of the National Power Survey report, then in the process of publication. It contained a comprehensive study of the nation's electric power industry. The survey's main aim was to promote the efficient provision of adequate supplies of low-cost electric power. Developed with the full cooperation and participation of the industry, the exhaustive report sought to map the future of the industry to 1980. Areas of emphasis included projected demand, patterns of fuel use and supply for generation, the technology of generation, and environmental problems. Given the policy objectives driving the report, emphasis was placed on attaining greater economies of scale in production and improved coordination in allocating supply and in transmission. The report was quite weak, however, in its consideration of the regulatory policy issues bearing on attainment of the objectives it sought.[32]

The rather relaxed and contemplative attitude of the 1964 task force and the report of the National Power Survey reassured policy makers about future energy supply. The blackout in the Northeast in 1965 temporarily raised the level of concern about electric power issues. There appeared to be a direct connection between the event and the formation of the Task Force on Electric Power in 1966. It was chaired by Donald K. Hornig, special assistant to the president for science and technology, and its membership was drawn from a number of departments and agencies. Califano asked the group to consider a number of specific issues. By and large, they turned around the need to rationalize policy in order to meet future electric power needs.[33] The task force concluded that more study was needed on a number of issues, including revision of the antitrust laws to facilitate mergers and joint ventures and whether the FPC should have jurisdiction over the intrastate aspects of electric power production and supply.[34] There was one important point on which there was substantial, but not unanimous, agreement within the task force and, it seemed for a time, agreement among presidential staff members. The task force was concerned with fragmentation in the electric power industry and its implications for meeting future supply needs. An approach emerged for dealing with the problem that involved materially strengthening the regulatory authority of the FPC. In the absence of voluntary industry action, it would empower the commission to create regional utility planning councils, to compel participation in them, to require interconnections and power wheeling, and to control utility operations in various other ways.[35]

Given the very large increase in regulatory authority contemplated in the approach and its political implications, it is not surprising that White House aides felt it necessary to "put the issue to the Pres."[36] Apparently the president was not comfortable with the proposal, and it did not become part of his legislative program in either 1967 or 1968.

There had been no consequential action as a result of these exercises, although they did contribute to a growing recognition that there were important policy problems that required attention. A decision was made to institute still another study. In a message to Congress in early 1967, Johnson announced that he was directing his science adviser and the Office of Science and Technology "to sponsor a thorough study of energy resources and to engage the necessary staff to coordinate energy policy on a government-wide basis."[37] The study was just getting underway in the last year of the Johnson presidency.

Agriculture

The most important agricultural policy reviews were directly connected to the submission of comprehensive legislation to Congress in 1965 and 1968, discussed later in the chapter. There was another, however, that is worthy of note. In his 1965 message, Johnson asserted that, although the main priority in agricultural policy that year was to pass the administration's farm bill, it was necessary to consider the "needs of tomorrow." Accordingly, he asked the Congress to establish the National Commission on Food and Fiber. Its charge was "to conduct a fundamental examination of the entire agricultural policy of the United States."[38] The Congress did so, and the commission came into being on 4 November 1965.

It was a classic example of the blue ribbon study group. More than half of its thirty-four members were drawn from academia, farm organizations, and agribusiness. There was additional representation from working farmers, labor organizations, and other relevant interests. The commission had its own staff and also drew upon consultants for support. Approaching their responsibilities with considerable energy, commission members held frequent work sessions and conducted seven hearings in various parts of the country.

A final report was submitted to the president in July 1967.[39] On the whole there was general agreement on key points. One was that the core problem of U.S. agriculture was excess production capacity. Current policy on a host of particular matters was considered appropriate for the moment. Program components treated in this context included parity, price supports, deficiency payments, acreage allotments, and quotas.

Looking ahead, however, there was a consensus among the members that there should be a movement away from a regulated agricultural economy to one in which market forces played the decisive role. The members were closely divided, however, in regard to timing. A narrow majority favored keeping controls and income supports in place until the excess capacity problem was solved, although the route to solution was not mapped with precision. The minority supported adopting market-oriented policies after a brief transition and the employment of temporary income support measures to ease the traumas of change.[40] Legislative proposals in 1968 reflected the majority view.

Communications

Johnson initiated a review of communications policies, especially their international aspects, in a message to Congress on 14 August 1967. The message reflected substantial policy uncertainty within the government, largely caused by technological developments. The most significant of these was communication satellites that were revolutionizing the transmission of words and images around the world. High-capacity transistorized underseas communication cables were also a new factor.

The complexity of arrangements for dealing with communications issues compounded the uncertainty. The Federal Communications Commission had a key role to play. The Commerce, Defense, and State departments had important interests, as did the Communications Satellite Corporation. Authorized in 1962, COMSAT, as the name indicates, was charged with developing a communications satellite system with capital raised through the sale of stock—half to the public and half to communications carriers—and other securities. It was headed by a board of directors. Three members were appointed by the president, six were elected by public stockholders, and six were elected by communications carriers. The act vested supervisory authority over COMSAT's international activities in the president. Subsequently, this was delegated to the Department of State and to the director of telecommunications management in the Office of Emergency Planning. The National Aeronautics and Space Administration was directed to provide launching and other technical services. Broad authority to regulate COMSAT was given to the FCC. In 1964 the International Telecommunications Union (INTELSAT) was formed on the basis of agreement among eighteen nations to own and manage a worldwide satellite system. Henceforward, COMSAT would not own satellites; it would own a share of INTELSAT's. In fact, it was the majority owner of the international system and the manager of the system's operations.[41]

Coordination problems caused by the complex arrangements were addressed in 1962. President Kennedy created a position designated as the director of telecommunications management, although the director was also to be a special assistant to the president. The new position and associated staff were located, as just noted, in the Office of Emergency Planning. In part because of organizational location, the director of telecommunications management during Johnson's presidency, James D. O'Connell, a retired Signal Corps general, was hampered in securing the resolution of policy issues.[42] In early 1965 he sent Johnson a lengthy survey of policy problems in which he argued that only the president could overcome policy fragmentation and bring about a much needed "over-all review of policy."[43] One positive step in this direction, O'Connell asserted, would be to establish in the Executive Office of the President a new unit devoted solely to communications matters.[44] About three months later the president explicitly said no to this proposition. In doing so, he rejected the recommendations of the director of the Office of Emergency Planning, the director of the Office of Science and Technology, the director and the deputy director of the Bureau of the Budget, and Bill Moyers.[45] In the face of Johnson's reaction, O'Connell and others attempted to make do with interagency groups and informal contacts for coordinating policy.

There were other instances in which the president shied away from efforts to get him more closely involved in communications issues. For example, late in September 1966 Robert Kintner made a low-key and unsuccessful effort to persuade him to establish a task force on communications policy.[46] The underlying problem was Johnson's sensitivity about his broadcasting interests. His standoffishness is underscored by the fact that O'Connell met with him for the first and only time in July 1964 shortly after his appointment.

O'Connell reports that Kintner later explained a fundamental fact to him that shaped his relations with the president and presidential involvement in communications matters: "You were brought here . . . not to bring telecommunications issues to the President's desk but to keep them from getting there."[47]

But problems such as those presented by communications satellite technology would not go away. The COMSAT legislation passed in 1962 was not a clear statement of policy. It was a framework that required policy elaboration. Consequently, a host of nagging issues arose that contributed to overcoming Johnson's sensitivities and to his announcement of a policy review in 1967. Three will be described for illustrative purposes. One was whether there should be a single "chosen instrument" for international communications. This was the preferred approach in most countries, whereas in the United States a variety of firms competed for international business. In addition to COMSAT, they included AT&T, International Telephone and Telegraph, Radio Corporation of America, Global Communications, and Western Union International, all of which traditionally relied upon cable or radio. There was some sentiment in favor of a single instrument, and even stronger sentiment for restructuring the private carriers through mergers in order to promote the more rational and efficient provision of services. In April 1966 an interagency committee recommended to Congress that legislation be enacted permitting mergers among the carriers, subject to FCC approval based upon a rather lax public interest standard.[48]

Another issue was the meaning of the vague "authorized user" language in the COMSAT legislation. It was intended to designate who could contract with COMSAT for use of its services and facilities. Private carriers claimed that they were the sole authorized users, and thus all international communications must go through them. The government claimed that it also was an authorized user and could contract directly with COMSAT for services, bypassing the private carriers. Obviously, a large amount of business was implicated.

When the Department of Defense sought to enter into a contract with COMSAT, the FCC instituted a proceeding to resolve the dispute. It issued a tentative decision on 23 June 1966 in which the commission affirmed the view that COMSAT was primarily "a carrier's carrier," but also held that in "unique or exceptional circumstances" the corporation could provide direct services to the government. Given the substantial budgetary stakes, the White House watched the proceeding closely and received advance notice of the

FCC's tentative decision.[49] Not satisfied with it, the White House made an effort to secure a more favorable result. O'Connell got Johnson's permission to talk with Rosel Hyde, chairman of the FCC.[50] He tried for a week to work out a compromise with Hyde, but he was unable to secure a different interpretation.[51]

The third issue concerned the scope of the FCC's regulatory authority over COMSAT. It was clear that the commission had the authority to approve the acquisition of satellites by the corporation. When the 1962 legislation was enacted, it was anticipated that COMSAT would own and operate its own satellites. Complications arose with the creation of INTELSAT. Under the new arrangement, COMSAT owned no satellites; it owned a share of the consortium's satellites. And, as the managing member, it was responsible for implementing INTELSAT decisions. In January 1966 INTELSAT decided to contract for six new satellites. COMSAT went to the FCC for approval on 25 February. On 13 April INTELSAT authorized COMSAT to execute the acquisitions contract. Under the circumstances, could the corporation go forward without regulatory approval?[52] Other nations in the consortium saw the FCC's insistence on the right of approval to be improper regulation of an international body by an entity of the U.S. government. The Department of State did not think that the FCC had authority over an INTELSAT decision.[53] The FCC's position was that COMSAT violated agreed-upon procedures when it placed new satellites on the consortium's agenda prior to securing FCC approval.[54] After a time, despite its reservations, the commission gave in to the State Department and let the acquisition go forward.[55]

It took a concerted effort on the part of some of his closest aides to overcome Johnson's skittishness about addressing communications issues. On 13 May 1967 Douglass Cater, Harry McPherson, and DeVier Pierson joined in a memorandum to the president urging that work begin on a national communications satellite policy.[56] After outlining some of the persisting issues, they recommended that a special message be sent to Congress, asking it to study the ownership and operation of a domestic satellite system, proposing permissive merger legislation, and announcing the establishment of a cabinet committee on satellite policy, chaired by the Department of State, to coordinate all relevant government activities.

The president approved the concept of a message, and White House aides began to develop its content. Several weeks passed before he was satisfied with what they produced. The message, dispatched on 14 August, committed him to no particular policy action. It contained four basic elements. The first was an affirmation of the U.S. commitment to INTELSAT. The second was a specification of some major issues that required attention, including the ownership of U.S. international carriers; the best uses of the electromagnetic spectrum; the nature and operations of a domestic satellite system; and the relationships among a domestic system, COMSAT, and the international carriers. The third element was announcement of a task force to study these and related issues, and the final element was announcement of a BOB study of government organization in the communications area.[57]

Task force membership was decided upon before the message was sent. It was chaired by Under Secretary of State for Political Affairs Eugene V. Rostow. O'Connell was vice chairman. There were fourteen additional members representing all the departments and agencies of government with a substantial interest in communications matters. DeVier Pierson was to serve as liaison with the White House, and a substantial number of staff members and consultants were scheduled to play supporting roles.

The work of the task force did not flow smoothly. An early omen came three days after the message, when Rostow asked for staff space in one of the executive office buildings. The president's irritated response was: "Tell him to run State and get out of bld. assignments."[58] But its major problems were the controversial nature of satellite issues and a necessity, in the interest of completeness, to delve into a wide range of related domestic communications issues.

At various points, Johnson heard rumblings that forecast a controversial reception for the task force report. For example, in early June 1968, not long before the report was to be completed, his old friend James Rowe cautioned him, "Your Task Force on Communications Policy . . . is going to cause a lot of problems."[59] In an attached paper, he spelled out a number of positions advocated by the task force's staff that concerned him. These included forcing carriers to divest their COMSAT stock, ending the corporation's management role in INTELSAT, and prohibiting the construction of additional international cables. He also reported that the staff was considering "a radical restructuring . . . of domestic communications." Rowe characterized the staff positions as generally based upon "untested ideological concepts" and as reflecting "a purely theoretical approach."[60]

Johnson asked for a report after receiving this information from Rowe. Pierson attempted to reassure him that the staff studies were preliminary, that the task force itself would make the final decisions, that the president controlled the release of the report, and that any legislative proposals would be considered only after he left office in 1969.[61] In response, the president indicated that he wanted completion of the report deferred beyond the 14 August target date. For this and other reasons, an extension was granted in early August. When he approved it, the president told Pierson that he wanted "to talk to them before they get so deeply involved that they can't change it."[62]

The president continued to receive periodic updates from Pierson. On 18 September he was given an outline of the major topics under consideration for inclusion in the report. In Pierson's view, "The report will [not] embarrass you or cause needless friction with the industry." It "will be a plus—not an irritant," and an important factor in shaping communications policy in the future.[63] Johnson was not convinced. His response was: "Please, please take *no* action staff or otherwise until we can discuss in accordance with my previous instructions."[64]

Contrary to Pierson's assurances, the work of the task force limped to a conflicted conclusion. Two of the most troublesome topics, arguably outside the task force's charter, were the domestic telecommunications and broadcasting industries. Because of the president's concerns, in late September his aides gave serious consideration to drastic steps. Possibilities included striking the chapters on these topics or even dissolving the task force and explaining the action in terms of the inability of members to reach consensus on major issues.[65] Neither of these strong steps was taken, but language critical of concentrated economic power in domestic telecommunications and broadcasting was softened.[66]

When completed, the final report contained nine lengthy chapters on various aspects of communications policy. In regard to matters included in the president's charge, it restated the U.S. commitment to INTELSAT and provided a basis for 1969 negotiations that would establish the organization on a permanent basis. Merger of U.S. international carriers into a single entity was strongly supported. Expanded use of satellite communications for educational purposes in developing countries was recommended. On the domestic application of satellite technology, the task force opted for a pilot program to be authorized by the FCC and managed by COMSAT. The report suggested a number of ways for improving governmental performance in communications. The most important were the consolidation of responsibility for spectrum management in a single organization and establishing a strong organizational center for policy planning, both to be located in the executive branch.[67]

As to the areas that had been the subject of controversy, the chapter on the domestic telecommunications industry focused on some modest means for enlarging competition without challenging basic industry structure and the predominant position of AT&T. Increasing diversity was the basic theme of the chapter on broadcasting. Promotion of cable television was seen as the most promising route to this end.

The impact of the report was weakened in two basic ways. It came to the White House on 9 December 1968 as a new president was preparing to take office. Also, there were questions as to whose views were represented. The process of collaboration had broken down some time before; in the months when the report was put together the task force did not meet to frame the issues clearly or to resolve differences. Pierson thought that the report essentially reflected the views of Rostow and the staff.[68] Indeed, only seven of seventeen members approved the report as a whole.[69] O'Connell and the representative of the Department of Commerce objected to large portions of it. The upshot, as Pierson told the president, was that the task force "did not reach agreement on a number of fundamental issues."[70] Consequently, the report was not heralded, but was quietly forwarded to the Bureau of the Budget for inclusion in transition materials.[71]

Antitrust

Approximately a week after the communications report was filed with the White House a decision had to be made there about the disposition of another policy review by a task force. This one focused on antitrust matters. During the 1950s and 1960s there was considerable discussion among academics and some politicians of structural changes in the economy, especially the emergence of conglomerates and other evidence of growing concentrations of economic power, and their implications for antitrust policy.[72] For most of Johnson's presidency, little systematic attention was given to basic questions of antitrust policy. The bank merger legislation discussed in chapter 5 hardly qualifies. Neither does legislation passed by Congress in 1966 exempting the merger of football leagues from the antitrust laws, nor legislation it considered giving antitrust relief to failing newspapers.[73]

Ernest Goldstein, the White House aide assigned to work with regulators, was principally responsible for the creation of the task force. The idea, he told Johnson, grew out of "a series of meetings with Rand Dixon of the Federal Trade Commission and Donald Turner of the Antitrust Division."[74] Three problems were of particular concern to them: "new merger patterns . . . apparently beyond the reach of existing legislation," "bigness," and "problems arising from resale price maintenance for drugs and related problems concerning restrictive use of drug patents."[75] The president gave Goldstein the signal to move ahead.

The next step was to select task force members. Goldstein worked with Matthew Nimetz of Califano's staff. They solicited nominations from Dixon, Turner, and a number of others.[76] The first choice for chairman was Phil C. Neal, dean of the University of Chicago Law School. He was joined on the task force by a distinguished group consisting of five other professors of law, three practicing attorneys, and three economists.[77]

Early problems were encountered when Nimetz learned that Turner had not been kept fully informed as to evolving plans for the task force. The antitrust chief, he told Califano, was "rather concerned that this group is designed to conduct an inquisition of his division."[78] This was not intended, and Califano took steps to reassure Turner, consulting with him on membership and inviting his cooperation. Califano and Turner had a meeting on 31 October 1967. Notes prepared for it emphasized that the task force was to study "bigness," conglomerate mergers, and the drug industry. It was not created as a result of criticism of the antitrust division.[79]

Seriousness of purpose marked the task force's work. It met eight times between 16 December 1967 and 15 June 1968, twice for two-day sessions. Minutes indicate fairly extensive consultations with other experts, preparation of papers by members to serve as the basis for discussions, and lively and sophisticated examination of policy options.[80]

The report was completed on 5 July 1968.[81] One of the problems encountered by the task force was a dearth of empirical analyses addressing questions relevant to antitrust policy. Consequently, it called for the collection of better data. It also called for further studies of the effect of tax laws on mergers and market concentration and of the possibility of substituting competition for regulation in various areas.

Other recommendations were more substantive. One set suggested modest adjustments in the enforcement of existing policy, such as requiring advance notification of mergers, establishing a statutory time limit for attacking mergers, and limiting the duration of antitrust decrees. Three recommendations called for adjustments in existing law to enhance competition. They involved liberalizing the Robinson-Patman Act, instituting certain reforms in the licensing of patents, and repealing federal law that sanctioned resale price maintenance agreements.

The two most significant recommendations dealt with oligopolies and conglomerate mergers. From the start most members of the task force considered these to be the most important matters for examination.[82] In regard to oligopolies, or highly concentrated industries, the task force's recommendation was premised on the view that concentration inevitably depressed competitive behavior. It proposed a Concentrated Industries Act. The legislation would require the breakup of leading firms in industries deemed to be concentrated according to specified criteria. In regard to conglomerate mergers, the task force urged legislation that would prohibit large firms from acquiring a leading firm of another industry. It specified rather precise criteria for defining large and leading firms.[83]

When the White House received the Neal task force report, the presidential campaign of 1968 was well underway, and Johnson was a bystander. It was decided at that point to ask a small group of officials to review it. They were Merton J. Peck, a member of the Council of Economic Advisers; Joseph W. Bartlett, general counsel of the Department of Commerce; Edwin Zimmerman, who recently had replaced Turner as head of the antitrust division; and Nimetz.

Califano sent their views to the president on 19 December. With the exception of Bartlett, who did not like the recommendation on conglomerates, the group generally applauded the task force's work on the major items. Further, the group recommended that Johnson send the concentrated industries and conglomerate merger proposals to Congress. Califano, however, advised the president against a message and legislative recommendations. His reasons were the controversial nature of the proposals, signs of division within the administration, and the unlikelihood of swift legislative action. Instead, he suggested a number of alternative courses, one of which was to have the CEA discuss the key ideas developed by the task force in the forthcoming economic report.[84] This was the route chosen by the president, and the report did, indeed, present them.[85]

Foreshadowings of Deregulation

I will recommend heavier reliance on competition in transportation.

LBJ, 4 January 1965 [86]

In the course of policy reviews and in other contexts, officials in the Johnson administration from time to time found themselves questioning the appropriateness of economic regulation in certain areas. Their somewhat tentative explorations foreshadowed the drive for deregulation that emerged with considerable force in the 1970s.

An important first step toward serious consideration of the deregulation option came during the Kennedy presidency. In a special message to Congress on transportation in 1962, Kennedy asserted that "less federal regulation and subsidization in the long run is a prime prerequisite" of a healthy transportation system.[87] A number of specific policy changes were proposed. The most significant was to exempt the transportation of certain commodities from minimum rate regulation, a step that would benefit the railroads and, presumptively, shippers and consumers. Reform of rate regulation was debated in Congress in 1963 and 1964, but no action ensued.

Deregulation, as such, was not a project of the Johnson presidency. There was no systematic effort to consider possibilities for deregulation across a range of activities, and there are no indications that Johnson himself was aware, except in the most general terms, of the views of economists who advocated competition as a desirable alternative to regulation. Although the deregulation movement can be linked to the Johnson presidency, it cannot be said to have started there.

To the extent that there was a keeper of the modestly flickering deregulation flame in the Johnson presidency, not surprisingly it was the Council of Economic Advisers. For example, in its 1965 report, the council observed, "Even where competition is imperfectly effective, it may sometimes be preferable to tolerate the imperfections if the only alternative is complicated government regulation."[88] In the 1967 report, although generally supporting economic regulation, the council said, "Regulation . . . must not be devoted to protecting the position of particular firms or industries at the expense of economic efficiency. . . . Regulatory policy must not forego the possibilities of introducing competition when technological change makes this economically desirable."[89] Furthermore, when specific issues arose for debate within the administration, the CEA ordinarily took a pro-market stance.

Random Manifestations

Several policy actions instituted at the agency level loosened regulatory restraints, although they were clearly idiosyncratic and not parts of an overall strategy. Nevertheless, they were factors in moving deregulation toward the policy agenda. The Civil Aeronautics Board gave supplemental carriers a broader scope of operations for their charter services.[90] In the *Carterfone* decision, the FCC held that AT&T could not bar attachments to telephones it did not provide, if they did no harm to the telephone system.[91] The Securities and Exchange Commission began the process of deregulating commissions on the sales of securities. The deregulation of residual fuel oil imports and the more relaxed regulation of national banks by the comptroller of the currency in regard to chartering, branching, investments, functions performed, lending authority, and other matters have already been discussed.

A number of task forces at least contemplated the possible value of cutting back regulation in certain areas. There was some discussion of removing natural gas prices from regulatory control.[92] The task force on communications recognized the importance of market forces in stimulating innovation and efficiency. In telecommunications, it asserted as a basic premise, "Unless clearly inimical to the public interest, free market competition affords the most reliable incentives for innovation, cost reduction, and efficient resource allocation."[93] The task force went on to call for the liberalization of regulation in several areas and criticized regulatory restrictions that hampered the development of cable television. At the first meeting of the antitrust task force, Turner expressed negative views on several regulatory programs.[94] In its report, the task force called for "a review of the extent to which competition may be substituted for regulation in the regulated industries."[95]

Toward Competition among Financial Institutions

In December 1965, with no warning or consultation, the Federal Reserve board of governors, by a four to three vote, altered Regulation Q and authorized member banks to increase the interest rate they paid on time deposits from 4.5 percent to 5.5 percent. In implementing the change, banks also began to offer low denomination certificates of deposit for the first time. There were complex reasons for the board's decision, but the proximate cause was to help its banks attract funds to meet increased demands for loans. This action forced a policy response from the administration that pointed toward increased competition for deposits among financial institutions.

Previously there had been a general understanding that the interest paid for time deposits should be the same for all thrift institutions, whether they were regulated by the FRB, the FDIC, or the FHLBB, with variations allowed for differing maturities and related factors. The other regulators did not follow the FRB's example in this instance, because they did not feel their institutions could safely offer the higher rates. The savings and loans, in particular, had their funds tied up in long-term home mortgages carrying low interest rates. Soon after the FRB's decision billions of dollars began flowing toward the higher rates paid by member banks, raising fears about the basic well-being of other institutions and the availability of funds for home mortgages.

For several months the concerned regulators met on the problem, as committees of the Congress discussed it without the benefit of an administrative position. As of May 1966, Joe Barr of the Treasury Department told the president, "They have gotten nowhere." He continued, "You will never get these regulatory agencies to agree on anything."[96] Johnson approved Barr's suggestion that he, BOB, and CEA officials tackle the problem. Barr told the president a day later that he and the others would "confer with the regulatory agencies but in the final analysis tell them what we want done."[97]

There was a meeting of the group on 14 May. Barr and his colleagues considered three basic options: to lower rates across the board, to allow the savings and loans to increase their rates, and to allow a differential to be paid, higher for larger certificates than for smaller ones. Ten thousand dollars was suggested as a dividing line. The last emerged as the preferred alternative.[98]

This remained the administration's basic position until legislation was enacted in September 1966. There was an important adjustment, however. The political implications of allowing higher interest rates for some depositors was difficult for some to accept. In the end, it was decided not to make a distinction in the legislation. Rather, regulators were given the discretion to set differential rates for various types and amounts of time and savings deposits. In this context, the FHLBB, for the first time, was given discretionary authority to regulate the interest paid on demand deposits by savings and loans. Taken together, these changes went a long way toward putting into law the Council of Economic Advisers' historic preference for standby authority to regulate interest rates and, under normal conditions, letting thrifts compete for deposits. At the least, the events of 1965 and 1966 weakened the notion that all types of institutions should be required to pay uniform interest rates and advanced the notion of competition.

The 1966 legislation was to expire in one year, but it was extended in each of the remaining years of Johnson's presidency. In the process, there were other moves toward a more competitive environment. James Duesenberry of CEA suggested that the standby authority be complemented by allowing savings and loans to grow beyond their specialized role in mortgage finance into more diversified institutions.[99] In reviewing Duesenberry's suggestion, the director of the Bureau of the Budget added that consideration also might be given to eliminating the prohibition of interest payments on demand deposits in banks.[100] The CEA continued to consider how thrifts might be made more competitive with banks.[101]

In 1967 the administration supported legislation reported by the House Banking and Currency Committee that, in limited but important ways, broadened the services that savings and loans might provide. The bill also authorized federal charters for mutual savings banks. This would allow them to operate around the country, instead of just in the eighteen states that then issued such charters. Opposition from the American Bankers Association prevented further action on the bill in that session of Congress.[102] In 1968, however, a law was passed that considerably enlarged the lending authority of federal credit unions and liberalized controls over other aspects of their operations, building further on the process that began in 1966.[103]

Surface Transportation

The most serious and sustained interest in deregulation was in surface transportation. Kennedy's 1962 initiative has already been noted. The legislation he recommended was still pending in Congress in 1964 and was a part of Johnson's inheritance. Very early in that year BOB director Kermit Gordon urged the new president not to back away from it: "This is the first major test of the Administration's position that competition—the free competition of private enterprise—really works, that management decisions are better than Government second-guessing."[104] He urged Johnson to send a letter to the chairmen of the two commerce committees urging action. In the letter he sent, the president endorsed a framework that "encourages constructive competition," but the commitment to deregulation was qualified somewhat by language added in the White House.[105] A rather weak compromise between the views of those favoring minimum rate-regulation for certain commodities and those opposing it failed to clear the House Rules Committee in April 1964.

Deregulation received a strong push from an outside transportation task force working on the 1965 legislative program. One of its charges was to consider whether it was "desirable for the United States to place much greater reliance on competition and lesser reliance on regulation."[106] The task force began its work on 20 July 1964. Dominated by academic economists, it was assisted in its work by an executive secretary drawn from the staff of the Bureau of the Budget. Myer Feldman and Douglass Cater served as liaisons with the White House.

Johnson gave an early boost to the task force when he met with its members on 21 July. In the talking points prepared for his use, it was suggested he say, "Regulation must be brought up to mid-century realities."[107] The task force certainly attempted to stimulate major reform. Its report recommended radical deregulation of rates and drastic reductions in control over entry and other aspects of operating rights.[108] The president responded in positive, albeit general, terms. He called for more competition in the State of the Union address.[109] The importance of "placing greater emphasis on competition" was reiterated in his economic report, again without specifying particulars.[110]

Despite these pledges, 1965 was to pass without any concrete presidential proposals for major changes in the regulation of transportation. It was not because of lack of effort. Extensive conversations within the administration ultimately led to the conclusion that there was no warrant that year for a message on transportation. In March Clarence D. Martin, Jr., the under secretary of Commerce for transportation, gave Moyers the results of his congressional soundings. The leadership thought it impossible to pass the rate legislation still pending. Martin felt, however, that proposals for modest change in regard to such matters as rail abandonments might be considered for submission.[111] The Bureau of the Budget objected, arguing that to promote the items suggested by Martin, generally favored by the railroads, would make it difficult to get their support for more meaningful reform later on.[112]

On 12 April Lee White summarized the situation for the president: real reform, with "basic deregulation of transportation rates" at its core, must be planned carefully and systematically. "I think," he continued, "we must reconcile ourselves to the fact it will require a very serious and well coordinated effort . . . , perhaps one planned over a couple of years."[113] White suggested that Johnson meet with key officials to begin work on an initiative for 1966.

He had the meeting on 5 May. In addition to the president and White, attending were John T. Connor and Clarence Martin, the secretary and under secretary of Commerce; Nicholas Johnson, the maritime administrator; Alan Boyd, the chairman of the CAB; Arthur Okun, a member of the CEA; and Bill Moyers. Okun later recalled that the president "told Connor and Boyd that he deeply regretted that we were not following through in 1965 on the pledge of the State of the Union message to produce . . . a deregulation program. The President made it clear that he wanted a bold and imaginative program in all areas of transportation for next January."[114] According to White, Johnson, among other things, "recommended a blend of a realistic view point of what could be achieved either late this year or early next year coupled with what our needs are, looking toward the end of the century."[115]

Policy development activity accelerated in August when an inside task force on transportation was formed. It was chaired by Boyd, who now held the transportation portfolio in Commerce. One of the tasks assigned to the task force was to "develop alternative proposals to achieve greater flexibility in the regulation of transport rates, routes, operating authorities, entry and exit . . . and mergers."[116] Department of Commerce staff played a leading role in these efforts, and those interested in real deregulation were disappointed at the results. Okun's sense of the situation in September was: "They pussyfoot . . . , recommending very little to change the situation in rates and nothing at all in operating rights."[117]

Califano echoed Okun's unhappy assessment in a report to the president a bit later: the "task force's proposals are not imaginative enough and will not give you the opportunity to select a variety of alternatives." Califano went on to note that there was much that might be done "that will not cost a lot of money."[118] He volunteered to talk to the principals and ask them to develop a program around four key ideas: a new Department of Transportation, reorganization of transportation regulation functions, deregulation, and highway safety.[119] Three days later, buttressed by staff support from BOB, Califano had a meeting on the task force report in the White House. It was agreed that papers would be prepared on Califano's items, plus other topics.[120]

In early December Boyd sent Califano the fruits of Commerce's work on deregulation, which were in striking contrast to the bold and clear recommendations of the 1964 task force. The proposals went in the direction of modest liberalization and did not constitute a decisive move toward deregulation.[121] At this point the White House began to take political soundings about the acceptability of a program to revise rate regulation to give more emphasis to costs and competition and to ease operating restrictions on common carriers.

Conversations were held with representatives of the carriers. The results were mixed. According to White, the railroads were generally positive toward the rate proposals and did not object to some liberalization of the operating authorities of motor carriers and inland waterway carriers, if they received similar consideration.[122] The motor carriers, however, took the position that "there is plenty of vigorous competition in the industry today, that the United States has the most efficient transportation system in the world and that any movement to deregulate would bring a return to chaos and irresponsibility."[123] The reaction of the water carriers was largely negative, but not as strong as that of the truckers.[124]

These conversations were the high-water mark of the effort to move transportation deregulation forward. Advocates of deregulation in the administration did not give up immediately, however. In late December Okun argued the case for deregulation for White and Califano in terms of gains in efficiency and innovation.[125] But in 1965 and 1966 the arguments of economists, no matter how meritorious, could not stand against a negative political climate. The basic situation was described by a Commerce official for White sometime later. Loosening regulatory restrictions "would be very controversial. The regulated industries, particularly motor and water carriers, would fight major proposals vigorously, while supporting groups, such as shippers and railroads, would not offer sufficient strength to offset the carrier groups' opposition."[126] The transportation message that went to Congress on 2 March 1966 gave tacit recognition to the political realities in its complete silence on deregulation.

Califano, in particular, attempted to keep the deregulation idea alive. In May 1966 he and his staff unsuccessfully proposed the creation of an outside task force on transportation regulation.[127] After the Department of Transportation was in operation, he asked the secretary, Alan Boyd, for his views on major issues in regulation. Boyd's response pointed to a number of general problems, such as the lack of a regulatory philosophy that transcended the interests of the various carrier groups, as well as specific issues in rate regulation and other areas. He did not, however, endorse deregulation as a major corrective.[128] Finally, in October 1968, Califano tried a last time, again without success. His proposal for a task force to examine ways to forge "a more efficient, integrated regulatory system," presumably with deregulation as a major means, went unheeded.[129]

Policy Refinements: Labor Issues

I don't see how I can *break* guideline.

LBJ, 9 February 1966[130]

The president was in the midst of an extended and heated debate over increasing the minimum wage. He was under strong pressure to raise it more than the 3.2 percent limit on wage increases his administration was attempting to promote generally throughout the economy. At issue was a change in a regulatory system originating in the 1930s.

Johnson's administration was instrumental in the consideration of only a small number of revisions in established schemes of regulation beyond those included in its consumer protection, health and safety, and environmental initiatives.[131] The authority of the ICC was enlarged in two respects. Several measures were enacted to fine tune the authority of those who regulated financial institutions and practices in regard to agricultural commodities futures, bank holding companies, savings and loan holding companies, unsound banking practices, and securities transactions. None of these generated much controversy. There were labor issues that did, however. These fall into two categories. The first category consisted of policy changes of special interest to organized labor. They were removal of section 14(b) from the Taft-Hartley Act and the legalization of common-site picketing. The second concerned fair labor standards, especially wage and hour controls.

Union Operations

Repeal of section 14(b), which provided that collective bargaining agreements could establish a union shop unless prohibited by state law, was a prime objective of organized labor from the moment it became law in 1947. A number of states had "right-to-work" laws that, consequently, barred union shops.

The problem of common-site picketing arose when there was more than one employer located at a work site, such as a construction project. In 1949 the NLRB held that picketing one employer at a work site was, in effect, picketing all. This constituted an illegal secondary boycott, if the intent or effect of a strike and picketing against one employer was to keep out the workers of other employers. The board's interpretation was upheld by the Supreme Court in 1951.[132] Reversal was of special importance to the building trades unions, and in this they were supported by the Eisenhower and Kennedy administrations.

Both section 14(b) and common-site picketing were politically sensitive issues. Liberal Democrats usually sided with labor on them, but conservatives of both major parties did not. In Johnson's presidency, the commitment to change was strongest on right-to-work. After his election in 1964, a repeal effort was initiated. Not surprisingly, within executive policy circles, its main advocate was the Department of Labor.[133] The Council of Economic Advisers did not have strong views, because, as its chairman told Bill Moyers, "The economic impact appears to be small, and it is mainly a political issue."[134] Repeal presented no problems for the Bureau of the Budget.[135]

With the concurrence of his advisers, Johnson announced to Congress that he supported repeal in his 1965 State of the Union message.[136] His position was reiterated four months later in a special message to Congress on labor matters.[137] After an acrimonious debate, the House of Representatives passed a repeal measure by a narrow margin of 221-203 on 28 July. In the Senate, a filibuster led by the Republican leader, Everett M. Dirksen, prevented a vote. In February 1966 another effort was made to secure Senate approval, but once again a filibuster prevailed.[138]

Not long afterward the president reflected on the repeal effort in a speech, saying, "I did my best to pass that bill in the House. We passed it by a few votes. I talked to 61 Senators that I thought we could influence . . . , and most of them were ready to support the measure. But there was a group that did not favor it. We will have to try again, and try again we will."[139] That proved to be a hollow promise; section 14(b) repeal languished for the remainder of Johnson's presidency. The main reason was that many Democrats in the House, having voted once in favor of repeal at some political cost to them, did not want to do so again, since passage in the Senate remained highly unlikely.

Failure to secure repeal of section 14(b) had an important bearing on the common-site picketing issue. Secretary of Labor Wirtz attempted without success to have the administration's position in support of removing the restriction included in the president's labor message in 1965.[140] Later, however, a bill pending in Congress to this effect was endorsed. Although reported by a House committee, the legislation stalled in the Rules Committee as the session ended. Another effort to clear the committee failed in early 1966. Shortly afterward Henry Wilson reported to Johnson that a number of freshmen Democrats feared being wounded by voting on the bill as a result of their section 14(b) experiences.[141] Furthermore, "other Members from labor districts will vote against it because of the animosity of certain other labor people toward the construction unions."[142] A week later Wirtz advised the president that AFL-CIO president George Meany probably realized that a common-site picketing bill could not be enacted and that "House *liberals* are urging *privately* that it not be pushed."[143] Although a bill was reported once more in the House in 1967, it again failed to advance beyond the Rules Committee. The committee was unwilling to move until the Senate acted, and the legislation was comatose there.

Organized labor's interests in the repeal of section 14(b) and resolution of the common-site picketing issue were real, but qualified by recognition of the political realities. The administration's support was based more on the important place of unions in the Democratic coalition than on real, substantive commitment. In the case of the minimum wage level and related issues, the interests of labor and the administration were more substantial, but they were not identical by any means. Labor was committed to securing the most generous revision in the Fair Labor Standards Act that it could manage. Johnson and his aides, although clearly in support of changes, had to temper their support in light of economic circumstances and the objectives of economic policy.

Fair Labor Standards

Revision of the law was one of the main accomplishments of the Kennedy administration in 1961. Congress increased the minimum wage from $1.00 to $1.25 per hour and, for the first time since 1938, extended the law's wage provisions to bring in an additional 3.6 million workers and enlarged coverage under the law's various restrictions on working conditions.[144] Still, approximately 17 million workers remained unprotected by the minimum wage requirement.

When Johnson became president in late 1963, changes in the law were again under consideration. From then until the Fair Labor Standards Act was reformulated in 1966, there was division within the administration on several related issues: the timing and the magnitude of minimum wage increases, the nature of the penalty to be applied to overtime work, and the extent of any expansion of coverage. The Department of Labor pushed for relatively generous changes. The Council of Economic Advisers, the Bureau of the Budget, and the Department of Commerce were more cautious.

Initial sparring extended from early December 1963 to late January 1964. On 7 December a presidential task force chaired by the CEA reported agreement on an extension of coverage, but irresolution on a number of other policy questions.[145] Less than a week later Labor provided its views. The department favored increasing the minimum wage to $1.50 and increasing the overtime penalty. Organized labor was then advocating a 35-hour work week as a means for increasing the number of jobs. Raising the overtime penalty was Labor's response.[146] The basic reactions of the CEA and the BOB were negative, arguing that the department's "proposals are objectionable because they would raise costs and prices in a year of increased inflationary danger when we must redouble our guard against rising prices."[147] The department responded with a revised industry-by-industry approach to overtime, but this failed to gain any converts among the president's other advisers.[148]

Johnson announced his decisions in his State of the Union address. He supported extending minimum wage coverage to an additional 2 million workers.[149] He also endorsed Labor's cumbersome industry-by-industry overtime penalty scheme. In the process, he explicitly rejected the idea of a 35-hour work week.[150] The two proposals were considered at the committee level in the House but not in the Senate, and the bills containing them died at the end of the session.

The conflicts of 1963 and 1964 were replayed in 1965, albeit in somewhat different terms. The president, in his State of the Union address, repeated his stance of the previous year on the extension of coverage.[151] Serious work on preparing a legislative proposal did not start until several weeks later, however. In mid-February, after several policy meetings in Bill Moyers's office, the Department of Labor proposed a rather ambitious undertaking. Its major components were to raise the minimum wage, effective September 1966, to $1.50 per hour (as opposed to organized labor's $2.00 proposal); to extend coverage to all of those constitutionally eligible, bringing an additional 13 million workers under the act's coverage; and to progressively increase the overtime penalty for large manufacturers.[152] Johnson was not persuaded, and he told Moyers that he did not want legislation prepared along those lines.[153]

Other reservations were entered almost immediately. Both the CEA and the bureau were firm in their opposition to raising the minimum wage to $1.50 at that time.[154] While sympathetic to extending coverage, both were dubious about the magnitude of Labor's proposal.[155] In addition, the council was uncomfortable with the overtime recommendation.[156]

After extensive analysis and discussion, an administration position began to emerge at about the time the president was scheduled to meet with union leaders on 9 March. Its essentials were to increase coverage by 4.6 million and to hold the minimum wage at the current level. There was agreement on double time for overtime after 48 hours, but not on Labor's plan to reduce the figure to 42 hours in four years.[157]

In a message to Congress on 18 May, the president asked for inclusion of an additional 4.5 million workers. The message was vague on the double time issue, indicating it would affect only some work, which was not specified. On the minimum wage, the president affirmed that the level should not be static. After asking Congress to consider carefully the economic effects of any proposed increase, he observed, "I do not think the time for change . . . has come."[158]

That view was not entirely persuasive with members of Congress, especially James Roosevelt, chairman of the subcommittee of the House Committee on Education and Labor with jurisdiction over labor standards. Rumored to be anticipating a race for statewide office in California, he produced a bill far more generous in some respects than the administration's proposal. The measure reported by his subcommittee in early August raised the minimum wage from $1.25 to $1.75 on 1 July 1968, extended coverage to 1.5 million more workers than suggested by the president, but did nothing on overtime. The CEA did not mince words in its evaluation of the bill. Overall, "the economy can ill afford to pay for Congressman Roosevelt's bill."[159] The bill reported by the full committee retained the $1.75 figure and increased coverage still more. For a variety of reasons, including the administration's reservations, the bill was not taken to the floor that session.

In the meantime, Johnson promised Walter Reuther, president of the auto workers, that in the following year, 1966, "amendment of the Fair Labor Standards Act must be given high priority." He instructed Joe Califano to see to the development of "a realistic bill . . . consistent with . . . guidelines for wage-price stability."[160]

Following the president's instruction, by mid-December 1965 some basic agreements had been reached within the administration. The most important was to raise the minimum wage to $1.40 and then to $1.60. There were differences on an implementation schedule. Wirtz favored making the first increase effective on 1 September 1966 and the second a year later. Gardner Ackley of the CEA and Secretary of Commerce John T. Connor argued for a more gradual approach, starting with $1.40 in 1966, moving to $1.50 in 1968, and to $1.60 in 1970.[161] Differences had not been resolved when the president delivered his State of the Union address and sent his economic message, and he made only brief and vague references to labor standards in them.[162]

The situation was somewhat different in Congress in 1966. Prospects for an accommodation were enhanced by Roosevelt's resignation and his replacement as subcommittee chairman by a more cooperative member. But the economic context was somewhat less favorable, particularly because of increasing inflationary pressures. The administration's wage guidepost, set at 3.2 percent, was under attack from a variety of quarters, including organized labor. Yet the administration remained stalwart in its commitment to the standard.[163]

Debate within the administration continued through February and into March. The main sticking point was contriving a schedule of increases that could be defended in terms of the guidepost, although any option would breach it to some degree.[164] Resolutions began to emerge on 11 February. Connor, Ackley, and Wirtz met in the office of Califano, who told them that Johnson wanted a unanimous recommendation. Under this pressure, Wirtz and Ackley compromised on $1.40 in September 1966 and $1.60 in September 1968.[165] Connor remained a holdout.[166] Wirtz immediately informed George Meany of the agreement. Meany, Wirtz told the president, seemed to accept the result, but the labor chieftain indicated that some of his colleagues would be unhappy.[167] Principal figures in Congress also expressed favorable reactions.[168]

Just a few days later, however, the AFL-CIO informed the White House that it would fight for $1.60 in 1967.[169] This precipitated a search for a new compromise. One which Johnson seemed to like for a time was for $1.40 in September 1966, $1.50 in September 1967, and $1.60 in September 1968.[170] Publicly, however, the administration continued to stand by the 1966–1968 schedule.[171] Next the CEA devised a new proposal that it was comfortable with and could defend in terms of the guidepost: $1.40 in February 1967 and $1.60 in February 1968.[172] The president received this proposal from Ackley on 8 March. That afternoon he met with Meany in the White House for an hour and fifteen minutes.[173] Shortly afterward labor grudgingly accepted the council's plan; after some difficulties were overcome Congress did so as well. It also extended coverage to an additional 9.1 million workers, including, for the first time, some agricultural workers.

Policy Extensions: Agriculture

> I was very reluctant to do it. I very hesitatingly, haltingly and grudgingly put my signature on it. I didn't want to sign it.
>
> LBJ, 14 October 1968[174]

The president was commenting on his recent approval of a one-year extension of basic agricultural legislation. The action in 1968 followed a controversial extension and revision initiative in 1965. Johnson's remarks to the cabinet on his feelings in 1968 are indicative of the discomfort he typically seemed to experience when dealing with agricultural policy issues. Dissatisfaction with established policy may partially explain his endorsement of one of the most radical ideas seriously considered by his administration for extending economic regulation: to empower agricultural producers—farmers—to organize and bargain collectively under national regulatory authority with the processors who bought their products. Essentially an extension of the agricultural cooperative idea, long established in federal law, and in some versions an adaptation of methods for regulating labor-management relations, the concept of collective bargaining in agriculture was not entirely new. However, it had not been strongly advanced previously as a national policy option.[175]

Bargaining Power for Farmers

A proposal for enhancing the bargaining power of farmers was brought to the White House by Secretary of Agriculture Orville Freeman in 1967.[176] The problem of the prices paid to farmers and the bargaining option were dramatized earlier in the year by the National Farmers Organization (NFO). The NFO, formed in 1955, had at the core of its strategy securing better prices for farmers through bargaining. When bargaining failed, it advocated withholding commodities from the market as the farmer's version of the strike.[177] The organization and its ideas gained national prominence when, in mid-March 1967, it instituted a coordinated fifteen-day milk withholding action in twenty-five states.[178]

During the remainder of 1967 unrest in agricultural areas grew as farm prices dropped and the cost of production increased. Early in August several thousand farmers gathered in Des Moines, Iowa, to discuss withholding as a means for pushing commodity prices up. On 18 August Johnson was asked at a news conference for his reaction. In the course of his response, the president said, "I think that this Government should give very serious consideration to evolving some kind of a program that will give the farmer an equity of fairness on the same basis for bargaining for . . . prices . . . as we have for the workers bargaining for . . . wages."[179] A week later Freeman had a draft bill ready for consideration.

The bargaining option presented complex problems. For several months various views and approaches were debated within the administration. Freeman's position was supported by the December report of an outside presidential task force that included a number of agricultural economists.[180] But he faced staunch opposition. The reaction of the Council of Economic Advisers was immediate and extremely negative. Its chairman, Gardner Ackley, the president was told, was "violently opposed."[181] Freeman's proposal, which covered livestock, poultry, fruits, and vegetables, was, he felt, "not collective bargaining but government-aided cartellization of agriculture. If it is effective, it may raise farm incomes, but it creates many other problems—as cartels always do."[182]

Despite these reservations, Johnson promised in his 1968 State of the Union address "to recommend programs to help farmers bargain more effectively for fair prices."[183] At this time, 17 January, administration officials were still trying to develop a coherent set of proposals. The Department of Agriculture was advocating a rather complex set of arrangements that combined elements of a labor-management relations model and the marketing order system. During the preparation of the address several aides involved expressed skepticism about the substantive and political value of the bargaining concept.[184] Nevertheless, the effort to find an acceptable formula continued.

Early in January the Bureau of the Budget circulated a draft bill, and early in February there were White House meetings. The antitrust division was opposed to legislation.[185] The CEA and the BOB did not oppose some aspects, but they were doubtful that the mechanisms proposed would have the desired effects or would draw broad support from the agricultural community. In addition, the two agencies strongly opposed a key element, production controls in connection with marketing orders, because they would push up consumer prices. Agriculture argued that production controls were the key to increasing the income of farmers.[186] The conflict between policy objectives was stark.

That was one reason why officials in the administration generally agreed that a collective bargaining bill should not accompany the president's forthcoming farm message. But there still was disagreement on the strength of the message's statement on bargaining. Freeman and Vice President Humphrey wanted a strong endorsement, DeVier Pierson reported to Johnson. However, "Budget Bureau, CEA and Justice . . . fear that a strong statement . . . will force us to support production controls. . . . So they would rather soft-pedal it in the message."[187] Pierson and Califano felt that "the passage of any legislation in the area is extremely unlikely. Consequently, we are more concerned with tactical handling of the issue rather than the merits of implementing the program."[188] Their view was that not expressing strong support would be bad politics, despite the bleak prospects for any proposal passing. Johnson accepted their recommendation that bargaining be supported in the message and that congressional hearings be encouraged. In the meantime, efforts would continue to resolve conflicts within the administration. There were hearings, but no administration proposal was forthcoming. The idea of dramatically enhancing the bargaining power of farmers slowly expired as the 1968 session of Congress drew to a close, leaving the regulation of agricultural production and prices still set in the framework of the 1930s.

This is not to suggest an absence of policy flux. The Democratic Party came to power in 1961 against a backdrop of considerable dissatisfaction with the agricultural policies of the Eisenhower administration. However, the Kennedy plans for tighter restrictions on production and marketing, together with more generous income support, encountered considerable resistance in Congress.[189] The task of policy reformation carried over into Johnson's presidency.

Basic Legislation

Despite some internal disagreements on several points, the Johnson administration was fairly consistent in its approach to basic agricultural policy, the flirtation with collective bargaining notwithstanding. One strong policy theme enthusiastically promoted by the Department of Agriculture was generally strengthening rural communities and their economies through the development and conservation of human and material resources.[190] The department created or redirected a wide array of nonregulatory programs toward these ends as Freeman and his colleagues struggled against the dominant urban concerns that permeated thinking within the Johnson presidency. In regard to commodities, there were several major objectives, including expanding markets for agricultural products in the United States and abroad, limiting production, raising farm income with a special emphasis on less affluent producers, and minimizing the costs of commodity programs to the Treasury.[191] General agreement on major points, however, masked clashing views on particulars.

Differences were worked out in the process of preparing commodity legislation. In general terms, it was a simple one. Proposals were devised by the Department of Agriculture, then subjected to intensive review at the presidential level. One characteristic of the process was that the president, although kept fully informed, was usually not an enthusiastic participant. Johnson's aloofness was a

source of considerable frustration for Freeman, who says, "I was operating with great uncertainties and very little assurance as to what
his real position was."[192] He suspected that Johnson had some basic
reservations about the programs due to the influence of conservative
Texas agricultural interests. In fact, Freeman considered resigning
several times in 1964, because he "found it very difficult to get any
feeling of where it [policy] was going."[193]

Another characteristic of the process was conflict between departmental and presidential perspectives on desirable program features.
DeVier Pierson explains the situation in this way: "There was always a good deal of disagreement between the Department and Budget Bureau and the Council of Economic Advisers. . . . The Budget
Bureau and CEA have a historic bias against the programs on the
basis that they're inefficient subsidies, and the President was very
torn by his economic advisers on one hand and Secretary Freeman,
usually joined by the Vice President, on the other hand."[194] According to Arthur Okun of CEA, there was "a constant battle going on
between the Budget Bureau and the Council on the one hand, and
Agriculture on the other."[195] This conflict may explain some of
Johnson's sensitivity in agricultural matters. In any case, the task of
mediating between the differing points of view was one of Pierson's
major responsibilities.

Both 1964 and 1965 were busy times for policy makers, although
legislative aims were less ambitious in the former year than in the
latter. Several recommendations were sent to Congress in 1964. Not
all of them were enacted, but two that passed addressed the most
critical problems of the moment. One was cotton, where there were
high support prices, overproduction, and massive carryover stocks
held by the Commodity Credit Corporation. The legislation gave
subsidies to U.S. textile mills for the purchase of domestic cotton.
Growers also were provided incentives to limit production voluntarily. The other problem was wheat, where the support price was
scheduled to drop from $2.00 to $1.25 per bushel as a result of the
rejection of mandatory production controls in a 1963 referendum.
The legislation avoided the decrease by a combination of voluntary
production limits, price supports, and certificates purchased from
producers by processors.[196] Johnson signed a bill covering cotton and
wheat on 11 April 1964.[197]

Two months later planning was underway for 1965, when several
legislative authorities would expire. It continued through the 1964
campaign. While on the hustings, Johnson spoke rarely and then
quite generally about agricultural issues. He made just one speech

devoted to agriculture, in which he said little about what farmers could expect from him, but placed great emphasis on what he characterized as a Republican promise to end commodity programs.[198]

The culmination of policy planning and legislative activity came in November 1965, when the president signed the Food and Agriculture Act of 1965.[199] Several commodity programs were reworked: cotton, wheat, feed grains, rice, wool, and milk. A cropland adjustment program sought by the administration was also included. It encouraged the long-term retirement of land from production.

In the process of formulating the legislation, some attention was given to basic options. Mandatory production controls cast in terms of quantities were viewed with considerable sympathy by some within the administration. They were thought to be more effective in holding down production and less expensive. At the same time, it was recognized that this approach was not feasible politically; it would not be accepted by the agricultural community and the congressional elders on the agricultural committees whose backing for any farm legislation was crucial and not easily obtained. Some time later Freeman observed that on the House committee, "The senior members [are] often irascible and more often than not against the Administration."[200] The major alternative was "buying out" production of major commodities through the voluntary acceptance of price supports, acreage limits, and diversion payments for planting less than acreage allotments. Despite the fiscal apprehension of BOB and CEA, they did not offer serious opposition, and this approach was selected for most commodity programs.[201]

In late January 1965 departmental officials and presidential staff reached agreement on basic program outlines, and a decision was made to seek the extension of existing programs with some modifications aimed at smoothing their operations and lowering costs.[202] A presidential message to Congress on 4 February set forth the administration's proposals in general terms.[203] Draft legislation followed approximately two months later. Several policy disagreements plagued decision makers in the period between the message and submission of legislation. Some were resolved through negotiations between the department and presidential staff, but others required the president to act.

One major point of disagreement was over the duration of the program extensions. Agriculture pressed forcefully for four years, whereas BOB and CEA officials argued in favor of one or, at the most, two years. They also wanted graduated price supports applied beyond cotton, where they had been introduced in 1964, to other commodities in order to give a special boost to low-income farmers. They strongly opposed Agriculture's plans for a strategic food reserve that would not be charged to its budget. CEA fought a proposal pushed by the vice president to increase the prices of commodities sold by the Commodity Credit Corporation. It also sought a reduction in Agriculture's proposed certificate price for wheat. Although the lower figure endorsed by CEA would increase the program's cost, it would put less pressure on the consumer price index. Johnson sided with his presidential aides on these issues, except for the certificate price of wheat.[204]

Cotton presented especially difficult problems. Freeman outlined two major options for the president early in March. One was to extend the existing program, and the other was to adopt the approach taken in the Humphrey-Talmadge bill. This bill, developed in Congress the previous year, set price supports at the world market level, then supplemented producer income through direct payments. It replaced the allotment then in force with a lesser allotment expected to yield 13 million bales and provided incentives for the voluntary retirement of substantial cotton acreage.[205] Freeman wanted to "go forward firmly and strongly with the Humphrey-Talmadge approach."[206] He was joined in this position by the vice president, the BOB, and the CEA.[207] Strong opposition to direct payments was likely, the secretary noted. In the Senate, Allan J. Ellender who chaired the Committee on Agriculture, was "cool" toward Humphrey-Talmadge, and another influential committee member, James O. Eastland, was "violently opposed."[208] Nevertheless, the secretary felt that his proposal could be pushed through if "the President gives it his definite, clear and vigorous support."[209] The next day Johnson decided that he did not like the prospects depicted by Freeman and indicated his preference for extending the cotton program then in place.[210]

Notwithstanding the president's reaction, Freeman continued to push for major revisions along the lines of Humphrey-Talmadge. Johnson expressed his irritation to Moyers on 27 March: "Bill—I've spent hours talking but never doing. I suggest get all Cong & Sen interested in House & Sen Com rooms & discuss various proposals & get agreement. Until Freeman et al. do this I'm wasting my time. Tell him so."[211] That same day he also indicated to Moyers that he did not want to act "until agreement can be produced by cotton leaders," despite new information that there was substantial support in Congress for Humphrey-Talmadge.[212]

The situation remained essentially unchanged for the next three months. Freeman, under pressure from Johnson and aided by the vice president and Buford Ellington, former governor of Tennessee and now director of the Office of Emergency Planning, engaged in extensive and wide-ranging negotiations on cotton in an effort to forge an accommodation among the various interests. Meanwhile, the president was largely unresponsive to the secretary's frequent entreaties that he become actively involved in the effort.[213] Finally, around the middle of June, a complex compromise was framed that combined elements of several approaches.[214] It was agreed to by presidential aides, accepted by Johnson, and worked into the farm bill when it was under consideration by the House committee.[215]

Even after this hurdle was overcome, the comprehensive bill's course to final passage was a difficult one. Regional conflicts broke out on the cotton provisions. As some had foreseen earlier, the wheat proposal, especially the certificate arrangements, stimulated accusations that the administration was attempting to impose a "bread tax."[216] Changes sponsored by members of Congress threatened to increase program costs dramatically.[217] Freeman and Johnson's other agents regularly sent detailed reports to him on their trials and tribulations. The secretary, in particular, continued to implore him to express public support for the administration's legislative package, but with no success.[218]

Despite Johnson's low profile, legislation eventually was passed. It generally conformed to the administration's recommendations, although there were departures on specifics. The programs were extended for four instead of two years, and their costs rose as a result of adjustments made by Congress. Passage of an unacceptable cotton program was narrowly averted on the Senate floor. Ellender's committee reported a version that appalled administration officials. In a dramatic move, Senator Herman Talmadge succeeded in amending the bill, replacing the committee language with cotton provisions preferred by Johnson's advisers.[219]

The basic agricultural policy framework as revised in 1965 carried through to the conclusion of Johnson's presidency. The legislation passed that year was due to expire in 1969. There was an internal debate as to whether to act in 1968 or to wait until after the election.[220] The proponents of action won, and in 1968 Congress was asked to extend the major commodity programs indefinitely, to create a strategic grain reserve, and to empower farmers to bargain collectively on prices.[221] Falling grain prices had led the administration to support the reserve concept in 1966 and 1967. In 1968 it was considered to be a short-term device to safeguard against low grain prices in an election year. BOB and CEA were very much against it. As reported previously, they also had reservations about the bargaining proposal.[222] The reserve proposal received about the same level of attention in Congress as the bargaining proposal and met the same fate.

The politics surrounding extension of the commodity programs were, as usual, complex and intense. Republicans pushed for a limited extension that would force a reexamination of policy when a new administration took office. Their hand was strengthened by extensive publicity given to the large subsidy payments received by some agricultural enterprises. They gathered sufficient support to add an amendment on the House floor that capped the amount a producer could be paid. Freeman was convinced that support for the bill as a whole would evaporate if this provision were not removed. A compromise was reached in which the limit was dropped and the commodity programs were extended for one year without change.[223]

The president was quite disturbed at the outcome. He did not sign the legislation until the last hour of the last day, and whether he would sign was very much in doubt until that moment. Returning from a visit to former president Harry S Truman in Missouri, he called Pierson from Air Force One on the evening of 11 October to say he was vetoing. Minutes later he called back to say that he had changed his mind and signed.[224] The source of the temptation to veto is not clear. One view is that Johnson was simply put off by the rejection of an indefinite extension. His real concern may be somewhat more substantive than that. Three days after the legislation became law, on 14 October, it was Agriculture's turn to provide Johnson with a cabinet review of the department's achievements during his presidency. As Freeman was speaking, the president broke in to comment on the signing. Although he wanted to veto, he was "worn down" by pressure from Freeman, the vice president, and others to give his approval.[225] He expressed irritation at Freeman for not preventing Congress from completing action on the measure as he had directed. "I thought it would be good for the farmer to put it up to January 20 and let the new President . . . work out a program."[226] His remarks suggest that it was not primarily the limited extension that prompted his reaction. He strongly implied that the difficulty in securing an extension caused him to doubt the soundness of the programs themselves. When Johnson concluded, Freeman resumed his narrative without a response, perhaps as uncertain of the president's views on agricultural policy in 1968 as he was in 1964.

Policy Extensions: Toward the "New" Regulation

> I was determined to protect the housewife against the huckster,
> the man of the house against the modern-day usurer, and the
> entire family against the sellers of tainted meat and dangerous
> merchandise.
>
> LBJ, 1971 [227]

The most significant policy contribution of Johnson's presidency
in regulation was the promotion of the extension of regulation to
deal with the social impact of economic activity and its externali-
ties. Specific objectives were to protect the interests of consumers,
to enhance public health and safety, and to safeguard environmental
quality. The main purpose, as Paul H. Weaver puts it, was to advance
the "overall welfare of the society."[228] In presidential rhetoric, this
translated into the concept of the "quality of life." In his consumer
message in early February 1964, Johnson pledged "to increase consumer well being—both the quality and comforts of life."[229] A year
later, in another message to Congress, he asserted that cleansing the
environment and protecting natural beauty "adds to the quality . . .
of life."[230] Improving the quality of life in new ways for all citizens,
in addition to enlarging opportunities for the disadvantaged, was accommodated easily, even centrally, in Johnson's ambition to push
the nation "forward to the Great Society."[231]

Of course, the "new" regulation was not entirely new. There were
established regulatory and other programs that touched upon consumer, health, safety, and environmental interests. What was different about the 1960s was the scope and pace of policy development
in regard to these areas of concern. As a result, the overall character
of regulation began to change in a number of ways. Most importantly, the regulatory reach of the national government started to
expand tremendously, and its power began to penetrate much more
deeply into the nation's life.

An Outline of Change

Regulatory legislation was passed during the Johnson presidency to
deal with twenty-three specific problems adversely affecting the
quality of life. In the case of both air and water pollution control,
there were two enactments, meaning that twenty-five measures became law. Almost all had presidential support. The problems and
the responses are indicated in table 5.

Table 5. *Problems Addressed by "New" Social Regulation: 1964–1968*

Problem	Enactment	Legislative Response
Consumers in the Marketplace		
Deceptive packaging	1966	Federal authority to regulate labels and designs
Inadequate consumer loan information	1968	Federal authority to require disclosure
Fraud in land sales	1968	Federal authority to require disclosure
Mail fraud	1968	Strengthened federal authority
Health and Safety		
Unsafe pesticides	1964	Strengthened federal authority
Cigarettes	1965	Federal labeling requirements
Exposure of children to hazardous substances	1966	Strengthened federal authority to label and ban
Unsafe passenger ships	1966	Strengthened federal authority
Unsafe coal mines	1966	Extended federal regulation to small mines
Unsafe mines and milling (other than coal and lignite)	1966	Federal-state regulation of metal and nonmetallic operations
Unsafe highways	1966	Federal authority to require states to meet federal standards
Unsafe motor vehicles	1966	Federal authority to set standards
Consumer product safety	1967	Federal study authorized
Suspect clinical laboratories	1967	Federal authority to license and set standards
Flammable fabrics	1967	Strengthened federal authority to set standards
Adulterated meat	1967	Federal-state regulation of meat in intrastate commerce
Adulterated poultry	1968	Federal-state regulation of poultry in intrastate commerce
Harmful radiation	1968	Federal authority to set standards for consumer electronic products
Unsafe gas pipelines	1968	Federal authority to set standards
The Environment		
Unsightly highways	1965	Federal authority to impose money penalties on states for ineffective control

Table 5. *Continued*

Problem	Enactment	Legislative Response
Polluted water	1965	Federal-state regulation of water quality
Polluted air	1965	Federal authority to set emission standards for motor vehicles
Polluted water	1966	Strengthened federal enforcement authority
Polluted air	1967	Federal-state regulation of air quality
Aircraft noise pollution	1968	Federal authority to set standards

Two major points are worth emphasizing. One is that the period of greatest achievement spanned the last three years of the Johnson presidency. During this time twenty of the twenty-five acts were passed. All four of the measures enacted in 1965, however, were important and somewhat controversial. They concerned cigarette labeling and advertising (not endorsed by the president), highway beauty, water pollution control, and control of motor vehicle emissions.[232]

The second point is that several approaches to regulation are evident in the enactments. In one case, that of cigarette labeling and advertising, there was direct legislative prescription, rather than the delegation of discretionary authority to an agency. In several instances, including protecting consumers against mail fraud and the public-at-large against dangerous pesticides, existing authorities were strengthened. Essentially new authorities were established in areas as diverse as motor vehicle safety and emissions and clinical laboratories.

A number of the new regulatory programs involved a combination of federal-state action or provided options for states to participate in a federal regulatory undertaking. Examples include mine safety, meat and poultry inspection, and air and water pollution control. Although there were variations in regard to the particulars, in each the core regulatory mechanisms were federal or federally approved standards that states could enforce. If they did not elect to assume responsibility, or if they did not perform satisfactorily, the federal government was to claim the enforcement function.

The Dynamics of Policy Activism

Michael Pertschuk, later chairman of the Federal Trade Commission, was on the staff of the Senate Commerce Committee when Johnson was in the White House. Commenting on the mid-1960s, he says, "The prevailing public mood . . . remained buoyant, confident, generous." Further, "The public agenda was the liberal agenda. . . . Government, preeminently the federal government, was the acknowledged and accepted instrument of social justice."[233] This mood began to grow among Democrats in Congress during the Eisenhower years. Especially in the Senate, issues were being shaped that would come to maturity in the 1960s. In most cases, attention stopped short of the enactment of legislation. One exception was water pollution control, where a measure was vetoed by President Eisenhower. Estes Kefauver of Tennessee was one of the most vigorous senators in exposing gaps in the regulatory scheme, holding well-publicized hearings on a number of topics, including drug safety.[234] Other senators highlighted problems involving environmental degradation along highways, highway safety, and consumer lending practices.[235]

The Democratic victory of 1960 that placed Kennedy in the White House created new possibilities for those who sought to correct perceived problems through innovative regulatory initiatives. Kennedy's assassination in 1963, Johnson's adeptness in the transition period, and his sweeping electoral victory in 1964 opened the way even further for policy change. Possibilities for change were enhanced by a growing number of policy activists advancing environmental and consumer causes. The most prominent was Ralph Nader, who, after his initial engagement with the automobile safety problem in 1965, continued as an advocate in other areas.

The "new" regulation enacted in the 1960s was usually, in the most meaningful sense, the joint product of the presidency and the Congress. Ideas were generated in both settings. The executive arguably can be credited with initiating action in several areas, including aircraft noise and improved inspection of meat, poultry, and fish. Mark V. Nadel, on the other hand, concludes that of the seventeen major consumer acts passed from 1962 through 1968 nine were introduced in Congress prior to presidential endorsement.[236] Even in cases of congressional initiation, the administration generally played a significant role in the process of securing passage. For example, Senator Paul Douglas of Illinois began a campaign in the 1950s to require full disclosure of information about interest rates and other matters in connection with consumer loans. Truth-in-lending was clearly a congressional initiative. Yet Treasury Department officials were active and important participants from 1964 through 1968 in negotiating the agreements that led to the approval of legislation.[237] During this period Johnson also gave strong public endorsement to the concept no less than ten times.[238] Another example is truth-in-packaging legislation. Hearings were first held in 1962 by Senator Philip A. Hart of Michigan. After the Senate passed his bill in 1966, he sent word to the president that "all the credit should go to you for the push you gave it."[239]

A few measures—mine safety legislation, for example—clearly were congressional products. In most cases, however, it is difficult to say that a particular measure owed more to the executive or to Congress. No matter what the original source of initiative, policy development took place concurrently at both ends of Pennsylvania Avenue. Congressional and executive policy entrepreneurs were both at work, usually in relative harmony. In cases of congressional initiation, once there was a presidential commitment, the executive leadership role tended to expand. This is illustrated in the emergence of regulation dealing with motor vehicle and highway safety.

In 1966 major legislation was enacted to cut the incidence of deaths and injuries on the nation's highways. The National Traffic and Motor Vehicle Safety Act authorized the establishment of federal motor vehicle safety standards. A companion piece, the Highway Safety Act, in effect required the states to establish highway safety programs that met federal requirements.

Safety on the highways had been a concern in Congress for some time. Periodically hearings were held on aspects of the problem. Between 1962 and 1964 there was incremental progress. Legislation was passed setting standards for hydraulic brake fluid, requiring federal standards for seat belts, and prohibiting purchase by the government of vehicles lacking safety devices specified by the General Services Administration. In the meantime, general interest in highway safety grew. The incubation period for the issue ended in 1965. A tire safety bill was pending in Congress and had attracted considerable support. That support quickened and broadened with the publication of Ralph Nader's book detailing a range of problems in auto safety centering on the Corvair. It expanded further when Senator Abraham Ribicoff of Connecticut began hearings on the problem, and it exploded in the wake of General Motors' clumsy investigation aimed at discrediting Nader.[240]

Early in 1966 Johnson recommended strong highway safety legislation to the Congress.[241] This was not simply a response to the public concerns raised by policy activists such as Nader and Ribicoff. Not long after becoming president, he had sent a letter to the secretary of Commerce directing him "to undertake immediately an accelerated attack on traffic accidents in this country."[242] In the aftermath of the president's letter, the Bureau of the Budget began to take a leadership role on the issue.

In December 1964 its director, Charles L. Schultze, advised the White House that "it is quite probable that an effective solution to the mounting highway safety problem will require a more aggressive role for the Federal Government."[243] One of the obstacles, he asserted, was the President's Committee on Traffic Safety, established in 1954. Its current chairman was newspaper publisher William Randolph Hearst, Jr. In Schultze's view, "Its main goal in life . . . is to assert States' rights and prevent Federal 'encroachment' in the highway safety area."[244] Approximately three weeks later the bureau recommended an "aggressive, expanded role in highway safety."[245] This was in late 1964, before the Ribicoff-Nader effects began to be felt in public opinion. In response, the president began the process that would lead to the 1966 legislation. He asked an interdepartmental highway safety group to submit a paper on the federal role in regard to the problem and instructed BOB to examine the organization and management of safety functions within the government.[246]

There was a contest within the executive branch in 1965 and into 1966 between the advocates of strong regulation and those who favored a go-slow approach. A task force on transportation preparing options for the 1966 legislative program thought further study was required.[247] The Department of Commerce tended to favor research, education, and incentives for voluntary action.[248] On the other side, the Bureau of the Budget and officials in the White House wanted considerably more. Toward the end of 1965 a decision was made to recommend strong measures in regard to both motor vehicle and highway safety the following year.

A number of issues were unresolved, however. One was whether the states should be penalized for noncompliance with highway safety requirements by a loss of federal aid funds. The Bureau of the Budget favored a 10 percent penalty.[249] The Department of Commerce objected, and the president endorsed its position.[250] As it turned out, the penalty provision was included in the version passed by the Congress. Another issue was whether motor vehicle safety standards should be set by the industry based upon performance criteria prescribed by the government or whether the government should set the standards. Again, the president opted for the more permissive approach, a position which was rejected by Congress in favor of mandatory standards, further evidence of the contributions of both the Congress and the president in policy making.[251]

Two sets of distinguishable policy development efforts were responsible for producing most of the "new" regulation associated with the Johnson presidency. One focused on environmental issues and the other on consumer issues defined broadly to include marketplace, health, and safety problems. Although the latter was the more productive in numerical terms, the more substantial achievements were in environmental regulation.

Environmental Initiatives

When Johnson became president, federal regulatory authority for enhancing environmental quality was quite weak. Congress took small steps in addressing water and air pollution problems in the 1940s and 1950s. In 1961 Kennedy asked Congress for water pollution control legislation that, among other things, strengthened federal regulation. Congress responded with a modest enlargement. In the following year he asked for an extension of expiring air pollution control legislation and the addition of a regulatory component. A measure along the lines sought by Kennedy was passed in 1963 and signed by Johnson on 17 December. In 1965 new water and air pollution measures were enacted, in 1966 there was the passage of a highway beauty measure and more water legislation, and in 1967 another major air pollution control bill became law.

Johnson did not ask for new environmental legislation in 1964; Congress was the point of initiative. The leading proponent of action was Senator Edmund S. Muskie of Maine. As chairman of the subcommittee of the Senate Public Works Committee with jurisdiction over pollution matters, he pushed energetically for strong federal programs. The Senate passed his ambitious water pollution control legislation in 1963, and the House passed its version in 1964, too late, however, for differences between the two bills to be resolved before the end of the session. Also in 1964 Muskie held hearings on air pollution around the country in an effort to build public support for major legislation.[252]

Prompted no doubt by congressional activism, the Johnson administration prepared for major environmental quality initiatives in 1965. When task forces were established in late summer 1964 to work on the legislative program for the following year, three focused on environmental matters. They dealt with natural beauty, natural resources, and environmental pollution. A study by a panel of the President's Science Advisory Committee, to be published in 1965, was also influential.[253] The result was a presidential message on 8 February 1965 in which Johnson called for stronger regulatory authority over both water and air pollution. He also asked for controls to enhance the beauty of lands bordering highways.[254]

Congress responded positively in all three areas, in some respects doing more and in some respects doing less than the president asked. It was most reluctant to act on the highway beauty initiative, despite the fact that there had been some concern among legislators for several years about the problem. Concern peaked in the 1950s when the interstate highway system was established. In 1958 legislation was enacted providing bonuses for states that controlled billboards. Extended in 1961 and 1963 and due to expire in 1965, it proved to be, at best, of questionable effectiveness. Against this background, the Task Force on Natural Beauty recommended that stringent regulation of billboards be a part of the 1965 legislative program. After an intense struggle with opponents in Congress and with the billboard industry, the administration was able to secure a modest, yet significant, result.[255]

In the segment of his message on air pollution, Johnson asked for an enlargement of the investigative powers vested in the secretary of HEW. He pledged, in addition, to begin discussions with industry representatives and others on reducing pollution from motor vehicles. Before the president's message was received, Muskie introduced legislation authorizing federal standards for emissions from new automobiles. During the course of Senate consideration of Muskie's bill, HEW suggested that the administration propose its own regulatory scheme. Johnson rejected the idea, preferring to seek voluntary action from the automobile industry. When an administration official testified against Muskie's bill, a storm of critical comment was generated. This caused a quick adjustment in official views, and the administration began to cooperate with Muskie. The result was legislation authorizing the secretary of HEW to regulate emissions along the lines proposed by the senator.

The most substantial achievement of the year was the Water Quality Act of 1965. There was a strong inclination within the administration to support major legislation in 1965. Some consideration was given to the employment of economic incentives for control purposes, but in the end the president endorsed a standards approach like that specified in Muskie's legislation. The bill signed by Johnson contained many elements. At the center was a regulatory scheme based upon water quality standards set by states and approved by the secretary of HEW.

The successes of 1965 did not stifle interest in pressing forward on environmental issues. Looking ahead to 1966, two task forces were established. The president's message in 1966 emphasized non-regulatory aspects of environmental programs, except for a modest strengthening of enforcement authority in water pollution control.[256] This was included in the water legislation enacted by Congress in that year.

Air pollution control was to be the centerpiece of the administration's environmental policy initiatives in 1967. In contrast to 1965, the executive moved into the forefront. The first item in the charge given to the Task Force on Environmental Quality in September 1966 as it began to develop measures to recommend to the upcoming Congress was to strengthen the air pollution control program.[257] In response, the task force recommended enlarged research and development efforts and financial assistance for the states to combat pollution. It also proposed injunctions against sources of pollution endangering public health, the control of additives to motor vehicle fuels, and uniform national air quality emission standards for certain industries. For the rest, the task force suggested that the federal government be authorized to establish regional air pollution control programs and standards of air quality if states did not act.[258] A serious air pollution episode in New York City in November 1966 gave impetus to the work of the task force, as did a December conference on the topic in Washington.

Air pollution control dominated Johnson's 1967 environmental message. It was the only area in which new regulatory authority was requested, and almost all of the task force's proposals were included.[259] Missing, however, were the injunction provision and the regulation of fuel additives, although registration of additives was sought. The legislation approved by the Congress—unanimously, in both houses—diverged significantly from administration proposals. The authority to seek injunctions was put back in, and the authority to set national industrial emission standards was excluded. There was a change in the approach to structuring control programs. The administration called for regional arrangements that could cross the boundaries of state and local governments. In areas where adequate regional programs did not come into being, the secretary of HEW was to establish, staff, and fund them. Although the scheme of regulation was complex, essentially the standards enforced by regional bodies were to be federal in character. In large part because of Muskie's reservations, a different approach was adopted in the law, one patterned on the water pollution control legislation passed in 1965. Although the federal role in standard setting remained important, state and local governments gained considerably more discretion in program matters than they were allowed in the administration's plan.

The Air Quality Act of 1967 was the last major environmental policy initiative enacted during Johnson's presidency, unless aircraft noise standards legislation passed in 1968 is included in this category. From agenda setting and policy development perspectives, however, 1967 and 1968 were active years. Without public presidential prodding, in 1967 the Senate passed omnibus water pollution control legislation that dealt with a number of problems, including the regulation of oil, vessel, and thermal pollution. In his message sent to Congress in early 1968, Johnson asked for the strengthening of the existing programs regulating water and air pollution and new regulatory restrictions on drinking water, aircraft noise, and surface mining.[260] Thus a number of matters were still pending on the congressional agenda when Johnson left office, as well as matters that were in the process of moving from the executive to Congress, such as the regulation of solid wastes.[261]

Consumer and Related Affairs

Environmental policy efforts were relatively focused. In part this was because of the nature of the problems addressed. The prominence of air and water pollution problems demanded that they top the agenda. There were also relatively few centers of expertise within the executive branch, limiting the range of interests to be dealt with in developing policy. The situation was different in regard to the protection of consumers in the marketplace and public health and safety. Once the idea of reflecting these interests in regulatory policy more expansively was established, there seemed to be no end to the number of particular problems that could be defined as warranting attention. Furthermore, a large number of government agencies had missions that affected the well-being of consumers and public health and safety and thus were positioned to offer policy suggestions.

Most of the administration's consumer protection, health, and safety proposals were presented in a series of consumer messages. Consumer protection policy development can be divided into two periods. In the first, extending from 1964 through most of 1966, efforts were less intense than in the second, which began in the latter part of 1966 when interest heightened in Congress as well as in the executive. The Senate Commerce Committee was an especially important participant.[262] Joe Califano attributes the surge to three factors: a growing interest in balancing the power of consumer and other economic forces, a perception that corporations are inherently unable to protect consumer interests, and a recognition by politicians that consumerism was a popular issue.[263]

Johnson's initial consumer message in 1964 was built principally on Democratic initiatives already launched in Congress and on the recommendations of his predecessor. It contained nine regulatory proposals. Perhaps the most important of them were for improved meat and poultry inspection and for truth in packaging and lending.[264] There was no message in 1965. The 1966 message was relatively limited. Its major new initiatives came from HEW and consisted of a number of measures to protect the safety of children in matters under the department's general jurisdiction.[265]

The legislative programs developed for 1967 and 1968 were more substantial; each contained ideas carried over from previous years as well as new ones. Efforts were spearheaded by the president's special assistant for consumer affairs, aided by her staff and by interagency task forces. Added to the agenda for consideration in 1967 were, for example, the regulation of mutual funds, based upon an SEC study and recommendations, the regulation of medical devices, the regulation of clinical laboratories, the regulation of gas pipeline safety, and strengthened regulation of flammable fabrics.[266]

In each of these two years suggestions for action, sifted at the task force level and by others in the White House, were numerous and covered a wide range of topics. For example, the task force working on the program for 1968 considered thirty-two proposals from eleven departments and agencies, some regulatory in nature and some not, in addition to those generated by the president's special assistant and her staff.[267] They received fairly rigorous scrutiny and a number were dropped, including the regulation of trading stamps, control of the quality of frozen foods, and a study of state regulation of automobile insurance that had the potential for promoting national regulation. The task force's report contained twenty-one recommendations.[268] Only five of these appeared in the president's message, accompanied by several others added independently in the White House.[269]

Even though Johnson did not seek reelection in 1968, a task force was asked to prepare a program for 1969. It submitted eighteen major recommendations. Among its regulatory targets were cosmetics, electric power rates, eggs and egg products, trading stamps, consumer finance interest rates, referral sales schemes, credit cards, and credit bureaus.[270] These, plus unenacted items previously placed on the agenda, provided a rather extensive range of options for policy makers if they wished to exploit them in the future.

Conclusions

Johnson did not enter the presidency with his own regulatory policy agenda or with particular major substantive policy objectives on his mind. In economic regulation, however, he inherited certain commitments. Changes in regard to section 14(b), common-site picketing, and fair labor standards were of special importance. The president was comfortable with following through with these, at least up to a point. Johnson also inherited an interest in the deregulation of surface transportation and again followed up on his predecessor's initiative without apparent reservations. Action on agricultural policy was forced by expirations of legislation. There were some efforts to develop a Johnson agenda in economic regulation. The principal vehicles were a number of task forces, especially those that conducted rather wide-ranging policy reviews. Those focusing on antitrust and communications, however, were completed shortly before Johnson left office, and a major energy policy study was just getting underway.

It was in the area characterized as the "new" regulation that a distinctly Johnsonian policy agenda emerged. In contrast to economic issues, in which the president's personal involvement and interest were at best restrained, he appeared to be more enthusiastically committed to attaining new policy objectives in connection with environmental, consumer, health, and safety problems.

The processes for making regulatory policy decisions within the executive branch, especially those requiring legislation, were centralized and dominated by presidential agents. Among the task forces, only the communications group went out of control. From time to time, however, but not with great frequency, presidential aides found that their policy preferences conflicted with those of departments and agencies as final decisions were being made. Differences were apparent, for example, in decision making on the deregulation of surface transportation, raising the minimum wage, giving bargaining power to farmers, enhancing highway beauty, and highway and motor vehicle safety. These tended to be differences in degree rather than principle. The president himself played a rather passive role and usually became involved at the last stages. He typically accepted the substantive advice of his aides, but at times, when there was conflict, he adopted the departmental perspective.

Ultimate policy results were shaped by the interaction of the president, the bureaucracy, Congress, and relevant interest groups. In a number of areas, notably on many environmental and consumer issues, most of the time the president and Congress worked and bargained as allies, not antagonists. The water and air pollution control measures are prime examples. There were other situations in which the executive, though successful, had to overcome strong congressional and interest group opposition. Examples include truth-in-packaging, truth-in-lending, and highway beauty. In still other areas, such as section 14(b) and common-site picketing, historic alliances opposed to policy change were able to prevail in the legislative process.

7. Grappling with Regulation

> In this system government is not a dictator or a master planner.
> Government is the great moderator—adjusting these differences
> and injustices which require its effort.
>
> LBJ, 23 July 1964[1]

IT IS well recognized that politicians enjoy distributing benefits
to their constituents. Yet, as Johnson's comments to a group of
business executives indicate, modern government must do more
than this. Although redistributing resources and refereeing disputes
among powerful interests are less attractive undertakings, regulation has been an important responsibility of the national government for many years. A rather close examination of regulatory affairs over approximately five years from the vantage point of the
presidency has been presented in previous chapters. Now it is time
to pull the various strands of analysis together and to frame a general
perspective on the Johnson presidency and regulation.

The President's Business

> I felt, very briefly, that this was a matter for them to settle by
> collective bargaining; that I did believe that the President of the
> country had an extreme responsibility for proclaiming the na-
> tional interest and serving the national interest; that I had a right
> to ask their complete cooperation; that I was asking for that and
> I expected to receive it and I believed I would.
>
> LBJ, 26 August 1965[2]

The president was reporting at a press conference on a meeting he
held that morning in the White House with representatives of the
steel industry and labor on negotiations then underway. They reveal
a duality that was near the center of Johnson's treatment of regula-

tion: a sense of the prerogative of the private sector joined with a sense of public responsibility. Dealing with the duality was an important aspect of the conduct of his business in regulation.

What, then, was the nature of that business? This is the central question introduced at the beginning of the analysis. The point of curiosity that animates the question is, what do presidents actually do and how do they go about doing it? Presidential and regulatory activities during a week in March 1965 were sampled as a basis for asking about connections. To broaden the illustration somewhat, it is useful to profile the flow of work on regulatory matters through the Johnson White House during the full month. A number of important discussions and decisions were on the agenda. The president and his aides gave a great deal of attention to agricultural legislation (discussed in chapter 4) throughout the month. Notification was received of a major FPC decision soon to be announced, about the Department of Justice's intention to file suit against a newspaper merger, and about the department's view of another antitrust problem on which the White House was being pressured by certain members of Congress. Problems in the Consumer Advisory Council and the regulation of international air fares were debated. The president and others were weighing minimum wage proposals to forward to Congress. Concurrently, the president decided not to move forward with deregulation of surface transportation that year. Five appointments to regulatory commissions were announced. The month ended with Johnson's unqualified and tenacious overruling of Udall's decision to end import controls on residual fuel oil.[3]

Regulatory matters, of course, did not dominate the White House agenda during the month. But they were neither absent nor insignificant in their presence. If March 1965 was reasonably representative, the president's business did include regulation as a notable and persistent component, though overshadowed by the great international and domestic issues of the day.

The nature and shape of the president's business in regulation at any given time are problematic, the product of interaction among a number of factors. One is the attitude of the president toward regulation. Johnson's is not easily discerned, but the evidence indicates that, like the man himself, it was complex. He was, at the same time, activist and restrained, involved and removed. He supported regulation, even its extension in important respects. At times he was an enthusiastic regulator, as the discussions of the wage-price guideposts, the balance-of-payments efforts, and various labor matters indicate. But overall his behavior and expressions often implied that, in his view, much of regulation was an irritant to be ignored if at all possible.

It is easiest to explain restraint and removal from established, ongoing regulatory programs. Although he basically accepted the regulatory system that had developed over the years, there appeared to be a side of Johnson that thought that regulation could go too far and be overly restrictive of economic activity. Belief in a measured approach to economic regulation, it should be remembered, was not a wholly unpopular one in the Democratic Party of the 1960s. Moderation was apparent in Congress. Furthermore, John Kennedy, Johnson's predecessor, Hobart Rowen says, "was not anti-business. . . . He leaned over backward for a long period to accommodate the criticisms and conservative views of businessmen and bankers."[4] Johnson's remarks to regulators soon after his investment in office and his insistence on judicious behavior reflect a similar sense that regulation should not be perceived as unreasonable or hostile to business.

Putting aside whatever philosophical views Johnson may have held on regulation, a number of political considerations contributed to his wariness. One of a president's basic problems is to husband his time and political resources for use in attaining policy objectives of prime importance to him. In Johnson's case, these were associated principally with Vietnam, civil rights, health, education, and the War on Poverty. There were dangers in regulation, especially in economic regulation, and the potential for political losses. It was not unreasonable for him to conclude that the greater his degree of perceived involvement, the greater the likelihood that losers in regulatory battles would withhold their general support from him. The momentary gratitude of winners would soon be forgotten. Johnson also carried special vulnerabilities, including his business interests in communications, his prior defense of oil and gas interests as a senator from Texas, and his reputation as a wheeler-dealer and expert manipulator of governmental machinery.

A president's desire to avoid or limit involvement in certain aspects of regulation, for whatever reasons, can only influence, not determine, his business in regulation. This is indicated by table 6, which summarizes the major areas of regulatory activity at the presidential level discussed in prior chapters. It excludes the generic wage-price guideposts effort and Johnson's execution of his responsibilities in labor disputes, but instances in which they produced relationships with other regulatory programs are included as discrete cases. In the table, activities are categorized along commis-

Table 6. *Areas of Involvement in Regulation*

Commission	*Executive*	*Both*
	SUBSTANTIVE	
High		Communications policy review
Air transportation rates	Railroad merger policy	Balance-of payments campaign
International air matters	Oil import policy	
Freight car problems	Agricultural prices	
Section 14(b)	Minimum wage	
	Antitrust uses to restrain prices	
Moderate		
Transportation deregulation	Agricultural programs	
Savings and loan interest rates	Environmental policy	
Common-site picketing	initiatives	
Airline strike response	Consumer and related	
	policy initiatives	
Low		
Recapture policy	Bank merger policy	
Energy policy reviews	Agricultural policy initiatives	
ICC rates	Antitrust policy review	
Casework	Casework	

ADMINISTRATIVE

High
Appointments
Deportment
Northeast blackout
  investigation

Moderate
Program Transfers
  from CAB and ICC
ICC reorganization
Budgets

Low
Interior-FPC
  conflicts

Appointments
Deportment
Organization for
  consumer affairs

Budgets

Scrutiny of financial institutions
Coordination of bank regulation
Organization for communications
  policy coordination

Generic management initiatives

sion-executive and substantive-administrative lines and according to the level of the president's personal involvement in them.

Distinguishing among levels of involvement is, admittedly, a subjective undertaking. In this instance, assignments were made with four criteria in mind: the magnitude of the interaction among Johnson and others in a particular case; the degree to which he appeared to have a real interest in how a matter was handled or resolved; the extent to which he initiated and directed action; and the weight of his participation as a decision maker rather than as a passive ratifier of the decisions of others. Generally speaking, areas of activity in the high column satisfy at least three of the criteria, those placed in the moderate category satisfy two, and cases in the low category satisfy one or none. Here the primary burden was carried by staff who played important roles in cases at all three levels.

In regard to the topics examined in previous chapters, a total of forty-two cases, or areas of activity, essentially made up the regulatory agenda of the Johnson presidency, in addition to his previously mentioned involvement in particular labor disputes and in the overall management of guideposts and balance-of-payments efforts. At least in regard to presidential work, they constituted his business in relation to the regulatory programs of commissions and executive agencies and related legislative initiatives.

Johnson, it is clear, was not always a passive observer. His level of involvement is judged to be high in seventeen instances, moderate in thirteen, and low in eleven. On the whole, there is a distinct emphasis on substantive policy matters as opposed to the purely administrative. In both the substantive and administrative realms, some agenda items concerned one-time problems or issues, such as a response to the strike in the airline industry that came and went in a matter of days. In many others, the presidency was involved periodically but regularly. Making decisions in international air transportation proceedings is a case in point. In still others, there was a fairly constant flow of business. Examples include making appointments to regulatory commissions and, for a protracted period, crafting a minimum wage proposal. Finally, the president's business was just about evenly divided between commission and executive regulation.

At first glance this agenda does not square with Johnson's limited regulatory objectives and the guarded and restrained stance he often took when presented with regulatory matters. Dissection of the cases provides insights into the sources of a seeming contradiction. It reveals countervailing forces, or factors, that in some instances press strongly in the direction of attention and may even make involvement attractive for reasons other than attaining a particular regulatory result. These essentially political forces play in and about a presidency; in the case of Johnson's, they contributed in important ways to shaping an agenda and to defining his business in regulation for him.

There are three basic factors at work on the presidency and on the president personally. Although distinguishable, in some ways they are not always mutually exclusive. Nevertheless, they appear to be useful in starting to think about what draws presidents into regulatory matters. These factors are duty, compulsion, and disagreement. The last is the easiest to define and identify. It is undimensional in nature and pertains to situations in which departments, agencies, or presidential staff members are unable to resolve disagreements on their own. Presidents and their aides may ignore disagreements and perhaps escape blame for their indifference. Some situations, however, are not easily ignored.

Duty involves de jure and de facto requirements for presidential attention that, essentially, are woven into the woof and warp of the office and take the form of obligations. Six stand out in importance:

1. Law: when statutes require the president to act, as in the case of appointments.

2. Consanguinity: when close political associations presumptively oblige the president to support or adopt the agenda of others to whom he is closely tied, as in the case of the core interests of important components of his electoral coalition or of leading members of his party in Congress.

3. Economic policy: when regulatory activities affect the attainment of basic economic policy objectives.

4. Foreign and national security policies: when regulatory activities have significant implications in these spheres.

5. Crisis management: when regulatory activities are related to a perceived crisis.

6. Executive management: when the president makes decisions based upon his constitutional responsibilities as chief executive about the general conduct of government, including regulation.

When viewed as a factor in defining the president's business in regulation, compulsion is admittedly difficult to separate from some of the other factors, especially consanguinity. The distinction made, and perhaps it is too fine, is between an obligation to act and political circumstances in which a president finds it is in his interest to respond or to act in a certain way. Compulsion assumes two forms: pressure, when demands focused on the White House in regard to regulatory matters are of such strength that they cannot be ignored,

Table 7. *Patterns of Involvement: Duty, Compulsion, and Disagreement Factors*

Level	Number of Factors Involved				
	One	Two	Three	Total	Average
High	3	8	6	17	2.18
Moderate	8	6	0	14	1.43
Low	8	3	0	11	1.40
Total	19	17	6	42	1.73

and support, when issues or situations related to regulation have implications for building and protecting the president's general political standing in the country, in the Congress, and in other places and for his store of political resources as they are related to central policy objectives.

Application of this schema illuminates the forces shaping the president's business in regulation and variations in Johnson's own involvement in regulatory processes. There are two basic questions to pursue. The first concerns the varied levels of presidential involvement. As might be expected, the number of factors present in a particular case often makes a difference. This is demonstrated in table 7. Of the seventeen areas of activity in which the level of his involvement is judged to be high, either two or three of the basic factors were present in fourteen. At the other two levels, there were no three-factor cases. The proportion of two-factor cases was significantly higher in the moderate category than in the low category. One-factor cases dominated this category: there were eight of this type and only three two-factor cases. To sum up the basic point of the table in a slightly different way, the more complex a case in terms of the number of factors involved, the more likely it was to draw Johnson's personal attention. This is indicated in a summary way by the average number of factors involved: 2.18 for the high involvement cases, 1.43 for the moderate involvement cases, and 1.40 for the low involvement cases.[5]

The question that follows has to do with the relative importance of duty, compulsion, and disagreement in shaping the president's business in regulation and his involvement. The basis for an answer is developed by taking a close look at the cases in which Johnson's personal involvement was high. A breakdown is presented in table 8. Compulsion factors are present in sixteen of the seventeen cases. In twelve of these, the problem of building and maintaining public

Table 8. *Profile of High Involvement Cases*

Cases	Number of Factors	Factors	Dimensions
Air transportation rates	1	Duty	Consanguinity Economic policy management
Deportment	1	Compulsion	Support
Organization for communications policy coordination	1	Compulsion	Support
International air matters	2	Duty	Law Economic policy management Foreign policy
		Compulsion	Pressure
Section 14(b)	2	Duty	Consanguinity
		Compulsion	Pressure Support
Railroad mergers	2	Compulsion Disagreement	Pressure
Antitrust uses to restrain prices	2	Duty	Economic policy management
		Compulsion	Support
Communications policy review	2	Compulsion Disagreement	Support
Appointments to commissions	2	Duty	Law
		Compulsion	Pressure Support
Northeast blackout	2	Duty	National security Crisis management
		Compulsion	Support
Scrutiny of financial institutions	2	Duty	Economic policy management
		Compulsion	Support
Balance-of-payments campaign	3	Duty	Economic policy management Foreign policy Crisis management
		Compulsion Disagreement	Support
Freight car problems	3	Duty	Economic policy management
		Compulsion	Pressure Support
		Disagreement	

Table 8. *Continued*

Cases	Number of Factors	Factors	Dimensions
Oil import policy	3	Duty	Law
			Economic policy management
			Foreign policy
		Compulsion	Pressure
			Support
		Disagreement	
Agricultural prices	3	Duty	Economic policy management
		Compulsion	Pressure
			Support
		Disagreement	
Minimum wage	3	Duty	Consanguinity
			Economic policy management
		Compulsion	Pressure
			Support
		Disagreement	
Coordination of bank regulation	3	Duty	Economic policy management
		Compulsion	Pressure
		Disagreement	

support was associated with presidential involvement. In many of the cases in which the support component of compulsion was present, there was the possibility that the president might be criticized for unpopular results associated with regulatory activities, such as increased food costs or bank failures. Johnson's interest in these situations, in part, was intended to prevent or limit political damage that might result from regulatory action or inaction. His sensitivity to the implications of regulation for his level of political support is also indicated in other ways. In two of the three one-factor cases, having to do with the deportment of commission regulators and organization for communications policy coordination, it was their implications for political support that defined their place on the agenda.

The necessity to manage pressures, in contrast, was evident in just nine cases. Business and labor interests were the principal sources of pressure in matters such as the repeal of section 14(b), increasing the minimum wage, and the coordination of bank regulation. There were also significant political pressures from governmental sources. Examples include Republicans in the Senate on commission appointments and the New England governors in the Penn-Central merger case.

Duty played a part in thirteen of the seventeen cases. There were legal requirements for presidential action in international air matters, in appointments to commissions, and in setting oil import policy. Far and away the most important dimension of duty, however, was economic policy management, a factor in ten cases. In several instances, such as freight car problems and setting the minimum wage, the main presidential focus was on limiting inflationary pressures. The international air, oil import, and balance-of-payments cases involved foreign policy dimensions, and Johnson had in mind national security considerations in his response to the Northeast blackout. Consanguinity, albeit a rather ambiguous notion having to do with political kinship, was present in three instances. The president's interest in supporting the CAB's effort to lower air fares was important from the standpoint of economic policy management, but it also seemed to be related to his long and close ties to the commission chairman. Johnson's engagement in the repeal of section 14(b) and in minimum wage issues was shaped in part by the important place of organized labor in the Democratic Party. In these cases, there was a certain obligation to the interests involved, but pressure from labor also contributed to shaping the nature of presidential involvement. As to the other aspects of duty, the president obviously perceived the Northeast blackout in crisis terms. His discretionary responsibilities as chief executive did not come into play in high involvement cases.

Disagreements figured in eight cases. Several patterns were evident. One was conflict between presidential aides and a department. This was a major element in handling the minimum wage issue. Another was conflict between departments, as in the case of railroad mergers. Still another involved a complex of conflicts among a fairly broad array of actors in oil import matters.

The pattern shifts in moderate and low level involvement cases, as shown in table 9. The most important factor in the instances of moderate presidential involvement was duty. It was present in thirteen out of fourteen cases, whereas compulsion figured in only five. Disagreements were evident in two cases. One of the interesting aspects of moderate involvement cases is the importance of consanguinity as a component of duty. Johnson opened his agenda to a number of matters that were neither distinctly his, at least initially,

Table 9. *Factor Incidence in Moderate and Low Involvement Cases*

Level	Factor		
	Duty	Compulsion	Disagreement
Moderate	13	5	2
Low	6	5	3
Total	19	10	5

nor forced upon him. Examples include transportation deregulation, a carryover from the Kennedy presidency, and environmental, consumer, and related policy initiatives. They first became a part of Johnson's business largely because they were the business of important Democrats in Congress.

When attention turns to low involvement cases, duty factors are still predominant, appearing in six of eleven cases. Compulsion factors are in second place with a score of five. In three areas of activity associated with compulsion, Johnson acted to limit his involvement in order to protect himself from political risks. In a sense, his business in these areas was to minimize perceptions of presidential connections. Disagreement figured in three cases. Presidential aides carried the entire burden in two of these. They involved the efforts to compromise differences between the Department of the Interior and the Federal Power Commission described in chapter 3.

The president's business in regulation—the portion that ascended to the White House, as opposed to that handled in presidential outposts, especially by the Bureau of the Budget—had a direct and immediate impact on only a small fraction of the total regulatory activity. Yet it cannot be characterized as insignificant. In reality, a distinction should probably be made between the president's business in regulation and presidential business, because of the vital role constantly played by staff across the whole agenda and Johnson's own selective involvement. In any case, vexing and sensitive problems regularly attracted and often demanded presidential attention. Duty in its various dimensions was a determinative factor, as was compulsion. Indeed, it is accurate to say that, for the most part, the content of the president's business in regulation was principally the product of what the president was required to handle and what seemed politically necessary to handle.

With few exceptions, the record in regulation is in stark contrast to Johnson's performance in other domestic policy areas; his legislative achievements in social policy generally were remarkable. He was similarly energetic in foreign policy and national security matters. This underscores a basic point. A president's business is variable in terms of the nature and intensity of his interests and the circumstances he confronts. An activist presidency, which Johnson's certainly was, is not necessarily activist in the same way or to the same degree in all matters.

A further word needs to be said about the areas where there was a high level of activism: wage-price guideposts, balance of payments, and selected labor negotiations. The first was the most important. A guidepost program was not required by law, but duty was involved. Consanguinity was present in that a program was in place when Johnson became president. It was a central element in economic policy management and had strong implications for foreign policy. In Johnson's mind, a high rate of inflation would have constituted a crisis. Obviously he felt pressure to restrain inflationary forces and realized full well the political costs of an unpopular rise in the cost of living. There were continuing disagreements within the administration on wage-price issues. For these reasons, notable activism on the part of Johnson personally was essential.

Much the same can be said for his involvement in the balance-of-payments issue and in certain labor disputes, as they had basic implications for general economic well-being and for the success of wage-price guideposts. There was a distinctive element in the latter, however. The Railway Labor and Taft-Hartley acts provided both a legal basis and an expectation that the president would act in crippling strike situations. In these and in wage-price guideposts, Johnson had tangible and vital regulatory purposes.

Working Relationships

> It has taken me a lifetime to learn the lessons of politics. . . . You can tell a man to go to hell, but you can't make him go. . . . Politics is the art and craft of dealing with people.
>
> LBJ, 1971[6]

Johnson brought more than three decades of experience in public life to his presidency, most of it served in the Congress. The political lessons he learned over the years were applied with positive effects in his work with people in the executive branch as well as in his dealings with the legislative branch.

His presidency was close to the major regulatory programs in a variety of senses as, directly and indirectly, he dealt with the people involved. One of the lessons he had learned was that, as he once put it, "A man's judgment on any subject is only as good as his information."[7] One aspect of closeness was that much information about regulatory activities was regularly available to Johnson and to those who assisted him. White House aides, Bureau of the Budget staff, and others monitored the agencies with some care. And through its actions, the presidency was frequently a meaningful presence in the undertakings of regulators. In short, the proximity of the presidency to both commission and executive regulation is better characterized as near, rather than distant, despite frequent indications of presidential hesitancy about involvement.

Clearly, the president and his aides were frustrated from time to time in their dealings with regulators. Nevertheless, the relationships between the presidency and the various agencies were ordinarily harmonious. There was a general propensity to respond positively to presidential interests and requests. Among the commissions, the ICC, although cooperative in some matters, presented the most difficulties. It was less than enthusiastic in assisting administration efforts to restrain price increases and to address the balance-of-payments problem. There were two other instances in which commissions were recorded as resisting administration importunings. One was the CAB's struggle to retain its role in airline subsidies when the Department of Transportation was being formed. The other was the FCC's refusal to adjust its stance in the authorized user question in connection with COMSAT services. The record, then, does not show a fervent insistence on independence and resentment of linkages to the presidency on the part of the commissions.

Resistance was just as likely to be experienced from executive agencies. Although usually cooperative in oil import control matters, the Department of the Interior showed an independent streak in others. The Department of Agriculture was slow to appreciate presidential concerns about rising prices. Then there were the continuing conflicts generated by the independent spirit of James J. Saxon when he served as comptroller of the currency, despite a clear presidential preference for cooperation. At the Department of Justice, Ramsey Clark did not hesitate to go against presidential preferences in antitrust decisions.

Beyond these few problem areas, relative harmony—or at least civilized behavior—generally marked relationships. There were instances too numerous to recount here in which both executive agencies and commissions cooperated fully with presidential requests and advanced presidential interests. Even when there were serious differences among key actors and no clear presidential position (as in the development of a policy on bank mergers), it was possible to work out accommodations. Other cases in which there were notable divisions to overcome include agricultural legislation in 1965, the termination of import controls on residual fuel oil, and minimum wage proposals. There were very few times in which a resolution satisfactory to the president was not reached, and they were in fairly inconsequential matters.

On the other side of the relationship, the president and his aides often supported the efforts of regulators and endorsed their decisions. For example, in almost every instance Johnson ratified the CAB's recommendations in international air certification proceedings and those of the Department of Agriculture in its commodity program actions. The major way in which the presidency, or at least the president, complicated the lives of regulators was when he avoided action, leaving his aides and regulators to flounder in uncertainty. This could happen even on major matters, such as cotton legislation in 1965, agricultural policy generally, and certain aspects of oil import control.

It can be argued that Johnson's largely successful relationships with regulators were due substantially to the manner in which he managed them. There was no explicitly articulated management philosophy, but certain basic precepts can be implied. Two are particularly relevant. One was that the president had a special responsibility to create a sense of an administration that reached out and incorporated all the departments and agencies of the government. An important correlate of this responsibility was to define the temper and tone of that administration. Johnson's primary methods in incorporating regulators into his administration were care in their selection, personal contact with them, letting officials know through various means that their efforts were recognized and appreciated, and periodically articulating through general and targeted expressions his views on appropriate orientations and conduct.

A second basic precept was that the president's business in regulation was circumscribed; it did not include everything. There was a distinction between the presidential and the nonpresidential. This view was reflected in a number of ways. For example, casework was discouraged. Departmental and agency prerogatives and legal responsibilities were recognized, and the value of the expertise of regulators was acknowledged, as the overall record in agriculture, antitrust, bank regulation, and oil import control indicates. Commissions were even freer in their undertakings.

Sorting out the presidential from the nonpresidential was an ongoing and relatively unsystematic effort. Johnson was a frequent contributor through initiating or resisting responses or action at the presidential level. Making the necessary distinctions was easy at times when there was a clear duty to act or when political implications were clear. Judgments had to be made in other circumstances. Framing the exact content of the legislative program was one. Another was in matters of lesser importance, where the question was whether the presidency could perform a critical service for regulators. Diverse services, in fact, were often provided in the name of promoting the sound conduct of government. They ranged from giving support to those who regulated financial institutions in their efforts to guard against failures to providing political guidance to the Department of Agriculture.

The identification of the presidential when attention at that level was not compelled was intuitive and rooted in particular circumstances, not calculated on the basis of specified criteria. Consequently, there were opportunities for presidential interference that might have been considered overly intrusive. Regulators may have resented the White House's interest in them from time to time, but in the flow of interactive relationships monitored in this analysis there are few, if any, indications of bruised sensibilities or of a sense on the part of regulators that the presidency overstepped its proper bounds.

Johnson was an active participant in managing his office's business in regulation, and in doing so he employed a style consisting of several distinctive elements. The president expected that he, and by extension those who assisted him, would be kept well informed about the flow of regulatory activity. Numerous sources of information were exploited, including the regulators themselves, presidential aides, task forces, contacts in Congress and in the business and labor communities, and media reports. He employed the constant and voluminous flow to monitor the regulatory agencies personally and to alert him to matters that required his or his aides' attention.

Another element in Johnson's style was his focus when engaged in his regulatory business. Typically it was on aspects of problems that related to his expertise—namely, the political. He was particularly interested in questions of political feasibility and the political consequences of action and inaction. In the process, Johnson insisted on realistic assessments; when there was doubt, he required thorough soundings in order to clarify the politics of the situation before determining a course of action. Especially in regard to legislation, he was not inclined to waste resources in fighting for hopeless causes.

As a decision maker, Johnson's style was adaptable, changing with the circumstances. He was publicly identified with some regulatory decisions, usually when it suited him. Much of his business, however, was conducted behind the scenes. As in the case of Eisenhower, his hand was often hidden when he attended to regulatory problems.[8] At times he was a decisive decision maker, as illustrated by his initiation of action on freight cars, his response to the Northeast blackout, his refusal to end residual oil import limits in 1965, and his order to resolve the Penn-Central merger situation without delay. At other times he was reluctant to make choices. He held back, for example, on some aspects of oil import control, on framing cotton legislation in 1964, and on bank merger legislation. Uncertainty or apprehension about the politics of a situation seemed to be the key to indecision, just as certainty seemed related to decisiveness.

In tending to his business in regulation, Johnson presided over a rather extensive complex of aides and advisers. It included White House staff and officials associated with the various units of the Executive Office of the President, especially the Bureau of the Budget and the Council of Economic Advisers. Within this complex, responsibilities were usually loosely defined, even fluid in nature. Working relationships, which often involved collaboration among a number of aides, were informal and flexible. At any given time a number of his White House assistants would be working on regulatory problems or issues. In most instances, responsibilities in regulation were implicit in general assignments rather than finely planned. Robert Kintner and Ernest Goldstein were exceptions in that the president explicitly directed them to look after the regulatory commissions.

The president gave his aides rather broad discretion in handling regulatory matters. By and large, their responses determined the degree and nature of presidential involvement, including, up to a point, Johnson's own participation. He was quite accessible to them and usually, but not always, was responsive to their suggestions and recommendations.

In the process of helping the president, staff members performed a variety of functions, all generally related to protecting and advancing his interests. First of all, they monitored the departments and agencies. Based upon information gathered through monitoring, they undertook a number of consequent activities. Their importance in keeping Johnson informed has been mentioned several times. This could include highlighting major problems, as when Kermit Gordon and Walter Heller presented the president with a strong characterization of flaws in the coordination of bank regulation and when several of his aides pointed out serious defects in communications policy, leading to a policy review. Going in the other direction, aides kept regulators informed of relevant presidential views and wishes, sometimes in the form of encouragement and requests to move in certain directions or to take particular steps.

An especially important variant of representing the president to regulators involved the mediation function. A good bit of the president's business in regulation was managing the resolution of conflict, as opposed to resolving conflict. Managing conflict resolution involves pressing for negotiated settlements among combatants, not pressing for a particular agreement or outcome that reflects a presidential preference. In many situations, there was no such preference to assert. The conflicts between the Department of the Interior and the Federal Power Commission illustrate the point. Other cases of this type are developing positions on bank merger legislation and on interest rate legislation in the wake of the Federal Reserve Board's revision of Regulation Q in late 1965. Seeking negotiated settlements often required, among other things, crafting strategy. This was the case in the situations just cited, as it was in attempting to improve coordination in bank regulation and in Califano's development of a scheme for phasing out residual oil import controls.

Assisting Johnson in decision making was, of course, a vital function of presidential aides. Their assistance took various forms. At times they were advocates. The most energetic were the special assistants for consumer affairs. Officials in the Bureau of the Budget and the Council of Economic Advisers were also prominent advocates. The bureau, for example, asserted stances protective of the president and the presidency on several occasions. It reminded people in the White House of the importance of keeping some distance from the commissions on particular proceedings. When Johnson expressed an interest in lessening his role in appointing commissioners, it demurred. And it insisted on the principle of presidential approval in the debate over regulating the rates of foreign air carriers. The bureau also strongly advocated ICC reorganization, transportation deregulation, more vigorous regulation to enhance highway safety, and agricultural policy changes that would lessen program costs. In this position it was supported by the Council of Economic Advisers. The council also expressed strong views on any number of other regulatory issues.

White House aides were much less likely to be advocates. When one of them, in the end, made a concrete recommendation to the president, it was typically based upon an agreement among the principals. When disagreement remained, the practice was to play the honest broker, briefly presenting the contending sides and leaving the choice to the president, or in some instances expressing a preference for an alternative in a reasoned way. A variant occurred when Johnson asked for the views of an aide not previously involved before he made a decision. Illustrations include Johnson's solicitation of Califano's opinion on the transatlantic certification proceeding and his inclusion of Jake Jacobsen in oil import control decisions.

His aides assisted Johnson in decision making in still other ways. In some instances they frontally challenged his inclinations. Mc-Pherson and White did so when they supported Udall's position on ending residual oil import controls in 1965. DeVier Pierson, it can be argued, at least softened the president's interest in stifling the communications policy study.

Another and more important form of assistance was to stimulate Johnson to act when he was reluctant to do so. This was not always possible, as the oil import case generally shows. However, the communications and antitrust policy reviews were instituted after aides persuaded him that there were problems that deserved examination.

Although Johnson relied heavily on his advisers, he was not overly dependent on them. By reason of his long tenure in government, he knew a great deal about the various regulatory programs. He did his homework with seriousness, devouring mounds of information, and, as a result, he was very much current on regulatory activities. Furthermore, he had a distinct preference for wide-ranging consultative processes reaching through and beyond the government. He continually promoted a form of multiple advocacy.[9] Advice from his most intimate associates was not always taken. When there was disagreement among his aides and department and agency officials, at times he sided with one and at times with the other.

It is generally asserted that a president's essential style in managing his business has broad implications which may be both positive and negative in their consequences. Johnson's style is usually characterized as flexible, unstructured, and essentially *ad hoc* in nature.[10] How well did this style work? The short answer is that it worked reasonably well in dealing with regulatory matters. From the presidential perspective, the major strength of an *ad hoc* style is that it enhances discretion. It provides maximum room for choice in when and how to become involved in the work of departments and agencies. Thus presidents and their aides can address the particular matters that they judge to be most important at the moment.

In the process, action can be geared to presidential priorities and resources, and demands on the president himself can be governed. Furthermore, timely, even decisive, responses to problems and circumstances requiring presidential attention are facilitated. All of these advantages were apparent as Johnson tended to his business in regulation.

One of the major limitations of this style, also demonstrated in the Johnson presidency, is that it makes it relatively easy for a president to duck matters that should receive attention. The availability of established structures and processes for dealing with important matters, on the other hand, promotes systematic and comprehensive attention to policy problems in a more or less regular and routine manner. Another potential problem is a persistent uncertainty about the presidential role and the nature of the president's business in a particular area. Uncertainty may contribute to a measure of unpredictability and inconstancy in relationships. This problem, too, was evident in the treatment of regulation in the Johnson White House.

A number of problems often associated with the *ad hoc* style did not emerge in serious form in the conduct of Johnson's business in regulation. The presidency was not overloaded or burdened by the pursuit of regulatory minutiae. Johnson's agenda in regulation was limited and for the most part consisted of matters that were presidential in character, even if not all of them were of great substantive moment. Indeed, much effort was devoted to keeping items off the agenda, including particular cases that were considered to be the business of the regulators. In these and other matters, aides generally were under control. They did not go into business for themselves in any meaningful sense; their actions were usually reported in full to the president and often were cleared by him before they were taken. Nor did aides attempt to manage lower-level operations. They were not prone to be directive or to give orders. Concentration was on assisting and advising the president and on the application of essentially noncoercive means for representing presidential interests to regulators.

Johnson's technique, or method, in conducting his presidency has been the subject of extensive comment. Larry Berman's summation is fairly representative. He asserts that there was "an emphasis on consensus, a tight rein on White House staff, an extreme sensitivity to criticism, a need for controlling information to and from the White House, and a preoccupation with secrecy."[11]

This characterization suggests considerably more order than was present in the conduct of Johnson's business in regulation. He and those who helped him did search for ultimate agreement on controversial matters, and he expected that once agreement was reached on a presidential position it would be supported by members of his administration. It is not uncommon for presidents to have such expectations. Up to the point at which a position was taken, however, there was wide latitude for the expression of diverse views. The White House staff was not kept on a tight rein. Contrarily, aides had wide latitude in the execution of their responsibilities and in their judgments. There was sensitivity in the White House to criticism, but not in a pathological sense. It was a reasonable sensitivity to criticisms of presidential actions and inactions, as well as of the work of departments and agencies, that had serious political implications. Insensitivity to such criticisms would be foolhardy and perhaps indicative of a tendency toward callous nonresponsiveness. The White House was not a prime source of information about regulation, and there were few indications of an unusual or abnormal concern for controlling its flow when the presidency was engaged in regulatory matters. Clearly, there was a desire for confidentiality in sensitive areas such as pending appointments, but hardly a "preoccupation with secrecy." In short, the Johnson White House, it seems, was much more relaxed and less convoluted and compulsive in regulation than it is depicted to have been in other areas.

Intentions and Effects

> I don't want to be a labor President or a business President or a bureaucratic President. I want to be an American President.
> LBJ, 20 August 1964[12]

In this statement, made relatively early in his presidency, Johnson laid out one of his basic objectives in regard to regulation. Beyond this, except for matters bearing broadly and directly on the general economic well-being of the nation in which the presidency was in the vanguard, Johnson's intentions in regulation were relatively limited. Underlying the particulars of the agenda he pursued was a basic interest in the conduct of regulation by commissions and executive agencies in ways that would not bring harm to his presidency. For Johnson, this meant regulation that, on the whole, was moderate in its aims, steered a middle course, and kept the inevitable conflicts from escalating to intense and sustained controversies. There were a few instances when problems flared, but the president and his aides were reasonably successful in avoiding major regulatory explosions that had serious and harmful consequences for them. It also meant regulation that gave support to his basic economic policies. The record of accomplishment here was, on the whole, positive. The Civil Aeronautics Board and the Federal Reserve Board, for example, cooperated fully in balance-of-payments efforts. There were, to be sure, secondary intentions in the policy realm, sometimes satisfied and sometimes not. The major accomplishment was in promoting new regulatory initiatives in the consumer, health, safety, and environmental areas. Other potentially innovative steps failed, such as the deregulation of surface transportation.

Johnson was equally successful in realizing his intentions in both commission and departmental regulation. There appeared to be no fundamental differences between the two types in regard to the kind and character of presidential interest or attention or in the quality of working relationships. In neither sphere did the presidency encounter serious difficulties in becoming engaged in matters of interest, although in some instances the results were not entirely satisfactory. Nevertheless, there are slight differences to note. Commission regulation drew marginally more extensive presidential attention, and a wider variety of matters were dealt with. The issues associated with executive regulation that rose to the presidential level tended to be more substantial and of greater policy significance.

What of the vast bulk of regulatory activity that did not receive direct presidential attention? To what degree was it affected by the Johnson presidency? From the overall climate of relations and evidence of general tendencies toward responsiveness that seemingly caused most regulators to behave as the president wished most of the time, one might infer that there were effects that corresponded with the president's basic intentions. There are some pieces of evidence to cite in support of the conclusion. In 1966 the president received a letter from the director of the Bureau of the Budget, which said, "The Federal Maritime Commission has been doing a noteworthy job in taking the heavy hand out of regulation by emphasizing settlements through informal agreements rather than by formal proceedings and litigation. . . . This achievement . . . represents less regulation, in accordance with your announced transportation policy."[13] At the CAB, according to its administrative history prepared at the conclusion of Johnson's presidency, "Despite the independent nature of the Board's function in the overall governmental scheme, the Board nevertheless seeks to accommodate and advance the basic policy objectives of the Administration wherever possible, consistent with its obligations under the statute."[14] Certainly when Charles Murphy was chairman of the board it acted in harmony with Johnson's policy objectives. Students of the FCC have noted Johnson's success in redirecting its regulatory efforts.[15] The FDIC, FHLBB, FPC, FTC, NLRB, and SEC, operating under the watchful eye of the presidency, functioned along lines generally acceptable to Johnson, if the absence of strong expressions of displeasure is an indication. Much the same could be said about the bulk of departmental regulation.

Governmental decisions are shaped by a complex of centripetal and centrifugal forces. Presidential influence on them is determined by the relative balance of forces pulling toward the center and forces pulling outward. During Johnson's presidency, in regulation the significance of several centripetal forces was apparent. First among them, especially in commission regulation, were the power to appoint members and the power, in most instances, to designate chairmen. In both commission and departmental regulation, there were the prestige of the presidential office and the deference which it often elicits. These forces were accentuated by the rather skillful and collaborative ways in which presidential aides and the president himself usually dealt with regulators.

This is not to suggest that centrifugal forces were inconsequential. Ingrained dispositions of regulators that were counter to presidential preferences were problems at times. Among the commissions, the ICC stands out as an example; among the departments, Agriculture, Justice, and the comptroller of the currency in the Treasury Department occasionally pulled against presidential traces.

Also at play was the influence of regulated interests. They no doubt reinforced traditional dispositions in some instances, but they also had independent effects. A few times presidential initiatives were thwarted by their opposition. One example is reorganization of bank regulation in 1965. Others involve the ICC and include deregulation, transfer of rail car functions, and strengthening the position of the chairman.

Regulatory politics, as they bear on the presidency, are usually more complex than the simplistic capture and congressional dominance models suggest. In situations of some political sensitivity, there were ordinarily a variety of interests for Johnson and his aides to sort through and, in some sense, manage. At times there was something resembling classic competitive regulatory politics in which a victory on the part of one interest meant a loss for others. The certification of U.S. air carriers to serve international routes is one example, and the struggle over the interest rates to be paid on time deposits is another. More frequently, a general interest, such as slowing price increases, collided with narrower interests. Cases of this sort include rail mergers, oil import controls, communications policy, and agricultural policy.

It can be argued that the more particularistic interests were of greater salience and carried more weight in congressional as opposed to presidential decision-making processes. This does not mean that the president and his aides were insensitive to pressure exerted by such interests. The conjunction of group pressures and the political interests of members of Congress clearly affected presidential appointments at times. They also affected presidential positions on, for example, agricultural legislation and the scheme for regulating motor vehicle emissions. In other instances, politics caused the modification of presidential initiatives in Congress. Among the many examples are the highway beauty and highway safety measures. The most adverse effects of regulatory politics on the conduct of the president's business in regulation were lost legislative battles, such as the failure to secure repeal of section 14(b), although there were few absolute defeats.

Johnson's congressional successes in altering economic regulation usually brought incremental changes of relatively minor importance. The only major innovative options seriously considered by the administration were in the regulation of cotton production, in revising the antitrust laws, in transportation deregulation, and in relations between farmers and the purchasers of their products. None of these were actually proposed to the Congress, except for the last, although the cotton scheme was first developed there.

New regulatory regimes reaching significantly beyond established boundaries to protect consumers, to enhance public health and safety, and to protect the environment are Johnson's largest and most enduring effect on the character of national regulation. A number of important measures were enacted, and still others were being developed or were under active consideration when he left office. In the process, the potential role of the president in regulation was enlarged, because most of the new programs that emerged were located in executive departments and agencies, not commissions.

There were also differences in the politics associated with these initiatives and the politics characteristic of economic regulation. In James Q. Wilson's formulation, the distinction is between interest group and entrepreneurial politics. Entrepreneurial politics form around policy proposals that promise general benefits but impose costs that are concentrated. Under such circumstances, political entrepreneurs are required to "mobilize latent public sentiment."[16] Members of Congress played important entrepreneurial roles in promoting the "new" regulation in its various specific forms. Although often following in their wake, Johnson used the distinctive and potent pulpit provided by his office to develop public support for new departures in policy.[17]

All in all, the politics of regulation in Johnson's presidency were essentially pluralistic in character. Managing the complex of forces at play was a continuing challenge and contributed to shaping how he played the presidential role in regulation.

On Being Chief Executive

> Energy in the executive is a leading character in the definition of good government. . . . It is . . . essential to the steady administration of laws.
>
> Publius, 18 March 1788[18]

Alexander Hamilton's familiar, yet ever-pertinent, admonition was certainly realized in the Johnson presidency. After leaving office, Johnson wrote, "I used the power of the Presidency proudly and I used every ounce of it I had."[19] Certainly the legislative record and many other aspects of his presidency clearly attest to this. In regard to the chief executive role, however, the precise nature and direction of the energy, or power, applied remain to be clearly delineated.

Presidents have important choices to make in their approach to the office and to the ways in which they play the chief executive role. Hugh Heclo points to the limits of administration and to the hazards of merely presiding. A president, he argues, must manage his relationship with aides and advisers in an attentive way. A major purpose is "to see to it that he is at the center of things when he wants to be and 'out of it' when he needs to be."[20] Johnson anticipated Heclo's prescription and rather adeptly managed the White House with this end in mind. As a result, not only could he govern the involvement of his aides in regulatory matters, but he could be somewhat selective in when and how he functioned as chief executive in relation to them.

There were, of course, limits to discretion. Some things had to be done, especially when required by law. But even in the realm of duty, as well as when compulsion and disagreement pressed for action, there was considerable room for choice. In other contexts, purpose, or focused policy objectives to which a president is personally committed, may motivate action. But there is discretion here as well, and this motivating factor was largely absent as Johnson went about his business in regulation.

When presidents elect to act as chief executive in particular situations, there are further choices to make as to means. A distinction is usually made between command, a technique appropriate in some situations, and leadership, or persuasion in Neustadt's terms. Leadership ordinarily is viewed as the more efficacious option for presidents. The essence of the leadership task is to mobilize and deploy influence as a means for obtaining presidential objectives and, in the process, provide necessary services to those at subordinate levels.

Executive leadership was on display most dramatically in regard to wage-price guideposts, balance of payments, and certain controversies in labor-management relations. The president employed a variety of tools that need not be reviewed again here. But note should be taken of a basic point: Johnson's executive leadership in regulation was a three-dimensional phenomenon with variations as to actuation, direction, and intention. When treated in presidential context, leadership is typically characterized as proactive in its actuation, as aimed at bringing about change in its direction, and, in intention, as seeking to realize particular results that the White House desires. In certain areas, Johnson's leadership fit this characterization. Transportation deregulation is an example. But much of Johnson's leadership in regulation followed a different course. As to actuation, it was more reactive to circumstances and pressures than proactive in the sense of seeking opportunities for involvement. In direction, it was not aimed at altering the status quo as much as it was employed to secure stability and to preclude the controversies often sparked by change, especially in economic regulation. Leadership often was exerted to prevent things from happening, rather than causing things to happen. In intention, it was often instrumental in character. That is to say, many of Johnson's engagements with regulation did not reflect an interest in influencing regulation per se. He cared naught, in his presidential role, for the licensing of broadcasting stations and motor carriers; for the enforcement of securities, meat and poultry inspection, and mine safety laws; or for the substance of many larger regulatory policy problems. Instead, influencing regulation was an instrument for protecting the president's capacities for leadership in matters of greater importance to him when there appeared to be a connection. When Johnson looked at most regulatory programs, it was largely in terms of how they might affect his power position in other areas and in the future.

All in all, Johnson conducted his business in regulation with shrewdness, adeptness, sophistication, and reticence. He led in a real sense, and in the process he demonstrated that there is more to the chief executive role and to executive leadership in that context than efforts to realize grand objectives. The test of success in the chief executive role and as executive leader is whether relevant presidential objectives are realized. By this measure, in regulation the presidency of Lyndon B. Johnson must be judged in quite positive terms.

Notes

1. The President's Business

1. Lyndon Baines Johnson, *The Vantage Point: Perspectives of the Presidency, 1963–1969* (New York: Holt, Rinehart and Winston, 1971), p. 566.

2. Data describing Johnson's week are taken from the Daily Diary material in the LBJ Library.

3. President's Committee on Administrative Management, *Report with Special Studies* (Washington, D.C.: GPO, 1937).

4. Joseph A. Califano, Jr., *A Presidential Nation* (New York: W. W. Norton, 1975), p. 24.

5. There is, of course, an extensive literature that treats presidential leadership in broad terms, headed by Richard E. Neustadt's *Presidential Power and the Modern Presidents: The Politics of Leadership from Roosevelt to Reagan* (New York: Free Press, 1990). Other notable works include James MacGregor Burns, *The Power to Lead: The Crisis of the American Presidency* (New York: Simon and Schuster, 1984); George C. Edwards III and Stephen J. Wayne, *Presidential Leadership: Politics and Policy Making* (New York: St. Martin's Press, 1990); Fred I. Greenstein (ed.), *Leadership in the Modern Presidency* (Cambridge: Harvard University Press, 1988); and Barbara Kellerman, *The Political Presidency: Practice of Leadership* (New York: Oxford University Press, 1984).

6. Richard Rose, *Managing Presidential Objectives* (New York: Free Press, 1976), p. 12.

7. Roger B. Porter, *Presidential Decision Making: The Economic Policy Board* (Cambridge: Cambridge University Press, 1980), p. 6.

8. Stephen Hess, *Organizing the Presidency* (Washington, D.C.: Brookings Institution, 1976), p. 146.

9. Godfrey Hodgson, *All Things to All Men: The False Promise of the Modern American Presidency* (New York: Simon and Schuster, 1980), p. 86.

10. The literature emphasizing the power of the centrifugal forces in and around the executive branch is vast. See especially Lawrence C. Dodd and Richard L. Schott, *Congress and the Administrative State* (New York: John Wiley, 1979); J. Leiper Freeman, *The Political Process: Executive Bureau–*

Legislative Committee Relations (New York: Random House, 1965); Hugh Heclo, "Issue Networks and the Executive Establishment," in Anthony King (ed.), *The New American Political System* (Washington, D.C.: American Enterprise Institute for Public Policy Research, 1978), p. 87; Theodore J. Lowi, *The End of Liberalism: The Second Republic of the United States* (New York: Norton, 1979); Arthur Maas, *Muddy Waters* (Cambridge: Harvard University Press, 1951); Grant McConnell, *Private Power and American Democracy* (New York: Alfred A. Knopf, 1966); Francis E. Rourke, *Bureaucracy, Politics and Public Policy* (Boston: Little, Brown, 1984); and Harold Seidman and Robert Gilmour, *Politics, Position, and Power: From the Positive to the Regulatory State* (New York: Oxford University Press, 1986).

11. John H. Kessel, *The Domestic Presidency: Decision-Making in The White House* (North Scituate, Mass.: Duxbury Press, 1975), pp. 9–11.

12. Louis W. Koenig, *The Chief Executive* (New York: Harcourt Brace Jovanovich, 1981), p. 189.

13. Porter, *Presidential Decision Making*, p. 230.

14. Richard E. Neustadt, "Politicians and Bureaucrats," in David B. Truman (ed.), *The Congress and America's Future* (Englewood Cliffs, N.J.: Prentice-Hall, 1965), p. 113.

15. See Norton E. Long, "Power and Administration," *Public Administration Review* 9/4 (1949): 257.

16. For an illustrative discussion, see Morton H. Halperin, *Bureaucratic Politics and Foreign Policy* (Washington, D.C.: Brookings Institution, 1974), pp. 239–242.

17. Rose, *Managing Presidential Objectives*, p. 5.

18. Koenig, *The Chief Executive*, p. 184.

19. See Richard L. Cole and David A. Caputo, "Presidential Control of the Senior Civil Service: Assessing the Strategies of the Nixon Years," *American Political Science Review* 73 (June 1979): 399.

20. See Kessel, *The Domestic Presidency*, pp. 4–7. For a general characterization of the president's role as chief executive that emphasizes both strengths and weaknesses, see Raymond Tatalovich and Byron W. Daynes, *Presidential Power in the United States* (Monterey, Cal.: Brooks/Cole, 1984), chapter 5.

21. Neustadt, *Presidential Power*, p. 251.

22. Joseph A. Califano, Jr., *The Triumph and Tragedy of Lyndon Johnson: The White House Years* (New York: Simon and Schuster, 1991); Robert A. Caro, *The Path to Power* (New York: Alfred A. Knopf, 1982); Robert A. Caro, *Means of Ascent* (New York: Alfred A. Knopf, 1990); Paul K. Conkin, *Big Daddy from the Pedernales: Lyndon Baines Johnson* (Boston: Twayne Publishers, 1986); Robert Dallek, *Lone Star Rising: Lyndon Johnson and His Times 1908–1960* (New York: Oxford University Press, 1991); Doris Kearns, *Lyndon Johnson and the American Dream* (New York: Harper and Row, 1976), esp. pp. 214–217. See also James David Barber, *The Presidential Character: Predicting Performance in the White House* (Englewood Cliffs, N.J.: Prentice-Hall, 1972), pp. 78–95.

23. Hess, *Organizing the Presidency*, p. 101.

24. "Special Message to the Congress: The Quality of American Government," 17 March 1967, *Public Papers of the President of the United States: Lyndon B. Johnson*, 1967 (Washington, D.C.: GPO, 1968), p. 358 (hereafter cited as *Public Papers*).

25. For an overview on the PPB experience, see Allen Schick, "A Death in the Bureaucracy: The Demise of Federal PPB," *Public Administration Review* 33 (March/April 1973): 146.

26. Norman C. Thomas and Harold L. Wolman, "The Presidency and Policy Formulation: The Task Force Device," *Public Administration Review* 29 (September/October, 1969): 459; Emmette S. Redford and Richard F. McCulley, *White House Operations: The Johnson Presidency* (Austin: University of Texas Press, 1986), chapter 5.

27. Emmette S. Redford and Marlan Blissett, *Organizing the Executive Branch: The Johnson Presidency* (Chicago: University of Chicago Press, 1981), p. 10. For a case study of presidential effect through structural change, see Robert R. Sullivan, "The Role of the Presidency in Shaping Lower Level Policy-Making Processes," *Polity* 3 (Winter 1970): 201–210.

28. G. Calvin Mackenzie, "The Paradox of Presidential Personnel Management," in Hugh Heclo and Lester M. Salamon (eds.), *The Illusion of Presidential Government* (Boulder, Colo.: Westview Press, 1981), p. 122. See also Richard S. Schott and Dagmar S. Hamilton, *People, Positions, and Power: The Political Appointments of Lyndon Johnson* (Chicago: University of Chicago Press, 1983).

29. Califano, *A Presidential Nation*, pp. 193–194.

30. Hugh Heclo, *A Government of Strangers: Executive Politics in Washington* (Washington, D.C.: Brookings Institution, 1977) p. 73.

31. Ibid.

32. James E. Anderson, "Presidential Management of the Bureaucracy and the Johnson Presidency: A Preliminary Exploration," *Congress and the Presidency* 1 (Autumn 1984): 137–164.

33. Neustadt, *Presidential Power*, p. 56.

34. Quoted in Califano, *A Presidential Nation*, p. 23.

35. James Gaither Oral History Interview, 17 January 1969, tape 4, p. 10, LBJ Library.

36. Ibid.

37. Hess, *Organizing the Presidency*, p. 110.

38. William D. Carey, "Presidential Staffing in the Sixties and Seventies," *Public Administration Review* 29 (September/October 1969): 454.

39. Hess, *Organizing the Presidency*, p. 110.

40. Thomas E. Cronin, " 'Everybody Believes in Democracy until He Gets to the White House . . .': An Examination of White House–Departmental Relations," in Norman Thomas and Hans W. Baade (eds.), *The Institutionalized Presidency* (Dobbs Ferry, N.Y.: Oceana Publications, 1972), p. 148.

41. Ibid., pp. 159–161.

42. Ibid.

43. Ibid., p. 148.

44. Califano, *A Presidential Nation*, p. 23.

45. Redford and Blissett, *Organizing the Executive Branch*, p. 208.

46. Numerous studies show that despite the enlargement and strengthening of the institutional presidency since the late 1960s Johnson's successors continued to experience frustration in playing the chief executive role. In addition to those already cited, the following analyses are illustrative: Joel D. Aberbach and Bert A. Rockman, "Clashing Beliefs within the Executive Branch: The Nixon Administration's Bureaucracy," *American Political Science Review* 70 (June 1976): 456; Joel D. Aberbach and Bert A. Rockman, "Mandates or Mandarins? Control and Discretion in the Modern Administrative State," *Public Administration Review* 48 (March/April 1988): 606; James G. Benze, Jr., *Presidential Power and Management Techniques: The Carter and Reagan Administrations in Historical Perspective* (New York: Greenwood Press, 1987); Ben W. Heneman, Jr., and Curtis Hessler, *Memorandum for the President: A Strategic Approach to Domestic Affairs in the 1980s* (New York: Random House, 1980); Herbert Kaufman, *The Administrative Behavior of Federal Bureaucrats* (Washington, D.C.: Brookings Institution, 1981); Lawrence E. Lynn, Jr., *Managing Public Policy* (Boston: Little, Brown, 1987); Richard P. Nathan, *The Administrative Presidency* (New York: John Wiley and Sons, 1983); Chester A. Newland, "The Reagan Presidency: Limited Government and Political Administration," *Public Administration Review* 43 (January/February 1983): 1; James P. Pfiffner, "Political Appointees and Career Executives: The Democracy-Bureaucracy Nexus in the Third Century," *Public Administration Review* 47 (January/February 1987): 57; Ronald Randall, "Presidential Power versus Bureaucratic Intransigence: The Influence of the Nixon Administration on Welfare Policy," *American Political Science Review* 73 (September 1979): 795; Elizabeth Sanders, "The Presidency and the Bureaucratic State," in Michael Nelson (ed.), *The Presidency and the Political System* (Washington, D.C.: Congressional Quarterly Press, 1988), p. 379; and Richard W. Waterman, *Presidential Influence and the Administrative State* (Knoxville: University of Tennessee Press, 1989).

47. "Special Message to the Congress on the Regulatory Agencies," 13 April 1961, *Public Papers*, p. 268.

48. The most thorough discussion of Johnson's broadcasting interests while in Congress is in Dallek, *Lone Star Rising*, pp. 247–251, 260, 265, 281, 283, 309, and 409–415.

49. Quoted in Dallek, *Lone Star Rising*, p. 371.

50. Joseph P. Harris, "The Senatorial Rejection of Leland Olds: A Case Study," *American Political Science Review* 45 (September 1951): 674.

51. His basic views are outlined in a speech on the Senate floor on 28 March 1950: *Congressional Record*, 81st Congress, 2d session, 1950, pp. 4189–4197.

52. James Q. Wilson, "The Politics of Regulation," in James Q. Wilson (ed.), *The Politics of Regulation* (New York: Basic Books, 1980), p. 388.

53. Kenneth J. Meier, *Regulation: Politics, Bureaucracy, and Economics* (New York: St. Martin's Press, 1985), p. 25.

54. Randall B. Ripley and Grace A. Franklin, *Congress, the Bureaucracy, and Public Policy* (Homewood, Ill.: Dorsey Press, 1984), pp. 24–26.

55. Randall B. Ripley and Grace A. Franklin, *Policy Implementation and Bureaucracy* (Chicago: Dorsey Press, 1986), chapters 5 and 6.

56. For example, Robert A. Katzman, "Federal Trade Commission," in Wilson (ed.), *The Politics of Regulation*, chapter 5; Paul J. Quirk, "Food and Drug Administration," in ibid., chapter 6; and Frances E. Rourke, "The Presidency and the Bureaucracy: Strategic Alternatives," in Michael Nelson (ed.), *The Presidency and the Political System* (Washington, D.C.: Congressional Quarterly Press, 1984), p. 339.

57. The literature on the point is voluminous. Two major and illustrative examples are Marver H. Bernstein, *Regulating Business by Independent Commissions* (Princeton: Princeton University Press, 1955), and Murray Edelman, *The Symbolic Uses of Politics* (Urbana: University of Illinois Press, 1964).

58. See, for example, Barry R. Weingast and Mark J. Moran, "Bureaucratic Discretion or Congressional Control? Regulatory Policymaking by the Federal Trade Commission," *Journal of Political Economy* 91 (1983): 765, and Barry R. Weingast, "The Congressional-Bureaucratic System: A Principal Agent Perspective," *Public Choice* 44 (1984): 147.

59. William E. Brigman, "The Executive Branch and Independent Regulatory Agencies," *Presidential Studies Quarterly* 11 (Spring 1981): 244; James O. Freedman, *Crisis and Legitimacy: The Administrative Process and American Government* (Cambridge: Cambridge University Press, 1978), pp. 62–65; Meier, *Regulation*, pp. 25–27; and Emmette S. Redford, "The President and the Regulatory Commissions," *Texas Law Review* 45 (December 1965): 288.

60. Martha Derthick and Paul J. Quirk, *The Politics of Deregulation* (Washington, D.C.: Brookings Institution, 1985). See also Howard Ball, *Controlling Regulatory Sprawl: Presidential Strategies from Nixon to Reagan* (Westport, Conn.: Greenwood Press, 1984); Anthony E. Brown, *The Politics of Airline Deregulation* (Knoxville: University of Tennessee Press, 1987); George C. Eads and Michael Fix (eds.), *The Reagan Regulatory Strategy: An Assessment* (Washington, D.C.: Urban Institute Press, 1984); Edward Paul Fuchs, *Presidents, Management and Regulation* (Englewood Cliffs, N.J.: Prentice-Hall, 1988); Marshall R. Goodman and Margaret T. Wrightson, *Managing Regulatory Reform: The Reagan Strategy and Its Impact* (New York: Praeger, 1987); Dorothy Robyn, *Braking the Special Interests: Trucking Deregulation and the Politics of Policy Reform* (Chicago: University of Chicago Press, 1987); Lester M. Salamon, "Federal Regulation: A New Arena for Presidential Power?" in Heclo and Salamon (eds.), *The Illusion of Presidential Government*, chapter 5; Susan J. Tolchin and Martin Tolchin, *Dismantling America: The Rush to Deregulate* (New York: Oxford University Press, 1983); and David M. Welborn, "Taking Stock of Regulatory Re-

form," paper presented at the annual meeting of the American Political Science Association, Washington, D.C., 1–4 September 1977.

61. Goodman and Wrightson, *Managing Regulatory Reform*, p. 26.

62. Ibid., p. 27.

63. U.S. Congress, Senate Committee on Commerce, *Appointments to the Regulatory Agencies: The Federal Communications Commission and the Federal Trade Commission (1949–1974)*, by James M. Graham and Victor H. Kramer, Committee Print (Washington, D.C.: GPO, 1976). Much of the literature on regulatory personnel is summarized in Barry M. Mitnick, *The Political Economy of Regulation: Creating, Designing and Removing Regulatory Forms* (New York: Columbia University Press, 1980), pp. 209–232.

64. William L. Cary, *Politics and the Regulatory Agencies* (New York: McGraw-Hill, 1967), pp. 8–9.

65. Major statements of this perspective include Emmette S. Redford, *The Regulatory Process: With Illustrations from Commercial Aviation* (Austin: University of Texas Press, 1969); Ripley and Franklin, *Congress, the Bureaucracy, and Public Policy*; and Paul A. Sabatier, "Regulatory Policy-Making: Toward a Framework of Analysis," *Natural Resources Journal* 17 (July 1977): 415.

66. Terry M. Moe, "Control and Feedback in Economic Regulation: The Case of the NLRB," *American Political Science Review* 79 (December 1985): 1094. Two other relevant articles by Moe are "Regulatory Performance and Presidential Administration," *American Journal of Political Science* 26 (May 1982): 197, and "An Assessment of the Positive Theory of 'Congressional Dominance,'" *Legislative Studies Quarterly* 12 (November 1987): 475.

67. Meier, *Regulation*, p. 27.

68. Roger G. Brown and Larry W. Thomas, "Reaganizing Federal Regulation: Presidential Impact on Enforcement Activities," paper presented at the annual meeting of the American Political Science Association, Washington, D.C., 30 August–2 September 1984; David W. Hedge, Donald C. Menzel, with George Williams, "Loosening the Regulatory Ratchet: The Reagan Administration and Coal Surface Mining," paper presented at the annual meeting of the American Political Science Association, Washington, D.C., 1–4 September 1983; Lawrence S. Rothenberg, "Presidential Management of the Bureaucracy: The Reform of Motor Carrier Regulation at the ICC," paper presented at the annual meeting of the Midwest Political Science Association, Chicago, April 1987; Seymour Scher, "Regulatory Agency Control through Appointment: The Care of the Eisenhower Administration and the NLRB," *Journal of Politics* 23 (November 1961): 667; Joseph Stewart, Jr., and Jane S. Cromartie, "Partisan Presidential Change and Regulatory Policy: The Case of the FTC and Deceptive Practices Enforcement, 1938–74," *Presidential Studies Quarterly* 12 (Fall 1982): 568; David M. Welborn, "Presidents, Regulatory Commissioners, and Regulatory Policy," *Journal of Public Law* 15 (1966): 3; and David M. Welborn, *Governance of Federal Regulatory Agencies* (Knoxville: University of Tennessee Press, 1977).

69. It should be noted, however, that even ambitious presidents may

meet with only qualified success. Two illustrative studies on the point are Roger G. Brown and Larry W. Thomas, "Reluctant Regulatory Reforms: Unanticipated Consequences of Reagan's Regulatory Federalism," paper presented at the annual meeting of the American Political Science Association, New Orleans, 29 August–1 September 1985, and B. Dan Wood, "Principals, Bureaucrats and Responsiveness in Clean Air Enforcement," *American Political Science Review* 82 (March 1988): 213.

2. The Fourth Branch

1. "Remarks at a Meeting with the Heads of Independent Regulatory Agencies," 3 December 1963, *Public Papers of the President of the United States: Lyndon B. Johnson, 1963–1964* (Washington, D.C.: GPO, 1965), p. 19 (hereafter cited as *Public Papers*).

2. For background, see Bernard Schwartz, *The Professor and the Commissions* (New York: Alfred A. Knopf, 1959).

3. David S. Black Oral History Interview, 12 November 1968, p. 13, LBJ Library.

4. Ibid., p. 11.

5. James M. Landis, *Report on Regulatory Agencies to the President-Elect*, printed by the Subcommittee on Administrative Practice and Procedure, Committee on Judiciary, U.S. Senate (86th Cong., 2d Sess., Committee Print, December 1960).

6. See David M. Welborn, "Presidents, Regulatory Commissioners and Regulatory Policy," *Journal of Public Law* 15/no. 1 (1966): 3.

7. "Remarks at a Meeting with the Heads of Independent Regulatory Agencies," 3 December 1963, *Public Papers*, p. 19.

8. Noted on memo, Jacobsen to Valenti, 11 May 1965, attached to letter, Jacobsen to Clark, 15 March 1965, Ex UT 2-1, WHCF, LBJ Library.

9. Letter, Clark to Jacobsen, 11 May 1965, Ex UT 2-1, WHCF, LBJ Library.

10. Memo, Jacobsen to Valenti, 11 May 1965, Ex UT 2-1, WHCF, LBJ Library.

11. Lee C. White Oral History Interview, 2 March 1971, tape 3, p. 27, LBJ Library.

12. Memo, Califano to president, 15 May 1967, "Pricing Files: Balance of Payments" folder, box 2, files of John Robson and Sanford Ross, LBJ Library.

13. Memo, McPherson to Alexander, 8 May 1968, "Office Files of Harry McPherson (A)" folder, box 46, files of Harry McPherson, LBJ Library.

14. Memo, White to Califano, 22 April 1966, Ex FG 200, WHCF, LBJ Library.

15. Memos, White to Watson, 11 April 1966, Ex FG 232; and Watson to president, 12 April 1966, Ex FG 232, WHCF, LBJ Library.

16. Memo, McPherson to president, 1 April 1966, "Memos for the President (1966)" folder, box 52, files of Harry McPherson, LBJ Library.

17. Comment, president to crm, 1 April 1966, attached to ibid.

18. Memo, Staats to Feldman, 16 October 1964, Ex FG 211, WHCF, LBJ Library.

19. Letter, Feldman to Hoyt, 19 October 1964, Ex FG 211, WHCF, LBJ Library.

20. Ibid.

21. Letter, Watson to Galland, 7 June 1965, Gen. CA/7 Island Airlines, WHCF, LBJ Library.

22. Memo, Kintner to files, 3 September 1966, Ex FG 228, WHCF, LBJ Library.

23. Letter, Ford to president, 5 January 1967, C.F. FG 234, WHCF, LBJ Library.

24. Memo, Califano to president, 19 January 1967, C.F. FG 234, WHCF, LBJ Library.

25. Memo, Valenti to president, 13 January 1967, Ex BE 4/Automotive, WHCF, LBJ Library.

26. Memos, Kintner to president, 13 January 1967, C.F. FG 234; and Schoen to Kintner, 13 January 1967, C.F. FG 234, WHCF, LBJ Library.

27. Memo, Watson to president, 16 January 1967, C.F. FG 234, WHCF, LBJ Library.

28. Memo, Califano to president, 19 January 1967, C.F. FG 234, WHCF, LBJ Library.

29. Memo, Kintner to files, 18 January 1967, C.F. FG 234, WHCF, LBJ Library.

30. Memo, Watson to president, 26 January 1967, Ex BE 4/Automotive, WHCF, LBJ Library.

31. Ibid.

32. Memo, Califano to president, 27 October 1965, C.F. UT 1-3, WHCF, LBJ Library.

33. Memo, Valenti to president, 6 December 1965, Ex UT 1-3, WHCF, LBJ Library.

34. Memo, Valenti to president, 11 May 1966, C.F. FG 228, WHCF, LBJ Library.

35. Memo, Watson to president, 24 May 1966, Ex FG 232, WHCF, LBJ Library.

36. Memo, Rowe to Watson, 2 June 1966, Ex FG 228, WHCF, LBJ Library.

37. Memo, Watson to president, 1 July 1966, Ex FG 232, WHCF, LBJ Library. Persons who dealt with Johnson usually learned that an obligation was created when they asked something of the president and it was granted. Approximately a year after seeing Johnson in 1966 Kappel was called upon to serve on a special board dealing with a difficult railway labor dispute. According to Califano, "Johnson wanted a report tilted toward labor with a distinguished businessman's endorsement. He got it" (Joseph A. Califano, Jr., *The Triumph and Tragedy of Lyndon Johnson: The White House Years* [New York: Simon and Schuster, 1991], pp. 194–195).

38. Memo, Califano to president, 14 July 1966, C.F. FG 228, WHCF, LBJ Library.

39. Ibid.

40. White Oral History Interview, tape 3, p. 26.
41. Ibid.
42. Recollection of Kenneth O'Donnell, quoted in U.S. Congress, Senate, Committee on Commerce, *Appointments to the Regulatory Agencies: The Federal Communications Commission and the Federal Trade Commission (1949–1974)*, by James M. Graham and Victor H. Kramer, Committee Print (Washington, D.C.: GPO, 1976), p. 243 (hereafter cited as *Appointments to the Regulatory Agencies*).
43. Letter, Mundt to president, 20 February 1965, Ex FG 263, WHCF, LBJ Library.
44. Noted on ibid.
45. Memo, Watson to president, 23 August 1966, Ex FG 251, WHCF, LBJ Library.
46. U.S. Congress, Senate, Committee on Government Operations, Study on Federal Regulation, vol. 1, *The Regulatory Appointments Process*, 95th Cong., 1st Sess. (Washington, D.C.: GPO, 1977) (hereafter cited as *The Regulatory Appointments Process*).
47. Letter, Burns to Watson, 12 May 1966, Ex FG 236, WHCF, LBJ Library.
48. John Harllee Oral History Interview, 24 March 1969, p. 5, LBJ Library.
49. Ibid.
50. *The Regulatory Appointments Process*, p. 101.
51. Memo, Macy to president, 16 March 1968, "Charles R. Ross" folder, box 501, files of John W. Macy, Jr., LBJ Library.
52. *The Regulatory Appointments Process*, p. 267.
53. Ibid., p. 243.
54. Memo, Macy to president, 12 June 1967, Ex FG 228 A, WHCF, LBJ Library.
55. *Appointments to the Regulatory Agencies*, pp. 259–260. Other indications of concern for pending cases are in memos, White to president, 26 January 1965, Ex FG 232; and Califano to president, 12 November 1966, Ex FG 251, WHCF, LBJ Library.
56. Black Oral History Interview, p. 11.
57. Noted on memo, Watson to president, 26 March 1966, Ex FG 263 A, WHCF, LBJ Library.
58. Memo, Macy to president, 25 July 1966, "Gerald A. Brown" folder, box 65, files of John W. Macy, Jr., LBJ Library.
59. Noted on memo, Califano to president, 18 April 1966, Ex FG 263, WHCF, LBJ Library.
60. Ibid.
61. Memo, Watson to president, 17 June 1966, Ex FG 263, WHCF, LBJ Library.
62. Memo, Califano to president, 18 July 1966, Ex FG 263, WHCF, LBJ Library.
63. Memo, Macy to Falcon, 19 July 1966, "Gerald R. Brown" folder, box 65, files of John W. Macy, Jr., LBJ Library.

64. Memo, McCulloch to Watson, 4 August 1966, Ex FG 263, WHCF, LBJ Library.

65. A somewhat similar situation arose in 1967 concerning Arnold Ordman, general counsel of the NLRB, whose four-year term expired in mid-May. Although he was supported for reappointment by McCulloch, the secretary and under secretary of Labor, and the AFL-CIO leadership (who, Califano told Johnson, "have been to see me three times this week about the problem") the president refused to act. Unless the post was filled, complaints could not be received or orders issued. At the last moment it was announced that Ordman would be continued, and he was designated as acting general counsel so the board could function while the Senate was considering his confirmation. See memos, Califano to president, 13 May 1967, Ex LA 3; and McPherson to president, 19 May 1967, "Memos for the President (1967)" folder, box 53, files of Harry McPherson, LBJ Library.

66. David M. Welborn, *Governance of Federal Regulatory Agencies* (Knoxville: University of Tennessee Press, 1977).

67. The chairman of the CAB serves a one-year term. There is legal uncertainty about the chairmanship of the FPC; one body of opinion is that its chairman could not be replaced before the completion of his term as a member. The chairman of the FRB serves a four-year term.

68. Memo, Jones to Watson, 15 June 1965, attached to memo, LBJ Library, Hopkins to Roberts, 29 June 1965, Ex FG 236A, WHCF, LBJ Library.

69. Memo, Falcon to Califano, 29 February 1967, Ex FG 234, WHCF, LBJ Library.

70. Memo, Marsh for the record, 17 March 1967, "Donald Turner" folder, box 604, files of John W. Macy, Jr., LBJ Library.

71. Memo, Macy to president, 19 August 1967, Ex FG 234 A, WHCF, LBJ Library.

72. *Broadcasting*, 11 April 1966, p. 134.

73. Interview with the author, 19 December 1973.

74. James L. Baughman, *Television's Guardians: The FCC and the Politics of Programming, 1958–1976* (Knoxville: University of Tennessee Press, 1985), pp. 133–150.

75. *Appointments to the Regulatory Agencies*, p. 251.

76. Ibid.

77. Memo, Macy to Watson, 26 April 1966, Ex FG 228, WHCF, LBJ Library.

78. White Oral History Interview, tape 3, p. 24.

79. Ibid.

80. Ibid. Swidler was not without his industry supporters, however. See letter, McElvenny to president, 19 May 1965, Ex FG 232, WHCF, LBJ Library. McElvenny was president of a natural gas company.

81. Comment, president to Jones, 17 October 1968, Ex FG 251, WHCF, LBJ Library.

82. Memo, Manatos to president, 1 September 1968, Ex FG 251, WHCF, LBJ Library.

83. Memo, Jones to president, 17 September 1968, Ex FG 251, WHCF, LBJ Library.

84. Richard L. Schott and Dagmar S. Hamilton, *People, Positions and Power: The Political Appointments of Lyndon Johnson* (Chicago: University of Chicago Press, 1983), pp. 14–17.

85. Memo, Macy to president, 30 September 1968, Ex FG 251, WHCF, LBJ Library.

86. Ibid.

87. Ibid.

88. Technically, the regulatory statutes place limits on the number of members drawn from one party. When Democrats are in the majority, it is not required that minority members be Republicans. They usually are, however.

89. *The Regulatory Appointments Process*, p. 145.

90. John Macy Oral History Interview, 26 April 1969, tape 3, p. 23, LBJ Library.

91. Memo, Gordon to president, 3 February 1964, Ex FG 200 A, WHCF, LBJ Library.

92. *Appointments to the Regulatory Agencies*, pp. 232–233.

93. Memo, Valenti to president, 8 January 1965, Ex FG 228, WHCF, LBJ Library.

94. *Appointments to the Regulatory Agencies*, p. 244.

95. Ibid., p. 245.

96. Ibid., p. 247.

97. Daily Diary, 25 March 1965, LBJ Library. The calls to Wadsworth were at 11:14 and 12:31 P.M.

98. Memo, Jones to president, 12 July 1968, Ex FG 232, WHCF, LBJ Library.

99. One Republican appointment, that of former representative Hamer Budge to the SEC, provoked considerable speculation. It was one of Johnson's first, and many saw the placement of a very conservative Republican on this agency as an inauspicious step. Budge's prime sponsor for a position was Representative Charles Halleck, House Minority Leader. Budge wanted a position to fill out his federal service for retirement program purposes. He and Halleck rebuffed suggestions of executive agency positions in favor of one for a term of office sufficient to guarantee the necessary years of service. Halleck had enough influence to get his way (memo, Dungan to president, 29 April 1964, Ex FG 200, WHCF, LBJ Library).

100. Memo, Macy to president, 8 December 1967, "Applications Recommendation—1967" folder, box 2, files of Harry McPherson, LBJ Library.

101. Macy Oral History Interview, tape 3, p. 21.

102. As shown, for example, in memos, Valenti to president, 17 March 1965, Ex FG 228; and Macy to president, 22 June 1968, Ex FG 228 A, WHCF, LBJ Library.

103. Noted on memo, McPherson to president, 13 August 1965, "Applications/Recommendations—1967" folder, box 2, files of Harry McPherson, LBJ Library.

104. *Appointments to the Regulatory Agencies*, p. 237.

105. *The Regulatory Appointments Process*, p. 232.

106. Ibid. The criteria employed in selecting regulators are quite similar to those applied in other areas (Schott and Hamilton, *People, Positions and Power*, pp. 203–209).

107. *Appointments to the Regulatory Agencies*, p. 237.

108. Sherwin J. Markman Oral History Interview, 21 May 1969, pp. 38–39, LBJ Library.

109. White Oral History Interview, tape 3, pp. 42–43.

110. Letter, Bennett to president, 7 February 1964, Ex FG 229, WHCF, LBJ Library.

111. "The President's News Conference, 10 July 1964," *Public Papers*, p. 854.

112. "Remarks at the Swearing In of Rear Admiral John Harllee and James V. Day as Chairman and Vice Chairman, Federal Maritime Commission," 20 July 1965, *Public Papers*, p. 768.

113. "Remarks at the Swearing In of Lee C. White as Chairman of the Federal Power Commission," 2 March 1966, *Public Papers*, p. 249.

114. This is not to suggest that policy views and policy expertise were not relevant, only that selection was not determined by such considerations. A study of subsequent administrations arrived at similar findings: Paul J. Quirk, *Industry Influence in Federal Regulatory Agencies* (Princeton, N.J.: Princeton University Press, 1981), pp. 87–95. There were other criteria as well. Johnson resisted appointing or reappointing persons who would become seventy prior to the expiration of their terms, although in a few instances he relented. Regional claims to representation were considered. Gender and racial balance were not factors. Only two women and one member of a racial minority were named by Johnson to initial terms on the boards and commissions dealt with here.

115. "Remarks at the Swearing In of Joseph W. Barr as Member, Board of Directors, Federal Deposit Insurance Corporation," 23 January 1964, *Public Papers*, p. 221.

116. James E. Anderson and Jared E. Hazleton, *Managing Macroeconomic Policy: The Johnson Presidency* (Austin: University of Texas Press, 1986), pp. 105–120.

117. RE: William J. [*sic*] Jones' review of Professor Neuner's book, attached to memo, Valenti to president, 20 April 1965, Ex UT 3, WHCF, LBJ Library. The book was Edward J. Neuner, *The Natural Gas Industry: Monopoly and Competition in Field Markets* (Norman: University of Oklahoma Press, 1960). The review was in the *Columbia Law Review* 61 (1961): 301.

118. Memo, Valenti to president, filed 22 April 1965, Ex UT 3, WHCF, LBJ Library.

119. There is evidence that health was a factor. Jones was later given serious consideration for the CAB chairmanship (memo, Falcon to Macy, 27 September 1967, "William Kenneth Jones" folder, box 293, files of John W. Macy, Jr., LBJ Library).

120. Memo, Dungan to president, 3 September 1964, Ex FG 234 A, WHCF, LBJ Library.

121. Ibid.

122. Memo, Watson to president, filed 5 May 1967, Ex TN, WHCF, LBJ Library.

123. Ibid.

124. Memo, Watson to president, 23 September 1966, Ex FG 234 A, WHCF, LBJ Library.

125. Memo, Watson to president, 22 August 1967, Ex FG 234 A, WHCF, LBJ Library.

126. Ibid.

127. Memo, Macy to president, 19 July 1967, Ex FG 211 A, WHCF, LBJ Library. There are hints of various places where loyalty to the administration included giving support to the chairman. To the extent there was a consideration, it resulted in very few decisions not to reappoint. Perhaps one explanation is that the realization of this, in addition to other factors, creates a strong natural inclination in members to support their chairman. See Welborn, *Governance of Federal Regulatory Agencies*, chapter 3.

128. The president was advised of some of the complications regarding the Permian Basin case by FPC chairman Swidler through Lee White (memo, White to president, 26 January 1965, Ex FG 232, WHCF, LBJ Library).

129. The president saw Bagge in the White House on 24 February 1965 (Daily Diary, 24 February 1965, LBJ Library).

130. *Washington Post*, 16 March 1965, p. A17. See also Rowland Evans and Robert Novak, *Lyndon B. Johnson: The Exercise of Power* (New York: Signet, 1966), pp. 508–510.

131. Ibid.

132. Ibid.

133. Other means also were used to strengthen ties at this stage. They ranged from major prizes such as a White House swearing in ceremony to small but significant acts such as the gift of an autographed presidential portrait. For an illustrative catalogue of presidential "graciousness and generosity" in the appointment process, see letter, Johnson to president, 7 July 1967, Ex FG 228, WHCF, LBJ Library.

134. Evans and Novak, *Lyndon B. Johnson*, pp. 510–512. The authors give no sources for their information, but Ross, in a personal conversation, indicates that it is accurate.

135. Letter, Ross to Valenti, 25 March 1965, Ex FG 232 A, WHCF, LBJ Library.

136. Letter, Bagge to Macy, 30 September 1965, Ex FG 232, WHCF, LBJ Library.

137. Ibid.

138. Letter, Bagge to Roberts, 3 June 1965, Ex FG 232, WHCF, LBJ Library.

139. *Appointments to the Regulatory Agencies*, p. 235.

140. Ibid., pp. 270–271.

141. Ibid., p. 254.

142. Memo, Pierson to president, 2 February 1968, Ex FG 211, WHCF, LBJ Library.

143. Noted on ibid.

144. For example, Johnson talked to Senator Monroney about his decision not to name Monroney's candidate for the FDIC (memo, Watson to president, 13 November 1967, Ex FG 229, WHCF, LBJ Library).

145. Memos, Macy to president, 11 September 1968, Ex FG 228; and Manatos to president, 12 September 1968, Ex FG 232, WHCF, LBJ Library.

146. Memo, Jones to president, 4 September 1968, Ex FG 232, WHCF, LBJ Library.

147. The White House kept close tabs on the situation (memos Manatos to O'Brien, 28 April 1965, Ex FG 232 A; and White to president, 28 April 1965, Ex FG 232 A, WHCF, LBJ Library).

148. Memo, Macy to president, 21 April, 1967, Ex FG 232 A, WHCF, LBJ Library.

149. Memo, Manatos to president, 8 August 1967, Ex PE 2, WHCF, LBJ Library.

150. Ibid.

151. Noted on ibid.

152. Letter, Bagge to president, 12 August 1967, Ex FG 232 A, WHCF, LBJ Library. Related materials are letter, president to Bagge, 22 August 1967, Ex FG 232 A; memo, jdr to president, 22 August 1967, Ex FG 232 A; and LBJ comment, 11 September 1967, Ex FG 232 A, WHCF, LBJ Library.

153. Memos, Watson to president, 19 February 1966, Ex FG 232 A; and Macy to president, 24 February 1966, Ex FG 232 A, WHCF, LBJ Library.

154. *Appointments to the Regulatory Agencies*, p. 250.

155. *New York Times*, 20 June 1966, p. 32.

156. Memo, Kintner to president, 20 June 1966, C.F. FG 228 A, WHCF, LBJ Library.

157. Memos, Kintner to president, 21 June, 1966, C.F. FG 228 A; and Kintner to Watson, 22 June 1966, C.F. FG 228 A, WHCF, LBJ Library. Kintner also arranged for Gould to see Nicholas Johnson (memo, Kintner to president, 27 June 1966, C.F. FG 228 A, WHCF, LBJ Library).

158. *New York Times*, 26 June 1966, p. D15.

159. *New York Times*, 3 July 1966, p. D11.

160. Ibid.

161. Ibid.

3. Attending to Commission Regulation

1. Note, president to Watson, 4 September 1965, Ex TN, WHCF, LBJ Library.

2. Letter, Bush to president, 3 September 1965, Ex TN, WHCF, LBJ Library.

3. In late summer 1967 one of the president's aides advised him, "For whatever other problems we have with Johnson, you should know that he is one of the people in government who never fails to give the president

appropriate recognition" (memo, Califano to president, 27 August 1967, Ex FG 228, WHCF, LBJ Library). But there were contrary perceptions. A month later another aide pointed out to a colleague that "Nick manages to do a whole speech without acknowledging that there is a President of the United States" (memo, Goldstein to Watson, 25 September 1967, Ex FG 228, WHCF, LBJ Library).

4. Memo, Wilson to O'Brien, 26 January 1965, Ex FG 251, WHCF, LBJ Library.

5. Memo, O'Brien to Wilson, 28 January 1965, Ex FG 251, WHCF, LBJ Library.

6. Memo, Wilson to Valenti, 10 February 1965, Ex FG 251, WHCF, LBJ Library.

7. Memo, Valenti to White, 13 February 1965, Ex FG 251, WHCF, LBJ Library.

8. Memo, White to Valenti, 15 February 1965, Ex FG 251, WHCF, LBJ Library.

9. Noted on ibid.

10. Letter, Dingell to Wilson, 25 January 1965, Ex FG 251, WHCF, LBJ Library.

11. "The President's News Conference," 31 March 1966, *Public Papers of the President of the United States: Lyndon B. Johnson, 1966* (Washington, D.C.: GPO, 1967), p. 388.

12. Larry E. Temple Oral History Interview, 12 June 1970, tape 2, p. 10, LBJ Library. For an overview of White House staff activities and Johnson's management style, see Emmette S. Redford and Richard T. McCulley, *White House Operations: The Johnson Presidency* (Austin: University of Texas Press, 1986).

13. W. DeVier Pierson Oral History Interview, 20 March 1969, tape 2, p. 10, LBJ Library.

14. E. Ernest Goldstein Oral History Interview, 10 December 1968, tape 2, p. 3, LBJ Library.

15. Ibid., p. 4.

16. Ibid.

17. Pierson Oral History Interview, tape 2, p. 12.

18. The Daily Diary materials are in the LBJ Library. On presidential relations with the Federal Reserve Board and its chairman, which were much more extensive than in the case of other regulatory bodies, see James E. Anderson and Jared E. Hazleton, *Managing Macroeconomic Policy: The Johnson Presidency* (Austin: University of Texas Press, 1986), especially chapter 4.

19. Goldstein Oral History Interview, tape 2, p. 16.

20. See, for example, memo, Watson to president, 13 January 1966, Ex FG 200, WHCF, LBJ Library. Watson told Johnson that an initial decision to exclude the FCC had been reversed. Similar meetings were also held with commission executive directors (memo, Watson to president, 31 January 1966, Ex FG 200, WHCF, LBJ Library). There are additional indications that Watson met with other staff groups. For example, he had lunch with several

SEC staffers on 28 February 1966 (letter, Watson to Becker, 28 February 1966, Ex FG 281, WHCF, LBJ Library).

21. Letter, Hearn to Califano, 5 June 1967, Ex TR 117, WHCF, LBJ Library.

22. Letter, Elman to Watson, 28 January 1966, Ex FG 234, WHCF, LBJ Library.

23. Letter, Fanning to president, 6 September 1966, Ex FG 263, WHCF, LBJ Library.

24. Personal interview with the author, 13 March 1981, Washington, D.C.

25. Goldstein Oral History Interview, tape 2, p. 18.

26. Ibid., p. 4.

27. Memo, Goldstein to Zwick, 19 September 1968, Ex FG 234, WHCF, LBJ Library.

28. Goldstein Oral History Interview, tape 2, p. 5.

29. Ibid.

30. Ibid.

31. Ibid., p. 18.

32. Ibid., p. 19.

33. Memo, White to Staats, 24 May 1965, Ex UT 2-1, WHCF, LBJ Library.

34. Memo, Staats to White, 3 June 1965, Ex UT 2-1, WHCF, LBJ Library.

35. Memo, Staats to White, 29 June 1965, Ex UT 2-1, WHCF, LBJ Library.

36. Ibid.

37. Memo, White to Staats, 2 August 1965, Ex UT 2-1, WHCF, LBJ Library.

38. Memo, Staats to White, 16 August 1965, Ex UT 2, WHCF, LBJ Library.

39. Ibid.

40. Memo, Sheplor to Staats, 25 August 1965, Ex UT 2, WHCF, LBJ Library.

41. Ibid.

42. Memo, Staats to White, 26 August 1965, Ex UT 2, WHCF, LBJ Library.

43. Memo, White to Staats, 28 August 1965, Ex UT 2, WHCF, LBJ Library.

44. Letter, Staats to Udall, 4 September 1965, Ex UT 2, WHCF, LBJ Library.

45. Letter, Udall to Staats, 9 September 1965, Ex UT 2, WHCF, LBJ Library.

46. Attached to ibid.

47. Unless otherwise indicated, information on the SEPA case is from memo, Roose to Staats, 18 May 1964, Ex FG 232, WHCF, LBJ Library.

48. Memos, Staats to White, 27 June 1964; and White to Staats, 7 July 1964, Ex FG 232, WHCF, LBJ Library.

49. 32 *F.P.C. Reports* 1523 (1964).

50. Memo, White to Staats, 6 January 1965, Ex FG 232, WHCF, LBJ Library.

51. Letter, White to Norwood, 6 January 1964, Ex UT 2-1, WHCF, LBJ Library.

52. Letter, Clark to White, 27 January 1964, attached to ibid.

53. Letter, Udall to White, 14 April 1964, attached to ibid.

54. Ibid.

55. Memo, White to Staats, 24 April 1964, attached to ibid.

56. Ibid.

57. Memo, Staats to White, 2 May 1964, attached to ibid.

58. Memo, Staats to White, 2 July 1964, attached to memo, White to Staats, 16 November 1965, Ex FG 232, WHCF, LBJ Library.

59. Memo, Staats to White, 19 November 1964, Ex FG 232, WHCF, LBJ Library.

60. Memo, Staats to White, 2 January 1965, attached to memo, White to Staats, 16 November 1965, Ex FG 232, WHCF, LBJ Library. Although the immediate procedural issue was resolved, important policy questions remained. What criteria should be employed in making recapture decisions? If there was recapture, what would be the basis for compensation? The need for an administration position on such matters to guide FPC decisions became evident to the commission, the bureau, and the White House in the discussions on procedure. The cooperative development of positions on these questions continued through 1968. In that year Congress enacted FPC legislation (P.L. 90-451) that streamlined the relicensing and recapture provisions of the Federal Power Act of 1920.

61. Letter, president to Meany, 16 December 1963, Ex FI 4/FG 263, WHCF, LBJ Library.

62. Notes, "For Independent Agencies," attached to the Presidential Appointments Schedule, Friday, 17 January 1964, Appointment File, Daily Diary Back-up, LBJ Library.

63. Memo, Schultze to Bush, 3 March 1966, "Interstate Commerce Commission—Director's Review Appeals 1967" folder, Series 52.12, Record Group 51, National Archives.

64. Noted on memo, Commerce and Housing Division to director, 20 November 1965, in ibid. One study, which includes the Johnson period, finds that the presidency generally is more supportive of commissions in budget matters than Congress: Joseph Stewart, Jr., James E. Anderson, and Zona Taylor, "Presidential and Congressional Support for Independent Regulatory Commissions: Implications of the Budgetary Process," *Western Political Quarterly* 25 (September 1982): 318.

65. Task Force on Government Organization, "Report," 6 November 1964, p. 27, task force collection, box 4, LBJ Library. The task force also proposed the consolidation of bank regulation into one agency (ibid., p. 16).

66. Emmette S. Redford and Marlan Blissett, *Organizing the Executive Branch: The Johnson Presidency* (Chicago: University of Chicago Press, 1981), p. 55. In late 1967 William H. Tucker, then chairman of the ICC,

spoke out in support of a National Transportation Commission to replace the ICC, FMC, and CAB. He drew the attention of BOB but generated no action (memo, Schnoor to Gallagher, 8 November 1967, "T9-3 National Transportation Commission" folder, Series 65.5, Record Group 51, National Archives).

67. Memos, Murphy to Califano, 24 January 1966; and Califano and White to president, 28 January 1966, Ex FG 211, WHCF, LBJ Library.

68. Letter, Webb to McClellen, 12 July 1966, attached to memo, Bush to commission, 11 July 1966, C.F. FG 175, WHCF, LBJ Library.

69. For details on the transfer of safety functions, see Redford and Blissett, *Organizing the Executive Branch*, pp. 67–69.

70. Interstate Commerce Commission, *Administrative History*, vol. 1, pp. 4–7, LBJ Library.

71. Letter, Gordon to Goff, 21 February 1964, attached to memo, Staats to Feldman, 29 January 1965, Ex FG 251, WHCF, LBJ Library.

72. Letter, president to Goff, 6 May 1964, Ex FI 2, WHCF, LBJ Library.

73. Memo, Staats to Feldman, 29 January 1965, Ex FG 251, WHCF, LBJ Library.

74. Memo, Schultze to president, 5 June 1965, attached to memo, Schultze to president, 16 June 1965, Ex FG 251, WHCF, LBJ Library. At Schultze's suggestion, Johnson sent a letter of gratitude to the ICC chairman (letter, president to Webb, 8 June 1965, Ex FG 251, WHCF, LBJ Library).

75. Memo, Staats to White, 5 January 1965, Ex FG 251, WHCF, LBJ Library.

76. Letter, Webb to Gordon, 27 April 1965, attached to ibid.

77. Memo, Gordon to president, 28 April 1965, attached to ibid.

78. Memo, Seidman to Moyers, 14 May 1965, attached to ibid.

79. Memo, Moyers to president, 25 May 1965, attached to ibid.

80. Memos, Califano to president, 5 January 1966, Ex FG 251; White to president, 10 January 1966 and 19 January 1966, Ex FG 251; and White to president, 25 January 1966, Ex FG 251, WHCF, LBJ Library.

81. Memo, Seidman to White, 27 January 1966, Ex FG 251, WHCF, LBJ Library.

82. Memo, Califano and White to president, 1 February 1966, Ex FG 251, WHCF, LBJ Library.

83. Memos, Califano to president, 22 February 1966, Ex SP 2-3/1966/TN; and Connor to Califano, 23 February 1966, Ex SP 2-3/1966/TN, WHCF, LBJ Library. See also memo, Califano to president, 25 February 1966, "Califano Reports on Transportation, Health and Education Messages" folder, box 38, files of Joe Califano, LBJ Library.

84. Memo, Southwick to Califano, 22 April 1966, attached to memo, Wilson to president, 25 April 1966, Ex FG 251, WHCF, LBJ Library.

85. Ibid.

86. Letter, Califano to Connor, 25 October 1966, C.F. FG 600/Task Force/T, WHCF, LBJ Library.

87. Memo, Boyd to Califano, 22 November 1966, Task Force on Transportation 1966, task force collection, box 20, LBJ Library.

88. Minutes, transportation meeting, 23 November 1966, Task Force on Transportation 1966, task force collection, box 20, LBJ Library.

89. Memo, Boyd to Levinson, 3 April 1967, Ex FG 251, WHCF, LBJ Library.

90. Memo, Boyd to Califano, 15 January 1968, "Interstate Commerce" folder, box 17, files of James Gaither, LBJ Library.

91. Ibid.

92. Memo, Robson to Nimetz, 10 April 1968, "Interstate Commerce" folder, box 17, files of James Gaither, LBJ Library.

93. "Memorandum concerning the Power Failure in the Northeastern United States," 9 November 1965, *Public Papers*, p. 1109.

94. Memo, Goldstein to president, 20 August 1968, Ex TN 5, WHCF, LBJ Library.

95. Memo, Goldstein to president, 25 June 1968, Ex FG 232, WHCF, LBJ Library. Clifford L. Alexander, Jr., of the Equal Employment Opportunity Commission earlier proposed a presidential memorandum to regulatory commissions saying that they should "emphasize" minority employment by those subject to their authority. The idea was rejected. It was feared that employment would then be construed as another factor to be taken into account in licensing and other regulatory decisions (memo, McPherson to Alexander, 8 May 1968, "Office Files of Harry McPherson [A]" folder, box 46, files of Harry McPherson, LBJ Library).

96. Memo, Califano to president, 2 January 1968, Ex FG 232, WHCF, LBJ Library.

97. Memo, Goldstein to president, 27 June 1968, Ex FG 234, WHCF, LBJ Library.

98. Memo, Barr to White, 13 July 1964, Ex FG 229, WHCF, LBJ Library.

99. For example, memo, Redmon to Moyers, 25 November 1964, Ex UT 1-3; letter, Swidler to White, 9 March 1965, FG 232, WHCF, LBJ Library.

100. Memos, Swidler to Peterson, 8 July 1964, Ex FG 232; and Kintner to White, Ex FG 232, WHCF, LBJ Library.

101. Memo, Swidler to Califano, 9 November 1965, Ex BE 4/Aluminum, WHCF, LBJ Library.

102. Memo, McKee to Watson, 28 September 1965, Ex CA 2, WHCF, LBJ Library.

103. Letters, Cohen to Moyers, 12 July 1965, Ex FG 281; and Cohen to Popple, 26 July 1965, Ex FG 281, WHCF, LBJ Library.

104. Goldstein Oral History Interview, tape 2, p. 6, LBJ Library.

105. Note from fs, 1 August 1965, Ex FG 251, WHCF, LBJ Library.

106. Letter, Hanner to Watson, 5 July 1967 and attached material, Ex UT 1-1, WHCF, LBJ Library.

107. Memo, Jones to Watson, 24 January 1967, Ex BE 2-4, WHCF, LBJ Library. There are almost no records of contacts such as these in the presidential papers. From the perspective of one regulator, the White House staff people were "extraordinarily sensitive . . . about not involving themselves in matters of the FCC" (Nicholas Johnson Oral History Interview, 18 July 1969, p. 45, LBJ Library).

108. Goldstein Oral History Interview, tape 2, p. 5; letter, Tierney to Goldstein, 13 September 1968, Ex FG 251, WHCF, LBJ Library.

109. Memo, White to president, 20 December 1965, Ex UT 2, WHCF, LBJ Library.

110. Memo, Cohen to Valenti, 20 April 1965, Ex FG 281, WHCF, LBJ Library.

111. Memo, White to president, 11 June 1965, Ex FI 3, WHCF, LBJ Library.

112. Letter, Cohen to Watson, 26 July 1965, attached to memo, Watson to president, 26 July 1965, Ex FG 281, WHCF, LBJ Library.

113. Memos, Watson to president, 22 July 1966, Ex FG 232; and Manatos to Watson, 19 March 1968, C.F. FG 232, WHCF, LBJ Library.

114. Memo, Henry to president, 11 January 1966, Ex UT 1-3, WHCF, LBJ Library.

115. Noted on memo, Goldstein to president, 17 April 1968, Ex UT 1, WHCF, LBJ Library.

116. Memo, Goldstein to president, 22 April 1968, "Federal Communications Commission" folder, box 5, files of Ernest Goldstein, LBJ Library.

117. Letter, Murphy to president, 13 September 1965, Ex FG 211, WHCF, LBJ Library.

118. Ibid.

119. James M. Graham and Victor H. Kramer, *Appointments to the Regulatory Agencies: The Federal Communications Commission and the Federal Trade Commission (1949–1974)*, Senate Committee on Commerce, Committee Print, 94th Cong., 2d Sess. (Washington, D.C.: GPO, 1976), p. 272.

120. Ibid.

121. Ibid., p. 271.

122. Ibid., p. 272.

123. Ibid.

124. Ibid.

125. Ibid.

126. Daily Diary, 14 December 1967, LBJ Library.

127. Lee White Oral History Interview, 3 March 1971, tape 4, p. 11, LBJ Library.

128. Ibid., p. 12.

129. Ibid.

130. Ibid.

131. Daily Diary, 9 November 1965, LBJ Library.

132. Ibid.

133. Ibid.

134. White Oral History Interview, tape 4, p. 12.

135. These relationships are treated throughout Anderson and Hazleton, *Managing Macroeconomic Policy*.

136. Kenneth A. Randall Oral History Interview, 14 March 1969, tape 1, p. 43, LBJ Library.

137. Suggestive of Johnson's continuing concern is memo, Fowler to president, 9 February 1966, C.F. FI 2, WHCF, LBJ Library.

138. Randall Oral History Interview, tape 1, p. 61.

139. Ibid.

140. Ibid., p. 63.

141. John F. Horne Oral History Interview, 22 July 1969, tape 1, p. 30, LBJ Library.

142. Ibid., p. 29.

143. Randall Oral History Interview, tape 1, pp. 47–48.

144. Anderson and Hazleton, *Managing Macroeconomic Policy*, p. 149.

145. Memo, Freeman to Califano, 3 August 1966, Ex BE 5-2; letter, Freeman to Dixon, 4 August 1966, Ex BE 5-2, WHCF, LBJ Library.

146. Memo, Robson to Califano, 24 October 1966, Ex BE 5-2, WHCF, LBJ Library.

147. Memo, Murphy to Califano, 7 October 1965, Ex CA, WHCF, LBJ Library. Earnings were to increase as a result of improved load factors. Murphy was also interested in expanding routes.

148. Memo, Murphy to president, 20 December 1965, Ex CA 3, WHCF, LBJ Library.

149. Memo, Murphy to president, 24 January 1966, Ex CA 3, WHCF, LBJ Library.

150. Memo, Murphy to president, 10 February 1966, Ex CA 3, WHCF, LBJ Library. The CAB did not have the authority to compel lower fares; it could only "persuade" carriers to file them.

151. Memo, Robson to Califano, 6 October 1966, Ex TN 5, WHCF, LBJ Library.

152. Ibid.

153. Memo, Robson to Califano, 14 November 1966, Ex FG 251, WHCF, LBJ Library.

154. Memo, Ross to Califano, 31 March 1967, Ex TN 4, WHCF, LBJ Library.

155. Memo, Ackley to president, 6 May 1967, Ex BE 5-2, WHCF, LBJ Library.

156. Memo, Ackley to president, 24 June 1967, Ex BE 5-2, WHCF, LBJ Library.

157. Ibid. Evan Murphy's response was criticized obliquely by Ackley.

158. Ibid.

159. Memo, Okun to Califano, 10 April 1968, Ex TN 5, WHCF, LBJ Library.

160. Ibid.

161. Noted on memo, Okun to president, 3 May 1968, Ex TN, WHCF, LBJ Library.

162. For an overview of the problem, see Interstate Commerce Commission, *Administrative History*, vol. 1, pp. 82–85, LBJ Library.

163. Memo, vice president to president, 5 October 1965, attached to note, Valenti to president, 6 October 1965, Ex TN 4, WHCF, LBJ Library.

164. Ibid.

165. Letter, Bush to Watson, 10 September 1965, Ex TN 4, WHCF, LBJ Library.

166. Memos, Watson to O'Brien, 10 September 1965; and O'Brien to Watson, 14 September 1965; attached to letter, Bush to Watson, 10 September 1965, Ex TN 4, WHCF, LBJ Library.

167. Memo, Valenti to president, 6 October 1965, Ex TN 4, WHCF, LBJ Library.

168. "Remarks upon Signing a Bill to Reduce Freight Car Shortages," 26 May 1966, *Public Papers*, p. 545.

169. Memo, Pfahler to regional directors, 9 September 1965, attached to letter, Bush to Watson, 10 September 1965, Ex TN 4, WHCF, LBJ Library.

170. Ibid.

171. Note, Bush to Califano, 4 October 1965, Ex TN 4, WHCF, LBJ Library.

172. Letter, Maxon to Robson, 16 August 1966, "Pricing Files: Railroads" folder, box 22, files of John E. Robson and Sanford Ross, LBJ Library.

173. Memo, Robson to Califano, 14 November 1966, Ex FG 251, WHCF, LBJ Library.

174. Ibid.

175. Letter, Tucker to Duesenberry, 8 February 1967, Ex TN 4, WHCF, LBJ Library.

176. "Statement by the President on the Breakdown of Negotiations on the Airline Strike," 7 July 1966, *Public Papers*, p. 712.

177. Memo, Califano to president, 8 July 1966, Ex FG 251; and letter, Bush to Califano, 18 July 1966, Ex FG 251, WHCF, LBJ Library.

178. Memo, Murphy to Moyers, 9 July 1966, Ex FG 211, WHCF, LBJ Library.

179. Memos, Murphy to president, 15 July 1966, Ex LA 6/Airlines; and Murphy to president, 22 July 1966, Ex LA 6/Airlines, WHCF, LBJ Library.

180. Memo, Califano to president, 25 August 1966, Ex FG 160, WHCF, LBJ Library.

181. Ibid.

182. Memo, Rowe to president, 12 September 1966, attached to memo, Yolanda to McPherson, 13 September 1966, "International Air (1)" folder, box 9, files of Harry McPherson, LBJ Library. The Federal Power Commission also advised the White House in at least two labor disputes. One instance involved a strike threatened against the Chicago Belt Railway. The FPC feared that it would disrupt the transport of coal for electric power production in Wisconsin and cause serious hardship (memo, Califano to president, 5 November 1968, Ex FG 232, WHCF, LBJ Library). The second involved a strike against the Consolidated Edison Company. White briefed the White House on the likelihood of operating difficulties if the strike were to go forward. He was, Califano assured the president, "watching . . . developments closely" (memo, Califano to president, 30 November 1968, Ex FG 232, WHCF, LBJ Library).

183. Memo, Califano to president, 15 May 1967, attached to memo, Ross to Califano, 15 May 1967, "Pricing Files: Balance of Payments" folder, box 2, files of John E. Robson and Sanford Ross, LBJ Library.

184. An example is letter, president to Cohen, 17 May 1967, Ex FG 281, WHCF, LBJ Library.

185. Memo, Levinson and Goldstein to president, 15 March 1968, Ex FG 281, WHCF, LBJ Library.

186. Memo, Margolin to Brown, 15 September 1967, Interstate Commerce Commission, *Administrative History*, vol. 2, appendix 13; and letter, Foley to Tanner, 8 November 1967, Interstate Commerce Commission, *Administrative History*, vol. 2, appendix 14, LBJ Library.

187. "Special Message to the Congress on International Balance of Payments," 10 February 1965, *Public Papers*, p. 177.

188. Ibid., pp. 175–176.

189. Memo, Boyd to White, 4 March 1965, Ex CA 5, WHCF, LBJ Library.

190. Memo, vice president to president, 14 March 1966, Ex FG 211, WHCF, LBJ Library.

191. Note, president to Jake, 29 October 1965, attached to memo, Murphy to president, 26 October 1965, Ex CA 3, WHCF, LBJ Library.

192. Letter, Califano to Murphy, 20 May 1966, Ex FG 211, WHCF, LBJ Library.

193. Ibid.

194. Letter, Murphy to Califano, 27 May 1966, Ex FG 211, WHCF, LBJ Library.

195. Memo, McPherson to Califano, 30 December 1966, "Joe Califano" folder, box 50, files of Harry McPherson, LBJ Library.

196. Although it is not treated here, the presidency was involved in a second important way in international air transport matters: the negotiation of agreements with other countries on landing rights, on fares, and on other matters. Central responsibility was in the Department of State, although the CAB was a participant.

197. Harry C. McPherson Oral History Interview, 19 December 1968, tape 3, p. 21, LBJ Library.

198. Memo, Pierson to president, 17 April 1968, "Office Files of DeVier Pierson (Transpacific Case)" folder 2, box 20, files of DeVier Pierson, LBJ Library.

199. Memo, Pierson to president, 22 November 1968, "Civil Aeronautics Board (1)" folder, box 2, files of DeVier Pierson, LBJ Library.

200. Note, McPherson to files, 5 December 1967, Ex CA, WHCF, LBJ Library.

201. Ibid.

202. For example, he allowed new charter authority for Caledonia Airways over the objections of BOB and Lee White, who argued that there were major policy issues involved that had not received sufficient airing (memo, White to president, 2 December 1965, Ex CA 7/United Kingdom–U.S., WHCF, LBJ Library).

203. *Air Afrique Foreign Air Carrier Permit*, 40 *CAB Reports* 759 (1964).

204. Letter, president to Crooker, 17 January 1969, Ex FG 211, WHCF, LBJ Library.

205. Such approval is shown in the response of CAB chairman Charles Murphy to questions put to him by the president about encouraging and liberalizing international air transportation (Murphy to president, 15 December 1965, Ex FO 5, WHCF, LBJ Library).

206. Letter, Murphy to president, 16 September 1966, attached to letter, Rowen to White, 29 September 1965, Ex CA 7/Transatlantic 11/19/65, WHCF, LBJ Library.

207. *Transatlantic Charter Investigation*, 40 *CAB Reports* 233 (1964).

208. Zwick to president, 17 December 1968, "Trans-Pacific Case" folder, box 19, files of James Gaither, LBJ Library.

209. Letter, president to Crooker, 17 December 1968, Ex CA 7/Transpacific, WHCF, LBJ Library.

210. Pierson Oral History Interview, tape 2, p. 1.

211. Ibid., p. 2.

212. Ibid.

213. Ibid.

214. Ibid., pp. 2–3.

215. Ibid., p. 3. The files indicate that the Johnson administration did try to expedite a decision in the case. See, for example, memo, Pierson to president, 18 December 1968, Ex CA 7/Transpacific, WHCF, LBJ Library. The decision made in the Nixon Administration is *Transpacific Route Investigation*, 51 *CAB Reports* 161 (1969).

216. Memo, Schultze to president, 22 June 1966, Ex CA 7/Transatlantic 2/12/66, WHCF, LBJ Library.

217. Rowe to McPherson, 13 May 1966, Ex CA 7/Transatlantic 2/12/66, WHCF, LBJ Library. Later McPherson reported to Johnson that the carrier opposition "has been very mild. I believe they consider it *fait accompli*" (memo, McPherson to president, 22 September 1966, Ex CA 7/Transatlantic 2/12/66, WHCF, LBJ Library).

218. Ibid.

219. Ibid.

220. Ibid.

221. This was the position set forth in a letter from Thomas K. Taylor, vice president of Trans World Airline, to Alan Boyd, 22 September 1965, attached to memo, Boyd to White, 27 September 1965, Ex CA 7/Transatlantic 11/19/65, WHCF, LBJ Library.

222. Letter, Rowe to McPherson, 19 March 1965, attached to memo, McPherson to White, 27 March 1965, Ex CA 7/Transatlantic 2/4/66, WHCF, LBJ Library.

223. Letter, Dillon to Gordon, 31 March 1965, attached to memo, Fowler to president, 18 August 1965, Ex CA 7/Transatlantic 11/19/65, WHCF, LBJ Library.

224. Memo, Capron to director, 25 March 1965, C.F. CA 7/Transatlantic, WHCF, LBJ Library.

225. Letter, Murphy to White, 11 August 1965, Ex CA 7/Transatlantic 2/4/66, WHCF, LBJ Library.

226. Memo, Solomon to Mann, undated, attached to memo, Mann to White, 1 January 1966, Ex CA 7/Transatlantic 2/4/66, WHCF, LBJ Library.

227. Letter, president to Murphy, 11 February 1966, *Public Papers*, p. 169.

228. Memo, McPherson to president, 7 December 1966, "Int'l Air" folder, box 27, files of Harry McPherson, LBJ Library.

229. *Transatlantic Route Renewal Case Reopened*, 46 *CAB Reports*, 75 (1966).

230. Memo, McPherson to president, 7 December 1966, "Int'l Air" folder, box 27, files of Harry McPherson, LBJ Library.

231. Ibid.

232. Memo, Califano to president, 10 January 1967, Ex CA 7/Ireland-U.S., WHCF, LBJ Library.

233. Pierson Oral History Interview, tape 2, p. 2.

234. Memo, White to president, 9 July 1965, Ex CA 4, WHCF, LBJ Library.

235. Memo, Rowen to White, 18 August 1965, Ex CA, WHCF, LBJ Library.

236. Memo, Rommel to Califano, 3 January 1968, Ex CA 3, WHCF, LBJ Library.

237. Draft memo, McPherson to president, 16 July 1968, Ex CA 3, WHCF, LBJ Library.

238. Memo, Boyd to McPherson, 3 April 1966, attached to note, Roth to McPherson, 5 May 1966, "Airlines" folder, box 18, files of Harry McPherson, LBJ Library.

239. Memo, Hughes to McPherson, 8 August 1966, "Office Files of Harry McPherson Int'l Air (1)" folder, box 9, files of Harry McPherson, LBJ Library.

240. Memo, McPherson to president, 2 September 1966, "Office Files of Harry McPherson Int'l Air (1)" folder, box 9, files of Harry McPherson, LBJ Library.

241. Letter, Murphy to Schultze, 20 April 1966, "Office Files of Harry McPherson: CAB (Sec. 213)" folder, box 20, files of Harry McPherson, LBJ Library.

242. Memo, Hamilton to Bator, 26 April 1966, "Office Files of Harry McPherson: Int'l Air (2)" folder, box 9, files of Harry McPherson, LBJ Library.

243. Memo, Murphy to Pierson, 25 May 1967, "CAB Cases" folder, box 10, files of DeVier Pierson, LBJ Library.

244. Letter, Crooker to McPherson, 19 September 1968, "Office Files of Harry McPherson: CAB (Sec. 213)" folder, box 19, files of Harry McPherson, LBJ Library.

4. Executive Regulation

1. Memo, Califano to president, 17 December 1965, Ex BE 5-2, WHCF, LBJ Library.

2. Among the other objects of Agriculture's regulatory efforts were

commodity exchanges, packer and stockyard operations, the marketing of perishable commodities, meat and poultry processing, and pesticides.

3. Conversation with the author. There was presidential disinterest despite the rather controversial stewardship of Dr. James L. Goddard as head of the Food and Drug Administration from late 1966 to mid-1968. An activist, Dr. Goddard was often involved in widely publicized conflict with the pharmaceutical industry. It should be said, however, that a tough regulator was sought when he was appointee (memo, Macy to president, 4 January 1966, "James L. Goddard" folder, box 214, files of John W. Macy, Jr., LBJ Library). Johnson appeared largely to ignore the controversies generated by Goddard. He did meet with the commissioner once on 26 June 1967 to review food and drug issues, at which time he was assured that the backlog in new drug applications would be eliminated expeditiously. This was accomplished (memo, Gardner to president, 16 June 1967, Ex HE 4, WHCF, LBJ Library).

4. Minimum wage policy issues (discussed in chapter 6) were of great interest to organized labor. Johnson frequently discussed them with top labor officials. See, for example, memo, Wirtz to Valenti, 19 March 1965, Ex LA 3, WHCF, LBJ Library.

5. "The President's News Conference," 9 August 1966, *Public Papers of the President of the United States: Lyndon B. Johnson, 1966* (Washington, D.C.: GPO, 1967), pp. 807–808 (hereafter cited as *Public Papers*).

6. Quoted in James E. Anderson and Jared E. Hazleton, *Managing Macroeconomic Policy: The Johnson Presidency* (Austin: University of Texas Press, 1986), p. 142. The discussion of guideposts here relies heavily on chapter 5 of this work.

7. Ibid., pp. 158–168.

8. Information on the balance-of-payments problem is derived principally from ibid., chapter 6.

9. "Special Message to the Congress on International Balance of Payments," 10 February 1965, *Public Papers*, p. 170.

10. "The President's News Conference at the LBJ Ranch," 1 January 1968, *Public Papers*, pp. 1–2.

11. Anderson and Hazleton, *Managing Macroeconomic Policy*, p. 208.

12. 48 *Stat.* 1185 and 49 *Stat.* 1189-91.

13. 61 *Stat.* 153.

14. U.S. Federal Mediation and Conciliation Service, *Annual Report, 1966* (Washington, D.C.: GPO, 1967), pp. 18–19.

15. "Televised Statement by the President Announcing Postponement of a Shutdown in the Steel Industry," 30 August 1965, *Public Papers*, p. 952.

16. "Televised Statement by the President Announcing Settlement of the Steel Dispute," 3 September 1965, *Public Papers*, p. 968.

17. U.S. Federal Mediation and Conciliation Service, *Annual Report, 1968* (Washington, D.C.: GPO, 1969), pp. 19–21.

18. Ibid.

19. "Talking Points of the President before Union and Company Negotiators in the Copper Strike," 4 March 1968, *Public Papers*, p. 333.

20. *Congress and the Nation: 1945–1964* (Washington, D.C.: Congressional Quarterly Service, 1965), p. 629.

21. Ibid., p. 627.

22. Background on the 1964 situation is drawn from *Congress and the Nation: 1945–1964*, pp. 620–621.

23. "Radio and Television Statement Announcing the Settlement of the Railroad Dispute," 22 April 1964, *Public Papers*, p. 517.

24. On the 1967 events, see *Congress and the Nation: 1965–1968* (Washington, D.C.: Congressional Quarterly Service, 1969), pp. 619–621.

25. Ibid., pp. 616–617.

26. "Remarks on Announcing an Agreement in the Airline Strike," 29 July 1966, *Public Papers*, p. 792.

27. Memo, Freeman to president, 7 April 1966, Ex FG 150, WHCF, LBJ Library.

28. Memo, Hughes to Maguire, 8 July 1966, Ex FG 150, WHCF, LBJ Library.

29. Memo, Freeman to president, 5 November 1964, Ex FG 150, WHCF, LBJ Library.

30. Memo, Ackley to Freeman, 2 July 1965, Ex BE 5-2, WHCF, LBJ Library.

31. Memo, Moyers to McPherson, 4 July 1965, attached to memo, Ackley to Moyers, 18 July 1965, Ex BE 5-2, WHCF, LBJ Library.

32. Memo, Ackley to Moyers, 18 July 1965, Ex BE 5-2, WHCF, LBJ Library.

33. Memos, Ackley to president, 25 August 1965 and 13 September 1965; attached to memo, Spellman to Redmon, 14 September 1965, Ex BE 5-2, WHCF, LBJ Library.

34. Memo, Freeman to president, 5 October 1965, Ex BE 5-2, WHCF, LBJ Library.

35. Memo, Ackley and Gordon to Califano, 14 October 1965, Ex FG 717, WHCF, LBJ Library.

36. Memo, Freeman to president, 29 October 1965, Ex BE 5-2, WHCF, LBJ Library.

37. Memo, Freeman to Califano, 19 November 1965, Ex BE 5-2, WHCF, LBJ Library.

38. Memo, Schnittker to Califano and McPherson, 22 November 1965, Ex BE 5-2, WHCF, LBJ Library.

39. Memo, Califano to president, 17 December 1965, Ex BE 5-2, WHCF, LBJ Library.

40. Memo, Freeman to president, 22 January 1966, attached to memo, Califano to president, 24 January 1966, Ex BE 5-2, WHCF, LBJ Library.

41. Ibid.

42. Memo, Jones to Watson, 28 April 1966, Ex WH 10, WHCF, LBJ Library.

43. Memo, Califano to president, 5 May 1966, Ex WH 10, WHCF, LBJ Library.

44. Memo, Freeman to president, 29 April 1966, Ex AG, WHCF, LBJ Library.

45. Memo, Freeman to president, 4 May 1966, Ex AG, WHCF, LBJ Library.

46. Memo, Freeman to president, 9 May 1966, Ex AG, WHCF, LBJ Library.

47. Memo, Freeman to president, 1 June 1966, attached to memo, Califano to president, 1 June 1966, Ex BE 5-2, WHCF, LBJ Library.

48. In one of his memos to the president pointing out how well farmers had done in recent years, Ackley asserted that the "farm community could lose a great deal and still be exceedingly well off" (memo, Ackley to president, 10 July 1967, Council of Economic Advisers, *Administrative History*, vol. 2, LBJ Library).

49. Memo, Freeman to president, 6 April 1967, Ex FG 150, WHCF, LBJ Library.

50. Memos, Ackley to president, 30 July 1966 and 6 August 1966, Ex BE 5-2, WHCF, LBJ Library.

51. Memos, Ackley to president, 8 November 1966 and 6 August 1966, Ex BE 5-2, WHCF, LBJ Library.

52. Memo, Ackley to president, 18 March 1967, Ex BE 5-2, WHCF, LBJ Library.

53. Memo, Connell to Watson, 2 May 1967, "Agriculture—General" folder, box 14, files of DeVier Pierson, LBJ Library.

54. Memo, Pierson to president, 25 May 1967, "Agriculture—General" folder, box 14, files of DeVier Pierson, LBJ Library.

55. Memos, Freeman to president, 11 August 1966, Ex BE 5-2; 6 October 1966, Ex AG; 6 April 1967, Ex FG 150; and 18 May 1967; attached to memo, Freeman to Watson, 25 May 1967, Ex AG, WHCF, LBJ Library. Also, memo, Freeman to president, 11 January 1968, "Agriculture—Freeman's Statements" folder, box 34, files of DeVier Pierson, LBJ Library.

56. George C. Mehren Oral History Interview, 18 February 1969, p. 58, LBJ Library.

57. Orville C. Freeman Oral History Interview, 14 February 1969, tape 1, p. 19, LBJ Library.

58. Memo, Okun to president, 23 March 1968, Ex BE 5-2, WHCF, LBJ Library.

59. "Remarks to Delegates to the Second Annual Conference on Farm Policy and Rural Life," 25 March 1968, *Public Papers*, p. 439.

60. Memo, Freeman to president, 28 March 1968, Ex FG 150, WHCF, LBJ Library.

61. Memo, Duesenberry to Califano, 13 May 1968, Ex AG 4, WHCF, LBJ Library.

62. The president was authorized by law to restrict imports by quotas or fees after study by the Tariff Commission. As of 1968 there were quotas on wheat, flour and other wheat products, cotton, sugar, peanuts, and certain dairy products (U.S. Department of Agriculture, *Administrative History*, vol. 1, pt. 1, p. 162, LBJ Library).

63. Mehren Oral History Interview, tape 2, p. 15.

64. Freeman Oral History Interview, tape 2, p. 18.

65. Charles L. Schultze Oral History Interview, 28 March 1969, tape 1, p. 21, LBJ Library.

66. Noted on memo, McPherson to president, 28 February 1966, "Memos for the President (1966)" folder, box 52, files of Harry McPherson, LBJ Library.

67. Memo, McPherson to president, 15 August 1966, Ex TA 6/Sugar, WHCF, LBJ Library.

68. Johnson did take a special interest in media discussion of decision matters, or leaks, and was inclined to be suspicious of the department on this score. See memos, Freeman to president, 12 June 1964, Ex FI 4/FG 150; Valenti to president, 27 November 1964, Ex FG 150; Hughes to Valenti, 14 January 1965, Ex Q1/FG 150; Schnittker to Califano, 9 February 1966, Ex FG 150; and Hughes to Jones, 24 March 1967, Ex FG 150, WHCF, LBJ Library.

69. Memo, Freeman to president, 2 December 1963, Ex TA 6/Beef, WHCF, LBJ Library.

70. For example, memo, Murphy to the president, 2 April 1964, Ex TA 6/Beef, WHCF, LBJ Library.

71. Letter, Schnittker to Pierson, 8 April 1968, "Agriculture—Milk" folder, box 14, files of DeVier Pierson, LBJ Library.

72. Memo, Schultze to president, 6 September 1967, "Agriculture—Milk" folder, box 14, files of DeVier Pierson, LBJ Library.

73. Memo, Pierson to president, 12 September 1967, "Agriculture—Milk" folder, box 14, files of DeVier Pierson, LBJ Library. The political game was an extended one. Charles J. Zwick, who followed Schultze as director of BOB, was puzzled by Mills's deep interest in milk, "until somebody pointed out that John Byrnes is from Wisconsin . . . Wilbur to carry the committee had to bring his counterpart, John Byrnes, along" (Byrnes was the ranking Republican member on the House Ways and Means Committee; Charles J. Zwick Oral History Interview, 1 August 1969, p. 8, LBJ Library). The headquarters of a very large milk cooperative, in fact, was in Mills's district.

74. Pierson Oral History Interview, tape 2, p. 32.

75. Memo, Schultze to president, 6 October 1967, Ex AG, WHCF, LBJ Library.

76. Memo, Pierson to president, 6 October 1967, Ex AG 4-1, WHCF, LBJ Library.

77. Noted on memo, Valenti to president, 4 April 1965, Ex TA 6/Oil, WHCF, LBJ Library.

78. Douglas R. Bohi and Milton Russell, *Limiting Oil Imports: An Economic History and Analysis* (Baltimore, Md.: Johns Hopkins University Press, 1978), p. 18. Much of the background on the topic is drawn from this excellent work. See also Edward H. Shaffer, *The Oil Import Program of the United States: An Evaluation* (New York: Frederick A. Praeger, 1968); and Yoram Barzel and Christopher D. Hall, *The Political Economy of the Oil Import Quota* (Stanford, Cal.: Hoover Institution Press, 1977).

79. Memo, Pierson to president, 1 May 1968, Ex TA 6/Oil, WHCF, LBJ Library.

80. Ibid.

81. Ibid.

82. Memo, Udall to Watson, 30 March 1965, Ex TA 6/Oil, WHCF, LBJ Library.

83. Bohi and Russell, *Limiting Oil Imports*, pp. 151–154.

84. Memo, Udall to Feldman, 28 April 1964, C.F. TA 6/Oil, WHCF, LBJ Library.

85. For example, memorandum of conversation, 9 March 1964, attached to memo, Pozan to Jenkins, undated, Ex TA 6/Oil; letter, Byrd to president, 11 March 1964, attached to note, Pauline to Mildred, undated, Ex TA 6/Oil, WHCF, LBJ Library.

86. Memo, Feldman to president, 5 June 1964, Ex TA 6/Oil, WHCF, LBJ Library.

87. Memo, Feldman to president, 5 June 1964, Ex TA 6/Oil, WHCF, LBJ Library.

88. Letter, Tuohy to president, 2 July 1964, Ex TA 6/Oil, WHCF, LBJ Library.

89. Secretary of the Interior, "Weekly Report to the President," attached to memo, Udall to Watson, 30 March 1965, Ex TA 6/Oil, WHCF, LBJ Library.

90. Memo, McPherson to president, 26 March 1965, "Memorandum for the President (1965)" folder, box 52, files of Harry McPherson, LBJ Library.

91. Memo, White to president, 30 March 1965, "Residual Oil Import Program" folder, box 78, files of Bill Moyers, LBJ Library.

92. Stewart Udall Oral History Interview, 29 July 1969, tape 3, p. 36, LBJ Library.

93. Ibid. McPherson says in regard to White House participation in oil decisions, "There has been absolutely none since Johnson became President." In the strict sense this is an erroneous statement. Placed in context, however, McPherson's point seems to be that there was no participation motivated by a desire to advance the interests of the oil industry. He emphasizes Johnson's apprehension about being involved in oil questions (Harry C. McPherson Oral History Interview, 9 April 1969, tape 6, p. 23, LBJ Library).

94. Memo, White to president, 31 March 1965, "Residual Oil Import Program" folder, box 78, files of Bill Moyers, LBJ Library.

95. Memo, White to president, 4 April 1965, Ex TA 6/Oil, WHCF, LBJ Library.

96. Daily Diary, 3 August 1965, LBJ Library.

97. Noted on letter, Hamon to president, 21 December 1965, Ex BE 4/Oil, WHCF, LBJ Library.

98. For example, see Gene T. Kinney, "Udall's Oil Policy Power Grows," *Oil and Gas Journal*, 27 December 1965: 57–59; and *Oil Daily*, 23 December 1965: 1.

99. Gene T. Kinney, "Watching Washington," *Oil and Gas Journal*, 27 December 1965: 67.

100. *Oil and Gas Journal*, 1 November 1965: 35–36.

101. Kinney, "Watching Washington," p. 67.

102. Memo, Udall to White, 17 May 1965, attached to memo, Katzenbach to White, 26 May 1965, Ex TA 6/Oil, WHCF, LBJ Library.

103. Memo, unsigned and undated, attached to memo, Katzenbach to White, 26 May 1965, Ex TA 6/Oil, WHCF, LBJ Library.

104. Letter, Ellington to Udall, 2 June 1965, attached to memo, Schultze to White, 24 June 1965, Ex TA 6/Oil, WHCF, LBJ Library.

105. Memo, Schultze to Udall, 24 June 1965, attached to memo, Schultze to White, 24 June 1965, Ex TA 6/Oil, WHCF, LBJ Library.

106. Other members were the departments of Commerce, Justice, Labor, State and Treasury; the Council of Economic Advisers; the Office of Emergency Planning; and the Office of Special Representative for Trade Negotiations.

107. Memo, Solomon to Bundy, 26 May 1965, attached to memo, Bator to White, 28 May 1965, C.F. TA 6/Oil, WHCF, LBJ Library.

108. Undated and unsigned paper, "The Oil Import Problem," "Oil Imports" folder, box 9, files of DeVier Pierson, LBJ Library.

109. Memo, White to president, 4 June 1965, Ex TA 6/Oil, WHCF, LBJ Library.

110. Memo, Watson to president, 26 August 1965, Ex TA 6/Oil, WHCF, LBJ Library.

111. Memo, White to president, undated, C.F. TA 6/Oil, WHCF, LBJ Library.

112. Memo, Udall to president, 30 November 1965, C.F. TA 6/Oil, WHCF, LBJ Library.

113. Memo, Udall and Mann to president, undated, attached to memo, Watson to president, 15 November 1965, C.F. TA 6/Oil, WHCF, LBJ Library.

114. Cable, Ball to Rusk, 19 November 1965, C.F. TA 6/Oil, WHCF, LBJ Library.

115. Memos, Udall to president, undated, attached to note, mjc to Juanita, 17 August 1965, Ex TA 6/Oil; and Solomon to Mann, 21 July 1965, attached to memo, White to president, 4 September 1965, C.F. TA 6/Oil, WHCF, LBJ Library.

116. Udall Oral History Interview, tape 3, p. 37.

117. These began to be expressed in the summer (memo, Ellington to Schultze, 19 August 1965, Ex TA 6/Oil, WHCF, LBJ Library).

118. Memo, Udall and Mann to president, undated, attached to memo, Watson to president, 15 November 1965, C.F. TA 6/Oil, WHCF, LBJ Library.

119. Memo, Udall to president, 19 November 1965, Ex TA 6/Oil, WHCF, LBJ Library.

120. Memo, Mann to White, 20 November 1965, C.F., TA 6/Oil, WHCF, LBJ Library.

121. Memo, Udall to Califano, 23 November 1965, Ex CM/Oil, WHCF, LBJ Library.

122. Memo, Ackley to White, 24 November 1965, Ex TA 6/Oil, WHCF, LBJ Library.

123. Memo, Ackley to Califano, 25 November 1965, Ex BE 4/Oil, WHCF, LBJ Library. Presidential-level interest in the consumer price aspects of oil continued in 1966 and beyond. At one point in 1966 administration inflation fighters attempted to change the pattern of oil import allocations to give small refiners a larger share, but Interior was successful in blocking the plan. See James L. Cochrane, "Energy Policy in the Johnson Administration: Logical Order versus Economic Pluralism," in Crawford D. Goodwin (ed.), *Energy Policy in Perspective* (Washington, D.C.: Brookings Institution, 1981), pp. 375–376.

124. Memo, Udall to president, 30 November 1965, C.F. TA 6/Oil, WHCF, LBJ Library.

125. Memo, Califano and White to president, 4 December 1965, attached to memo, Jacobsen to president, 6 December 1965, Ex TA 6/Oil, WHCF, LBJ Library.

126. Memo, Jacobsen to president, 6 December 1965, Ex TA 6/Oil, WHCF, LBJ Library.

127. Memo, Califano to president, 7 December 1965, C.F. TA 6/Oil, WHCF, LBJ Library.

128. Memo, Califano to president, 20 December 1965, attached to memo, Califano to Udall, 21 December 1965, C.F. TA 6/Oil, WHCF, LBJ Library.

129. Ibid.

130. Memo, Udall to Califano, 23 December 1965, C.F. TA 6/Oil, WHCF, LBJ Library.

131. Memos, Ackley to Califano, 3 January 1966, Ex TA 6/Oil; and Ackley to president, 4 January 1966, Ex CM/Oil, WHCF, LBJ Library.

132. Memo, Califano to Ackley, 6 January 1966, C.F. TA 6/Oil, WHCF, LBJ Library.

133. Memo, Ackley to Califano, 14 January 1966, Ex TA 6/Oil, WHCF, LBJ Library.

134. Memo, Udall to president, 1 February 1966, attached to memo, White to Udall, 3 February 1966, Ex TA 6/Oil, WHCF, LBJ Library.

135. Memo, Read to Watson, 1 February 1966, C.F. TA 6/Oil, WHCF, LBJ Library.

136. Note re conversation with White by vm, attached to memo, White to president, 1 February 1966, Ex CM/Oil, WHCF, LBJ Library.

137. Memo, Watson to White, 1 February 1966, attached to memo, Read to Watson, 1 February 1966, C.F. TA 6/Oil, WHCF, LBJ Library.

138. Memo, White to Udall, 3 February 1966, Ex TA 6/Oil, WHCF, LBJ Library.

139. Memos, Nicoll to Moore, 10 February 1966, C.F. TA 6/Oil; and Solomon to Ackley, 10 February 1966, C.F. TA 6/Oil, WHCF, LBJ Library.

140. Bohi and Russell, *Limiting Oil Imports*, p. 156.

141. Memo from Katzenbach, 21 February 1966, attached to memo, Nicoll to Moore, 10 February 1966, C.F. TA 6/Oil, WHCF, LBJ Library.

142. Memo, Udall to president, 15 March 1966, attached to memo, Califano to president, 16 March 1966, Ex FG 145, WHCF, LBJ Library.

143. Noted on memo, Califano to president, 17 March 1966, Ex TA 6/Oil, WHCF, LBJ Library.

144. Noted on memo, Califano to president, 22 March 1966, Ex TA 6/Oil, WHCF, LBJ Library.

145. Memo, Udall to Califano, 23 March 1966, attached to memo, Califano to president, 23 March 1966, Ex CM/Oil, WHCF, LBJ Library.

146. Memo, Califano to president, 23 March 1966, Ex CM/Oil, WHCF, LBJ Library.

147. Noted on memo, Fowler to president, 17 July 1965, attached to memo, Busby to Fowler, 20 July 1965, Ex FI 2, WHCF, LBJ Library.

148. Ibid.

149. Memo, Gordon and Heller to president, 28 February 1964, attached to letter, Feldman to Kelly, 22 April 1964, Ex FI 2, WHCF, LBJ Library.

150. For an overview, see Emmette S. Redford, "Dual Banking: A Case Study in Federalism," *Law and Contemporary Problems* 31 (Autumn 1966): 749.

151. Memo, Gordon and Heller to president, 28 February 1964, attached to letter, Feldman to Kelly, 22 April 1964, Ex FI 2, WHCF, LBJ Library.

152. Ibid.

153. Status memorandum, "Reorganize Bank Supervisory Agencies," 18 February 1965, "Reorganization and Economy, 14 March 1965," folder, box 3, files of Bill Moyers; and memo, Gordon and Heller to president, 28 February 1964, attached to letter, Feldman to Kelly, 22 April 1964, Ex FI 2, WHCF, LBJ Library.

154. Memo, O'Donnell to Jenkins, 10 February 1964, attached to letter, O'Donnell to Babington, 19 May 1964, Gen. FG 110-5, WHCF, LBJ Library.

155. William Bacon Camp Oral History Interview, 12 December 1968, tape 1, p. 28, LBJ Library.

156. Department of the Treasury, *Administrative History*, Office of the Comptroller of the Currency, vol. 1, pp. 69–70, LBJ Library.

157. "Interagency problems among Federal bank supervisory agencies since April, 1963," attachment A to memo, Gordon and Heller to president, 28 February 1964, attached to letter, Feldman to Kelly, 22 April 1964, Ex FI 2, WHCF, LBJ Library.

158. Memo, Gordon and Heller to president, 28 February 1964, attached to letter, Feldman to Kelly, 22 April 1964, Ex FI 2, WHCF, LBJ Library.

159. "Interagency problems among Federal bank supervisory agencies since April, 1963," attachment A to memo, Gordon and Heller to president, 28 February 1964, attached to letter, Feldman to Kelly, 22 April 1964, Ex FI 2, WHCF, LBJ Library.

160. Memo, Gordon and Heller to president, 30 January 1964, attached to letter, O'Donnell to Babington, 29 May 1964, Gen. FG 110-5, WHCF, LBJ Library.

161. Letter, Babington to president, 30 January 1964, attached to letter, O'Donnell to Babington, 29 May 1964, Gen. FG 110-5, WHCF, LBJ Library.

162. Letter, Kelly to president, 14 February 1964, attached to letter, Feldman to Kelly, 22 April 1966, Ex FI 2, WHCF, LBJ Library.

163. Memo, Dillon to O'Donnell, 19 March 1964, C.F. FG 110-5, WHCF, LBJ Library.

164. Letter, Saxon to Kelly, 11 February 1964, attached to ibid.

165. Interview by the author with Joseph W. Barr, 21 October 1981. Dillon felt that the comptroller was "right in most of his basic objectives." See memos, Dillon to O'Donnell, 19 March 1964, attached to note, Dillon to O'Donnell, 19 March 1964, C.F. FG 110-5, WHCF, LBJ Library; and Walter Jenkins to O'Donnell, 11 February 1964, attached to letter, O'Donnell to Babington, 29 May 1964, Gen. FG 110-5, WHCF, LBJ Library.

166. Memo, Jenkins to Valenti, 14 May 1964, attached to letter, Jenkins to Schooley, 21 May 1964, Gen. FG 110-5, WHCF, LBJ Library.

167. For example, letter, Schooley to Jenkins, 17 March 1964, attached to letter, Jenkins to Schooley, 30 March 1964, Gen. FG 110-5, WHCF, LBJ Library.

168. Memo, Dillon to Moyers, 26 February 1964, attached to memo, Busby to Fowler, 20 July 1965, Ex FI 2, WHCF, LBJ Library. The president had a general session with an American Bankers Association group in mid-December 1963, but there are no indications that regulatory problems were discussed (letter, Kelly to president, 13 February 1964, attached to letter, Feldman to Kelly, 22 April 1964, Ex FI 2, WHCF, LBJ Library).

169. Memo, Gordon and Heller to president, 28 February 1964, attached to letter, Feldman to Kelly, 22 April 1964, Ex FI 2, WHCF, LBJ Library.

170. Ibid.

171. Barr interview.

172. "Letter to Secretary Dillon on the Need for Coordinating Federal Actions in the Field of Bank Regulation," 2 March 1964, released 18 March, *Public Papers*, p. 393.

173. Memo, Dillon to president, 13 March 1964, Ex FI 2, WHCF, LBJ Library.

174. Letter, Dillon to Martin, Saxon and Barr, 3 March 1964, attached to memo, Dillon to O'Donnell, 19 May 1964, C.F. FG 110-5, WHCF, LBJ Library.

175. Memo, Gordon to Dillon, 13 March 1964, attached to memo, Busby to Fowler, 20 July 1965, Ex FI 2, WHCF, LBJ Library.

176. Memo, Gordon to president, 14 March 1964, attached to memo, Busby to Fowler, 20 July 1965, Ex FI 2, WHCF, LBJ Library.

177. *New York Times*, 17 March 1964, p. 45.

178. Memo, Gordon to O'Donnell, 19 March 1964, Ex FG 110-5, WHCF, LBJ Library.

179. Memo, Dillon to O'Donnell, 19 March 1964, attached to memo, Dillon to O'Donnell, 19 March 1964, C.F. FG 110-5, WHCF, LBJ Library.

180. Ibid.

181. Memo, Feldman to president, 26 March 1964, Ex FG 110-5, WHCF, LBJ Library.

182. Ibid.

183. Barr as FDIC chairman was not asked specifically by the White

House to stand between Saxon and Federal Reserve officials, but he made a serious effort to do so (Barr interview).

184. Letter, Saxon to Gordon, 28 April 1964, Ex FI 2, WHCF, LBJ Library.

185. Department of the Treasury, *Administrative History*, Office of the Comptroller of the Currency, vol. 1, p. 74, LBJ Library.

186. Memo, Gordon to president, 5 August 1964, Ex FI 2, WHCF, LBJ Library.

187. Letter, Schooley to Moyers, 9 November 1964, attached to letter, Schooley to Moyers, 17 November 1965, Gen. FI 2, WHCF, LBJ Library.

188. Memo, Grubb to Jenkins, 6 October 1964, Gen. FG 100-5, WHCF, LBJ Library.

189. *New York Times*, 12 April 1965, p. 53.

190. Memo, Dillon to president, 13 January 1965, C.F. FG 110-5, WHCF, LBJ Library.

191. Memo, Watson to president, 5 November 1965, Ex FI 8, WHCF, LBJ Library. Not long afterward Johnson also learned of Senator John McClellan's attitude. The senior Democrat did not ask for Saxon's removal, but he did indicate that he intended to "take after" the comptroller in hearings (memo, Manatos to president, 24 January 1966, Ex FG 229 A, WHCF, LBJ Library).

192. Memo, Gordon to president, 5 August 1964, Ex FI 2, WHCF, LBJ Library.

193. *New York Times*, 27 October 1964, p. 53.

194. Memo, Cater to president, 3 November 1964, Ex FG 600, WHCF, LBJ Library. Barr proposed another alternative in early 1965: the creation by statute of a committee made up of the comptroller and the FDIC and FRB chairmen. It would receive notice of proposed regulatory action and, in the event of conflict, resolution would be by majority vote. The plan was opposed by the Bureau of the Budget for several reasons, but basically because it added to organizational complexity and confusion (memo to Moyers, undated, "Reorganization and Economy, 14 March 1965" folder, box 3, files of Bill Moyers, LBJ Library).

195. Status memorandum, "Reorganize Bank Supervisory Agencies," 18 February 1965, "Reorganization and Economy, 14 March 1965" folder, box 3, files of Bill Moyers, LBJ Library.

196. Memo, Moyers to Gordon, 21 March 1965, "Reorganization and Economy, 14 March 1965" folder, box 3, files of Bill Moyers, LBJ Library.

197. "The President's News Conference," 1 April 1965, *Public Papers*, p. 367.

198. *New York Times*, 2 April 1965, p. 45.

199. Letter, Oldin to president, 9 April 1965, attached to letter, president to Oldin, 11 May 1965, Ex FI 2, WHCF, LBJ Library.

200. *Congressional Quarterly Almanac* (Washington, D.C.: Congressional Quarterly Service, 1965), pp. 850–851.

201. Letter, president to Oldin, 11 May 1965, Ex FI 2, WHCF, LBJ Library.

202. Memo, Califano to president, 31 December 1966, C.F. FG 110-5,

WHCF, LBJ Library. Reorganization was suggested as an agenda item for a proposed task force on financial institutions in November 1966, but a task force was not created (memo, Schultze to Califano, 19 November 1966, FG 600/Task Force/F, WHCF, LBJ Library).

203. Memo, Fowler to president, 25 June, 1965, Ex FI 2, WHCF, LBJ Library.

204. Barr interview.

205. Department of the Treasury, *Administration History*, Office of the Comptroller of the Currency, vol. 1, p. 9, LBJ Library.

206. Memo, Randall to Moyers, 13 July 1965, "Banks—San Francisco National" folder, box 5, files of Harry McPherson, LBJ Library.

207. Memo, Barr to Califano, 10 January 1966, Ex FI 2, WHCF, LBJ Library.

208. Letter, Fowler to Saxon, 24 June 1965, attached to memo, Fowler to president, 25 June 1965, Ex FI 2, WHCF, LBJ Library.

209. Ibid.

210. See, for example, memos, Fowler to president, 9 February 1966, C.F. FI 2, and 26 May 1966, Ex FI 2, WHCF, LBJ Library. See also "Annual Message to the Congress: The Economic Report of the President," 26 January 1967, *Public Papers*, p. 87.

211. Camp Oral History Interview, tape 1, p. 40.

212. Department of the Treasury, *Administrative History*, Office of the Comptroller of the Currency, vol. 1, pp. 79–80, LBJ Library.

213. Camp Oral History Interview, tape 1, p. 32.

214. Barr interview.

215. Memo, Fowler to Jacobsen, 7 November 1966, attached to memo, Smith to Jacobsen, 28 October 1966, Ex FI 2, WHCF, LBJ Library. Saxon became associated with the Indianapolis bank of Robert McKinney, long a prominent Democrat.

216. *New York Times*, 9 November 1966, p. 55. A number of possibilities were considered, including FDIC chairman William Sherrill (memo for the record, 4 November 1966, "William B. Camp" folder, box 83, files of John W. Macy, Jr., LBJ Library).

217. Ibid., and 12 March 1965, section 3, p. 5. There are also a number of indications of this in Camp's oral history.

218. Camp Oral History Interview, tape 1, p. 39.

219. Ibid., p. 27.

220. "Annual Message to Congress: The Economic Report of the President," 26 January 1967, *Public Papers*, p. 87.

221. Camp Oral History Interview, tape 1, pp. 22, 39.

222. Ibid., pp. 37, 39.

5. Tenuous Ties: The Case of Antitrust Enforcement

1. Noted on memo, Califano to president, 5 May 1968, Ex TN 4, WHCF, LBJ Library.

2. *Wall Street Journal,* 16 May 1968, p. 28.

3. "Annual Message to the Congress: The Economic Report of the President," 27 January 1966, *Public Papers of the President of the United States: Lyndon B. Johnson, 1966* (Washington, D.C.: GPO, 1967), p. 98 (hereafter cited as *Public Papers*).

4. "The Annual Report of the Council of Economic Advisers," in *Economic Report of the President* (Washington, D.C.: GPO, 1965), pp. 131–135 (hereafter cited as *Economic Report*).

5. *Economic Report,* 1967, pp. 113–115.

6. Robert M. Goolrick, *Public Policy toward Corporate Growth: The ITT Merger Cases* (Port Washington, N.Y.: Kennicat Press, 1978), p. 39.

7. Mark J. Green with Beverly C. Moore, Jr., and Bruce Wasserstein, *The Closed Enterprise System* (New York: Bantam Books, 1972), pp. 32–44, 80–81; Department of Justice, *Administrative History,* Antitrust Division, introduction, vol. 1, p. 8, LBJ Library (hereafter cited as *Antitrust Division Administrative History*).

8. Suzanne Weaver, *Decision to Prosecute: Organization and Public Policy in the Antitrust Division* (Cambridge, Mass.: MIT Press, 1977), pp. 157–159. Katzenbach was reported to have "conceded" that the effects of some proposed mergers on competition may be less important to Justice than jobs lost (Harold B. Meyers, "Professor Turner's Turn at Antitrust," *Fortune,* September 1965, p. 171).

9. Interview by the author with Donald F. Turner, Washington, D.C., 21 January 1982.

10. Turner interview; interview by the author with Edwin M. Zimmerman, Washington, D.C., 21 January 1982.

11. *New York Times,* 27 June 1965, p. 41.

12. Goolrick, *Public Policy toward Corporate Growth,* p. 45; Green et al., *The Closed Enterprise System,* p. 97.

13. Green et al., *The Closed Enterprise System,* p. 98.

14. The raw figures are provided in Richard A. Posner, "A Statistical Study of Antitrust Enforcement," *Journal of Law and Economics* 13 (October 1970): 366.

15. A concise summary of key developments is found in *Antitrust Division Administrative History,* pp. 1–7.

16. Meyers, "Professor Turner's Turn at Antitrust," p. 170.

17. *Antitrust Division Administrative History,* subsection d, pp. 1–3.

18. Richard A. Posner, *Antitrust Law: An Economic Perspective* (Chicago: University of Chicago Press, 1976), pp. 230–231.

19. On Turner's tenure at the antitrust division, see generally Green et al., *The Closed Enterprise System,* pp. 82–97; and Weaver, *Decision to Prosecute,* chapter 6.

20. Noted on memo, Valenti to president, 8 April 1965, Ex JL 2-1, WHCF, LBJ Library.

21. Memo, Valenti to president, 18 March 1965, Ex JL 2-1, WHCF, LBJ Library.

22. Ibid.

23. Letter, White to Ribicoff, 25 March 1965, attached to letter, White to Katzenbach, 6 April 1965, Ex JL 2-1, WHCF, LBJ Library.

24. Ibid.

25. Letter, Ribicoff to president, 14 April 1965, Ex JL 2-1, WHCF, LBJ Library.

26. Green et al., *The Closed Enterprise System*, p. 42.

27. Nicholas deB. Katzenbach Oral History Interview, 11 December 1968, p. 5, LBJ Library.

28. Memo, Katzenbach to president, 15 April 1965, box 604, files of John W. Macy, Jr., LBJ Library.

29. Turner interview.

30. Memo, Valenti to president, 22 April 1965, Ex BE 2-4, WHCF, LBJ Library.

31. "The President's News Conference," 27 April 1965, *Public Papers*, p. 451.

32. Larry Temple Oral History Interview, 12 June 1970, tape 7, pp. 1–2, LBJ Library.

33. Harry C. McPherson, Jr., Oral History Interview, 9 April 1969, tape 8, p. 8, LBJ Library.

34. Ibid., pp. 8–9.

35. Ibid., p. 7.

36. Ramsey Clark Oral History Interview, 3 June 1967, p. 27, LBJ Library.

37. Turner and Zimmerman interviews.

38. Turner interview.

39. Letter, Woodward to Valenti, 19 May 1964, Ex BE 2-4, WHCF, LBJ Library.

40. Memo, vice president to Califano, 13 April 1967, Ex BE 2-1, LBJ Library.

41. Turner interview.

42. Green et al., *The Closed Enterprise System*, p. 42.

43. The cases concerned Broadcast Music, Inc., and the Scripps Howard Newspaper chain (ibid.).

44. Memo, Katzenbach to president, 2 March 1965, Ex JL 2-1, WHCF, LBJ Library.

45. Memo, Walter to Jack, 21 April 1964, Ex JL 2-1, WHCF, LBJ Library.

46. The president's response was written on a coverslip from Bill Moyers, attached to letter, Salinger to president, 14 July 1965, attached to memo, Katzenbach to White, 29 July 1965, Ex JL 2-1, WHCF, LBJ Library.

47. Memo, Katzenbach to White, 29 July 1965, Ex JL 2-1, WHCF, LBJ Library.

48. Memo, Feldman to Jenkins, 17 September 1964, Ex JL 2-1, WHCF, LBJ Library.

49. *Newsweek*, 25 July 1966, pp. 24–25.

50. *New York Times*, 14 July 1966, p. 16; 15 July 1966, p. 15.

51. Memo, Watson to president, 25 September 1967, Ex FG 135, WHCF, LBJ Library.

52. The president saw Miller on other matters, for example on 21 January, 11 March, and 15 June 1967 (Daily Diary Index, LBJ Library).

53. *Wall Street Journal*, 5 December 1967, p. 31.

54. Memo, Jacobsen to president, 12 April 1966, attached to memo, Katzenbach to president, 9 April 1966, C.F. BE 2-4, WHCF, LBJ Library.

55. Letter, Abram to McPherson, 30 August 1966, "Antitrust Cases" folder, box 2, files of Harry McPherson, LBJ Library.

56. Daily Diary Index, LBJ Library.

57. Memo, Temple to president, 8 February 1968, Ex JL 2-1, WHCF, LBJ Library.

58. On the management of wage-price policy generally, see James E. Anderson and Jared E. Hazleton, *Managing Macroeconomic Policy: The Johnson Presidency* (Austin: University of Texas Press, 1986), chapter 5.

59. Memo, Katzenbach to president, 1 October 1965, Ex BE 5-2, WHCF, LBJ Library.

60. Memo, Califano to president, 1 October 1965, Ex BE 5-2, WHCF, LBJ Library.

61. Memo, Schultze to Califano, 8 October 1965, Ex BE 5-2, WHCF, LBJ Library.

62. Memo, Ackley to president, 6 March 1966, Ex FG 11-3, WHCF, LBJ Library.

63. Memo, Turner to Califano, 18 February 1966, Ex BE 4/Construction, WHCF, LBJ Library.

64. Memo, Robson to Califano, 14 October 1966, "Pricing Files: Presidential Authorities" folder, box 16, files of John E. Robson and Sanford Ross, LBJ Library.

65. Memo, Califano to president, 9 August 1966, Ex JL 2-1, WHCF, LBJ Library.

66. Memo, Levinson to Califano, 13 October 1966, C.F. CM/Food, WHCF, LBJ Library.

67. Draft attached to memo, Robson to Califano, 14 October 1966, "Pricing Files: Presidential Authorities" folder, box 16, files of John E. Robson and Sanford Ross, LBJ Library.

68. Ibid.

69. Ibid.

70. Ibid.

71. Ibid.

72. Letter, Saxon to Reuss, 10 January 1966, Ex LE/FE 2, WHCF, LBJ Library.

73. Memo, Katzenbach to Califano, 14 September 1965, Ex LE/FI 2, WHCF, LBJ Library.

74. Department of Justice, *Administrative History*, vol. 8, part 12, sec. F, Legislative Matters, pp. 1–4, LBJ Library.

75. Memo, Califano to president, 2 February 1968, Ex SP 2-3/1968/AG, WHCF, LBJ Library.

76. "Special Message to the Congress: Prosperity and Progress for the Farmer and Rural American," 27 February 1968, *Public Papers*, pp. 276–277.

77. Memo, Ackley to president, 29 June 1967, Ex BE 2-4, WHCF, LBJ Library.

78. Memo, White to president, 19 February 1966, Ex LE/FI 2, LBJ Library.

79. Ibid.

80. P.L. 86-463.

81. *United States* v. *Philadelphia National Bank*, 347 U.S. 321 (1963).

82. Background and basic information about the congressional struggle over bank merger legislation are drawn from *Congressional Quarterly Almanac* (Washington, D.C.: Congressional Quarterly Service, 1967), vol. 22, pp. 767–772; and *Antitrust Division Administrative History*, "Bank Mergers," subsection B, p. 1, LBJ Library.

83. *United States* v. *First National Bank (Lexington)*, 376 U.S. 665 (1964).

84. Turner and Zimmerman interviews.

85. "Memorandum concerning the Legislation to Place the Regulation of Bank Mergers in the Bank Supervisory Agencies," p. 6, attached to memo, Moyers to president, 20 April 1965, Ex LE/FI 2, WHCF, LBJ Library.

86. Memo, Hughes to Moyers, 19 April 1965, Ex LE/FI 2, WHCF, LBJ Library.

87. Memo, Moyers to president, 20 April 1965, Ex LE/FI 2, WHCF, LBJ Library.

88. Letter, Robertson to Mansfield, 17 September 1965, attached to memo, Califano to president, 25 September 1965, Ex LE/FI 2, WHCF, LBJ Library.

89. Memo, Valenti to president, 25 May 1965, Ex BE 2-4, WHCF, LBJ Library.

90. Memo, Hughes to White, 1 July 1965, "Bank Mergers" folder, box 5, files of Harry McPherson, LBJ Library.

91. Ibid.

92. Memo, McPherson to White, 14 June 1965, "Bank Mergers" folder, box 5, files of Harry McPherson, LBJ Library.

93. Memo, Hughes to White, 1 July 1965, "Bank Mergers" folder, box 5, files of Harry McPherson, LBJ Library.

94. Memo, McPherson to Watson, 2 July 1965, Ex LE/FI 2, WHCF, LBJ Library.

95. Ibid.

96. Memo, Watson to president, 15 July 1965, Ex LE/FI 2, WHCF, LBJ Library.

97. Letter, Walker to Watson, 19 August 1965, Ex FG 135, WHCF, LBJ Library.

98. Letter, Saxon to Patman, 24 August 1965, Ex LE/FI 2, WHCF, LBJ Library.

99. Memo, O'Brien to Wilson, 30 August 1965, attached to memo, Wilson to president, 30 August 1965, Ex LE/BE 2-4, WHCF, LBJ Library.

100. Memo, Wilson to president, 31 August 1965, Ex LE/FI 2, WHCF, LBJ Library.

101. Letter, Walker to Watson, 19 August 1965, Ex LE/FI 2, WHCF, LBJ Library.

102. Memo, Wilson to president, 31 August 1965, Ex LE/FI 2, WHCF, LBJ Library.

103. Letter, Katzenbach to Califano, 14 September 1965, Ex LE/FI 2, WHCF, LBJ Library.

104. Memo, Hughes to Califano, 14 September 1965, Ex LE/FI 2, WHCF, LBJ Library.

105. Memo, Califano to president, 14 September 1965, Ex LE/FI 2, WHCF, LBJ Library.

106. Ibid.

107. Memo, McPherson to Watson, 2 July 1965, Ex LE/FI 2, WHCF, LBJ Library.

108. The final version of the letter is attached to memo, Katzenbach to Califano, 24 September 1965, Ex LE/FI 2, WHCF, LBJ Library. Differences in views are filed with it in memos, Fowler to Califano, 18 September 1965; and Katzenbach to Fowler, 19 September 1965.

109. Memo, Califano to president, 20 September 1965, attached to memo, Califano to president, 25 September 1965, Ex LE/FI 2, WHCF, LBJ Library.

110. Noted on ibid.

111. Memo, Califano to president, 21 September 1965, attached to memo, Califano to president, 25 September 1965, Ex LE/FI 2, WHCF, LBJ Library.

112. Memo, Califano to president, 21 September 1965, Ex FI 2, WHCF, LBJ Library.

113. Ibid.

114. Memo, Barr to president, 7 October 1965, Ex LE/FI 2, WHCF, LBJ Library.

115. The draft with the changes, probably in Califano's hand, is attached to memo, Katzenbach to Califano, 24 September 1965, Ex LE/FI 2, WHCF, LBJ Library.

116. Memo, Califano to president, 25 September 1965, Ex LE/FI 2, WHCF, LBJ Library.

117. Memo, Barr to president, 7 October 1965, Ex LE/FI 2, WHCF, LBJ Library.

118. Ibid.

119. Ibid.

120. *New York Times*, 6 November 1965, p. 35; 9 November 1965, p. 61; and 13 November 1965, p. 35.

121. Letter, Saxon to Reuss, 10 January 1966, Ex LE/FI 2, WHCF, LBJ Library.

122. Memo, White to president, 19 February 1966, Ex LE/FI 2, WHCF, LBJ Library.

123. The most important decisions were in *United States* v. *First City*

National Bank of Houston, 386 U.S. 361 (1967), and *United States* v. *Third National Bank of Nashville,* 390 U.S. 171 (1968).

124. Department of the Treasury, *Administrative History,* Office of the Comptroller of the Currency, vol. 1, p. 20, LBJ Library.

125. Memo, Ackley to Califano, 28 November 1966, attached to memo, Graham to Califano, 12 December 1966, Ex FG 678, WHCF, LBJ Library.

126. "Criteria to Implement the Merger Provisions of the President's Transportation Message," attached to memo, Graham to Califano, 12 December 1966, Ex FG 678, WHCF, LBJ Library.

127. See Richard Saunders, *The Railroad Mergers and the Coming of Conrail* (Westport, Conn.: Greenwood Press, 1978).

128. *Seaboard Air Line R. Co.* v. *U.S.,* 382 U.S. 154 (1966).

129. Memo, Prettyman to Feldman, 9 January 1964, Ex BE 2-4, WHCF, LBJ Library.

130. Daily Diary Index, LBJ Library.

131. Letter, Saunders to president, 14 July 1964, Ex TN 4, WHCF, LBJ Library.

132. Memo, attorney general to files, attached to letter, Katzenbach to Saunders, 4 September 1964, Ex BE 2, WHCF, LBJ Library.

133. Ibid.

134. Memo, Okun to White, 26 July 1965, Ex BE 2-4, WHCF, LBJ Library; memo, Okun to Turner, 17 June 1966, "Transportation" folder, box 16, files of Harry McPherson, LBJ Library.

135. Memo, Levinson to Califano, 26 November 1966, Ex BE 2-4, WHCF, LBJ Library.

136. Memo, Boyd to Clark, 21 November 1966, Ex BE 2-4, WHCF, LBJ Library.

137. "Memorandum re Participation of Department of Justice in Penn-Central Proceeding," 21 November 1966, prepared by counsel for the Norfolk & Western Railway Company, attached to letter, Katzenbach to Saunders, 4 September 1964, Ex BE 2, WHCF, LBJ Library.

138. Memo, Califano to president, 21 November 1966, Ex BE 2-4, WHCF, LBJ Library.

139. Ibid.

140. Noted on ibid.

141. Joseph A. Califano, Jr., *The Triumph and Tragedy of Lyndon Johnson: The White House Years* (New York: Simon and Schuster, 1991), pp. 161–162.

142. Memo, Ackley to Clark, 26 November 1966, Ex BE 2-4, WHCF, LBJ Library.

143. Ibid.

144. Ibid.

145. Ibid.

146. *Baltimore & Ohio R. Co.* v. *United States,* 386 U.S. 372 (1967), pp. 384–385.

147. Memo, Clark to president, 5 December 1966, Ex PU 1/FG 135, WHCF, LBJ Library.

148. *Baltimore & Ohio R. Co.* v. *United States,* 386 U.S. 372 (1967).

149. *Antitrust Division Administrative History*, p. 16.

150. Zimmerman interview.

151. Green et al., *The Closed Enterprise System*, p. 43.

152. "Press Briefing with the Governors Following the New England Governors Conference," 15 May 1967, *Public Papers*, pp. 533–534.

153. Ibid.

154. Ibid.

155. Zimmerman interview.

156. Memo, Watson to president, 9 June 1967, Ex BE 2-4, WHCF, LBJ Library.

157. A synopsis of the government's brief is found in 19 L. Ed. 2d 1507 (1967).

158. *Penn-Central Merger and N & W Inclusion Cases*, 389 U.S. 486 (1968). Associate Justice Fortas participated in the 1967 decision and wrote this decision, despite the role he played in shaping the government's brief two years previously.

159. *New Haven Inclusion Cases*, 399 U.S. 392 (1970).

160. Memo, Ackley to Califano, 28 November 1966, attached to memo, Graham to Califano, 12 December 1966, Ex FG 678, WHCF, LBJ Library.

161. Letter, Ross to solicitor general, 27 November 1968, attached to memo, Pierson to Temple, "Memos for the President" folder, box 20, files of DeVier Pierson, LBJ Library.

162. Memo, Robson to Califano, 8 May 1968, attached to memo, Califano to president, 8 May 1968, Ex TN 4, WHCF, LBJ Library.

163. Memo, Clark to Temple, 4 May 1968, Ex FG 251, WHCF, LBJ Library.

164. Attached to memo, Temple to Califano, 18 December 1967, Ex BE 2-4, WHCF, LBJ Library.

165. *Washington Star*, 12 May 1968, p. D13.

166. Temple Oral History Interview, tape 7, p. 6.

167. *United States* v. *Interstate Commerce Commission, et al.*, 396 U.S. 491 (1969).

6. Further Explorations of Policy

1. Noted on memo, Califano to president, 31 May 1967, HE 8-1, WHCF, LBJ Library.

2. Erwin C. Hargrove and Michael Nelson, *Presidents, Politics and Policy* (New York: Alfred A. Knopf, 1984), chapter 3.

3. Memo, Califano to Ackley, 22 September 1966, Task Force on the Quality of the Environment 1966, box 19, task force collection, LBJ Library.

4. Randall B. Ripley and Grace A. Franklin, *Congress, the Bureaucracy and Public Policy* (Pacific Grove, Cal.: Brooks/Cole, 1991).

5. James E. Sundquist, *Politics and Policy: The Eisenhower, Kennedy and Johnson Years* (Washington, D.C.: Brookings Institution, 1968).

6. The use of task forces is treated in a number of studies. Among them

are Hugh Davis Graham, *The Uncertain Triumph: Federal Education Policies in the Kennedy and Johnson Years* (Chapel Hill: University of North Carolina Press, 1984); Emmette S. Redford and Richard T. McCulley, *White House Operations: The Johnson Presidency* (Austin: University of Texas Press, 1986), chapter 5; and Norman C. Thomas and Harold L. Wolman, "The Presidency and Policy Formulation: The Task Force Device," *Public Administration Review* 29 (September/October 1969): 459.

7. "Special Message to the Congress on Protecting the Consumer Interest," 15 March 1962, *Public Papers of the President of the United States: John F. Kennedy, 1962* (Washington, D.C.: GPO, 1963), p. 235 (hereafter cited as *Public Papers*).

8. Memo, Heller to president, 31 July 1963, Council of Economic Advisers, *Administrative History*, vol. 2, LBJ Library.

9. Ibid.

10. Ibid.

11. Council of Economic Advisers, *Administrative History*, vol. 1, p. 21, LBJ Library.

12. Memo, Heller to president, 12 December 1963, Council of Economic Advisers, *Administrative History*, vol. 2, LBJ Library.

13. Esther Peterson Oral History Interview, 25 November 1968, pp. 5–9, LBJ Library.

14. Memo, Heller to president, 28 December 1963, Ex FI, WHCF, LBJ Library.

15. "Statement by the President upon Establishing the President's Committee on Consumer Interests," 3 January 1964, *Public Papers*, p. 108.

16. Peterson Oral History Interview, p. 3.

17. Ibid., pp. 14–17.

18. Note, Peterson to president, 22 February 1965, attached to letter, Watson to Peterson, 25 February 1965, Ex FG 717, WHCF, LBJ Library.

19. Memo, Okun to White, 2 March 1965, Ex AG 3-1, WHCF, LBJ Library.

20. Ibid.

21. Memo, Peterson to Macy and Schultze, 28 October 1965, attached to memo, Levinson to Okun, 31 January 1967, C.F. FG 717, WHCF, LBJ Library.

22. Note, CEC to Joe, undated, C.F. FG 717, WHCF, LBJ Library.

23. Noted on ibid.

24. Noted on memo, Moyers to president, 4 April 1966, Ex FG 717, WHCF, LBJ Library.

25. Memo, Califano to president, 25 June 1966, attached to memo, Watson to Califano, 27 June 1966, Ex FG 717, WHCF, LBJ Library.

26. Memo, Bohen to Califano, 26 January 1967, attached to memo, Levinson to Okun, 31 January 1967, C.F. FG 717, WHCF, LBJ Library.

27. Memo, Califano to president, 1 May 1967, C.F. FG 717, WHCF, LBJ Library. The Furness appointment was a puzzle to Macy. Macy says that Johnson wanted a female and someone who could deal with Congress. After he and Califano interviewed her she met with the president, who "obvi-

ously was impressed by her knowledge of the field and her intense determination to make good" (John W. Macy, Jr., Oral History Interview, 26 April 1969, tape 3, p. 27, LBJ Library).

28. Memo, Cater, McPherson and Pierson to president, 13 May 1967, "Memos for the President" folder, box 20, files of DeVier Pierson, LBJ Library.

29. James L. Cochrane, "Energy Policy in the Johnson Administration: Logical Order versus Economic Pluralism," in Crawford D. Goodwin (ed.), *Energy Policy in Perspective: Today's Problems, Yesterday's Solutions* (Washington, D.C.: Brookings Institution, 1981), p. 343.

30. "Natural Resources," 17 June 1964, p. 8, "Task Forces on the 1965 Legislative Program, June 17, 1964" folder, box 94, files of Bill Moyers, LBJ Library.

31. Task Force on Natural Resources, "Report," 1964, pp. 80–90, box 2, task force collection, LBJ Library.

32. Federal Power Commission, *National Power Survey* (Washington, D.C.: GPO, 1964).

33. Memo, Califano to Hornig, 14 October 1966, "Task Force on Electric Power" folder, box 13, task force collection, LBJ Library.

34. Task Force on Electric Power, "Report," 1966, pp. 13–14, box 13, task force collection, LBJ Library.

35. Ibid., pp. 3–10.

36. Notes, White House meeting on electric power, 3 December 1966, box 13, task force collection, LBJ Library.

37. "Special Message to the Congress: Protecting Our Natural Heritage," 30 January 1967, *Public Papers*, p. 100.

38. "Special Message to the Congress on Agriculture," 4 February 1965, *Public Papers*, pp. 147–148.

39. National Advisory Commission on Food and Fiber, *Food and Fiber for the Future* (Washington, D.C.: GPO, 1967).

40. Ibid., p. 17.

41. On U.S. satellite policy in international context, see Jonathan F. Galloway, *The Politics and Technology of Satellite Communications* (Lexington, Mass.: Lexington Books, 1972).

42. Francis E. Rourke and Roger G. Brown, "The President and Telecommunications Policy: The Failure of An Advisory System," paper presented at the annual meeting of the American Political Science Association, Washington, D.C., 28–31 August 1980, pp. 2–15.

43. Memo, O'Connell to president, 13 January 1965, "Telecommunications Management/OEP" folder, box 134, files of Bill Moyers, LBJ Library.

44. Ibid.

45. Memo, Valenti to president, 8 April 1965, Ex FG 11-2, WHCF, LBJ Library.

46. Memo, Kintner to president, 7 September 1966, Ex UT 1, WHCF, LBJ Library.

47. Quoted in Rourke and Brown, "The President and Telecommunications Policy," p. 13.

328	*Notes to Pages 214–218*

48. "Report and Recommendations to Senate and Home Commerce Committees," 29 April 1966, Ex FG 11-6-2, WHCF, LBJ Library.

49. Memo, O'Connell to Semer, 16 June 1966, Ex PQ 2, WHCF, LBJ Library.

50. Memo, Kintner to president, 5 July 1966, C.F. FG 228/A, WHCF, LBJ Library.

51. 4 FCC 2d 421 (1966).

52. Letter, O'Connell to Hyde, 1 June 1966, attached to memo, O'Connell to president, 3 June 1966, Ex UT 1, WHCF, LBJ Library.

53. Letter, Loy to Hyde, 2 June 1966, attached to memo, O'Connell to president, 3 June 1966, Ex UT 1, WHCF, LBJ Library.

54. Letter, Hyde to O'Connell, 7 June 1966, attached to memo, O'Connell to Semer, 8 June 1966, Ex UT 1, WHCF, LBJ Library.

55. Federal Communications Commission, *Administrative History*, pp. 27–28, LBJ Library.

56. Memo, Cater, McPherson and Pierson to president, 13 May 1967, "Memos for the President" folder, box 20, files of DeVier Pierson, LBJ Library.

57. "Special Message to the Congress on Communications Policy," 14 August 1967, *Public Papers*, p. 763.

58. Noted on memo, Cater and McPherson to president, 17 August 1967, "Memos for the President (1967)" folder, box 53, files of Harry McPherson, LBJ Library.

59. Memo, Rowe to president, 21 June 1968, C.F. FG 600/Task Force/C, WHCF, LBJ Library.

60. Ibid.

61. Memo, Pierson to president, 27 June 1968, Ex FG/Task Force/C, WHCF, LBJ Library.

62. Comment, 8 August 1968, attached to letter, Rostow to president, 7 August 1968, attached to ibid.

63. Memo, Pierson to president, 18 September 1968, Ex FG 600/Task Force/C, WHCF, LBJ Library.

64. Noted on ibid.

65. Memo, Marks, Cater, and Pierson to president, 26 September 1968, Ex FG 600/Task Force/C, WHCF, LBJ Library.

66. Memo, Morrill to director, 14 November 1968, "T8-1, vol. 3, Task Force on Telecommunications (September–December 1968)" folder, Series 65.5, Record Group 51, National Archives.

67. President's Task Force on Communications Policy, *Final Report* (Washington, D.C.: GPO, 1968).

68. Memo, Pierson to president, 9 December 1968, Ex FG 600/Task Force/C, WHCF, LBJ Library.

69. Ibid.

70. Ibid.

71. Memo, Pierson to Zwick, 18 December 1968, Ex FG 600/Task Force/C, WHCF, LBJ Library.

72. There were a number of congressional hearings on these matters. In

addition, see, for example, Carl Kaysen and Donald F. Turner, *Antitrust Policy: An Economic and Legal Analysis* (Cambridge: Harvard University Press, 1959); Estes Kefauver, *In a Few Hands: Monopoly Power in America* (New York: Pantheon Books, 1965); Mark S. Massel, *Competition and Monopoly: Legal and Economic Issues* (Washington, D.C.: Brookings Institution, 1962); and Gardner C. Means, *The Corporate Revolution in America: Economic Reality vs. Economic Theory* (New York: Collier Books, 1962).

73. *Congress and the Nation 1965–1968* (Washington, D.C.: Congressional Quarterly Service, 1969), pp. 292–293.

74. Memo, Goldstein to president, 6 October 1967, Ex FG 600/Task Force/A, WHCF, LBJ Library.

75. Ibid.

76. Memo, Nimetz to Califano, 17 October 1967, "Task Force on Antitrust" folder, box 199, files of James Gaither, LBJ Library.

77. The law professors were William F. Baxter of Stanford, Robert H. Bork of Yale, Carl H. Fulda of Texas, William K. Jones of Columbia, and James A. Rahl of Northwestern. The attorneys were Dennis G. Lyons, George D. Reycroft, and Richard Sherwood. The economists were Paul W. MacAvoy of MIT, James W. McKie of Vanderbilt, and Lee E. Preston of the University of California at Berkeley. S. Paul Posner served as staff director.

78. Memo, Nimetz to Califano, 28 October 1967, "Task Force on Antitrust" folder, box 199, files of James Gaither, LBJ Library.

79. "Agenda—Meeting with Don Turner," undated, "Task Force on Antitrust" folder, box 199, files of James Gaither, LBJ Library.

80. "Task Force on Antitrust" folder, box 199, files of James Gaither, LBJ Library.

81. Task Force on Antitrust Policy, "Report," 5 July 1968, attached to letter, Neal to president, 5 July 1968, C.F. FG 600/Task Force on Antitrust, WHCF, LBJ Library.

82. Memo, Posner to task force, 9 January 1968, "Material for January 13 Meeting of Task Force" folder, box 394, files of James Gaither, LBJ Library.

83. The oligopoly proposal was not supported by Bork or Sherwood. They, together with MacAvoy, also dissented from the majority's position on conglomerates. In both cases, their basic criticism was the lack of evidence to support the premise that bigness per se caused anticompetitive behavior. See Robert H. Bork, *The Antitrust Paradox: A Policy at War with Itself* (New York: Basic Books, 1978), esp. pp. 175–197 and 246–262.

84. Memo, Califano to president, 19 December 1968, "1967–68 Outside Task Force on Antitrust #2" folder, box 200, files of James Gaither, LBJ Library.

85. Council of Economic Advisers, *The Annual Report of the Council of Economic Advisers* (Washington, D.C.: GPO, 1969), pp. 106–109 (hereafter cited as *Report*).

86. "Annual Message to the Congress on the State of the Union," 4 January 1965, *Public Papers*, p. 6.

87. "Special Message to the Congress on Transportation," 5 May 1962, *Public Papers*, p. 292.

88. Council of Economic Advisers, *Report*, 1965, p. 132.

89. Council of Economic Advisers, *Report*, 1967, p. 117.

90. This was ruled unlawful by the Supreme Court, but Congress quickly conferred the necessary authority on the board (P.L. 90-514).

91. 13 FCC 2d 420 (1968).

92. Task Force on Natural Resources, "Interim Report," pp. 86–87, attached to memo, Fisher to Moyers, 18 September 1964, Ex FG 600/T, WHCF, LBJ Library.

93. President's Task Force on Communications Policy, *Final Report*, chapter 6, p. 7.

94. Minutes, meeting of 16 December 1967, attached to minutes, meeting of 13 January 1968, "Minutes, Task Force Meetings" folder, box 200, files of James Gaither, LBJ Library.

95. Task Force on Antitrust Policy, "Report," 5 July 1968, p. 11, attached to letter, Neal to president, box 6, task force collection, LBJ Library.

96. Memo, Barr to president, 12 May 1966, Ex FI 2, WHCF, LBJ Library.

97. Memo, Barr to president, 13 May 1966, attached to memo, Barr to president, 14 May 1966, C.F. FG 600/Task Force/5, WHCF, LBJ Library.

98. Memo, Barr to president, 14 May 1966, C.F. FG 600/Task Force/5, WHCF, LBJ Library.

99. Memo, Duesenberry to Califano, 21 October 1966, attached to memo, Schultze to Califano, 19 November 1966, Ex FG 600/Task Force/F, WHCF, LBJ Library.

100. Memo, Schultze to Califano, 19 November 1966, Ex FG 600/Task Force/F, WHCF, LBJ Library.

101. Council of Economic Advisers, *Report*, 1967, pp. 66–67.

102. *Congress and the Nation: 1965–1968* (Washington, D.C.: Congressional Quarterly Service, 1969), p. 272.

103. Ibid., p. 278. See Thomas H. Hammond and Jack H. Knott, "The Deregulation Snowball: Exploring Deregulation in the Financial Industry," *Journal of Politics* 50 (February 1988): 3.

104. Memo, Gordon to president, 27 January 1964, attached to memo, Feldman to Jenkins, 12 February 1964, Ex TN 5, WHCF, LBJ Library.

105. "Letter to Senate and House Committee Chairmen on Various Legislative Proposals Relating to Transportation," 27 January 1964, *Public Papers*, p. 241.

106. "Task Force Issue Paper Transportation," 17 June 1964, p. 1, attached to memo, Gordon to Cater, 22 June 1964, C.F. FG 600/T, WHCF, LBJ Library.

107. "Remarks of the President to the Presidential Task Force on Transportation," attached to memo, Murray to Feldman, 18 July 1964, Ex FG 600/Task Force/T, WHCF, LBJ Library.

108. Task Force on Transportation Policy, "National Transportation Policy," November 1964, Ex FG 600/Task Force on Transportation Policy, WHCF, LBJ Library.

109. "Annual Message to the Congress on the State of the Union," 4 January 1965, *Public Papers*, p. 6.

110. "Annual Message to the Congress: The Economic Report of the President," 28 January 1965, *Public Papers*, pp. 115–116.

111. Memo, Martin to Moyers, 12 March 1965, "Transportation 3/2/65" folder, box 7, files of Bill Moyers, LBJ Library.

112. Memo, Capron to White, 27 March 1965, Ex LE/TN, WHCF, LBJ Library.

113. Memo, White to president, 12 April 1965, "Transportation 3/2/65" folder, box 7, files of Bill Moyers, LBJ Library.

114. Memo, Okun to Ackley, 11 September 1965, attached to memo, Ackley to Califano, 13 September 1965, Ex TN, WHCF, LBJ Library.

115. Memo, White to files, 10 May 1965, Ex LE/TN, WHCF, LBJ Library.

116. Memo, Califano to Boyd, 12 August 1965, C.F. FG 600/T, WHCF, LBJ Library.

117. Memo, Okun to Ackley, 11 September 1965, attached to memo, Ackley to Califano, 13 September 1965, Ex TN, WHCF, LBJ Library.

118. Memo, Califano to president, 22 September 1965, Ex LE, WHCF, LBJ Library.

119. Ibid.

120. Memo, Califano to Boyd, 25 September 1965, C.F. TN, WHCF, LBJ Library.

121. Memo, Boyd to Califano, 3 December 1965, FG 600/T, WHCF, LBJ Library.

122. Memo, White to files, 14 December 1965, Ex TN, WHCF, LBJ Library.

123. Ibid.

124. Memo, White to files, 16 December 1965, Ex TN, WHCF, LBJ Library.

125. Memo, Okun to White and Califano, 28 December 1965, Ex TN, WHCF, LBJ Library.

126. Memo, Birdwell to White, 1 February 1966, Ex TN, WHCF, LBJ Library.

127. Memo, Gaither to Califano, 17 May 1967, "Transportation—General" folder, box 43, files of James Gaither, LBJ Library.

128. Memo, Boyd to Califano, 10 July 1967, "Price Files Transportation Costs" folder, box 28, Files of John Robson and Sanford Ross, LBJ Library.

129. Memo, Califano to president, 8 October 1968, Ex TN, WHCF, LBJ Library.

130. Noted on memo, Califano to president, 9 February 1966, Ex LE/LA, WHCF, LBJ Library.

131. Of course, Congress considered much legislation concerning economic regulation that was not of presidential interest.

132. *NLRB* v. *Denver Building and Construction Trade Council*, 341 U.S. 675 (1951).

133. Memo, Powers to Redmon, 13 January 1965, "Fair Labor Standards—Minimum Wage" folder, box 6, files of Bill Moyers, LBJ Library.

134. Memo, Ackley to Moyers, 19 April 1965, "Fair Labor Standards—Minimum Wage" folder, box 6, files of Bill Moyers, LBJ Library.

135. Memo, Gordon to Moyers, 21 April 1965, "Fair Labor Standards—Minimum Wage" folder, box 6, files of Bill Moyers, LBJ Library.

136. "Annual Message to the Congress on the State of the Union," 4 January 1965, *Public Papers*, p. 6.

137. "Special Message to the Congress on Labor," 18 May 1965, *Public Papers*, p. 535.

138. *Congress and the Nation: 1965–1968*, pp. 602–606, 611.

139. "Remarks to Members of the International Labor Press Association," 23 May 1966, *Public Papers*, p. 542.

140. Message from Wirtz, undated, Ex SP 2-3/1965/LA, WHCF, LBJ Library.

141. Memo, Wilson to president, 24 February 1966, Ex LE/LA, WHCF, LBJ Library.

142. Ibid.

143. Memo, Wirtz to president, 3 March 1966, attached to memo, Califano to president, 8 March 1966, Ex LE/LA, WHCF, LBJ Library.

144. *Congress and the Nation: 1945–1964* (Washington, D.C.: Congressional Quarterly Service, 1965), pp. 633–651.

145. Memo, Lewis to Sorensen, 7 December 1963, Ex LE/LA, WHCF, LBJ Library.

146. Memo, Wirtz to president, 11 December 1963, attached to memo, Wirtz to Sorensen, 11 December 1963, Ex LE/LA, WHCF, LBJ Library.

147. Memo, Gordon and Heller to president, 21 December 1963, Ex LE/LA, WHCF, LBJ Library.

148. Memo, Gordon and Heller to Sorensen, 24 December 1963, Ex LE/LA, WHCF, LBJ Library.

149. "Annual Message to the Congress on the State of the Union," 8 January 1964, *Public Papers*, p. 114.

150. Ibid., p. 116.

151. "Annual Message to the Congress on the State of the Union," 4 January 1965, *Public Papers*, p. 6.

152. Memo, Wirtz to Moyers, 17 February 1965, attached to memo, Moyers to president, 16 February 1965, "Fair Labor Standards—Minimum Wage" folder, box 6, files of Bill Moyers, LBJ Library.

153. Noted on ibid.

154. Memos, Eckstein to Moyers, 17 February, "Fair Labor Standards—Minimum Wage" folder, box 6, files of Bill Moyers; and Gordon to Moyers, 24 February 1965, "Fair Labor Standards—Minimum Wage" folder, box 6, files of Bill Moyers, LBJ Library.

155. Memo, Eckstein to Moyers, 18 February 1965, "Fair Labor Standards—Minimum Wage" folder, box 6, files of Bill Moyers, LBJ Library.

156. Memo, Eckstein to Moyers, 25 February 1965, Ex LA 3, WHCF, LBJ Library.

157. Memo, Wirtz to president, 7 March 1965, attached to memo, Wirtz to Valenti, 9 March 1965, Ex LA 3, WHCF, LBJ Library. The Department of Commerce wanted to hold the extension of coverage to 2 million, the immediate coverage of these at $1.25, and the double-time proposal (letter,

Connor to Gordon, 28 April 1965, "Fair Labor Standards—Minimum Wage" folder, box 6, files of Bill Moyers, LBJ Library).

158. "Special Message to the Congress on Labor," 18 May 1965, *Public Papers*, p. 554.

159. Memo, Eckstein to president, 4 August 1965, Ex LE/LA, WHCF, LBJ Library.

160. Memo, Califano to Wirtz, Connor and Ackley, 1 December 1965, C.F. LE/LA 3, WHCF, LBJ Library.

161. Memo, Wirtz to Califano, 14 December 1965, attached to memo, Wilson to president, 12 January 1966, Ex LE/LA, WHCF, LBJ Library.

162. "Annual Message to the Congress on the State of the Union," 12 January 1966, *Public Papers*, p. 5; "Annual Message to the Congress: The Economic Report of the President," 27 January 1966, *Public Papers*, p. 107.

163. Memo, Ackley to president, 28 December 1965, Ex LA 8, WHCF, LBJ Library.

164. Memo, Ackley to Califano, 4 February 1966, attached to memo, Califano to president, 9 February 1966, Ex LE/LA, WHCF, LBJ Library.

165. Memo, Wirtz to president, 12 February 1966, C.F. LE/LA, WHCF, LBJ Library.

166. Memo, Connor to president, 12 February 1966, Ex LE/LA, WHCF, LBJ Library.

167. Memo, Wirtz to president, 12 February 1966, attached to memo, Califano to president, 12 February 1966, Ex LE/LA, WHCF, LBJ Library.

168. Memo, Wilson to president, 17 February 1966, Ex LE/LA, WHCF, LBJ Library.

169. Ibid.

170. Memo, Califano to president, 22 February 1966, Ex LE/LA, WHCF, LBJ Library.

171. Memo, Wirtz to president, 3 March 1966, attached to memo, Califano to president, 8 March 1966, Ex LE/LA, WHCF, LBJ Library.

172. Memo, Ackley to president, 8 March 1966, Ex LE/LA, WHCF, LBJ Library.

173. Daily Diary, 8 March 1966, LBJ Library. Califano provided the president with discussion material for the meeting with Meany (memo, Califano to president, 8 March 1966, Ex LE/LA, WHCF, LBJ Library).

174. Transcript, "Review with Orville Freeman," 14 October 1968, p. 5, Cabinet Review: Department of Agriculture, Special Files—Cabinet Papers, LBJ Library.

175. Don Paarlberg, "Proposed and Existing Organizational Efforts for Farmers," in Vernon W. Ruttan, Arley D. Waldo, and James P. Honck (eds.), *Agricultural Policy in an Affluent Society* (New York: W. W. Norton, 1969), p. 201.

176. Memo, Freeman to Califano, 25 August 1967, C.F. AG 3, WHCF, LBJ Library.

177. Ross B. Talbot and Don F. Hadwiger, *The Policy Process in American Agriculture* (San Francisco: Chandler Publishing Company, 1968), pp. 64–67.

178. Charles Walters, *Holding Action* (New York: Halcyon House, 1968).

179. "The President's News Conference," 18 August 1967, *Public Papers*, p. 793.

180. Task Force on Agricultural Bargaining, "Report," 11 December 1967, box 5, task force collection, LBJ Library.

181. Memo, Pierson to president, 26 August 1967, Ex AG, WHCF, LBJ Library.

182. Memo, Ackley to Califano, 25 August 1967, Ex AG, WHCF, LBJ Library.

183. "Annual Message to the Congress on the State of the Union," 17 January 1968, *Public Papers*, p. 31.

184. Memo, Pierson to Califano, 21 December 1967; and attached views of the CEA and the BOB, Ex SP 2-3/1968/AG, WHCF, LBJ Library.

185. Department of Justice, *Administrative History*, vol. 3, part 12, sec. F, Legislative Matters, pp. 14–16, LBJ Library.

186. Memo, Pierson to president, 9 February 1968, Ex SP 2-3/1968/AG, WHCF, LBJ Library.

187. Ibid.

188. Ibid.

189. *Congress and the Nation 1945–1964*, pp. 711–724.

190. James L. Sundquist with David W. Davis, *Making Federalism Work* (Washington, D.C.: Brookings Institution, 1969), chapter 4.

191. For a broad review of the politics of agriculture, see Talbot and Hadwiger, *The Policy Process in American Agriculture*.

192. Orville C. Freeman Oral History Interview, 14 February 1969, tape 1, p. 18, LBJ Library.

193. Ibid., p. 15.

194. W. DeVier Pierson Oral History Interview, 20 March 1969, tape 1, pp. 3–4, LBJ Library.

195. Arthur Okun Oral History Interview, 15 April 1969, interview II, tape 2, p. 3, LBJ Library.

196. *Congress and the Nation: 1965–1968*, pp. 724–730.

197. P.L. 88-297. Also in 1964, over the administration's objections, Congress passed meat import legislation requiring the president to set limits under certain circumstances.

198. "Remarks at the State Capitol in Des Moines," 17 October 1964, *Public Papers*, p. 1227.

199. P.L. 89-321. Also in that year P.L. 89-12 revised the tobacco program and P.L. 89-331 altered the sugar program.

200. Memo, Freeman to president, 29 August 1967, "Agriculture—Freeman's Statements," box 7, files of DeVier Pierson, LBJ Library.

201. Memo, Gordon to president, 5 November 1964, Ex AG 4, WHCF, LBJ Library.

202. Memo, Freeman to Moyers et al., 26 January 1965, Ex AG, WHCF, LBJ Library.

203. "Special Message to the Congress on Agriculture," 4 February 1965, *Public Papers*, p. 139.

204. Memo, Gordon to Moyers, 15 March 1965, Ex LE AG, WHCF; memo, Moyers to president, 16 March 1965, "Omnibus Farm Bill" folder, box 2, files of Bill Moyers, LBJ Library. However, Okun says that, in conflicts with Agriculture, BOB and CEA "probably lost three battles out of four" (Okun Oral History Interview, interview II, tape 2, p. 3, LBJ Library).

205. Memo, Freeman to president, 4 March 1965, "Omnibus Farm Bill" folder, box 2, files of Bill Moyers, LBJ Library.

206. Ibid.

207. Memo, Murphy to Valenti, 12 March 1965, "Agriculture 4/65" folder, box 4, files of Bill Moyers, LBJ Library.

208. Memo, Freeman to president, 15 March 1965, Ex LE AG, WHCF, LBJ Library.

209. Ibid.

210. Memo, Moyers to president, 16 March 1965, "Omnibus Farm Bill" folder, box 2, files of Bill Moyers, LBJ Library.

211. Written on memo, Moyers to president, 27 March 1965, "Omnibus Farm Bill" folder, box 2, files of Bill Moyers, LBJ Library.

212. Ibid.

213. For example, memos, Freeman to president, 7 April 1965, attached to memo, Valenti to Freeman, 14 April 1965, Ex FG 150; Freeman to president, 20 May 1965, Ex CM/COTTON; and Valenti to Moyers, 15 June 1965, Ex LE AG, WHCF, LBJ Library.

214. Memo, Schnittker to vice president et al., 16 June 1965, Ex LE/CM/COTTON, WHCF, LBJ Library.

215. Memos, Freeman to president, 17 July 1965, Ex LE/AG, WHCF, LBJ Library; and Freeman to president, 9 July 1965, Ex LE/AG, WHCF, LBJ Library.

216. Memo, Freeman to president, 16 July 1965, Ex LE/AG, WHCF, LBJ Library.

217. Memo, Schultze to president, 31 August 1965, Ex LE/AG, WHCF, LBJ Library.

218. Memo, Freeman to president, 29 July 1965, attached to memo, Freeman to president, 13 August 1965, Ex LE/AG, WHCF, LBJ Library.

219. Freeman Oral History Interview, tape 1, pp. 29–30.

220. Memo, Pierson to Freeman and Schnittker, 5 January 1968, "Agriculture—Freeman's Statements" folders, box 7, files of DeVier Pierson, LBJ Library.

221. "Special Message to Congress: 'Prosperity and Progress for the Farmer and Rural America,'" 27 February 1968, *Public Papers*, p. 271.

222. Memos, Pierson to president, 1 December 1967, Ex LE/AG 7; Duesenberry to Califano, 21 December 1967, attached to Pierson to Califano, 21 December 1967, Ex SP 2-3/1968/AG; and Zwick to Califano, 21 December 1967, Ex SP 2-3/1968 Ag Farm Message, Backup Material I, WHCF, LBJ Library.

223. *Congress and the Nation: 1965–1968*, pp. 580–581.

224. P.L. 90-559; Pierson Oral History Interview, tape 1, pp. 4–5.

225. Transcript, "Review with Orville Freeman," 14 October 1968, p. 5, Cabinet Review: Department of Agriculture, Special Files—Cabinet Papers, LBJ Library.

226. Ibid., p. 6.

227. Lyndon Baines Johnson, *The Vantage Point: Perspectives of the Presidency, 1963–1969* (New York: Holt, Rinehart and Winston, 1971), p. 341.

228. Paul H. Weaver, "Regulation, Social Policy, and Class Conflict," *Public Interest* (Winter 1978): 59. For other formulations, see William Lilley III and James C. Miller III, "The New 'Social Regulation,'" *Public Interest* (Spring 1977): 49; Michael D. Reagan, *Regulation: The Politics of Policy* (Boston: Little, Brown, 1987), p. 86; and David Vogel, "The 'New' Social Regulation in Historical and Comparative Perspective," in Thomas K. McCraw (ed.), *Regulation in Perspective: Historical Essays* (Cambridge: Graduate School of Business Administration, Harvard University, 1981), p. 155.

229. "Special Message to the Congress on Consumer Interests," 5 February 1964, *Public Papers*, p. 263.

230. "Special Message to the Congress on Conservation and Restoration of Natural Beauty," 8 February 1965, *Public Papers*, p. 156.

231. "Remarks at the University of Michigan," 22 May 1964, *Public Papers*, p. 704.

232. The cigarette issue was extraordinarily controversial. Even after the legislation passed, the White House avoided involvement. When the surgeon general's third report on smoking and health was released in 1968, White House aide Douglass Cater was quoted as saying "he wouldn't touch it with a 40 foot filter tip" (memo, Maguire to Christian, 2 July 1968, Ex CM/Cigarettes, WHCF, LBJ Library).

233. Michael Pertschuk, *Revolt against Regulation: The Rise and Pause of the Consumer Movement* (Berkeley: University of California Press, 1982), p. 13.

234. Richard Harris, *The Real Voice* (New York: Macmillan, 1964).

235. On the development of a congressional agenda, see Mark V. Nadel, *The Politics of Consumer Protection* (Indianapolis, Ind.: Bobbs-Merrill, 1971), chapter 2; and James L. Sundquist, *Politics and Policy: The Eisenhower, Kennedy, and Johnson Years* (Washington, D.C.: Brookings Institution, 1968), chapter 8.

236. Nadel, *The Politics of Consumer Protection*, p. 242.

237. Barr to president, 7 February 1968, Ex LE/FI 5, WHCF, LBJ Library.

238. Memo, Furtado to Nimetz, 24 May 1968, Ex LE/FI 5, WHCF, LBJ Library.

239. Memo, Califano to president, 9 June 1966, Ex LE/BE 2-1, WHCF, LBJ Library.

240. The background is taken from *Congress and the Nation: 1965–1968*, pp. 782–785.

241. "Special Message to Congress on Transportation," 2 March 1966, *Public Papers*, pp. 256–259.

242. "Letter to Secretary Hodges on Highway Safety," 23 March 1964, *Public Papers*, p. 413.

243. Memo, Schultze to Valenti, 10 December 1964, Ex SA 2, WHCF, LBJ Library.

244. Ibid.

245. Memo, Capron to White, 7 July 1965, attached to memo, White to president, 3 September 1965, Ex SA 2, WHCF, LBJ Library.

246. Memo, White to president, 3 September 1965, Ex SA 2, WHCF, LBJ Library.

247. "Agenda for Transportation Meeting," attached to note, Capron to Califano, 24 September 1965, Ex TN, WHCF, LBJ Library.

248. Memo, Boyd to Califano, 2 November 1965, Ex LE/SA 2, WHCF, LBJ Library.

249. Memo, Hughes to Califano, 12 February 1966, Ex LE/FA 3, WHCF, LBJ Library.

250. Noted on memo, Califano to president, 18 February 1966, Ex LE/SA 2, WHCF, LBJ Library.

251. *Congress and the Nation: 1965–1968*, pp. 784–786, 790–791.

252. The discussion of air and water pollution control efforts draws extensively on J. Clarence Davies III, *The Politics of Pollution* (Indianapolis, Ind.: Pegasus, 1970), chapter 2; and Sundquist, *Politics and Policy*, chapter 8.

253. Environmental Pollution Panel, President's Science Advisory Committee, *Restoring the Quality of Our Environment* (Washington, D.C.: White House, 1965).

254. "Special Message to the Congress on Conservation and Restoration of Natural Beauty," 8 February 1965, *Public Papers*, pp. 161–163.

255. Lewis L. Gould, *Lady Bird Johnson and the Environment* (Lawrence: University Press of Kansas, 1988), chapters 7 and 8.

256. "Special Message to the Congress Proposing Measures to Preserve America's Natural Heritage," 23 February 1966, *Public Papers*, p. 195.

257. Memo, Califano to Ackley, 22 September 1966, in Task Force on the Quality of the Environment material, box 19, task force collection, LBJ Library.

258. Task Force on the Quality of the Environment, "Report," 21 November 1966, box 19, task force collection, LBJ Library.

259. "Special Message to the Congress: Protecting Our Natural Heritage," 30 January 1967, *Public Papers*, p. 93.

260. "Special Message to the Congress on Conservation: To Renew a Nation," 8 March 1968, *Public Papers*, p. 355.

261. Task Force on Quality of the Environment, "Report," October 1968, box 29, task force collection, LBJ Library.

262. David E. Price, *Who Makes the Laws? Creativity and Power in Senate Committees* (Cambridge, Mass.: Schenkman Publishing Company, 1972), chapter 2.

263. Joseph A. Califano, Jr., *A Presidential Nation* (New York: W. W. Norton, 1975), pp. 129–131.

264. "Special Message to the Congress on Consumer Interests," 5 February 1964, *Public Papers*, p. 263.

265. "Special Message to the Congress on Consumer Interests," 21 March 1966, *Public Papers*, p. 336.

266. "Special Message to the Congress: 'To Protect the American Consumer,'" 16 February 1967, *Public Papers*, p. 196.

267. Memo, Furness to president, 9 October 1967, "Consumer Protection" folder, box 18, files of Joe Califano, LBJ Library.

268. Task Force on Consumer Protection, "Report," 14 November 1967, box 21, task force collection, LBJ Library.

269. "Special Message to the Congress: 'To Protect the Consumer Interest,'" 6 February 1968, *Public Papers*, p. 173.

270. Task Force on Consumer Protection, "Report," December 1968, attached to memo, OLR (Frey/Devall) to director, 6 December 1968, in Task Force on Product Information material, box 28, task force collection, LBJ Library.

7. Grappling with Regulation

1. "Remarks at a Luncheon for a Group of Businessmen," 23 July 1964, *Public Papers of the President of the United States: Lyndon B. Johnson, 1963–64* (Washington, D.C.: GPO, 1965), p. 881 (hereafter cited as *Public Papers*).

2. "The President's News Conference," 26 August 1965, *Public Papers*, pp. 934–935.

3. Based on an analysis of the Daily Diary for March 1965, LBJ Library.

4. Hobart Rowen, *The Free Enterprisers: Kennedy, Johnson and the Business Establishment* (New York: G. P. Putnam's Sons, 1964), pp. 16–17.

5. A similar association between complexity and level of involvement is evident when the average numbers of duty and political dimensions are computed. The results are 2.28 dimensions for high involvement cases, 1.64 for moderate involvement cases, and 1.0 for low involvement cases.

6. Lyndon Baines Johnson, *The Vantage Point: Perspectives of the Presidency, 1963–1969* (New York: Holt, Rinehart and Winston, 1971), pp. 460–461.

7. Ibid., p. 327.

8. Fred I. Greenstein, *The Hidden-Hand Presidency: Eisenhower as Leader* (New York: Basic Books, 1982).

9. See Alexander L. George, *Presidential Decisionmaking in Foreign Policy: The Effective Use of Information and Advice* (Boulder, Colo.: Westview Press, 1980).

10. See generally, Richard Tanner Johnson, *Managing the White House: An Intimate Study of the Presidency* (New York: Harper and Row, 1974).

11. Larry Berman, "Lyndon B. Johnson: Paths Chosen and Opportunities Lost," in Fred I. Greenstein (ed.), *Leadership in the Modern Presidency* (Cambridge, Mass.: Harvard University Press, 1988), pp. 137–138.

12. "Remarks at a Reception for Small Businessmen," 20 August 1964, *Public Papers*, p. 994.

13. Letter, Schultze to president, 2 April 1966, Ex FG 236, WHCF, LBJ Library.

14. Civil Aeronautics Board, *Administrative History*, p. 6, LBJ Library.

15. James L. Baughman, *Television's Guardians: The FCC and the Politics of Programming 1958–1976* (Knoxville: University of Tennessee Press, 1985), pp. 133–150; Francis E. Rourke, "The Presidency and the Bureaucracy: Strategic Alternatives," in Michael Nelson (ed.), *The Presidency and the Political System* (Washington, D.C.: Congressional Quarterly Press, 1984), p. 342.

16. James Q. Wilson, "The Politics of Regulation," in James Q. Wilson (ed.), *The Politics of Regulation* (New York: Basic Books, 1980), p. 370.

17. In the process, he contributed to altering the interest group landscape in ways that contributed to further regulatory expansion. See Jeffrey M. Berry, *Lobbying for the People: The Political Behavior of Public Interest Groups* (Princeton: Princeton University Press, 1977).

18. "The Federalist No. 70," in Edward Mead Earle (ed.), *The Federalist* (New York: Modern Library), p. 454.

19. Johnson, *The Vantage Point*, p. 433.

20. Hugh Heclo, "The Changing Presidential Office," in James P. Pfieffer (ed.), *The Managerial Presidency* (Belmont, Cal.: Brooks/Cole, 1991), p. 39.

Index

Johnson, Lady Bird, 15, 84
Johnson, Lyndon Baines, 283 n.1;
336 n.227; 338 n.6; business in
regulation, 20, 25–26, 55–57,
105–109, 159–161, 256–270,
280–281; concepts of commission and executive regulation,
161; effects on regulatory system,
203–204, 228, 242–244, 253,
275–279; and executive leadership, 279–281; record in regulation as member of Congress,
14–16; regulatory issues and
presidential sensitivities, 23–32,
43, 62, 82–84, 126–127, 134,
136, 138–139, 239–241; views
on regulation, 19–21, 45–53, 56–
57, 255–257, 275–276; and
White House staff, 20–21, 59,
60–63, 170–171, 270, 273–275
Johnson, Nicholas, 54, 59, 64, 82–
83, 225
Johnson, Richard Tanner, 332 n.10
Jones, Mary Gardner, 49, 52, 83
Justice, Department of: and agriculture, 178, 235; antitrust enforcement, 163–179, 200, 256; bank
mergers, 179–190; bank regulation, 147–148; FCC, 67, 178;
FPC, 71–72, 178; oil import controls, 140, 143–144; presidency,
relations with, 277, and rail mergers, 191–199; wage-price stability, 108, 175–176

Kappel, Frederick R., 28, 30–32, 82
Katzenbach, Nicholas de B.: and
antitrust enforcement, 165–175,
200; bank mergers, 177, 182,
184–189; oil import controls,
134, 143–144; rail mergers, 194–
195; wage-price stability, 108, 175
Katzman, Robert A., 287 n.56
Kaufman, Herbert, 286 n.46
Kaysen, Carl, 170, 329 n.72
Kearnes, Dorothy, 284 n.22
Kefauver, Estes, 245, 329 n.72

Kellerman, Barbara, 283 n.5
Kelly, William F., 149
Kennedy, John F., 245; and agriculture, 118, 236; balance of payments, 6, 93; and bank regulation, 146–147, 158; business
community, relations with, 257;
communications policy, 213;
consumer protection, 206–207;
Fair Labor Standards Act, 230; international aviation, 94, 104; on
presidents and regulation, 14; and
rail mergers, 191–193; regulatory
commissions, 23–24; transportation deregulation, 221, 224, 266;
wage-price stability, 6, 110; water
pollution control, 248
Kennedy, Robert F., 165, 193–194,196
Kessel, John H., 284 nn.10,11,20
King, Charles, 43–44
Kinney, Gene T., 312 nn.98,99,
313 n.101
Kintner, Robert E., 28–29, 55, 62,
213–214, 271
Koenig, Louis W., 9–10,
284 nn.12,18
Knott, Jack H., 330 n.103
Kramer, Victor H., 288 n.63,
291 n.42, 302 n.119

Labor, Department of: and con-
sumer protection, 208; labor leg-
islation, 228–232; rail mergers,
191; wage-price stability, 108,
111. *See also* Wirtz, Willard
Labor-management relations, 92–
93; 113–118
Labor policy, 227–233
Landis, James M., 23
Langdon, Jim C., 134, 139–140
Leaks, 45, 187–188
Lee, H. Rex, 53
Lee, Robert E., 36–37
Leedon, Boyd, 35
Leoni, Raul, 136
Levinson, Lawrence E., 78, 94, 176,
196, 208